Bruce Nauman: Topological Gardens

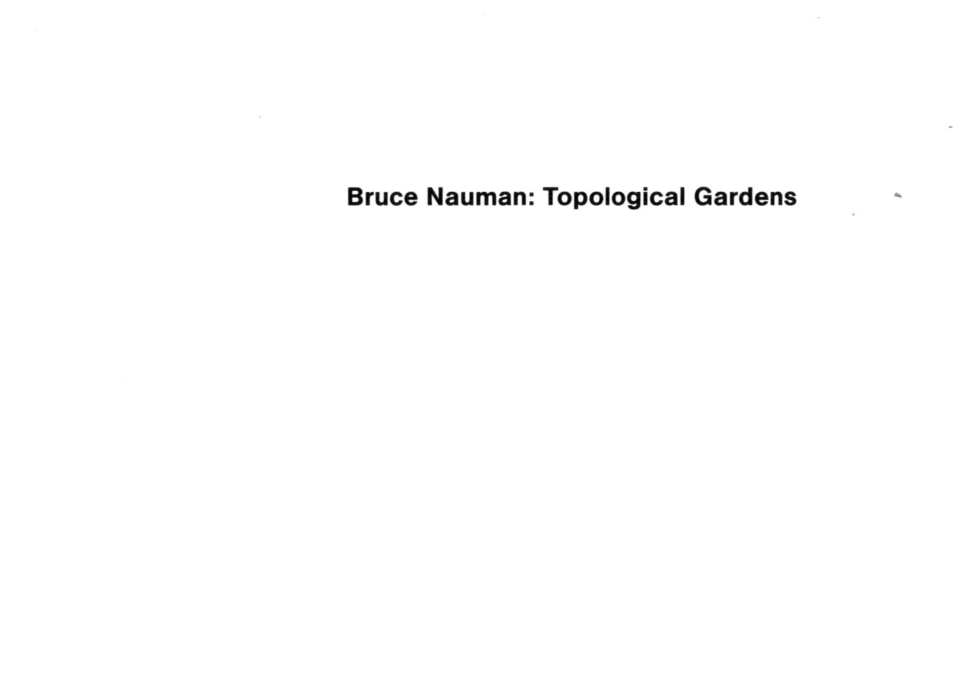

Bruce Nauman: Topological Gardens

Carlos Basualdo and Michael R. Taylor
U.S. Commissioners, 53rd International Art Exhibition—La Biennale di Venezia

Catalogue organized by Carlos Basualdo

Essays by Carlos Basualdo, Erica F. Battle, Marco De Michelis, and Michael R. Taylor

Philadelphia Museum of Art
in association with
Yale University Press, New Haven and London

Bruce Nauman: Topological Gardens, the official United States entry in the 53rd International Art Exhibition—La Biennale di Venezia, is presented by the Bureau of Educational and Cultural Affairs of the U.S. Department of State, in cooperation with the U.S. Embassy in Rome and the Peggy Guggenheim Collection, Venice.

The exhibition has been organized by the Philadelphia Museum of Art and presented in collaboration with the Università Iuav di Venezia and the Università Ca' Foscari di Venezia.

U.S. Pavilion at the Giardini della Biennale, Venice
June 7—November 22, 2009

Università Iuav di Venezia at Tolentini
June 7—October 18, 2009

Exhibition Spaces at Università Ca' Foscari
June 7—October 18, 2009

Major support for the exhibition was provided by the Commonwealth of Pennsylvania, the Henry Luce Foundation, The Pew Charitable Trusts, and the Bureau of Educational and Cultural Affairs of the U.S. Department of State.

This publication has been made possible by Isabel and Agustín Coppel.

Additional funding for the project was generously provided by the Friends of Bruce Nauman: Maja Oeri and Hans Bodenmann, Agnes Gund, and Sperone Westwater Gallery; the Donald Young Gallery, Chicago, and Dr. Friedrich Christian Flick; Barbara B. and Theodore R. Aronson, The Broad Art Foundation, Melva Bucksbaum and Raymond Learsy, Carlos and Rosa de la Cruz, Jaimie and David Field, Gemini G.E.L., Glenstone, Jeanne and Michael Klein, Jill and Peter Kraus, Rachel and Jean-Pierre Lehmann, Emily Rauh Pulitzer, Patrizia Sandretto Re Rebaudengo, the Sender Collection, Peter and Mari Shaw, and Sotheby's; Dorothee Fischer/Konrad Fischer Galerie, Marion Stroud Swingle, Selma and Joseph Vandermolen, and Robin Wright and Ian Reeves.

[Credits complete as of April 28, 2009]

This publication was funded in part by a grant from the U.S. Department of State. The opinions, findings, and conclusions stated herein are those of the authors and do not necessarily reflect those of the U.S. Department of State.

For more information on the exhibition, see www.naumaninvenice.org

Back cover: Bruce Nauman, *The True Artist Helps the World by Revealing Mystic Truths (Window or Wall Sign)*, 1967 (plate 22)

Produced by the Publishing Department
Philadelphia Museum of Art
2525 Pennsylvania Avenue
Philadelphia, PA 19130
USA
www.philamuseum.org

Published in association with Yale University Press
302 Temple Street
P.O. Box 209040
New Haven, CT 06520-9040
www.yalebooks.com

Editing by David Frankel
Editorial assistance by Jennifer Wilkinson
Translation by Elena Cimenti
Italian proofreading by Roberta Nuzzaci
Design by Jenny 8 del Corte Hirschfeld, Franck Doussot, and Mischa Leiner of CoDe. New York, Inc.
Color separations, printing, and binding by Conti Tipocolor S.p.A., Florence, Italy

Library of Congress Control Number: 2009927214

ISBN 978-0-87633-217-7 (PMA)
ISBN 978-0-300-14981-4 (Yale)

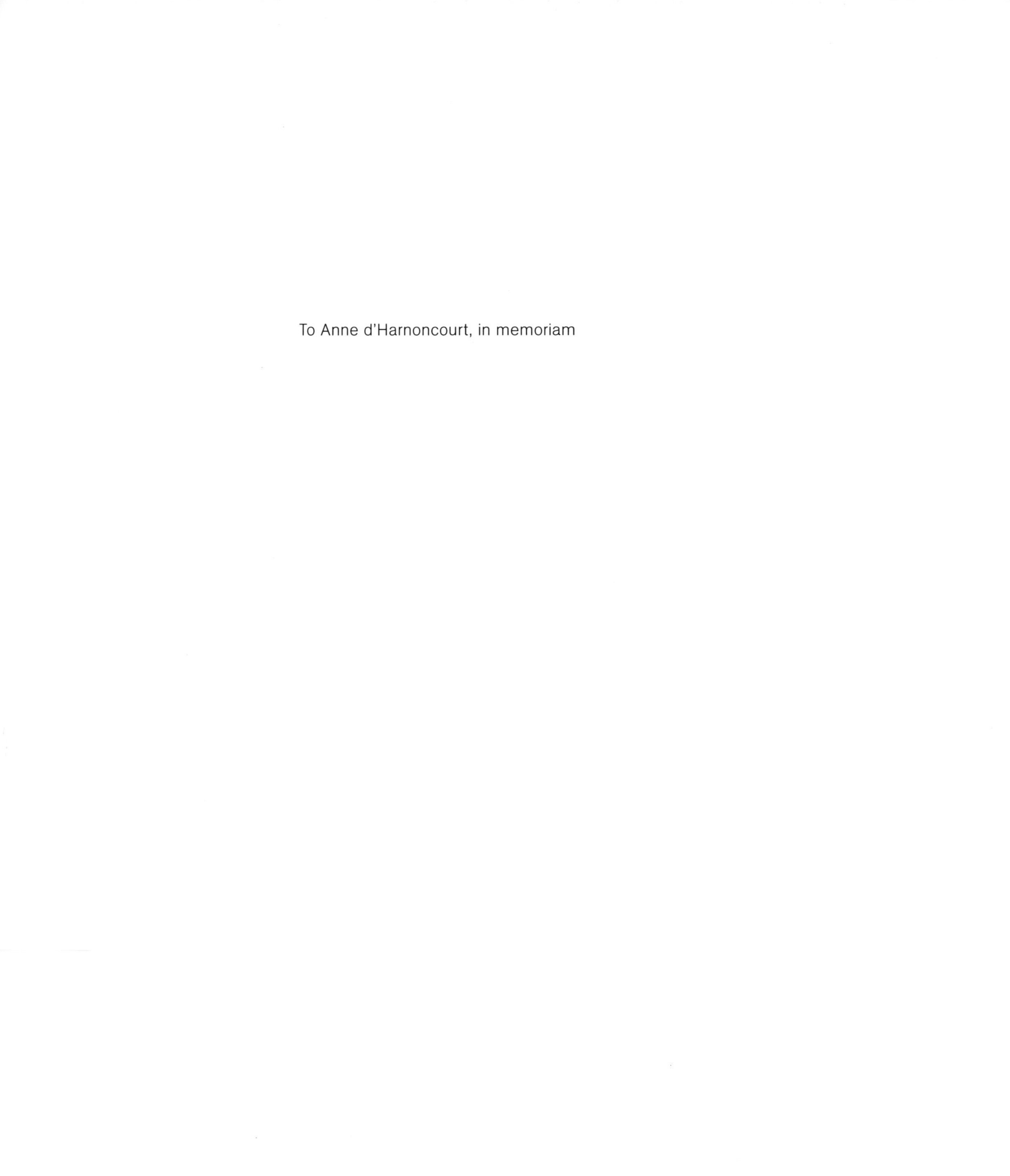

To Anne d'Harnoncourt, in memoriam

Lenders to the Exhibition

Bruce Nauman

Centre Georges Pompidou, National Museum of Modern Art – Center for Industrial Creation, Paris

CIAC: Colección Isabel y Agustín Coppel

Collection Dorothee and Konrad Fischer

Friedrich Christian Flick Collection

Hirshhorn Museum and Sculpture Garden, Smithsonian Institution, Washington, D.C.

Emanuel Hoffmann Foundation, permanent loan to the Öffentliche Kunstsammlung Basel

Indianapolis Museum of Art

Collection Rachel and Jean-Pierre Lehmann

Museum Boijmans Van Beuningen, Rotterdam

Museum of Contemporary Art, Chicago

The Museum of Modern Art, New York

Philadelphia Museum of Art

François Pinault Foundation

Private collection. Courtesy Hauser & Wirth, Zurich and London

Private collection, Madrid. Courtesy Donald Young Gallery, Chicago

Solomon R. Guggenheim Museum, New York. Panza Collection

Sperone Westwater, New York

Staatliche Museen zu Berlin, Nationalgalerie. Sammlung Marx

Stedelijk Museum, Amsterdam

Marc and Livia Straus Family Collection

Stuart Collection at the University of California, San Diego

Tate and National Galleries of Scotland

Collection Jack and Nell Wendler, London. Courtesy Sperone Westwater, New York

Collection Donald Young, Chicago

Contents

Foreword

The Philadelphia Museum of Art is deeply honored to have been chosen by the U.S. Department of State to organize *Bruce Nauman: Topological Gardens*, the official U.S. representation at the 53rd International Art Exhibition—La Biennale di Venezia. The last time the Museum organized an exhibition for the Venice Biennale was 1988, and the artist whose work was chosen to be shown at the U.S. Pavilion was Jasper Johns. Nauman and Johns, two of the most influential artists of the second half of the twentieth century, share a keen intelligence, an absolute devotion to their art, and an aura of inscrutability. Their fiercely personal work defies easy categorization and invites discourse and introspection in equal measure. The Museum is privileged to have had, in both of its Venice presentations, the opportunity to work with such distinguished artists.

This catalogue is dedicated to the late Anne d'Harnoncourt, who directed the Philadelphia Museum of Art with such grace, acumen, and passion from 1982 until her untimely passing in June 2008. She was a fervent champion of Nauman's work and was overjoyed when the Museum's proposal to organize a Nauman exhibition for the Venice Biennale was accepted. We are profoundly sad that she is not here to reap the rewards of the project that emerged from her inspirational tutelage.

While Bruce Nauman, born in Fort Wayne, Indiana, is quintessentially American, the two U.S. Commissioners, Carlos Basualdo and Michael R. Taylor, are Argentinean and British, respectively. They brought to this project an international perspective that epitomizes the Venice Biennale. Carlos, the lead organizer of the exhibition and the Museum's Keith L. and Katherine Sachs Curator of Contemporary Art, has developed with Nauman the kind of probing yet mutually trusting relationship that is essential between a living artist and the person responsible for presenting his art to the public. Carlos's longstanding and intimate familiarity with the city of Venice, which is so evident in his illuminating essay for this catalogue, was a stroke of good fortune and key to the success of this project. His ability to navigate, almost single-handedly and always graciously, among the many Italian and American officials, agencies, galleries, and institutions that played a part in executing the U.S. presence at the Biennale, not to mention all of the lenders and myriad staff involved, was nothing short of miraculous. Most importantly, his courage and determination to realize this project after the devastating loss of Anne d'Harnoncourt would have made her very proud.

Michael Taylor, Carlos's esteemed colleague and the Muriel and Philip Berman Curator of Modern Art at the Museum, brought to his eloquent essay in this catalogue, and to the project as a whole, the grounded perspective of a scholar who places Nauman's work in the broad context of art history. Michael's formidable intellect, though clearly evident, is tempered by a remarkable talent for presenting dense ideas and arguments with a lucidity that captivates even the most uninformed reader. Together, Carlos and Michael, ably assisted by the wonderfully talented Erica F. Battle, who also contributed an essay to the catalogue, deserve enormous credit for the spirit of collegiality that they have demonstrated in this enterprise, and, with the rest of the staff in the Department of Modern and Contemporary Art, in their broader roles at the Museum. Such genuine partnerships are rare.

The many Museum staff members and others who played important roles in bringing this exhibition and catalogue to fruition are acknowledged elsewhere in this publication, and we join in saluting their contributions. We are also particularly grateful to the lenders, who are individually listed above, not only for their generous loans but for their patience in proffering the unending assistance required when borrowing such technically complex works of art.

To the staff of the Peggy Guggenheim Collection in Venice, particularly its Director, Philip Rylands, and its Manager of Publications and Special Projects, Chiara Barbieri, we extend our warmest thanks for all their help on this complex project, particularly with regard to the U.S. Pavilion, which they care for and administer so capably.

We are also delighted and honored that two distinguished universities in Venice agreed to present portions of the exhibition, allowing us to install the works according to the themes of the exhibition. Both Magnifico Rettore Carlo Magnani and Magnifico Rettore Pier Francesco Ghetti, rectors of the Università Iuav di Venezia and the Università Ca' Foscari di Venezia, respectively, were extremely generous in allowing us the use of their galleries and the time of their staffs; we are also grateful for the support of Medardo Chiapponi, Dean of the School of Art and Design at Iuav, and Professor Giuseppe Barbieri. We are fortunate indeed that Professor Marco De Michelis of Iuav has contributed an enlightening essay to this book. We are particularly pleased that Nauman's work will provide a rich experience for the students of these two universities, and that the universities' presence in this project has provided intellectual sustenance.

Exhibitions and catalogues of this scale require substantial underwriting, and we are enormously grateful for the moral support as well as the financial assistance that we have received from a partnership of government, foundation, gallery, and private sources. First of all, we would like to thank the Bureau of Educational and Cultural Affairs at the U.S. Department of State for giving us the privilege of bringing Nauman's work to this celebrated international venue, and for providing the initial funding for the project. Colombia Barrosse, Cultural Programs Division Chief, Office of Citizen Exchanges, was particularly helpful and delightful to work with. The U.S. Department of State was quickly followed by the Commonwealth of Pennsylvania and The Pew Charitable Trusts, both steadfast supporters of the Museum and the arts. They were joined by the Henry Luce Foundation, which has so often helped to promote the cause of American artists. Isabel and Agustín Coppel, who not so very long ago joined the Museum's Modern and Contemporary Art Committee, very generously agreed to support the publication that accompanies the exhibition when it became clear that this would be a major scholarly undertaking. And lastly, we are delighted by the enthusiastic help of the Friends of Bruce Nauman, an international group of art lovers, collectors, and admirers of Bruce Nauman who joined forces to bring this ambitious project to completion in full measure: Maja Oeri and Hans Bodenmann, Agnes Gund, and the Sperone Westwater Gallery each provided substantial leadership gifts; the Donald Young Gallery, Chicago, and Dr. Friedrich Christian Flick made significant contributions; and generous gifts were also provided by Barbara B. and Theodore R. Aronson, The Broad Art Foundation, Melva Bucksbaum and Raymond Learsy, Carlos and Rosa de la Cruz, Jaimie and David Field, Gemini G.E.L., Glenstone, Jeanne and Michael Klein, Jill and Peter Kraus, Rachel and Jean-Pierre Lehmann, Emily Rauh Pulitzer, Patrizia Sandretto Re Rebaudengo, the Sender Collection, Peter and Mari Shaw, and Sotheby's.

Finally, we wish to pay tribute to the heart and soul of this project, Bruce Nauman, a true artist who, in his own words, and for more than forty years, has "helped the world by revealing mystic truths."

Alice Beamesderfer
Associate Director for Collections and Interim Head of Curatorial Affairs

Gail Harrity
Chief Operating Officer and Interim Chief Executive Officer

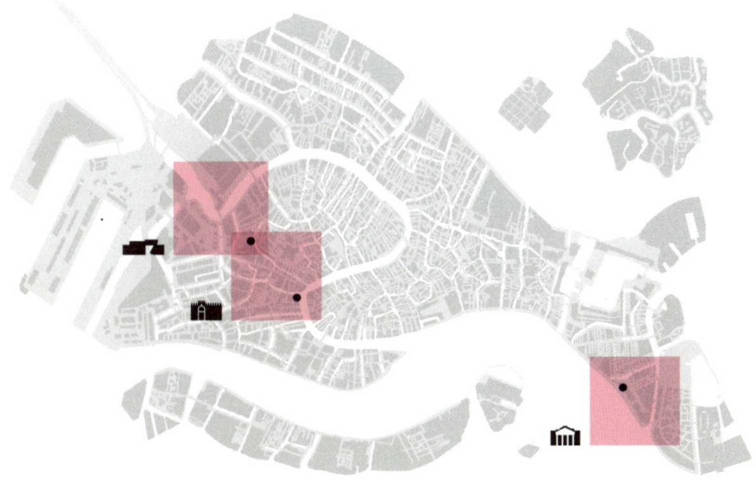

A Key to the Threads and Exhibition Sites

The Threads

Bruce Nauman: Topological Gardens proposes three points of entry, or "threads," with which to access and experience four decades of work by Bruce Nauman: Heads and Hands, Sound and Space, and Fountains and Neons. The threads are discussed at length in the essays by Carlos Basualdo and Erica F. Battle included in this book. Since these recurrent threads can be traced through much of Nauman's art, the exhibition checklist points toward a larger possible selection of works that were continuously part of our overall thought process. For the purposes of making these provisional categories—which have no order or hierarchy—clear to the reader, we have color-coded all images of Nauman's works, those on view in the exhibition and otherwise, throughout the catalogue. It must be noted that any number of threads could potentially be developed in the interpretation of Nauman's oeuvre, and that these organizing principles should not be considered either exclusive or exhaustive, but strategically useful for the purposes of this exhibition.

- Heads and Hands
- Sound and Space
- Fountains and Neons

Exhibition Sites

With three exhibition sites—the U.S. Pavilion at the Giardini della Biennale, the Università Iuav di Venezia at Tolentini, and the Exhibition Spaces at Università Ca' Foscari—*Bruce Nauman: Topological Gardens* requires visitors to traverse Venice, allowing the fabric of the city to become part of their experience of the exhibition and the work of Bruce Nauman. The icons featured next to the captions in the Plates section of this book indicate the placement of the different works through the sites.

- U.S. Pavilion at the Giardini della Biennale
- Università Iuav di Venezia at Tolentini
- Exhibition Spaces at Università Ca' Foscari

Bruce Nauman: Topological Gardens

Carlos Basualdo

Understand nothing about this "town" where everything is traveling except the pigeons.
Marcel Duchamp, postcard to Jacques Doucet, Venice, May 23, 1926

1. Fingers and Holes

Venice seems stale—and at least in terms of its urban structure, that impression is not entirely misguided. The topographic map of the city drawn by Bernardo and Gaetano Combatti in 1847, and updated eight years later, shows few major differences from the plan today (fig. 1). In the century and a half that saw the most dramatic expansion in history in the sizes and populations of Europe's capitals, Venice remained physically almost unchanged and its population in fact shrank. Today, the traveler returns to the city as confident as a lover going back to old letters hidden in a trunk. Not only bridges, churches, and *campos* will still be there, but very likely also that butcher's shop, that hidden bookstore, that ice cream parlor. It is a city that one doesn't so much encounter as interminably rediscover, and even the feeling of getting lost in its narrow passages and impossibly beautiful yet painfully indistinguishable vistas becomes a reverie, an expected part of the experience of the visit. The same visitor who responds with excitement to the ever-changing landscapes of Mexico City or New York comes to abhor any changes on the lagoon. Venice should stay as it is, as a false guarantee of our unlikely immutability. If it should change, we might lose our memory.

Before Venice had memory, though, its landscape was as chaotic as life when it begins. Tradition states that the town was settled on the island of Rivoaltus (Rialto) in 421 A.D., by citizens of neighboring Padua escaping Attila's armies. The first surviving plan of the city, an orthographic projection by Paolino da Venezia that appears in the *Chronologia Magna*—an illuminated manuscript that dates from 1346—reveals a formless territory, fragmented, resembling the anxious expression on the face of a diver emerging from the water, gasping for air (fig. 2). The Grand Canal is there, clearly visible, and so is the Giudecca Canal, but the city remains a collection of patches, disorderly and unstructured. Since the still-astonishing bird's-eye view miraculously drawn by Jacopo de' Barbari in 1500—the first plan of the city to be printed—we have grown accustomed to imagining a reclining Venice, leaning gracefully on its side (fig. 3). The city is read from west to east and from left to right, like a fantastically knitted page. The earlier *Chronologia Magna*, though, instead depicts it erect, hands over feet, with the east pointing to the top of the page and the west at the bottom, oriented perhaps to allow its rulers

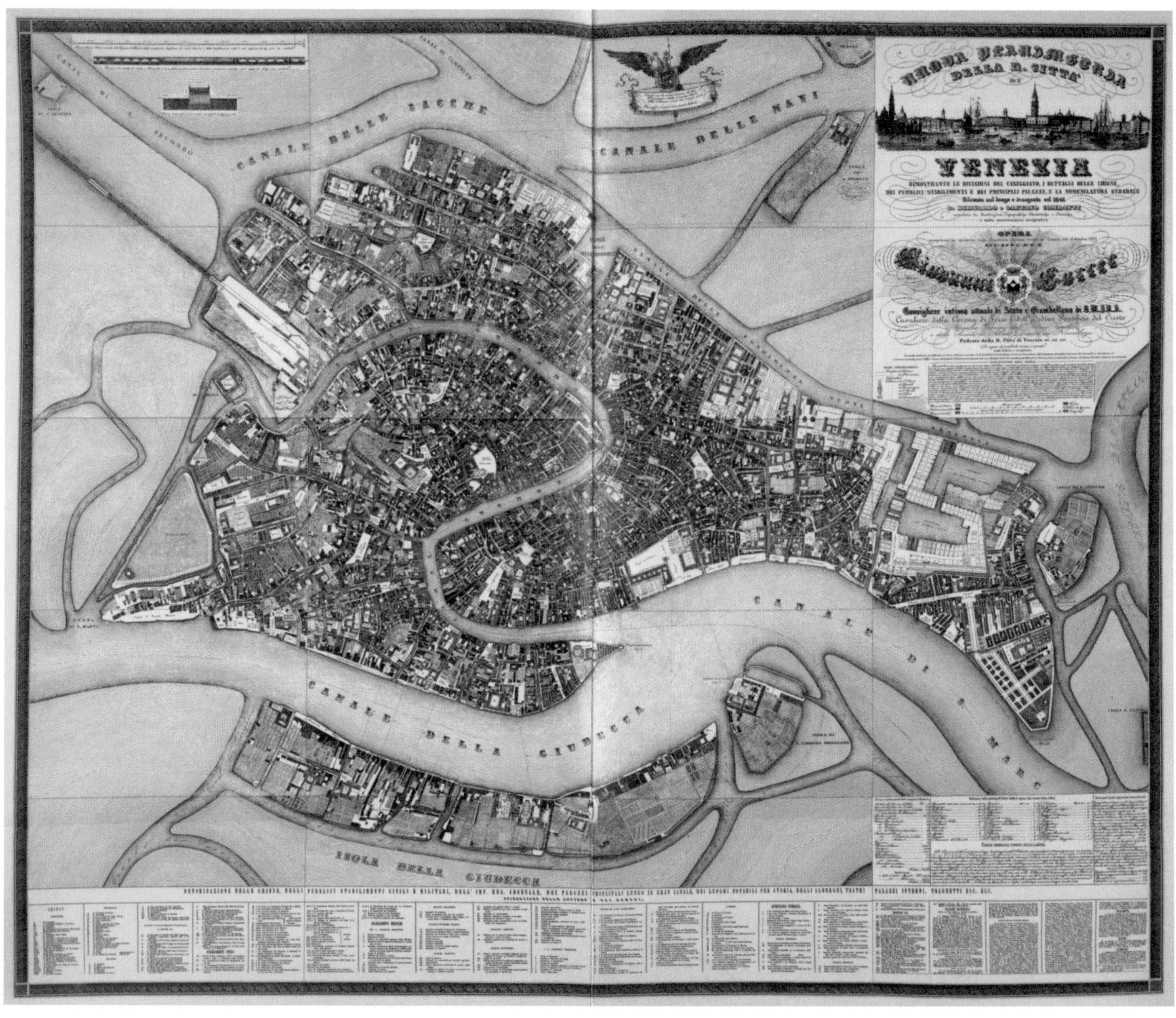

Fig. 1 Designed by Bernardo and Gaetano Combatti. *Pianta topografica della città*, 1847–55. Copper engraving, 50 1/4 x 57 1/2 inches (127.5 x 146 cm). Edition of 20. From Giocondo Cassini, *Piante e vedute prospettiche di Venezia: 1459–1855* (Venice: La Stamperia di Venezia Editrice, 1982), pp. 196–97, pl. 115

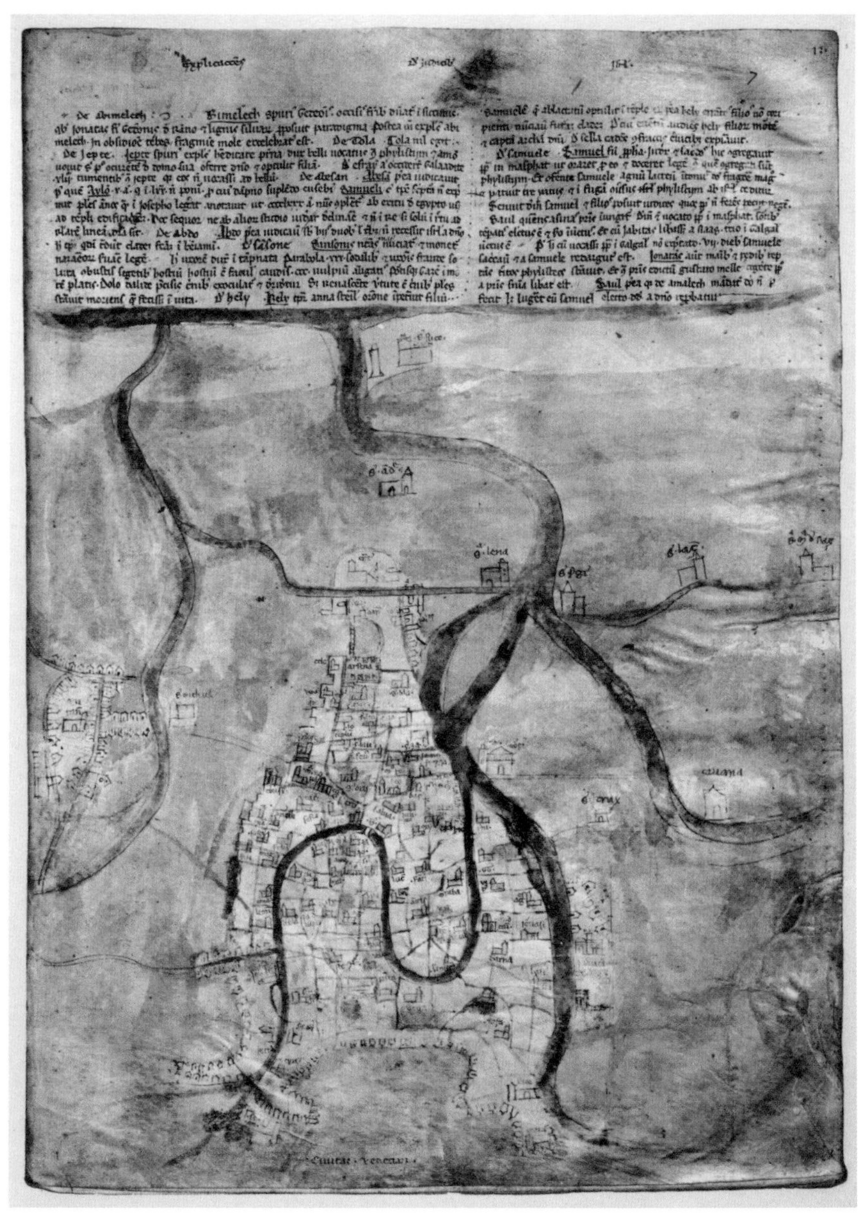

Fig. 2 Paolino da Venezia. *La Pianta di Venezia*, 1346. Insert in his *Compendium*, also known as *Chronologia Magna*. Biblioteca Marciana, Venice, Ms. lat. Zan. 399.
18 3/8 x 13 1/4 inches (46.8 x 33.6 cm).
From Giocondo Cassini, *Piante e vedute prospettiche di Venezia: 1459–1855* (Venice: La Stamperia di Venezia Editrice, 1982), repro. p. 8

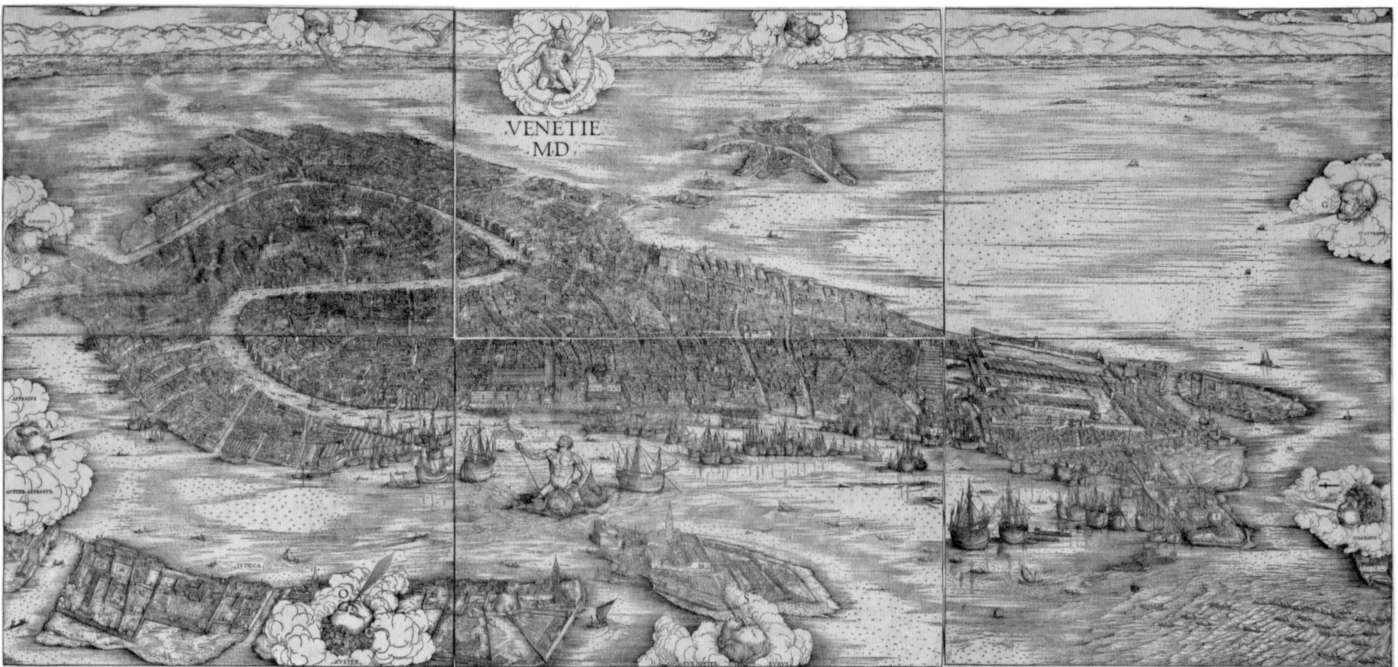

to imagine that geography was destiny and that their duchy would prevail over its past and advance toward the heart of Europe. The quivering land seems to have been less important for the cartographer than the darker, undulating streaks signaling the waterways between Venice and the mainland—the latter being indicated in the upper section of the map, which incidentally is also occupied by two columns of text. It is the water that shapes the land, as if giving it both form and nurture. Rather than depicting a frozen, ideal city, the map speaks to the unending negotiations among shores and tides that constitute the very substance of Venice, where nothing has ever been still. It shows Venice standing like an idol of mud surrounded by the watery branches of a growing tree, with fragments clinging to its hesitating feet, ready to lose or gain a piece of land. And in fact, for the next three hundred years the city would constantly perform a dance of greed and desire with the fluid embrace of the lagoon, gaining territory and solidity, incessantly moving toward its current structure.

That unstable Venice, mired in its moorings, still exists today. It is not blatant, it eludes easy observation, but it can nevertheless be felt, and those who find themselves walking through the city's streets, unaided by maps or the sedative regularity of the *vaporetti*, are doomed to discover it: getting from here to there always proves harder than expected, or even harder than

Fig. 3 Jacopo de' Barbari (Italian, 1460/70–1516). Published by Anton Kolb (German, active Venice 1500–1536). *View of Venice*, 1500.
Woodcut printed from six blocks, 52 3/16 x 110 5/8 inches (132.7 x 281.1 cm).
The Cleveland Museum of Art. Purchase from the J. H. Wade Fund, 1949.565.1–6

yesterday or the night before. Like a velvety curtain the city guards its folds with a slow and indifferent zeal, and then, all of a sudden, it opens them in a hurry. What determines the distances between places is the mood of the walker, rather than any objective unit of measure detached from the circumstances and accidents of the route. In the mind, the city constantly expands and contracts, like a grasping hand, or a prone body responding with perceptible shudders to the fleeting touch of underground currents of water. Feeling the tides and rivers running below the ground, we walk guided by them, but their direction keeps changing and so do our steps, so we lose ourselves in a multitude of mutable thoughts and views and impressions, until we approach an unexpected destination that we nonetheless recognize as intended, simply because it is there, waiting for our arrival. We then conclude that the city is not the extended mesh of wonders that most renderings depict but a moving target on which we incessantly project our emotions, our changing experience of ourselves.

***

Most dictionaries define topology dryly as a branch of mathematics that studies the qualitative properties of space. It is concerned not with measurements or distances but with the *structure* of space, and with the way in which space functions. The *Encyclopædia Britannica* defines topology as the mathematical study of the properties of a geometric object that remains unchanged by deformations such as bending, stretching, or squeezing but not breaking. A sphere is topologically equivalent to a cube of the same relative dimension because if they were made, for example, of modeling clay, each could be deformed into the other without being broken. A sphere is not equivalent to a doughnut because it would have to be broken to put a hole in it. Topological concepts and methods underlie much of modern mathematics, and the topological approach has clarified basic structural concepts in many of its branches. A topologist, it is commonly said, cannot distinguish a coffee mug from a doughnut, since one can be made into the other by simple deformation. The urban structure of Venice, for example, might be better understood through topology than a map, since the representational language of a map is restricted to the abstract and simplified language of two-dimensionality. A bird's-eye view of Venice like de' Barbari's, with its stress on the morphology of the urban fabric, could be described as topological in relation to an orthographic projection, where the shapes of buildings and the relations between different parts of the city are sacrificed to exact measurements and scale—and interestingly enough, after Paolino's inspired early plan, generations would pass before orthographic projections of Venice would become the norm, progressively replacing bird's-eye views at the dawn of the Enlightenment. Venice seems to call for an emotional topology instead of a map—a topology that could correspond to the work of an artist.

As Joan Simon writes in her brief, enlightening catalogue essay on Bruce Nauman's *Fingers and Holes* prints from 1994, the subject of hands has recurred in his work since he deliberately left fingerprints in the surfaces of his first fiberglass sculptures, in the mid-1960s. In *Fingers and Holes*, a series of eight prints, Nauman laid down what seems to be a vocabulary of hand gestures, as if intent on creating the basis for a secret, wordless language. A precise, sexual meaning may be ascribed to an image in just one case: index finger and thumb of one hand make a circle that the other hand's index finger hungrily penetrates (fig. 7). The configuration

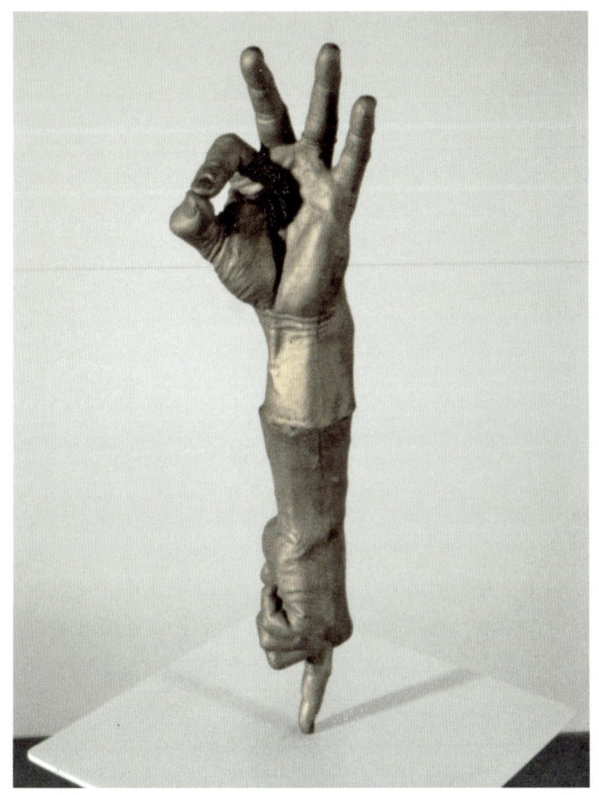

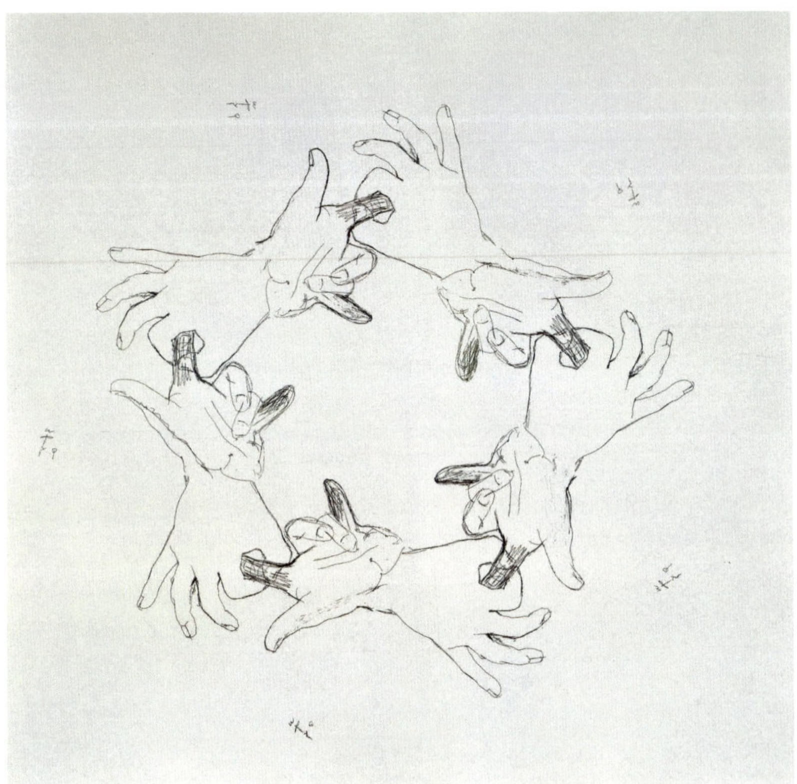

had appeared before, in the small yellow-and-green neon *Human Sexual Experience* of 1985 (plate 14), and the print in which it resurfaces, the largest in the series, seems to have been made by sequentially repeating that earlier drawing along the margins of an imaginary circle (fig. 5). Two years later the curious form this repetition created would be cast in bronze, in *Untitled (Hand Circle)* (1996; plate 25). Six of the prints in the *Fingers and Holes* series represent two hands, left and right, schematically but precisely drawn, fingers touching in various positions (figs. 6–11). In one print we see instead two series of hands, as if representing two different moments of the same gesture (fig. 12). Nauman told Simon that "the series was not about the holes at first," but then, after he realized "what was going on," he started thinking about topology, which he had studied as an undergraduate math student at the University of Wisconsin-Madison. Incidentally, Jasper Johns, another artist in whose work hands figure

Fig. 4 Bruce Nauman. Detail of *Fifteen Pairs of Hands*, 1996 (plate 7).
White bronze with painted steel base; each pair of hands variable dimensions.
Courtesy the artist and Sperone Westwater, New York

Fig. 5 Bruce Nauman. *Untitled*, 1994. From the series *Fingers and Holes*.
Monoprint produced from screen matrix, with coloring of each print varying, on Rives BFK paper; 35 x 35 inches (88.9 x 88.9 cm).
Gemini G.E.L., Los Angeles. BN94-192

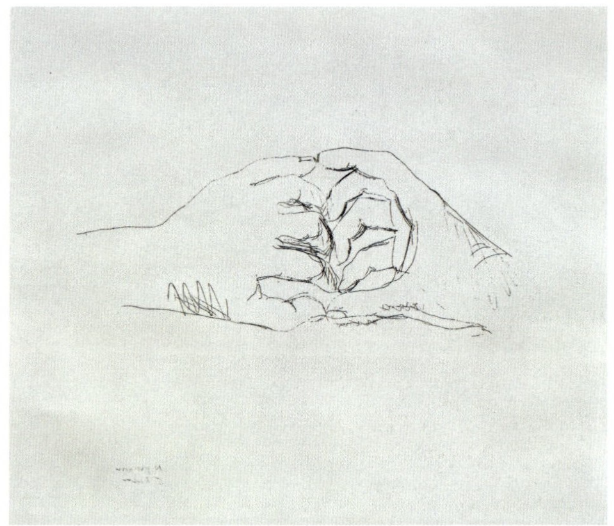

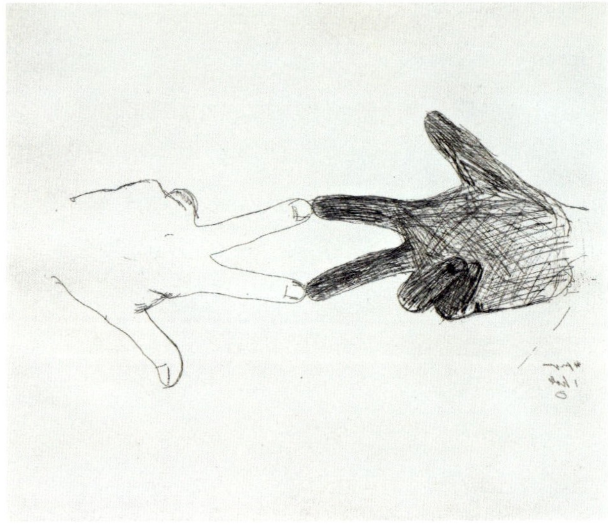

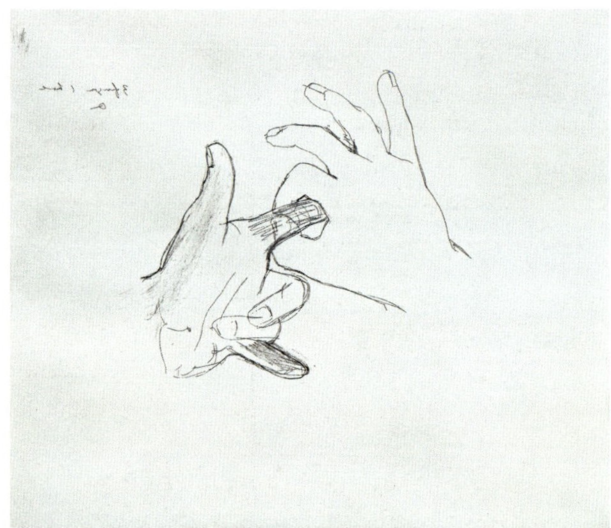

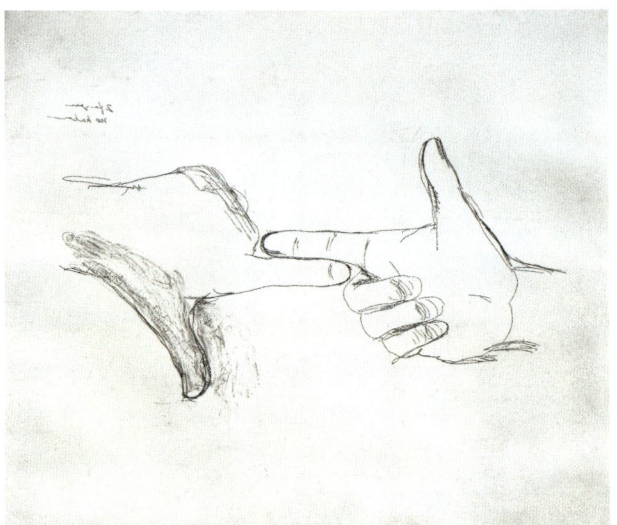

Fig. 6 Bruce Nauman. *Untitled*, 1994. From the series *Fingers and Holes*. Etching on Lana gravure paper, 20 x 22 inches (50.8 x 55.9 cm). Edition of 50. Gemini G.E.L., Los Angeles. BN93-3207

Fig. 7 Bruce Nauman. *Untitled*, 1994. From the series *Fingers and Holes*. Etching on Lana gravure paper, 20 x 22 inches (50.8 x 55.9 cm). Edition of 50. Gemini G.E.L., Los Angeles. BN93-3201

Fig. 8 Bruce Nauman. *Untitled*, 1994. From the series *Fingers and Holes*. Etching on Lana gravure paper, 20 x 22 inches (50.8 x 55.9 cm). Edition of 50. Gemini G.E.L., Los Angeles. BN93-3205

Fig. 9 Bruce Nauman. *Untitled*, 1994. From the series *Fingers and Holes*. Etching on Lana gravure paper, 20 x 22 inches (50.8 x 55.9 cm). Edition of 50. Gemini G.E.L., Los Angeles. BN93-3206

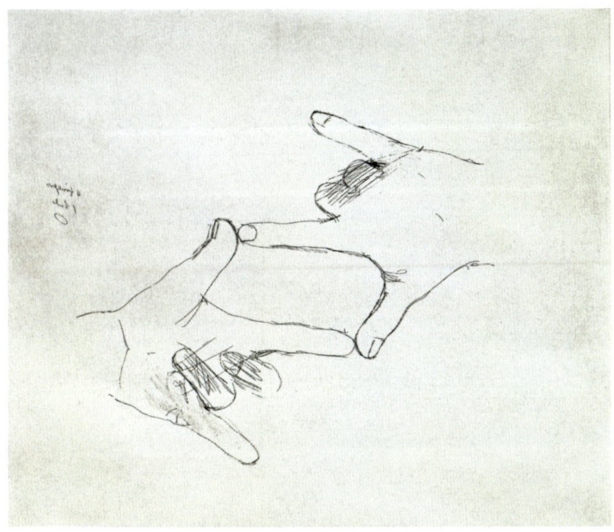

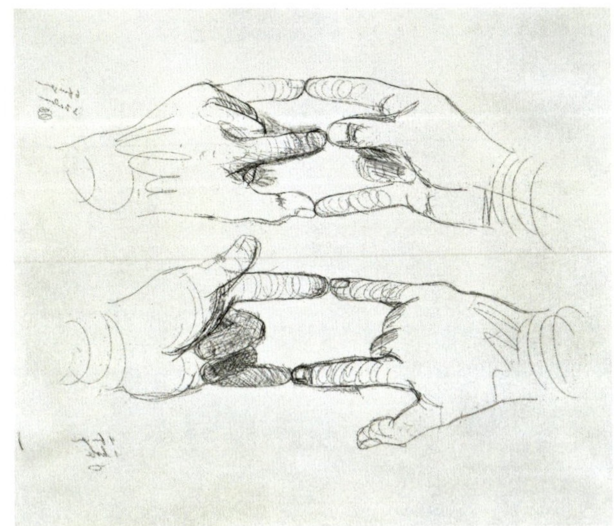

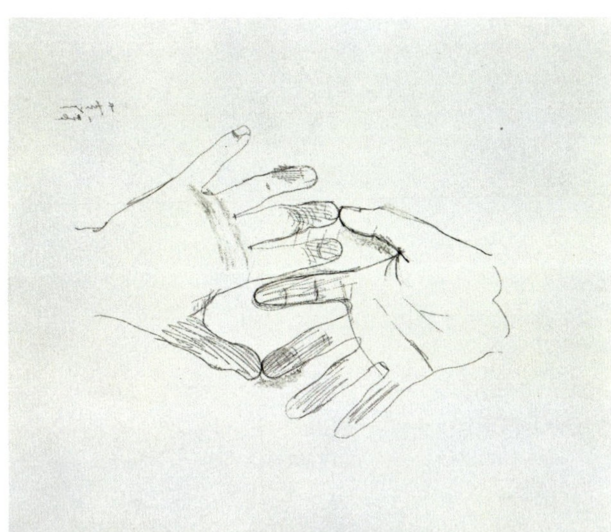

Fig. 10 Bruce Nauman. *Untitled*, 1994. From the series *Fingers and Holes*. Etching on Lana gravure paper, 20 x 22 inches (50.8 x 55.9 cm). Edition of 50. Gemini G.E.L., Los Angeles. BN93-3204

Fig. 11 Bruce Nauman. *Untitled*, 1994. From the series *Fingers and Holes*. Etching on Lana gravure paper, 20 x 22 inches (50.8 x 55.9 cm). Edition of 50. Gemini G.E.L., Los Angeles. BN93-3203

Fig. 12 Bruce Nauman. *Untitled*, 1994. From the series *Fingers and Holes*. Etching on Lana gravure paper, 20 x 22 inches (50.8 x 55.9 cm). Edition of 50. Gemini G.E.L., Los Angeles. BN93-3202

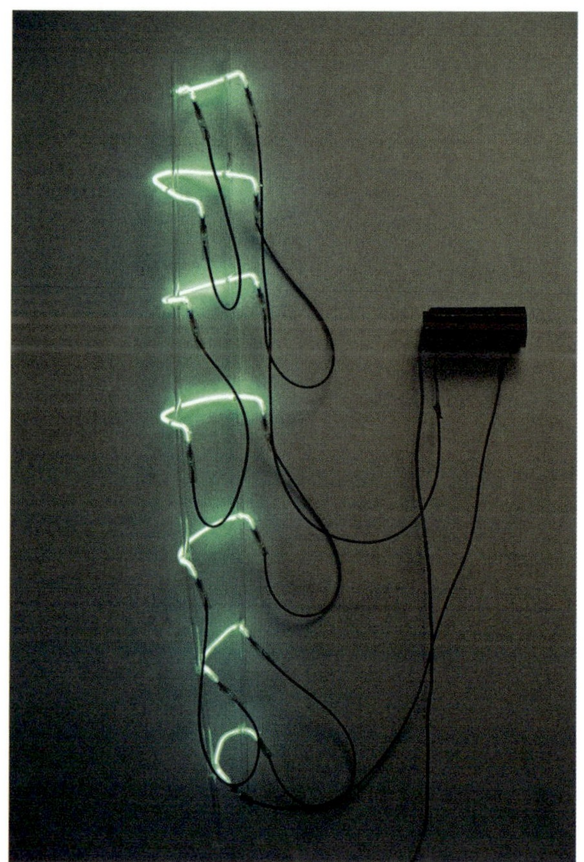

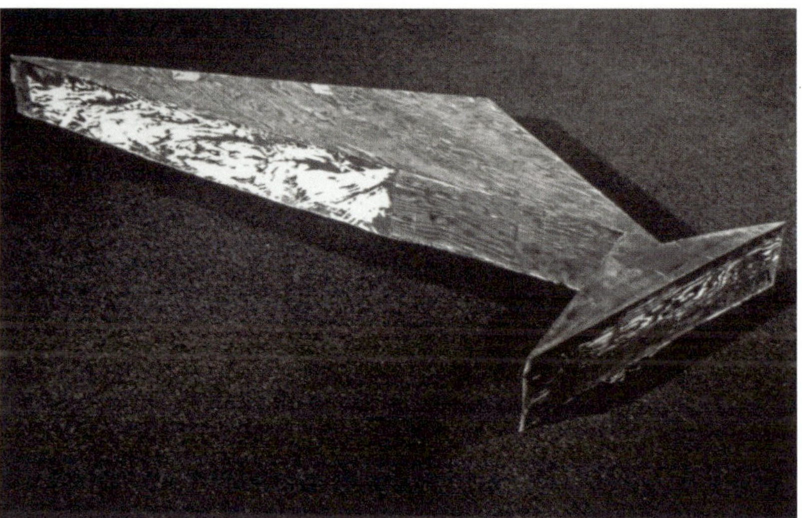

prominently—since at least his print series *Skin* of the early 1960s, in which he mapped the surface of his face and hands two-dimensionally—is equally preoccupied with the conceptual mapping of a paradoxical topological space in many of his paintings.

Nauman has explored the sculptural presence of negative space since very early on. His *Neon Templates of the Left Half of My Body Taken at Ten-Inch Intervals* from 1966 (fig. 13) is an early example of this insistence, and negative space acquires a clear physical manifestation in *Platform Made Up of the Space Between Two Rectilinear Boxes on the Floor* of the same year (fig. 14). In both cases the titles are precise descriptions of the process involved in the sculptures' conception and execution. Only a year later Nauman would use the *moulage*

Fig. 13 Bruce Nauman. *Neon Templates of the Left Half of My Body Taken at Ten-Inch Intervals,* 1966.
Neon tubing with clear glass tubing suspension frame, 70 x 9 x 6 inches (177.8 x 22.9 x 15.2 cm).
The Estate of Philip Johnson, courtesy of the National Trust for Historic Preservation

Fig. 14 Bruce Nauman. *Platform Made Up of the Space Between Two Rectilinear Boxes on the Floor,* 1966.
Fiberglass and polyester resin, 7 1/2 x 86 5/8 x 42 7/8 inches (19 x 220 x 110 cm).
Kröller-Müller Foundation, Otterlo, The Netherlands, formerly in the Visser collection. Purchased with support from the Mondriaan Foundation

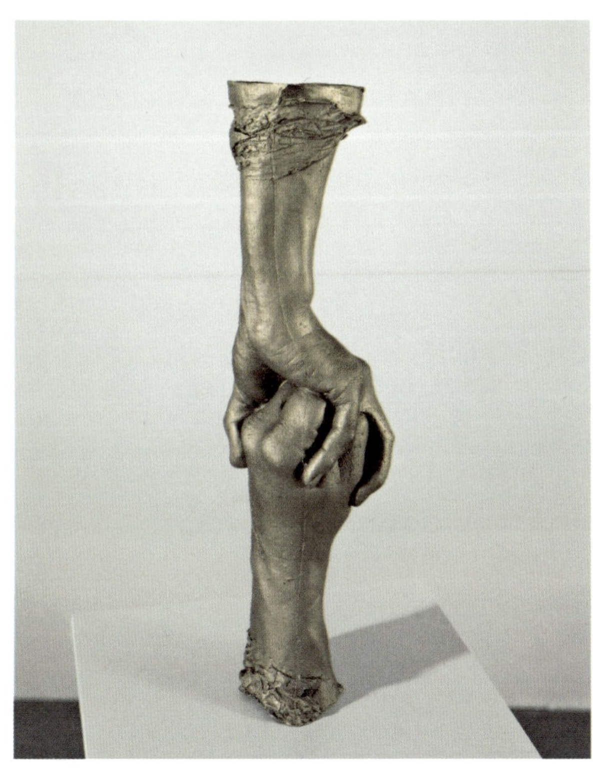

technique to cast in a porous and delicate green wax a part of the body of his then-wife, Judy, extending from the tip of her right hand all the way up her arm to her neck, chin, and mouth. The work's title, *From Hand to Mouth* (plate 11), makes a figure of speech literal and in doing so manages to make the relation between two parts of the body that would reappear throughout the artist's work both abstract and concrete. The eerie, somewhat disturbing presence of a fragment plucked out of the body seems nonetheless to insistently call attention to the absent whole. In this work, more powerfully than in *Neon Templates* or *Platform Made Up of the Space*, Nauman ties a fragmented presence indissolubly to an absence, creating a continuum that unravels the boundaries between a sculptural body and its physical context.

Simon puts topology to further account in discussing the formal operation at play in the *Fingers and Holes* prints, suggesting that a like rationale might be at play in similar works by Nauman. Michael Auping too cites Nauman's interest in topology as a math student in his essay for the catalogue of the *Raw Materials* exhibition at Tate Modern, London, in 2005. In Auping's account, topology is useful to explain the way in which Nauman navigates different mediums and disciplines in his work, "twisting without tearing an idea of form." Finally, in his "Topological Pathways of Post-Minimalism," Eric de Bruyn describes how Dan Graham arrived at topology as a critical

Fig. 15 Bruce Nauman. Detail of *Fifteen Pairs of Hands*, 1996 (plate 7).
White bronze with painted steel base; each pair of hands variable dimensions.
Courtesy the artist and Sperone Westwater, New York

model after first encountering an untitled latex sculpture of Nauman's from 1965–66, then witnessing one of his early performances, a variation of his *Bouncing in a Corner* videos of 1968–69, at the *Anti-Illusion* exhibition at the Whitney Museum of American Art, New York, in 1969.

It is somewhat possible to represent Venice by shaping one's right hand as a horizontal U, then holding one's left fist inside it, leaving a sinuous space between the two hands—an evocation of the puzzling twists and turns of the Grand Canal. Coincidentally, a similar gesture can be found in one of the sculptures that is a part of Nauman's *Fifteen Pairs of Hands* (1996; fig. 15). The mimetic power of a pair of hands seems to express the complexity of the site in a way that maps do not. Only the early plans in which the islands' contours primarily result from the demarcation of the waterways around them—a scheme more relevant to the maps' original users, whom it allowed an understanding of the navigational routes in and around the city—express the topological nature of the urban space to the same extent. Discussing those bird's-eye views of Venice, in which the point of view is clearly located in the San Marco Basin, Egle Trincanato underlines a willingness on the part of the cartographers to assign equal importance to the built city and to the water surrounding it, as if tacitly but firmly declaring that in Venice no distinctions should be established between land and water. The Grand Canal both divides and gracefully connects the land on its shores. The fluidity of Venice is as passing as a gesture, and seems equally to imply an unfulfilled promise of meaning. The "holes" that Nauman finally saw between the fingers, not as negative space but as the very substance of which the gestures are made, correspond accurately, in a topological logic, to the profound instability that still articulates our contemporary experience of Venice. It is Venice that makes us think of Nauman's work as topological, but, symmetrically, it is the experience of Nauman's work that allows us to make sense of the city. They seem to correspond to each other inevitably, like a pair of hands.

2. Topological Gardens

The summer is negligent in Venice, and this is nowhere better seen than at the Giardini di Castello, near the eastern tip of the island. Here, in the years when there is no exhibition, the grass grows freely and indolently among the boarded doors and windows of the Biennale's pavilions. In the long and tortuous history of the archipelago, the Public Gardens, or Giardini Pubblici, are a recent and dramatic addition. In 1797 the Venetian republic, by then fragile, fell to Napoleon's troops. Its demise came about not as the outcome of a bloody battle but as the unlikely result of a vote and the consequent resignation of the last doge, Ludovico Manin, a somewhat shameful turn of events that would weigh on that distinguished Venetian family for generations. From 1805 to 1814, Venice was still part of Napoleon's swelling empire, and it was during this period, and as one of the many changes and challenges that the city and its citizens faced at the time, that its first public gardens were created. Commissioned to design new gardens as part of Napoleon's expansionist plans for the island, the Venetian architect Giannantonio Selva followed dogmatic neoclassical ideas ill-adapted to a city that remained profoundly strange to them in every possible way. Giorgio Fossati's panoramic view of Venice of 1743—the last original record of Venice's appearance before the republic's fall—shows a densely inhabited cluster of buildings where the new gardens were to be laid out (fig. 16).

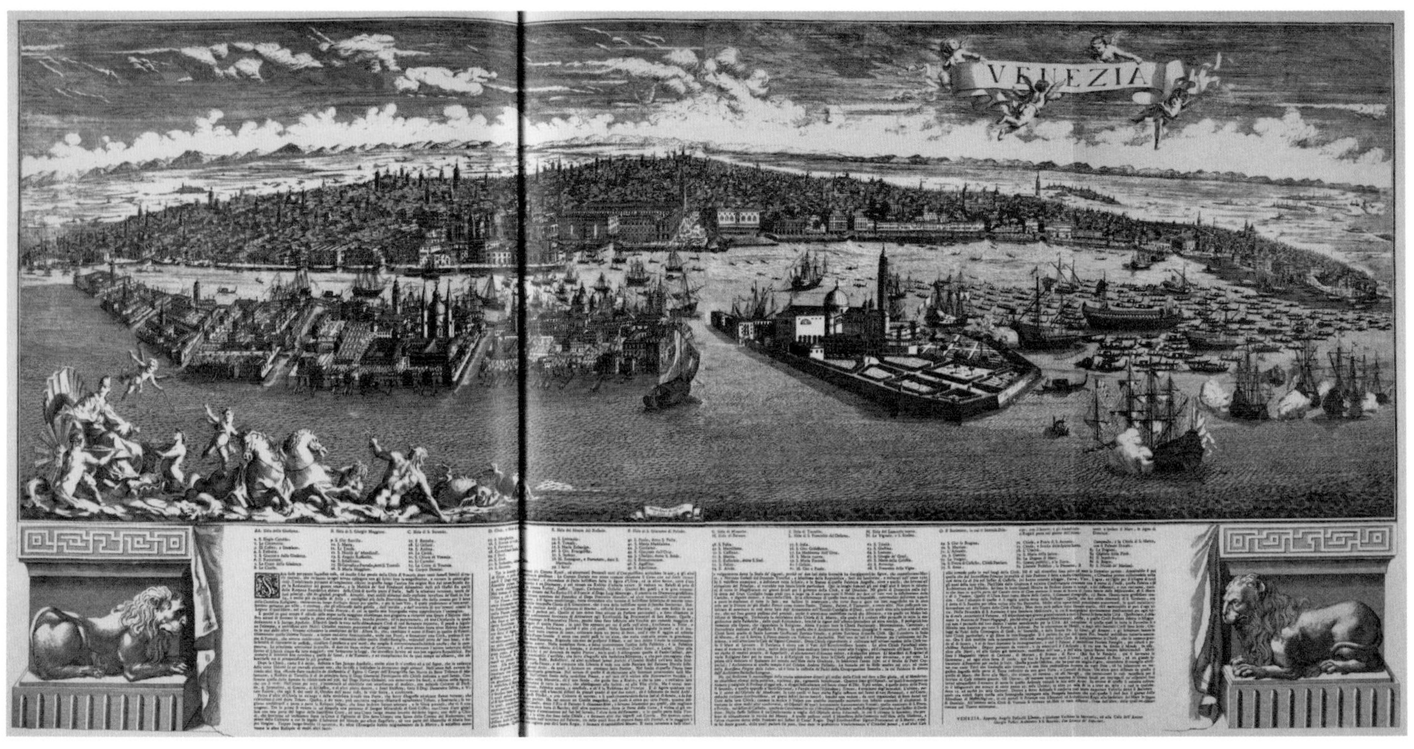

Fig. 16 Designed and engraved by Giorgio Fossati (Italian, 1706–1778). *Pianta-veduta prospettica*; Venice, 1743.
Copper engraving, 17 13/16 x 50 15/16 inches (45.2 x 129.3 cm).
From Giocondo Cassini, *Piante e vedute prospettiche di Venezia: 1459–1855* (Venice: La Stamperia di Venezia Editrice, 1982), pp. 146–48, pl. 76

Between 1808 and 1812, houses, churches, and convents were razed, and canals were filled, to make way for the bucolic park, initially a precise arrangement of long pathways and symmetrical parterres.

The Venetians at first found little use for their new public gardens. To the visitor, Venice looks like a city of stone and brick and mortar. A few scattered trees languish here and there in some of the larger *campos*, a doubtful relief for children and dogs but certainly not enough to modify the character of a city that seems to have been created as a refusal of nature. Behind walls and gates, though, Venice unfolds grass and trees immodestly and reveals an oblique but intense communion with the very nature that its foundations seem to negate. Large parts of the Dorsoduro neighborhood actually served for centuries as orchards, and the eastern tip of the island in the Castello neighborhood, where the public gardens would be laid out, also contained orchards, along with some of the oldest churches in the city. Seen from our vantage point, it could be said that gardens were mostly "private" in Venice, and some of them remain silent and secret until today, accessible only to those who own them. More importantly, the abstract notions of "public" and "private" are hard to impose on the entangled urban structure of a city that seems blatantly to ignore them, as if the distinction were unsophisticated and base in the context of Venice. Since early times the Piazza San Marco has been both ceremonial and utilitarian, and the many *campos*—truly the magnetic poles that organize the life of the city—were and are used in the most complex and enchanting ways, alternately or simultaneously markets, meeting places, stages, playgrounds, and extended living rooms where people of all ages casually or deliberately meet. It is easy to imagine that these open spaces were once still more deeply integrated into the sociality of the city's inhabitants, whose lives would have unfolded in the open, in squares where they both became their very selves and acted in the larger drama of life in the republic. With the modern notion of public and private came a strict compartmentalization of daily activities. The public gardens were part of that design, which the urban structure of Venice contradicts. In a topological city there is no space to isolate forms from their possible uses.

It may be a sign of Venice's deep resistance to the rationalistic organization of life imposed by the heavy mantle of the Napoleonic rules and regulations that the city at first found no use for its newly created site of solace, set beyond the past glories of the Arsenale, closer than the rest of the city to the protective shores of the elongated island of the Lido. Not until more than half a century later, after the Unification of Italy, when a site was required for the *First National Exhibition of Art (Esposizione Nazionale d'Arte di Venezia)* in 1887, did the Giardini finally find their use: to display. The success of that first event took Venice by surprise, and motivated the establishment of a more enduring and lasting presence in Venice, the Biennale, initially conceived to attract visitors, educate the masses, and stimulate a floundering art market. In 1895 Mario de Maria designed the exhibition's first building, the Palazzo delle Esposizioni, or Exhibition Palace, known as the Padiglione Italia, and recently rechristened as the Palazzo della Biennale. Since then the Biennale has become internationally celebrated, has taken place almost uninterruptedly, and has made a profound and lasting impact on the life of the city.

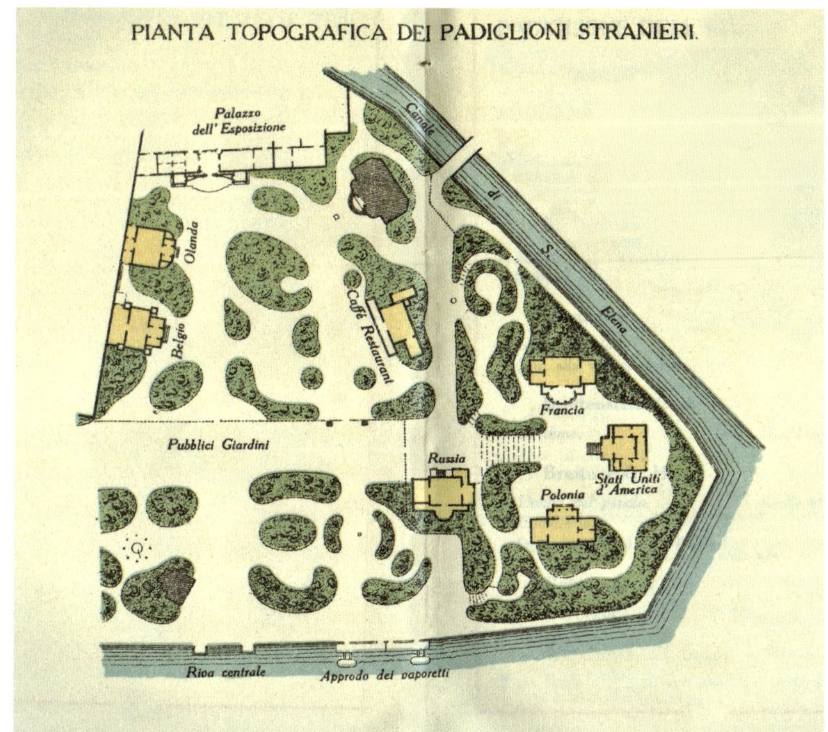

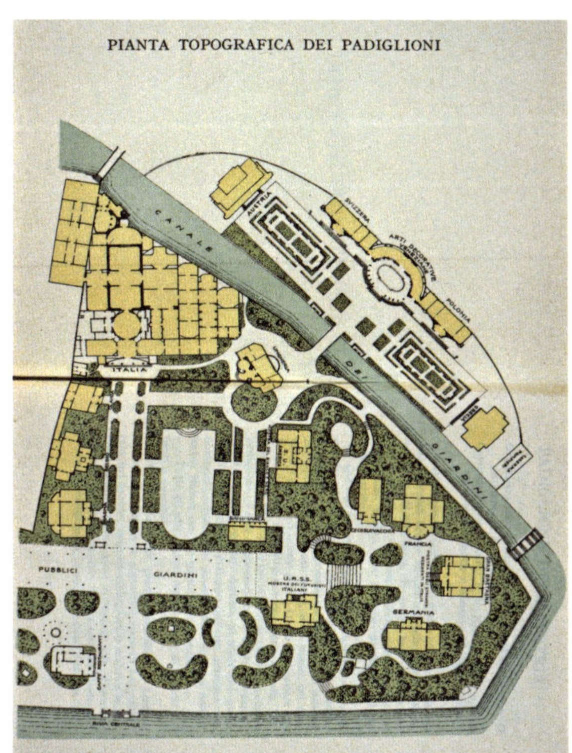

When Belgium built its National Pavilion on the grounds of the Giardini in 1907, the Biennale was following a path prepared in 1867, when the *Exposition Universelle* in Paris for the first time used separate buildings for the display of the products of the different nations. Then, at the height of colonialism, the paradoxical solidity of the impermanent pavilions was called on to represent the power of the nation-state and the indissoluble link between its culture and its identity, which was conceived mostly in ethnic terms. Each pavilion served as a monument to the intimate linkage of bodies, ideas, and race on which the modern notion of the nation-state was founded. The Giardini would soon become peppered with such buildings. A plan of the gardens dating from 1910 also shows British and Bavarian pavilions (the latter would later become the German Pavilion). By 1932, two years after the United States built its pavilion, Hungary, Spain, the Netherlands, the Soviet Union, Czechoslovakia, and Denmark had joined the ranks of the nations represented on the high grounds of what had been the ancient orchards of the Most Serene Republic. The increase in the number of the national pavilions in the Giardini becomes evident by comparing plans from the 1920 (fig. 17) and 1934 (fig. 18) editions of the Biennale catalogue.

***

Fig. 17 *Giardini della Biennale,* 1920. From *Esposizione internazionale d'arte della città di Venezia, 1920,* 2nd ed. (Rome: Bestetti & Tumminelli, 1920), repro. p. 128

Fig. 18 *Giardini della Biennale,* 1934. From *Esposizione internazionale d'arte della città di Venezia, 1934,* 2nd ed. (Venice: Ferarri, 1934), repro. p. 208

Nauman has repeatedly mentioned his fascination with telephone booths. Inside them, he has said, you are both exposed and secluded, in a space of your own that does not protect you from being on exhibit. In this paradoxical entanglement, which could be better described using the language of topology, Nauman has found devices that have triggered many of his most successful sculptures, videos, and installations, starting from the first sculptures, made of ceramic, listed in his catalogue raisonné and dated 1965. The first one, called *Cup and Saucer Falling Over* (fig. 19), might perhaps be said to evoke Raymond Duchamp-Villon's *Horse* (1914; fig. 20) as it likewise represents an attempt to depict motion and time through a system of intersecting planes that compose a virtual volume. *Cup Merging with Its Saucer* (fig. 21) is similar, but in this case the movement seems not to have originated in an external action; instead the cup literally unfolds in its saucer, both objects embraced in a spiraling expansive gesture. In the second object the interior of the cup becomes its enveloping saucer; in the first both cup and saucer dissolve in the concrete representation of their fall. As in a phone booth, a condition of possibility that enables a subjective experience of interiority is paradoxically determined by the subject's exposure. As in the cups and saucers—or the fingers and holes—what's outside results not from its separation from the inside, or from a clear cut or divorce, but from an unfolding, an unraveling, a momentary disentanglement that never reaches stillness or equilibrium. As Nauman said in an interview with Ian Wallace and Russell Keziere in 1979, "What I want to do is use the investigative polarity that exists in the tension between the public and the private space and to use it to create an edge"—an edge of experience, one might add, in which the boundaries between object and viewer are equally intended to be dissolved.

Nauman has explored this topological logic through a number of operations, some of them precisely oblique, others extremely literal. In *Flayed Earth Flayed Self (Skin Sink)* (1973; plate 9) he allows the viewer to occupy the metaphorically "peeling" center of a room marked with six radiating lines of masking tape emanating from the center of the floor and creeping up the walls, dividing the space into six equal sections. In the center of the room the isolated viewer finds the center of her body, which twists and turns in the imagination until its surface is plastered on the receding walls, "stretching and expanding" until the room becomes her disembodied self. Entering *Double Steel Cage Piece* (1974; plate 3), the viewer, now seduced into active participation in the work, walks laterally inside, her body compressed between two steel meshes that allow only enough space to move laterally, away from the cage's entrance and around its claustrophobic perimeter, while the empty interior remains inaccessible but visibly at hand. The inner core and the physical structure of the work are clearly revealed, so that she can imagine herself inside it, where to find a way out she would have to unravel that structure in her mind, at the same time eroding the certainty of her separate self.

A similar operation is at play in the composer Steve Reich's *Piano Phase* of 1967, as two piano players constantly repeat a certain pattern, one gradually increasing the tempo to move slowly ahead of the other. What is required to play the piece, Reich remarks, is listening attentively rather than reading a musical score. Performing the work requires the musicians to become intimately involved with its structure, listening and remembering it while playing it. The work enacts memory as the living condition of the possibility of action. It is memory,

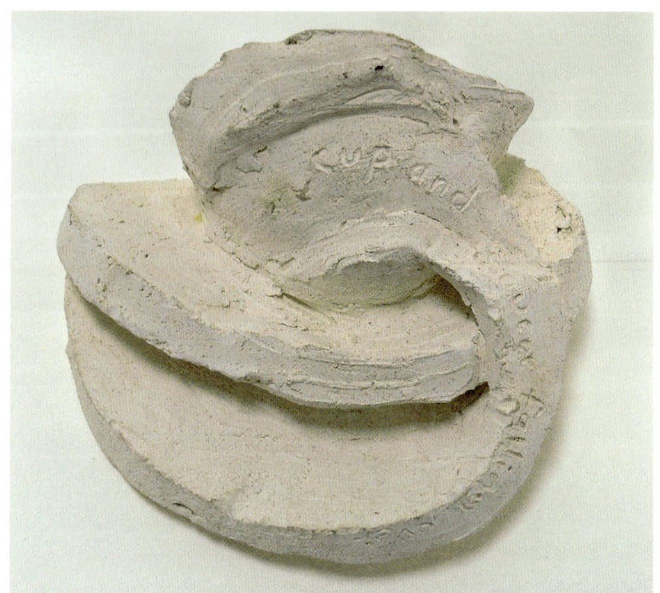

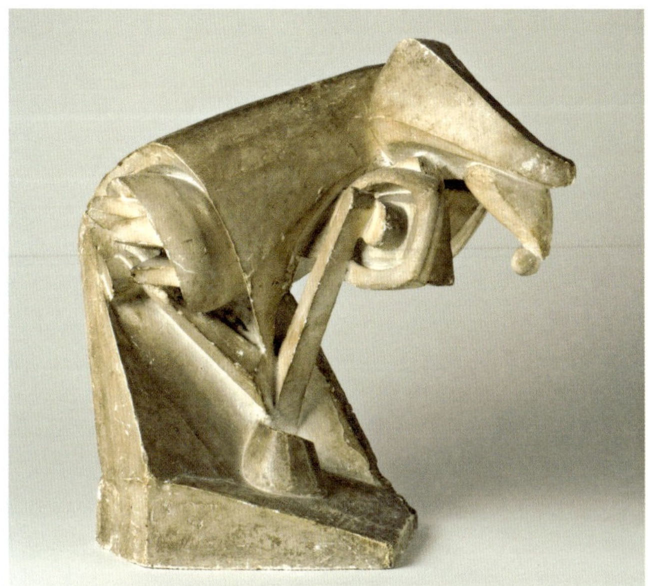

which lies at the foundation of our sense of self, that Nauman's works insist on evoking and distorting, fusing experience and environment in a move toward the impermanent invention of a topological self.

3. Forced Perspective

In 1927 the Italian sculptor, art critic, and vocational diplomat Antonio Maraini was appointed Secretary General of the Venice Biennale, a position that he would keep for almost a quarter of a century. Under Maraini, the Biennale became closely dependent on the cultural politics of the fascist state, and its mission was clearly defined as the promotion of "Italian art," conceived in a totalizing and unifying way. The first Biennales had been very different. A few years after the Unification, Italy was still a federation of quite distinct regions with their own dialects, histories, and cultures. The Biennale initially mirrored these differences, assigning to each of these regions its own room in the Palazzo delle Esposizioni, so that each could appear in glorious singularity before the others, in a gesture intended to enhance mutual knowledge and understanding. The fascist approach was quite the opposite: local differences were subsumed under the banner of a singular national identity, with the Biennale becoming the institution officially in charge of performing that task in the visual arts.

Fig. 19 Bruce Nauman. *Cup and Saucer Falling Over*, 1965.
Unglazed ceramic and graphite, 4 x 5 1/2 x 5 1/2 inches (10.2 x 14 x 14 cm).
Richard L. Nelson Gallery and The Fine Arts Collection, University of California, Davis

Fig. 20 Raymond Duchamp-Villon (Pierre-Maurice-Raymond Duchamp) (French, 1876–1918). *The Horse*, 1914.
Plaster, 17 1/2 x 17 1/2 inches (44.5 x 44.5 cm).
Philadelphia Museum of Art. Gift (by exchange) of Miss Anna Warren Ingersoll, 1999-5-1

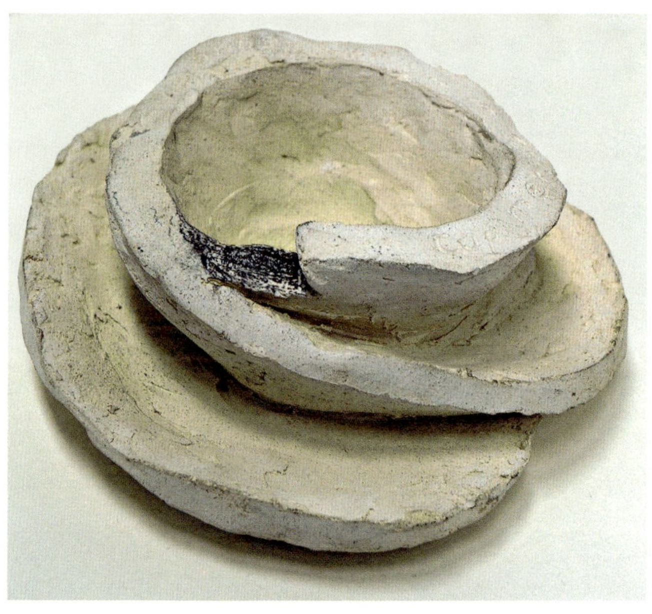

The stage for this demiurgic transformation was the Palazzo delle Esposizioni, which was rechristened the Italian Pavilion (fig. 22). The nations that initially exhibited in that building alongside the Italian regions then started a process of migration, from cosmopolitan co-existence in the rooms of the Palace to homes scattered through the bucolic landscape of the former public gardens. In 1927, when Maraini became the Director of the Biennale, there were only nine national pavilions in the Giardini. By 1934, the number had increased to fifteen. As the Italian Pavilion became the container for a certain idea of what Italian art could or should be, a signifier of the peninsula's newly fashioned identity, so too were the national pavilions, under Maraini, asked to become the heralds of their respective cultures and peoples, with art's assignment being that of clarifying and distilling their national identities. Maraini pursued this political goal through a careful selection process, assigning only a marginal role to the Futurists, for example, and stressing instead a more conservative, romantic form of realism. He also made the new role of the Italian Pavilion explicit by modifying its architectural features, including a renewed facade (which the Pavilion still has) and a simplified sequence of internal rooms organized along a narrative axis so as to clarify visitors' itinerary—and overdetermine the meaning of the art on exhibit (fig. 23). Perhaps not coincidentally, there seems to be a correspondence between Maraini's objective of making the maze of rooms in the Palazzo delle Esposizioni—which had grown chaotically in the Biennale's first decades—into a coherent whole and Napoleon's plans to turn Venice's complex urban structure into a legible modern city. Maraini would only attain his presumptive goals toward

Fig. 21 Bruce Nauman. *Cup Merging with Its Saucer*, 1965.
Unglazed ceramic and graphite, 2 x 5 1/2 x 6 inches (5.1 x 14 x 15.2 cm).
Richard L. Nelson Gallery and The Fine Arts Collection, University of California, Davis

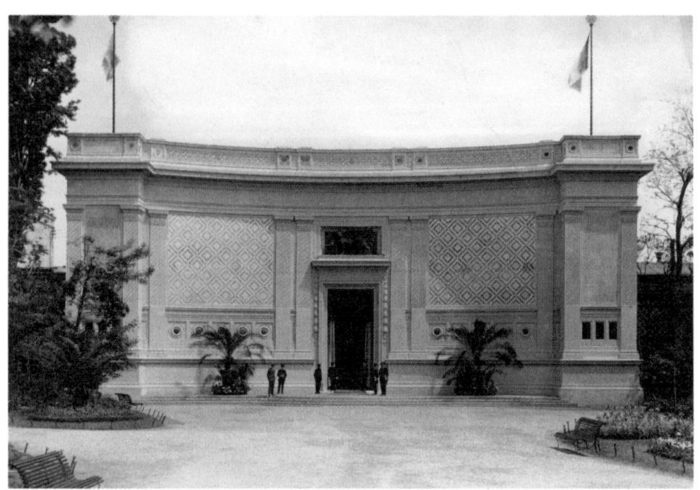

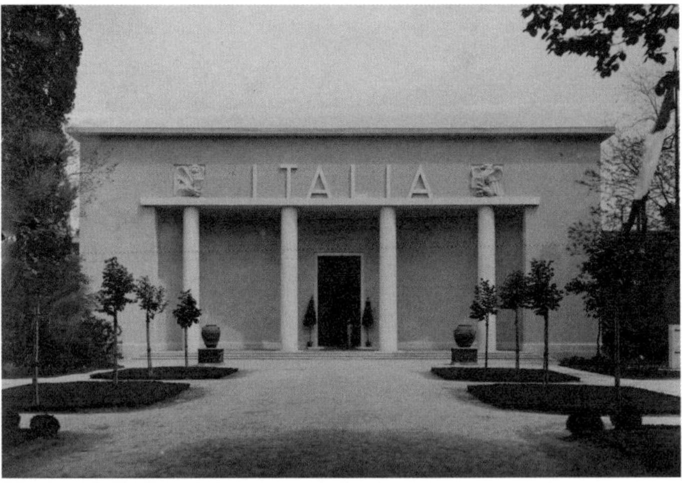

the last two editions of the Biennale under his supervision, in 1940 and 1942. The highest degree of control over the meaning of the exhibition in the Italian Pavilion, which was implemented through its architecture and the organization of the exhibition itinerary so that it would be firmly impressed upon the viewer, would paradoxically coincide with the disintegration of the political regime that made that objective desirable.

The coincidence of politics and art under the same roof at the Venice Biennale could not have had a more dubious pedigree: it was a direct inheritance of the colonialist project that had propelled the nineteenth-century British and French universal exhibitions, a legacy manifest in Belgium's erection of the first national pavilion at the height of that country's colonial power. Under Maraini this already objectionable content was further tainted by the authoritarian tendencies of an arguably fascist cultural project, intended to redress the undesirable diversity of Italian culture soon after the country's unification. Only blind determination made it possible to imagine that art could stand for the identity of a nation as the ultimate cultural expression of a specific ethnic group.

Nothing could be farther from this idea than the plural and ever-changing realities that have always characterized the territory of the United States. The U.S. Pavilion was designed in 1929 by the architects William Adams Delano and Chester Holmes Aldrich, known for their neo-Georgian New York town houses and clubs (fig. 24). They chose for the building the neoclassical style that was something like a norm for cultural buildings in the United States at the time—the sprawling neoclassical building of the Philadelphia Museum of Art, for example, was built around the same period. Designed with a similar neoclassical footprint, the U.S. Pavilion cuts

Fig. 22 *Italian Pavilion,* 1930. Silver gelatin print, 7 x 9 5/16 inches (18 x 24 cm)

Fig. 23 *Italian Pavilion,* 1932. Silver gelatin print, 7 x 9 5/16 inches (18 x 24 cm)

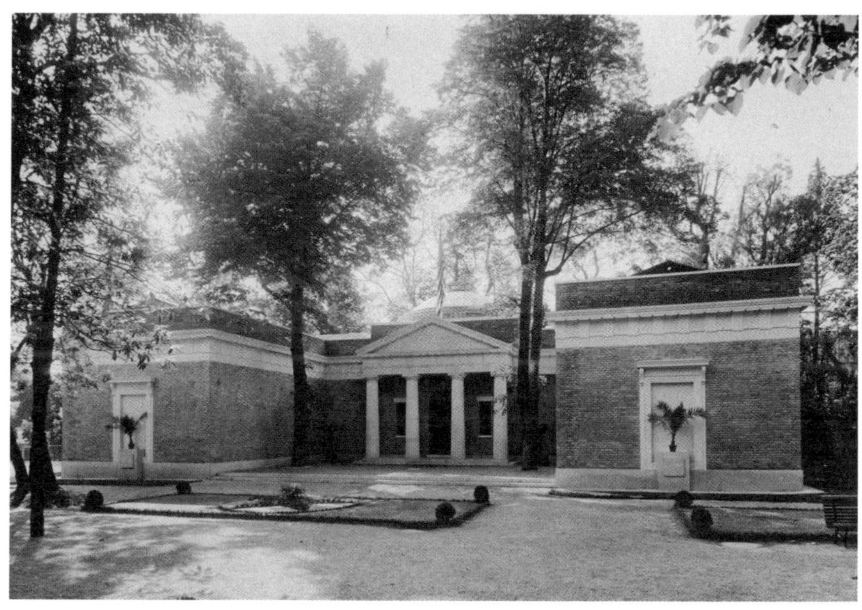

a somewhat quaint figure amid more challenging architectural company such as Josef Hoffmann's Austrian Pavilion of 1934, Gerrit Rietveld's Dutch Pavilion of 1954, Carlo Scarpa's Venezuelan Pavilion of 1956, and Alvar Aalto's beautiful Finnish Pavilion of 1956.

The U.S. Pavilion has been used for the American contributions to the Biennale almost continuously since 1930, with a few exceptions, notably that of the 1942 Biennale, when the world was at war. Only on a couple of occasions have U.S. exhibitions been extended outside the building to the city beyond. In 1964, for example, when Robert Rauschenberg famously won a controversial Gran Prix in Painting, the show representing the United States, organized by Alan Solomon, was in fact a group exhibition comprised of two parts, and took place in both the Pavilion and the recently closed U.S. Consulate, a building adjacent to the Palazzo Venier dei Leoni, which houses the Peggy Guggenheim Collection. In 1990—the first time the United States won the Golden Lion, for its Jenny Holzer exhibition—the Pavilion show was complemented by outdoor projections in the Lido, although the commissioner, Michael Auping, had originally planned a more extended occupation of the city. Never before 2009, we believe, has the U.S. exhibition been conceptually and programmatically conceived to exceed the physical and ideological limitations of the national pavilions and to establish deeper consonances among the work of the artist shown, the urban fabric of Venice, and the social, ethnic, and cultural constitution of the nation that it is supposed to represent. Exhibiting work like Nauman's that has systematically explored and eroded the boundaries between public and private, in a city where those boundaries have been, and still are, under negotiation, unequivocally requires a novel approach to the exhibition itself.

 Fig. 24 *U.S. Pavilion,* 1930. Silver gelatin print, 7 x 9 5/16 inches (18 x 24 cm)

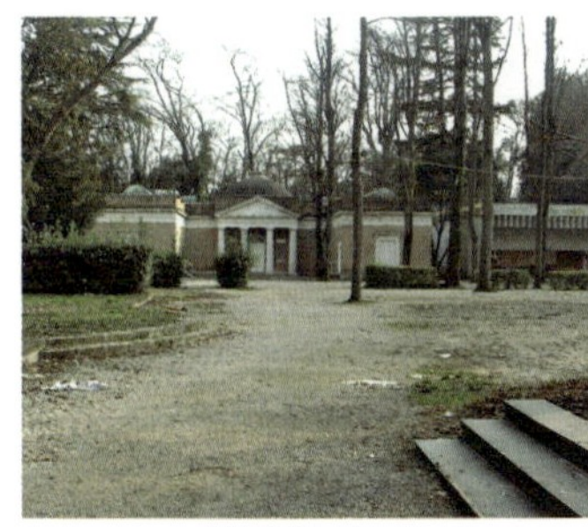
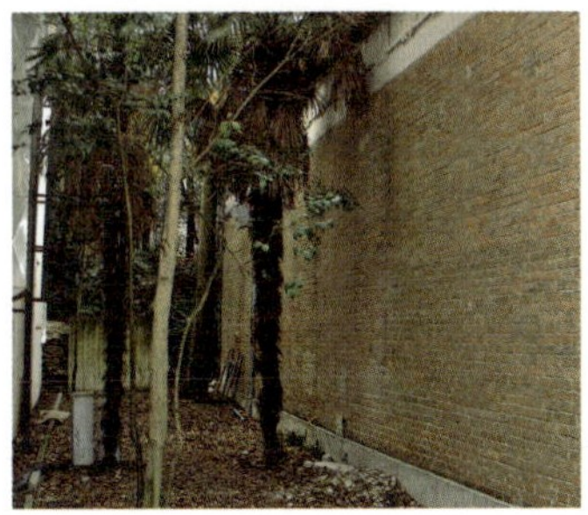
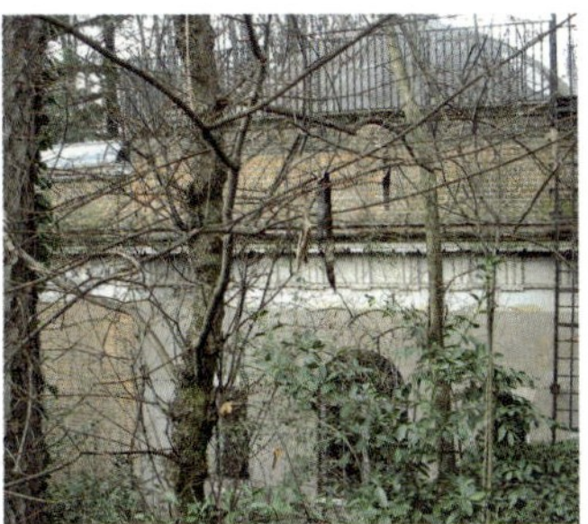
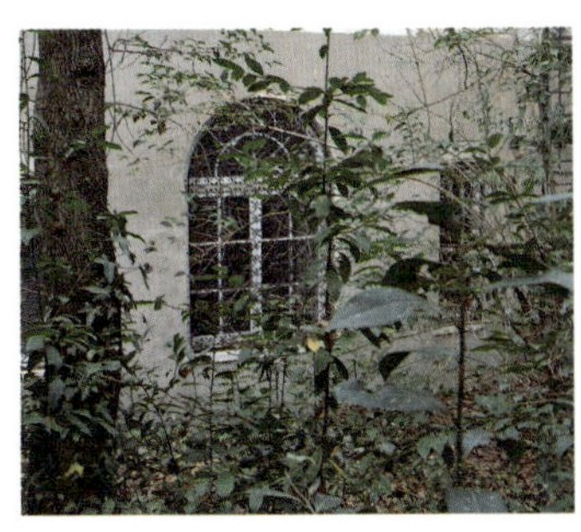

4. Vices and Virtues

The point of departure for *Bruce Nauman: Topological Gardens* has been to ask whether an exhibition, through its very structure, could help the viewer relate to both the work it presents and the context in which it takes place. In the case of an exhibition that sets out from the start to achieve the impossible task of representing a country, the challenge is to acknowledge that impossibility productively by making it integral to the logic of the show. It is as hard to imagine that a country could be represented by the work of a single artist—even work with the complexity of Nauman's—as it is feasible to organize a single exhibition presenting the totality of Nauman's practice in an exemplary and exhaustive way. An exhibition that *is* possible to imagine, though, is one whose structure allows it an active relation with both its subject and its context. In trying to produce such an exhibition, we have used the model of topology to propose a specific, contextually bounded way of approaching Nauman's practice and also of interpreting the urban structure of the city in which the exhibition is set. By allowing the audience to use its experience of the city to relate to Nauman's work, and vice versa, the exhibition sets out to question the ideological foundations of the national pavilions that frame it. Topology is used to establish these connections, to poke into these seemingly discrete territories so that their mutual resonance engenders a more intense relation between them and the audience.

Incorporating two venues outside the Giardini as well as the Delano & Aldrich building, the U.S. Pavilion imagined in *Bruce Nauman: Topological Gardens* is bound not so much territorially as aesthetically to the city of Venice, to its history, its inhabitants, and the actual uses of its spaces. The renovated interior of a Gothic palazzo on the Grand Canal, which previously housed the administrative offices of the Università Ca' Foscari, and the cloisters and main lecture hall—originally a refectory—of the Università Iuav, in the former convent of the Tolentini church, exemplify the palimpsest of public and private spaces upon which the fabric of Venice is built (figs. 25, 27, 28, 30). In this sense their inclusion as exhibition sites is intended to amplify the contradictions in the creation of the Giardini in the nineteenth century and their later use as the site of an exhibition still closely associated with a well-defined political and

Fig. 25 U.S. Pavilion at the Giardini della Biennale

economic project. Together, the three sites of *Topological Gardens* compose a kind of phrase, which parses through cases of the structural instability between the public and the private that characterizes the urban fabric of Venice.

If the exhibition's three sites are called on to stand as a visible manifestation of the topological nature of the city's urban structure, then the three conceptual threads around which the show has been conceived are intended to let the viewer imagine a topological logic in Nauman's work. Each thread is organized, once again, like a sentence, in which works take the place of words, or like the clusters of notes in a musical score. The threads are intended, not to exhaust the possibilities of any specific artistic operation, but to indicate its directionality, to point to a path rather than follow it to its conclusion. A thread is not a collection of evidence but the manifestation of an aesthetic possibility.

The threads' mode of operation is simple. First, each thread is just a connector between two terms. Although more could have been found in the case of this exhibition, three were identified: Hand to Head, Space to Sound, and Fountains to Neons. These elements are clearly of different status; it is unimportant for the terms a thread connects to belong to the same order of things. These terms exist only as tentative examples of polarities that the threads represent. The threads are not exhaustive—rather than pretending or intending to constrain the constantly surprising open-endedness of Nauman's work, they are open categories. Nor are the elements in one thread precluded from becoming part of another—a work like *Three Heads Fountain (Three Andrews)* (2005; fig. 26), for example, could exist in several of these conceptual parameters or, more properly, between them. The threads are imaginary, evolving paths among individual works, taking the viewer visually, experientially, and conceptually from one term to another, as if they were metonymically linked. More properly, the relation between the elements of one thread could be described as topological, in the sense that it always seems possible to imagine a passage from one to the other by stretching and twisting, shrinking and contracting—again to quote words used by Nauman, in the text he wrote to accompany *Flayed Earth Flayed Self (Skin Sink)* (1973; plate 9). That the transformations of the body in Heads and Hands seem to mimic the transitions from Sound to Space, and the fact that both echo the passages from image to language exemplified in the thread that leads from Fountains to Neons, testifies to the consistency of Nauman's work across time and mediums.

In the trajectory from hand to head, it is the mouth that one finds first. Yet if *From Hand to Mouth* (1967; plate 11) begins the first thread, it is only because its greenish surface, full of detail and somewhat macabre associations, evokes precisely the totality of the body that the casting process has subtracted. The tender hand hangs, fingers extended, grasping nothing. Its five fingers multiply in the gestures of *Fifteen Pairs of Hands* (1996; plate 7), which take to three dimensions the topological movement started by the *Fingers and Holes* prints referenced above (figs. 5–12). The relation between these two works may be used to exemplify the passage from one term of a thread to the other. One of the bronze sculptures in *Fifteen Pairs of Hands* (1996; fig. 4) comprises two hands welded at the wrist, so that they aim in opposite directions. Their gestures resemble those of the neon hands in *Human*

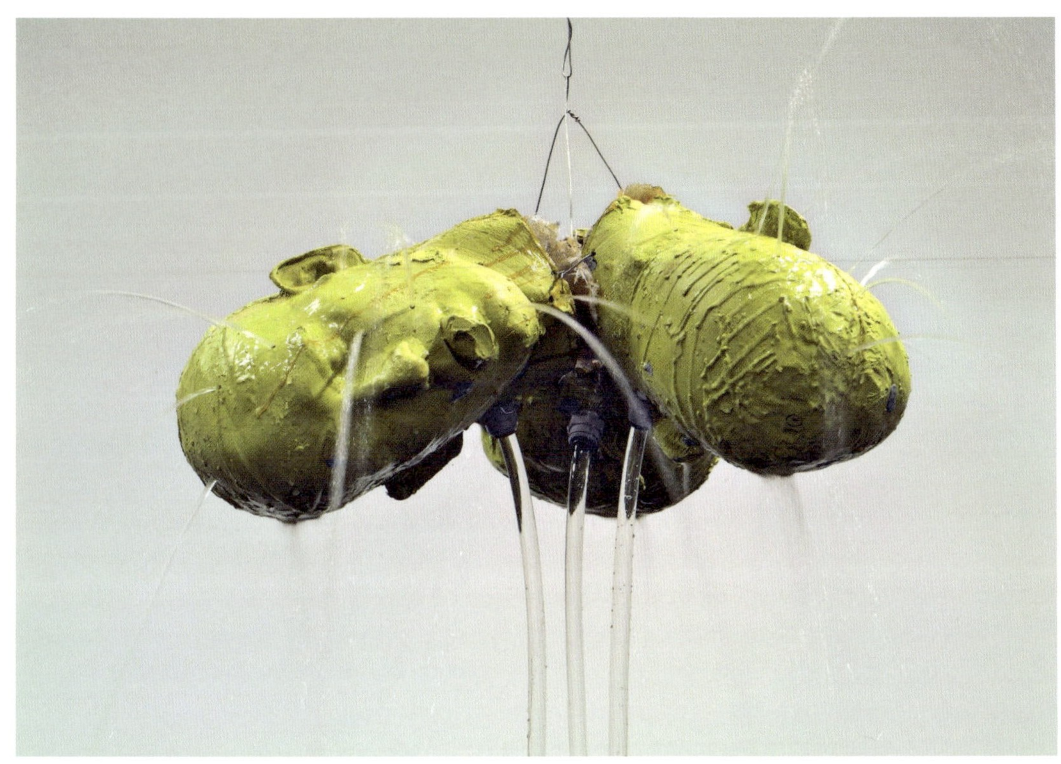

Sexual Experience (1985; plate 14), but now they are turned around: the index finger of one hand, instead of penetrating the hole created by the finger and thumb of the other, points to the base, while the other hand, inverted, seems to signal that everything is fine. The gestures are isolated and recombined, changing their meaning. More importantly, that instability of meaning seems to extend to the other pairs of hands, as if all fifteen pairs were words in an unintelligible phrase. Form promises meaning only as pure promise, always unfulfilled, while meaning is revealed as an accident of form.

Hands and heads multiply in divergent series. *Untitled* (1970/2009; plate 24) began as the performance of two dancers, the fingers of their hands slightly touching, a subtle contact that helped them to define the space traced by the circular motion of their bodies on the marked surface of the floor. Their performance was filmed, and a video projection recording their unraveling movement, like an endless circle of bodies, twisting and spiraling, was shown in the empty room in which it had taken place. Mutely gesturing, constantly moving hands are the sole protagonists of *Washing Hands Normal* (1996; plate 28), while hands move in slow motion in *Coffee Spilled and Balloon Dog* (1993; plate 2), spilling coffee or stretching and bending a long balloon to make a dog. This folding and unfolding of both the hands and the object

Fig. 26 Bruce Nauman. Detail of *Three Heads Fountain (Three Andrews)*, 2005 (plate 21). François Pinault Foundation.

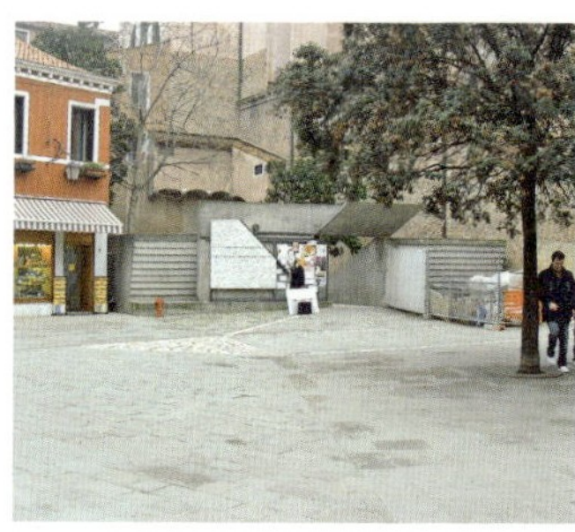

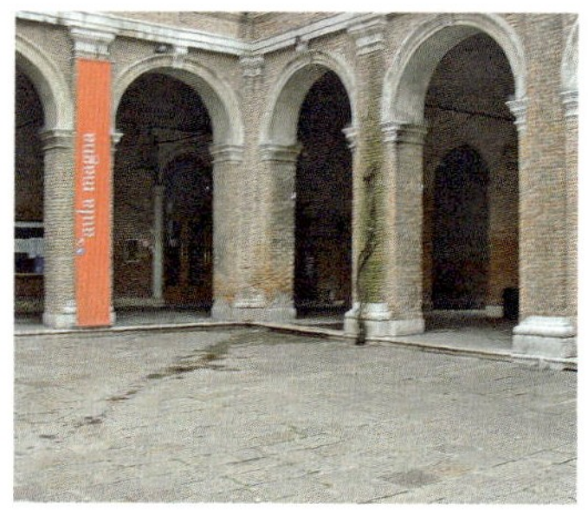

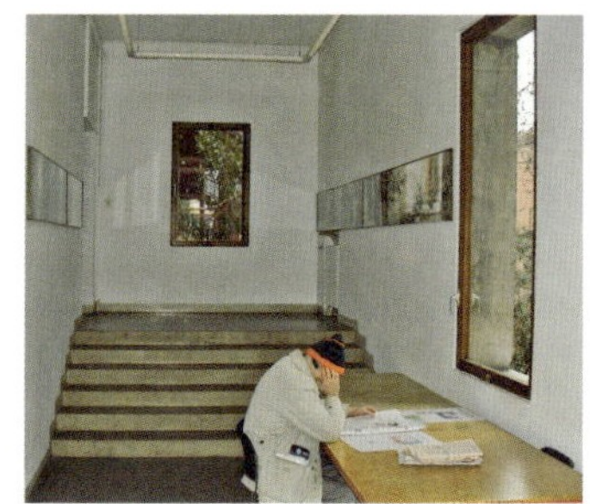

they handle anticipates the gestures of *Fifteen Pairs of Hands*, "screwing in, screwing out." Meanwhile, heads appear in wax (*Four Pairs of Heads [Wax]*, 1991; plate 10), bronze (*Hanging Head for Leo*, 1990; plate 13), or neon (*Double Poke in the Eye II* and *Eating Buggers*, both 1985; plates 4 and 5, respectively). Silent heads face a blank wall in a corner of the room (*Five Pink Heads in the Corner*, 1992; plate 8), screaming heads jump on video screens (*Think*, 1993; plate 20), and when we find heads hanging ripe from plastic tubes, spitting and sputtering water, a threshold has been crossed and we are stepping into the pool of a fountain (*Three Heads Fountain* works of 2005; plate 21; fig. 26).

The thread that leads from Sound to Space may start in the emptiness of the artist's studio, where Nauman "spent a lot of time . . . kind of reassessing, or assessing, why, why are you an artist and what do you do," as he told Michele de Angelus in 1980. An empty studio in which nobody works is what there is to see in the video *Sound for Mapping the Studio Model (The Video)* (2001; plate 19), where, although no artist is seen the work is done, nonetheless, perhaps implying that whatever we accomplish is always done behind our backs, as if by somebody else. The artist's studio is a relentless presence in Nauman's work, sometimes standing in for the source of all creativity, which at times Nauman seems to understand as the effect of a language game, so that the studio becomes in fact the place for testing the limits of any definition of art. It is also where the artist may or may not choose to work, the preferred space where his ideas, projects, and activities come together or unravel—an unraveling externalized and literalized in the movements of the two dancers in *Untitled* of 1970/2009 (plate 24).

In Nauman's work any investigation of the physical qualities of the studio seems to coincide with a psychological and literal mapping of the artist's body. Often, this mapping will be done through the use of sound, as in *Sound for Mapping the Studio Model (The Video)*, which exemplifies the protagonism that sound acquires in this process. The work is a single-channel video lasting just over an hour in which Nauman extracted and edited together all the video segments that included sound events from the much longer *Mapping the Studio I (Fat Chance John Cage)* (2001; fig. 31). As the title of the single-channel version suggests, it is sound and

 Fig. 27 Università Iuav di Venezia at Tolentini

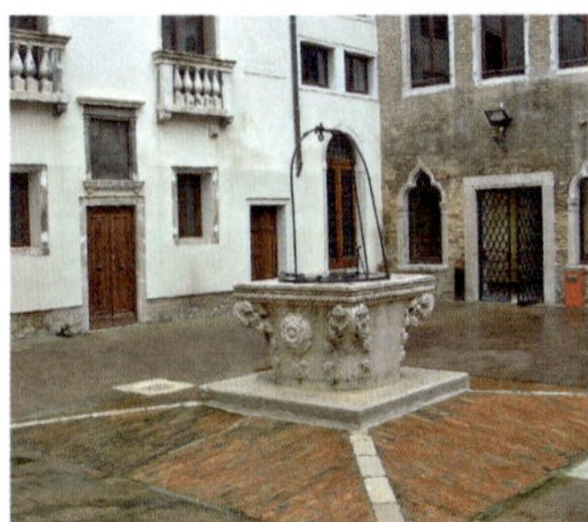
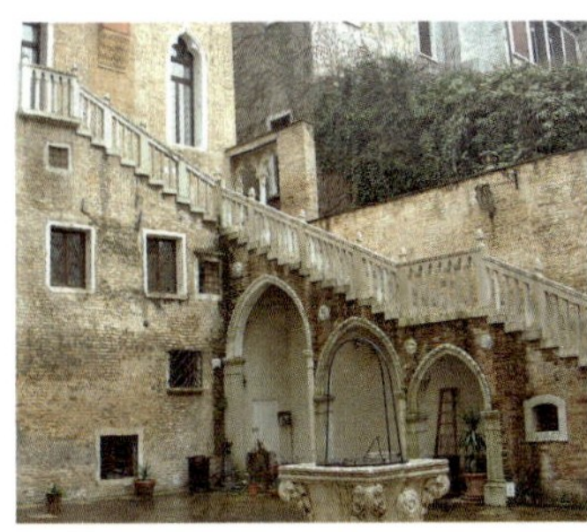
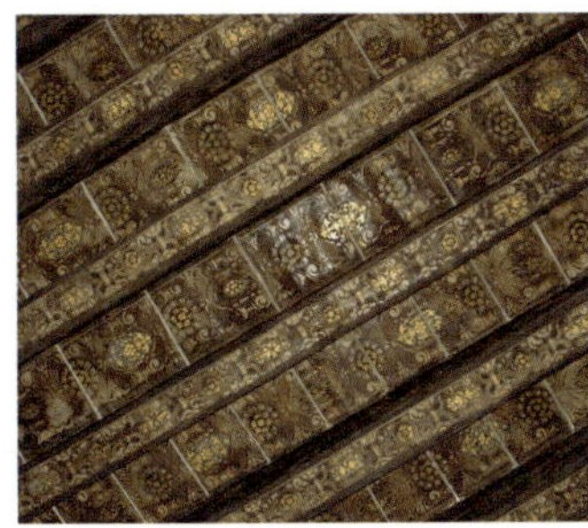

sound alone that allows for a precise understanding of the literal and metaphorical space of the studio. Sound punctures the physical boundaries of a body or space, reconfiguring the audience's experience of the work and its surroundings. From *Studio Aids II* (1967–68; checklist 21) to *Days* (2009; checklist 16; see the section elsewhere in the catalogue), it is for Nauman a privileged tool of investigation and a way to short-circuit the boundaries between spaces, bodies, and language, turning these discrete entities into topological wholes.

If the studio is empty like the artist's head—or is it the viewer's?—then it is because it is indeed a head or a cage. Installations like *Audio Video Piece for London, Ontario* (1969–70; plate 1) and *Double Steel Cage Piece* (1974; plate 3) are literally set up so that they can trap the viewer through seductive visual counterpoints and twisted formal resonances. If the head is empty like an empty space, then by twisting and stretching it may unfold into a room, its walls contracting and expanding until they turn themselves inside out. An empty head sinking in on itself, until it spits itself out, like water in a fountain. If the jet of water is the head's interior, it is because its empty space has been translated into a liquid language. Language becomes fluid, water resting patiently inside ourselves so it can be expelled in the form of meaning, illuminating us. Language endlessly enlightening, itself a spiraling truth leading nowhere.

Maybe as a sign of Nauman's many happy coincidences with the work of Marcel Duchamp—and specifically with his final piece, *Étant donnés: 1° La chute d'eau, 2° Le gaz d'éclairage (Given: 1. The Waterfall, 2. The Illuminating Gas)* of 1946–66—the "given" passage from neon (which is certainly an "illuminating gas") to fountains (or waterfalls), or vice versa, is always mediated by language. This transition is first and foremost exemplified by the transition between an early neon, *The True Artist Helps the World by Revealing Mystic Truths (Window or Wall Sign)* of 1967 (plate 22), to *Untitled (The True Artist Is an Amazing Luminous Fountain)* of 1968 (plate 26), in which cut-out letters are installed on the perimeter of a preexisting architectural detail of a threshold, window, or doorway. The earlier, extraordinarily evocative photograph *Self-Portrait as a Fountain* of 1966–67 (fig. 29) retroactively confirms this. What is at stake in the passage from one work to the other is the very definition of art, which is interrogated through

Fig. 28 Exhibition Spaces at Università Ca' Foscari

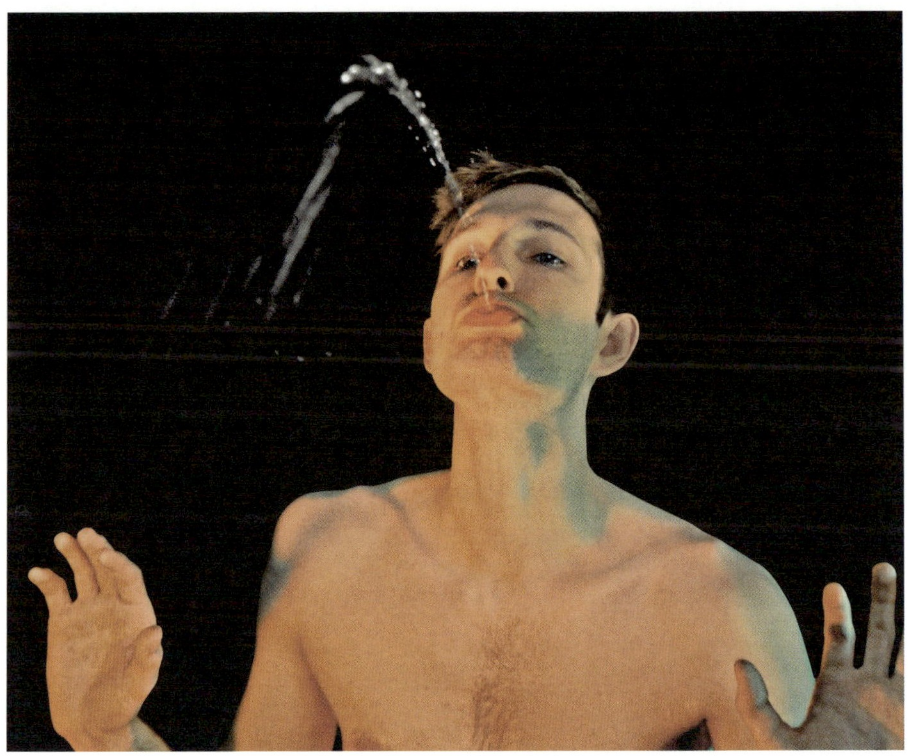

an examination of the artist's role initially—and literally—embodied by Nauman but also posed insistently to the viewer. The fluctuating and disorienting glare of *Pink and Yellow Light Corridor (Variable Lights)* from 1972 (plate 17), for example, twists and distorts the viewer's perception as a literal manifestation—both affirmative and ironic—of the presumed powers of art. The definition of art becomes a matter of the viewer's experience in a continuously unfolding topological logic. Together with sound—from which it is indissociable—language is used and abused by Nauman to create fluctuating continuities out of the discrete singularities of mediums, disciplines, bodies, and spaces.

Finally, it is the tension between private and public spaces in Venice that constitutes a fourth thread. As a city that allows for the systematic confusion between outside and inside, its urban structure and the subjective way in which it is experienced, Venice is ideal for lending itself to dialogue and interplay with Nauman's works. As is the case with the negative spaces in *Fingers and Holes*, the spaces between the three sites of the exhibition should not be considered

Fig. 29 Bruce Nauman. *Self-Portrait as a Fountain,* from the portfolio *Eleven Color Photographs*; 1966–67/1970/2007.
Ink-jet print exhibition copy (originally chromogenic development print). Edition 8/8.
Image 19 7/8 x 23 3/4 inches (50.9 x 60.3 cm).
Museum of Contemporary Art, Chicago. Gerald S. Elliott Collection, 1994.11.k

empty, but an integral part of the structure of the show. It is in those uncharted passages between works of art and buildings, where the viewer's imagination allows her to piece together her experiences, reinventing the work in her mind while traversing the city. There is no hierarchical arrangement of the exhibition sites. Like Leibnitzian monads, each could be seen independently or in any combination, thus precluding the need for a mandatory or preferred order in which to go from one to the other. The space between them counts, though, as does the individual process of finding them. They are the fingers to the city's holes, and both are part of the experience.

It should be noted that the works included in each of the three sites do not exemplify the individual composition of any one thematic thread. Each site instead includes a combination of threads in which no single one prevails over the others. The sites are organized to show works that resonate with each other, so that formal and conceptual features that dictate the transition from one work to another become transparent to the viewer—the only condition, as always with Nauman's work, being to pay attention. In this way, visiting only one of the three sites would still allow the audience to experience the logic that organizes the entire exhibition.

As the exhibition intends to suggest that the relationships among mediums and disciplines that comprise Nauman's work are also topological in nature, each of the sites allows for both the widest possible variety of formal and conceptual solutions to the problems posed by the different threads and the inclusion of works from the longest possible span of the artist's career. Writing about Marcel Duchamp's *Étant donnés*, Anne d'Harnoncourt and Walter Hopps argue that "the limited number of things Duchamp made constitutes an oeuvre of such concentration and density that it reads not only forward in time with the chronological progression of his career, but backwards and even sideward." The same could be said of Nauman, and that criterion underlies the guiding principle in the selection and presentation of the works included in this project. In a way, by choosing not to display Nauman's works chronologically, the exhibition condemns itself—and the work—to a circular logic. Or, put differently, it condemns the viewer—just as any visitor to Venice—to start *in media res*, to be always, inescapably, in the middle of everything.

5. Caffeine Dreams (Epilogue)

By midsummer, the Giardini becomes heavy with decadent magnolia trees, ripe with bees and perfume. Miniature jasmines are ready to be plucked; delicate lavender and shadowy alleys find themselves peppered with dense clusters of grass in shades of violent green. The grass is carefully manicured only during Biennale years, so that the rest of the time it grows uncontrolled, covering as much territory as the weather permits, and the result is delightful. Yet, when there is no show on display, few people visit. There are the occasional young couples, film crews, unavoidable and lost tourists escaping the weary summer crowds, or groups of children hiding from the blinding light reflecting on the shallow waters of the lagoon. Once at the iron fences whose limited use is designed to deter visitors with no tickets from entering the Biennale grounds, very few walk inside the gardens and even fewer approach the silent buildings of the national pavilions. Most seem content simply to peek at the unruly grasses and the slender silhouettes of distant trees. With nothing to display, the reason for the gardens to be exposed quietly recedes. Discreetly, they fold back upon themselves—skin peeling, sinking, thinking, spiraling away—and they restitute their secret self to a city for which they never had a proper use. Their casual visitors seem to unknowingly know that. Intent on retracing their steps back to the city, they hesitate and start to walk toward the Grand Canal, leaving behind the iron fence, until they stop. For a brief moment, they look back at the gardens as if looking down at their truest reflection in a distant, impossible mirror. And then they turn away.

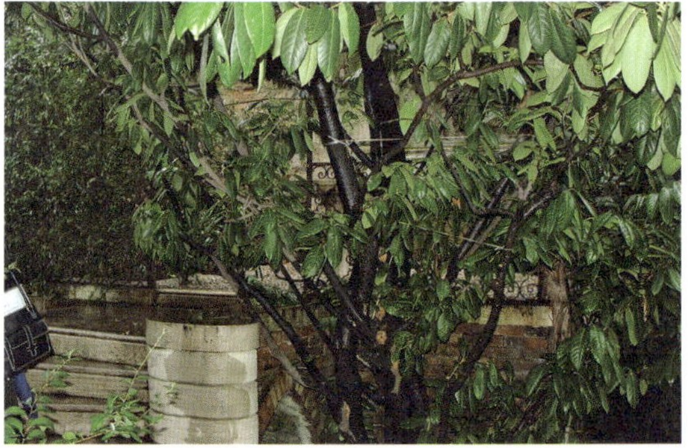

 Fig. 30 Palazzo Brandolini

Sources

Auping, Michael. "Metacommunicator." In *Bruce Nauman: Raw Materials*, exh. cat. London: Tate, 2004

Cassini, Giocondo. *Piante e vedute prospettiche di Venezia: 1459–1855.* Venice: La Stamperia di Venezia Editrice, 1982

Dammicco, Mariagrazia, and Marianne Majerus. *Jardins secrets de Venise.* Paris: Flammarion, 2006

de Bruyn, Eric. "Topological Pathways of Post-Minimalism." *Grey Room* 25 (Fall 2006)

De Sabbata, Massimo. *Tra diplomazia e arte: le Biennali di Antonio Maraini (1928–1942).* Udine: Forum, 2006

d'Harnoncourt, Anne, and Walter Hopps. "Étant donnés: 1° La chute d'eau, 2° Le gaz d'éclairage: Reflections on a New Work by Marcel Duchamp." *Philadelphia Museum of Art Bulletin* 64, nos. 229 and 300 (1969)

Gough-Cooper, Jennifer, and Jacques Caumont. "Effemerides on and about Marcel Duchamp and Rrose Sélavy, 1887–1968." In *Marcel Duchamp*, exh. cat. Milan: Bompiani, Palazzo Grazzi, 1993

Goy, Richard. *Venice: The City and Its Architecture.* London: Phaidon, 1997

Howard, Deborah. *The Architectural History of Venice*, rev. and enlarged ed. New Haven: Yale University Press, 2002

Martini, Maria Vittoria. "A Brief History of I Giardini." In *Muntadas: On Translation: I Giardini, Spanish Pavilion, 51 Venice Biennale*, ed. Bartomeu Marí and Marc Augé. Barcelona: Actar, 2005

Nauman, Bruce. *Please Pay Attention Please: Bruce Nauman's Words: Writings and Interviews*, ed. Janet Kraynak. Cambridge, Mass.: MIT Press, 2002

Rylands, Philip, and Enzo di Martino. *Flying the Flag for Art: The United States and the Venice Biennale, 1895–1991.* Richmond, Va.: Wyldbore and Wolferstand, 1993

Schulz, Jürgen. *Saggi e memorie di storia dell'arte 7: The Printed Plans and Panoramic Views of Venice (1486–1797).* Florence: Casa Editrice Leo S. Olschki, 1972

Simon, Joan, in *Bruce Nauman: Fingers and Holes.* Los Angeles: Gemini G.E.L., 1994

Simon, Joan, et al. *Bruce Nauman: Exhibition Catalogue and Catalogue Raisonné.* Minneapolis: Walker Art Center, 1994

Bruce Nauman: Mapping the Studio, Changing the Field

Michael R. Taylor

In the summer of 2000 Bruce Nauman spent seven weeks recording one-hour segments of footage in his studio, on the ranch in the New Mexico desert, where he has worked since 1989. He filmed seven different locations within the studio for seven nights each, letting the equipment record the nocturnal sights and ambient sounds of his work space. This real-time transcription of events Nauman then edited into a film, *Mapping the Studio I (Fat Chance John Cage)* (2001; fig. 31), which lasts five hours and forty-five minutes and was first shown using seven video projectors and multiple audio tracks in a room-sized installation at the Dia Center for the Arts, New York, in 2002. The title's reference to the American composer John Cage, known for his use of chance operations to determine the form of his music, underscores the aleatory aspect of the piece, in which the cameras and microphones registered what took place both inside and outside the studio without the artist's hand or vision to guide them—except in the editing process, where Nauman condensed, rather than added to, the greenish-gray images of his work space at night.

Nauman also created a Cage-like soundtrack of buzzing flies, howling coyotes, barking dogs, neighing horses, and the whistles of distant trains to accompany the film. The discombobulated viewer suspects that these eerie noises come from outside the rough, shacklike studio, while inside it the stillness of the empty space is sporadically punctuated by scurrying mice, flickering moths, and a tailless black cat, with incandescent eyes, who skulks among the electrical cords, tools, and other studio debris. The sound and presence of these nocturnal creatures enliven what would otherwise have been a banal recording of an empty studio akin to the nonaction films of Andy Warhol, which were a powerful influence on Nauman's early video work. The static blankness of Warhol's 1964 film *Empire*, for example, is replaced here by unsettling surveillance techniques, with every movement of the trespassing field mice and prowling black cat being observed and recorded, thus extending the interest in animal behavior seen in, say, Nauman's *Learned Helplessness in Rats (Rock and Roll Drummer)* (1988). Every now and then the fleeting image of Nauman himself appears on camera, turning the equipment on and then leaving the room. Mostly, though, he is absent, leaving the studio itself as the work's subject.

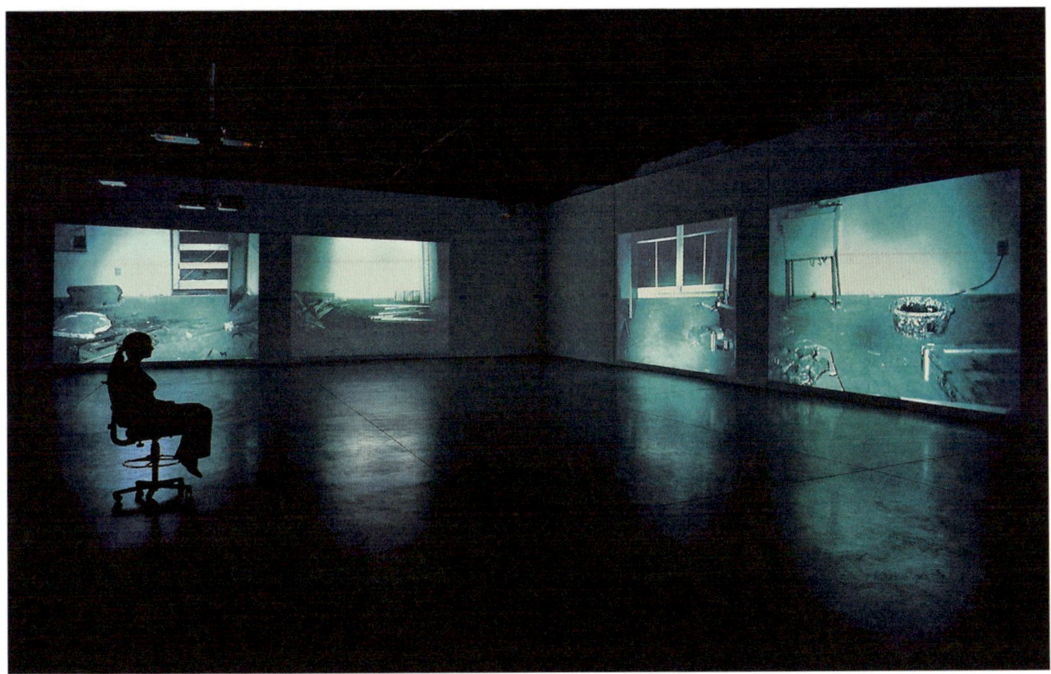

According to Nauman, *Mapping the Studio I (Fat Chance John Cage)* was triggered by the rodents:

> We had a big influx of field mice that summer, in the house and in the studio. They were so plentiful even the cat was getting bored with them. I was sitting around the studio being frustrated because I didn't have any new ideas, and I decided that you have to work with what you've got. What I had was this cat and the mice, and I happened to have a video camera in the studio that had infrared capability. So I set it up and turned it on at night and let it run when I wasn't there, just to see what I'd get.[1]

This emphasis on the studio as the primary site of creativity—a place where ideas are generated by simply working "with what you've got"—has been one of the dominant themes of Nauman's work since the mid-1960s. In the immense and diverse body of work that he has produced over the ensuing decades, the studio has functioned variously as a theater, a prison, and a laboratory for repeated, task-oriented experiments that are carefully staged yet utterly inconsequential. In the process, Nauman's studio has often become a mute witness to surveillance, interrogation, and even torture, as the artist channels his frustration and anger with the human condition into extraordinary works of art of great originality and raw emotional power.

Fig. 31 Bruce Nauman. Installation view of *Mapping the Studio I (Fat Chance John Cage)*, 2001.

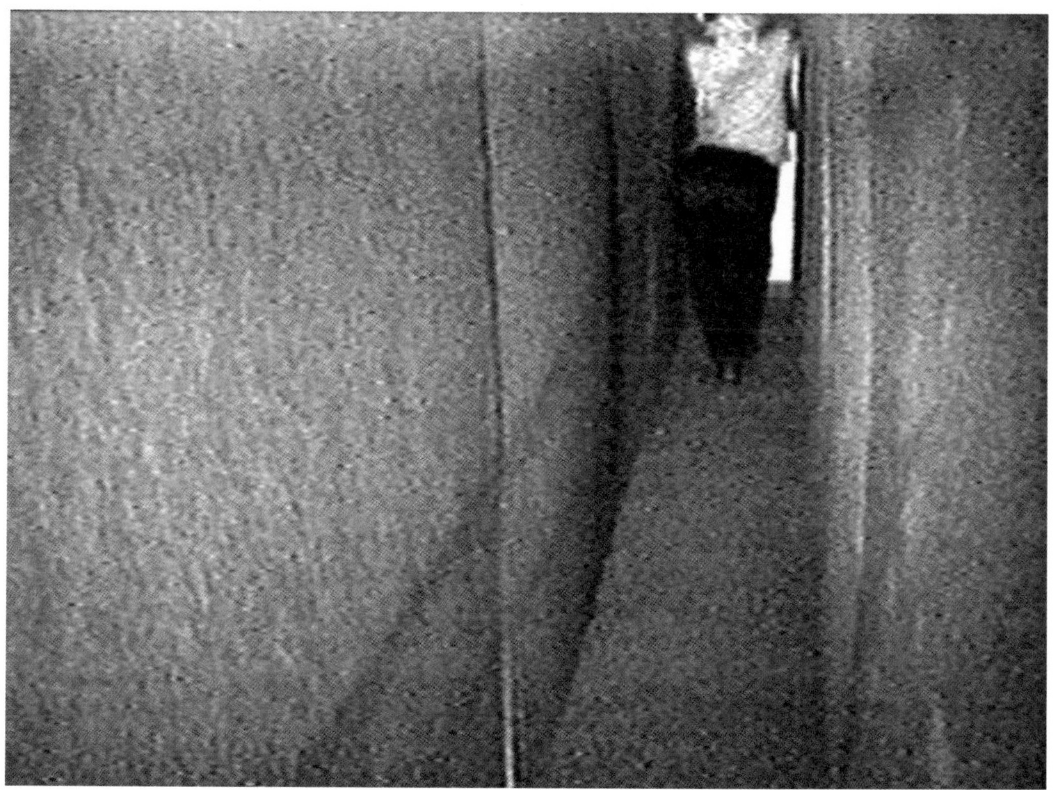

The studio has appeared in various guises over the course of Nauman's long career and often seems to have an ambiguous and multivalent meaning for him, depending on the specific work and context. In the 1968 sound installation *Get Out of My Mind, Get Out of This Room* (checklist 20), for example, the repeated title phrase, uttered by the artist in a variety of intonations from speakers sunk in the wall of an empty space, projects onto the gallery visitor the solitude and alienation of the studio where the work was created. The work suggests that the loneliness of the artist's vocation, which requires spending countless hours alone in the studio, can induce paranoid delusions that transform the work space into a threatening and disquieting place, as well as a metaphor for the artist's tortured mind.

In Nauman's work the studio can be an alluring place of intimacy and reflection, an escape from the everyday world, but more often than not it is oppressive, like the claustrophobically narrow corridors that the artist initially conceived as a prop for *Walk with Contrapposto* (fig. 32). In that video work, filmed in his studio in 1968, he sashayed down the long, narrow

Fig. 32 Bruce Nauman. *Walk with Contrapposto*, 1968. Videotape (black-and-white) and sound; 60 minutes

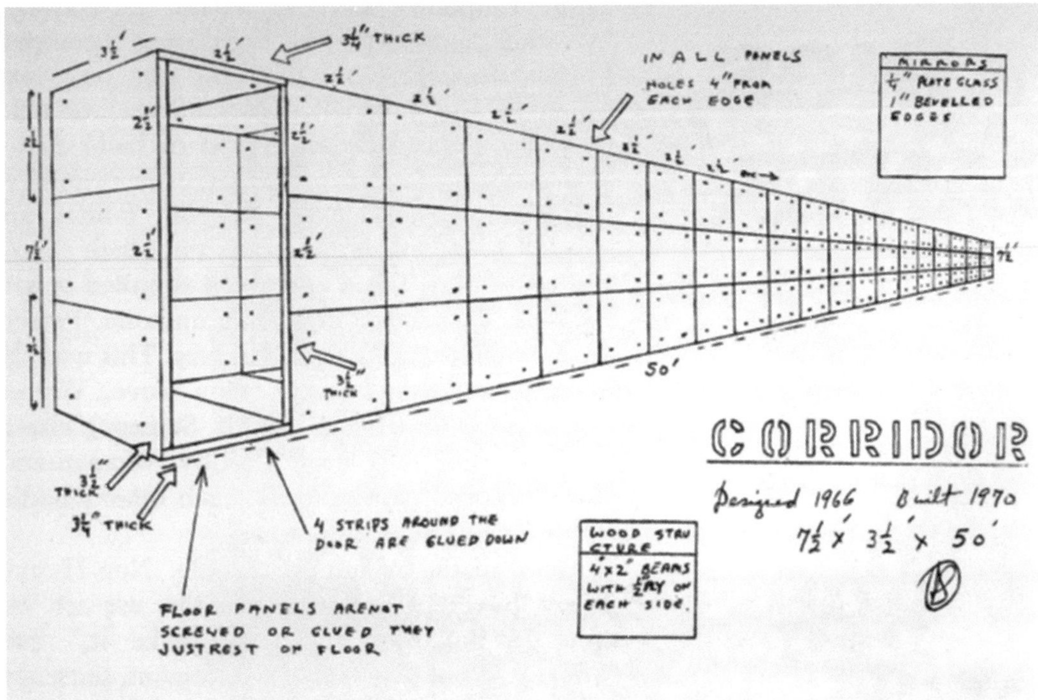

passageway in an exaggerated manner akin to the stylized poses of classical sculpture. In May 1969 this corridor—two long, parallel walls placed twenty inches apart—was reconstructed at the Whitney Museum of American Art, New York, under the title *Performance Corridor* (see fig. 49), as part of the exhibition *Anti-Illusion: Procedures/Materials*. Because the work received a restricted space in the exhibition, it became longer and much narrower, prohibiting all but the skinniest visitor from entering the space between them.

These architectural works, later variations of which would include fluorescent lights, mirrors, cameras, and videotape monitors, initiated the artist's lifelong interest in destabilizing the viewer's perception of space and of the body through works of art that challenge the mind and assault the senses. These corridors and other room-sized environments can be understood as surrogates for the artist's body, suggesting that Nauman took the implied narcissism of Lucas Samaras's contemporaneous mirrored corridor (fig. 33), conceived in a 1966 drawing but not built until 1970, to its logical extreme by using the measurements and proportions of his own body to determine the tall and narrow format of these constricted passageways, which correspond to the artist's thin, lanky physique and are just wide enough to accommodate someone of his build.[2]

Fig. 33 Lucas Samaras (American, born Greece, 1936). *Corridor;* designed 1966, built 1970. Collection of the artist. From *Arts Magazine* 48, no. 3 (December 1972–January 1973), repro. p. 55

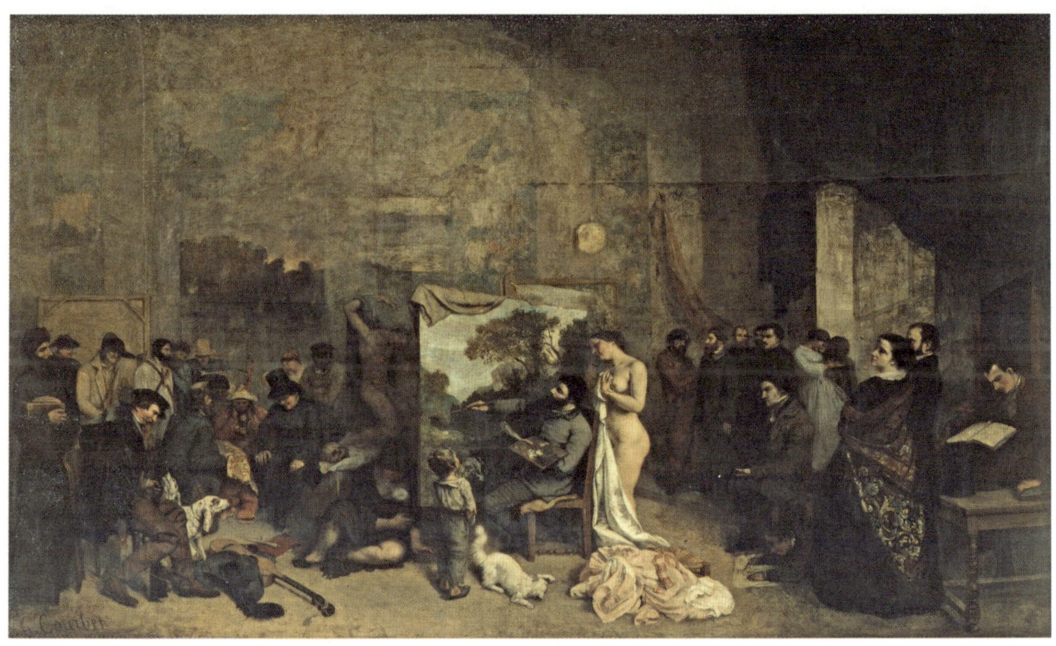

Nauman's work thus simultaneously challenges and reinforces the twentieth-century notion of the artist's studio as a private, almost sacred space, where the creative act takes place within an atmosphere of solitude and reflection. Until the end of the nineteenth century, the artist's studio was often used as a public venue of exchange between the painter or sculptor and his collectors, critics, friends, and models, as seen in Gustave Courbet's allegorical self-portrait *The Artist's Studio: A Real Allegory Summing up Seven Years of My Artistic and Moral Life* (fig. 34), of 1854–55, where the burly artist, brushes, knife, and palette in hand, holds center stage in the cavernous, sparsely furnished atelier. Courbet is clearly aware that he is on continuous display in this overpopulated interior, which he has depicted as the crossroads of contemporary French society, whole sections of which have been brought into the studio and then divided by the pivotal figure of the artist. Never before had the studio been accorded such consummate importance.[3]

This situation changed in the early twentieth century, when the move toward abstraction led many modern artists—especially inward-looking, quasi-mystical individuals like Vasily Kandinsky and Piet Mondrian, who equated their art with spiritual transcendence—to value their privacy and guard against outside interference. The studio was swiftly transformed into a laboratory for experimentation, replete with antiseptic white walls, in which only the privileged few were permitted entry, but also a place for aesthetic contemplation, where

Fig. 34 Gustave Courbet (French, 1819–1877). *The Artist's Studio: A Real Allegory Summing up Seven Years of My Artistic and Moral Life*, 1854–55.
Oil on canvas, 142 1/8 x 235 7/16 inches (361 x 598 cm).
Musée d'Orsay, Paris

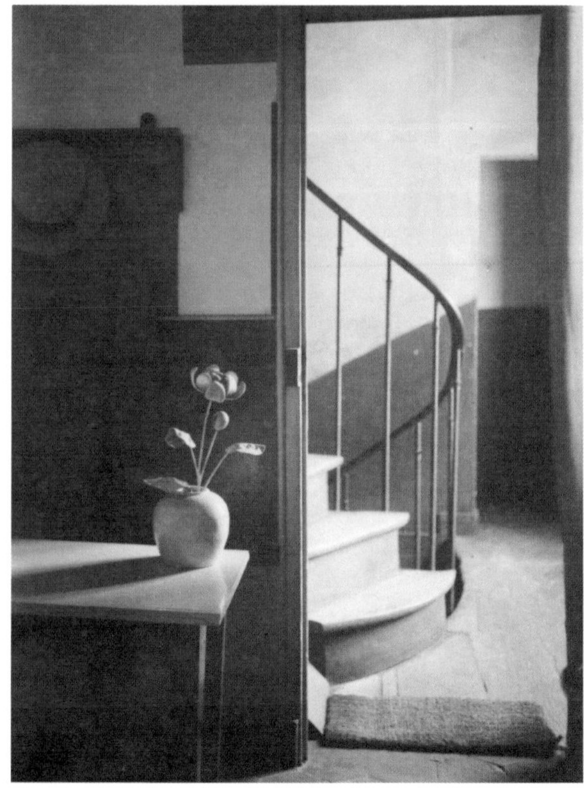

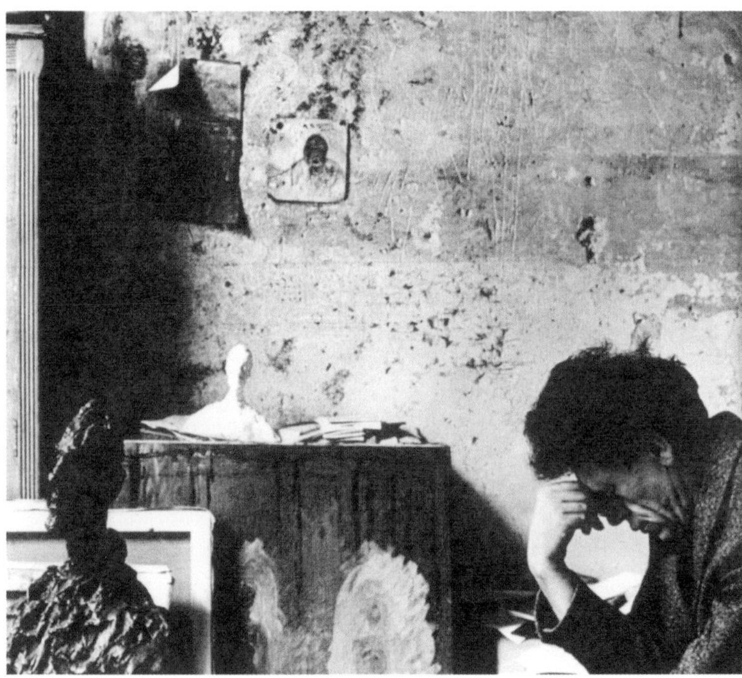

the formal austerity of the artist's creations was echoed in their pristine and often Spartan surroundings. One thinks of the pared-down simplicity of Mondrian's Paris apartment at 26, rue du Départ, as captured in André Kertész's extraordinary 1926 photograph (fig. 35), where even the leaves and petals of the single red tulip that the artist kept in a vase by the entrance to the studio were painted white, lest their fading bloom spoil the immaculate perfection of the space.[4]

By the early 1960s, when Nauman was studying art, initially as a painter and later as a Conceptual artist and process-based sculptor working in a variety of mediums at the University of California, Davis, the modern artist's studio had been romanticized through its photographic representation to the point where the artist no longer needed to be present for the space to signify the presence of artistic genius. On the contrary, the atmosphere of the

Fig. 35 André Kertész (American, born Hungary, 1894–1985). *Chez Mondrian, Paris 1926.* Gelatin silver print; image: 4 5/16 x 3 1/8 inches (10.9 x 7.9 cm); sheet: 5 3/4 x 3 3/16 inches (13.3 x 8.1 cm). The J. Paul Getty Museum, Los Angeles

Fig. 36 Alexander Liberman (American, born Russia, 1912–1999). *Concentration* (Alberto Giacometti in his studio, sometime between 1951 and 1955). From Alexander Liberman, *The Artist in His Studio* (1960; reprint, New York: Random House, 1988), p. 130, repro. D

studio as a place of creativity and illumination, where things are both made and revealed, was dramatically enhanced by the absence of the artist, whose recently used tools and unfinished works invested the space with a potent creative charge surpassing that of the individual sculptor or painter.[5]

Since World War II, the mystique of the artist's atelier had been widely disseminated in the United States through the publication in popular magazines, such as *Life*, *Vogue*, and *Harper's Bazaar*, of images of the homes and studios of famous modern artists such as Pablo Picasso, Henri Matisse, Pierre Bonnard, and Alberto Giacometti. Taken by a wide range of photographers, most notably Brassaï, Alexander Liberman, and Ugo Mulas, these images used the visual language of documentary photography to construct a highly romanticized account of the prewar Paris avant-garde through their current living quarters and ateliers. This process reached its apogee with the publication in 1960 of Liberman's *Artist in His Studio*, a "cultic" photography book that soon became a ubiquitous presence in art school libraries and the homes of aspiring artists.[6] Liberman, who worked for many years as a photographer and art director for *Vogue* magazine (and later as editorial director for all of the Condé Nast magazines), devoted nearly two decades to this book, whose rationale was "to show the creative process itself, and thereby to relate painting and sculpture with the mainstream of man's search for truth. Painters and sculptors, like poets and scientists, are seekers of truth."[7]

Liberman's book juxtaposes photographs of carefully posed modern artists such as Picasso, Matisse, Giacometti (fig. 36), Georges Braque, and Marcel Duchamp working or relaxing in their studios with dramatic images of the studios themselves. The photographs are accompanied by biographical sketches based on interviews and verbal anecdotes, and the result is a collective portrait of the Paris avant-garde, including heroic, often far-fetched personal exploits that the book unhesitatingly presents as fact. More important for this study, the images, like Brassaï's before them, promulgate the notion of the artist's studio as a place of enchantment, creativity, and self-expression, a private refuge imbued with almost magical qualities that Liberman seeks to capture, like lightning in a bottle, through the medium of photography. Encouraged by the exalted prose of the written vignettes, the reader feels privileged to enter the inner sancta of the artists' studios through photographs that attempt to transport us to the center of their private world, the world that Picasso believed to be the focal point of the whole artistic universe.[8]

That Nauman was not unaware of, or even immune to, the cultural construction of the studio in the 1960s as a mysterious, isolated personal realm in which the artist enjoyed a supreme and almost God-given authority can be seen in one of his earliest works in neon. In 1967 Nauman created a spiraling neon sign entitled *The True Artist Helps the World by Revealing Mystic Truths* (plate 22), which he installed in the large window of the studio he had recently established in a disused grocery store in San Francisco. The patently romantic message, emblazoned in pink and blue neon letters, looked back to the mystical dimension of early-twentieth-century abstraction, but at the same time questioned whether such a statement could still ring true in an age of mass consumerism, the Vietnam War, and the struggle for civil rights, an age when the ironic, parodist stance of Pop and Conceptual art had undermined the notions of aesthetic purity and the redeeming value of art. Nauman later spoke of his desire to test the veracity of this statement, which was

> on the one hand a totally silly idea and yet, on the other hand, I believed it. It's true and it's not true at the same time. It depends on how you interpret it and how seriously you take yourself. For me it's still a very strong thought.[9]

The placement of this illuminated credo in the storefront window no doubt confused and perplexed passersby as they tried to understand what product was being promoted by the brightly colored neon advertising sign. The ambiguous message thus served to demarcate Nauman's studio, like Mondrian's before it, as a site of radical creative experimentation and, just possibly, of spiritual transcendence, a place where the artist-prophet or seer divined mystic revelations.

Nauman had moved to San Francisco shortly after receiving his master's degree from the University of California, Davis, in 1966, where his teachers had included William T. Wiley and Robert Arneson. These nonconformist artists, then leading members of the nascent Bay Area Funk movement, inculcated in their young protégé the notion that a strong dedication to his work, especially time spent in the studio, would be as meaningful as the objects he made there. Taking this idea a step further, Nauman decided in 1966 that if

> I was an artist and I was in the studio, then whatever it was I was doing in the studio must be art. And what I was in fact doing was drinking coffee and pacing the floor. It became a question then of how to structure those activities into being art, or some kind of cohesive unit that could be made available to people. At this point art became more of an activity and less of a product.[10]

Nauman began to make work that came out of his routine daily activities in the studio, as well as from specific, often fruitless tasks that he assigned himself as a way of keeping busy and killing time, nevertheless performing and documenting them with the clinical detachment and precision of a scientist conducting experiments in a laboratory. These repetitive tasks included making a different sculpture out of a pile of flour on the studio floor every day for more than a month in 1966 (*Flour Arrangements*; see fig. 47); performing with overlaborious intensity in *Dance or Exercise on the Perimeter of a Square (Square Dance)* in 1967–68 (see fig. 63); and pacing or stomping about the studio in a forced and exaggerated manner in 1968 (*Slow Angle Walk [Beckett Walk]*, see fig. 50; and *Stamping in the Studio*). The last two were filmed at a studio owned by Roy Lichtenstein and Paul Waldman in Southampton, Long Island, using video equipment supplied by Nauman's New York dealer, Leo Castelli, which recorded the artist performing the titular repetitive actions continuously over the course of an hour.[11] Asked about these methodical exercises a few years later, Nauman would recall that it was "a tedious, complicated process to gain even a yard"[12]—a comment that could as easily be applied to the daily grind of his artmaking in the 1960s as to his efforts to move around the studio within such self-imposed limits. Alone with his video camera, in a studio space almost completely devoid of furniture let alone of art objects, Nauman used the nearest thing to hand—his body—as the raw material both for sculpture and for films without beginning or end, for they were intended to be played on a continuous loop, emphasizing the absurdly banal nature of the repetitive tasks being performed in front of the camera.

This interest in the human body as a vehicle for ideas appears again in the extraordinary 1967 sculpture *From Hand to Mouth* (plate 11), a wax body-cast taken from Nauman's first wife. As the title suggests, the impression begins at the fingers of Judy Nauman's right hand, continues up her arm, and ends with her chin and mouth. As a three-dimensional embodiment of a colloquial expression, this work has often been compared with Duchamp's *With My Tongue in My Cheek* (fig. 37), of 1959,[13] whose title embodies the older artist's irreverent, tongue-in-cheek approach to "serious" artmaking, as well as with Jasper Johns's use of colored body fragments in his 1955 painting *Target with Plaster Casts* (fig. 38), which features a row of wooden boxes filled with casts of lips, nose, ears, fingers, and male genitalia.

Nauman was especially interested in Johns's use of body parts and anatomical fragments in the form of wax and plaster casts or physical imprints, for example in the skin-print drawings of the early 1960s, which bear the indexical trace of the artist's face and hands. Like Johns, Nauman took a depersonalized approach to the body, which functioned for him as a measuring device, tool, or template, or an object that could be used and manipulated at will. This interest in body casting helps to explain Nauman's desire to obtain an impression of Judy Nauman's hand, arm, and lower jaw, but the title, which refers to the couple's shared existence just above the poverty line, bears a closer affinity to the punning yet literal titles of Duchamp and Man Ray.

Although Nauman has been reticent in acknowledging the extent of Duchamp's influence on his early work, its presence is undeniable, even though the older artist's iconoclastic ideas were often mediated through the work of contemporaries like Johns, Samaras, Joseph Kosuth, and Robert Morris. Duchamp's rejection of the "retinal" art of painting, together with the open-ended nature of his work, his embrace of contradiction, his use of working notes and diagrams and of quirky, unconventional materials such as glass, lead, wire, and dust, and his provocative invention of the readymade, all offered a profound challenge to existing definitions of the work of art and would have important ramifications for Nauman's work, despite his later claims that such ideas were simply in the air during his early years in California. Nauman was one of the few artists of his generation to heed Duchamp's call for artists to "go underground,"[14] a call that resonates strongly with Nauman's lifelong, self-enforced artistic isolation in his various studios in San Francisco, Mill Valley, and Pasadena, California, and later in two locations in New Mexico, where he continues to practice "withdrawal as an art form."[15]

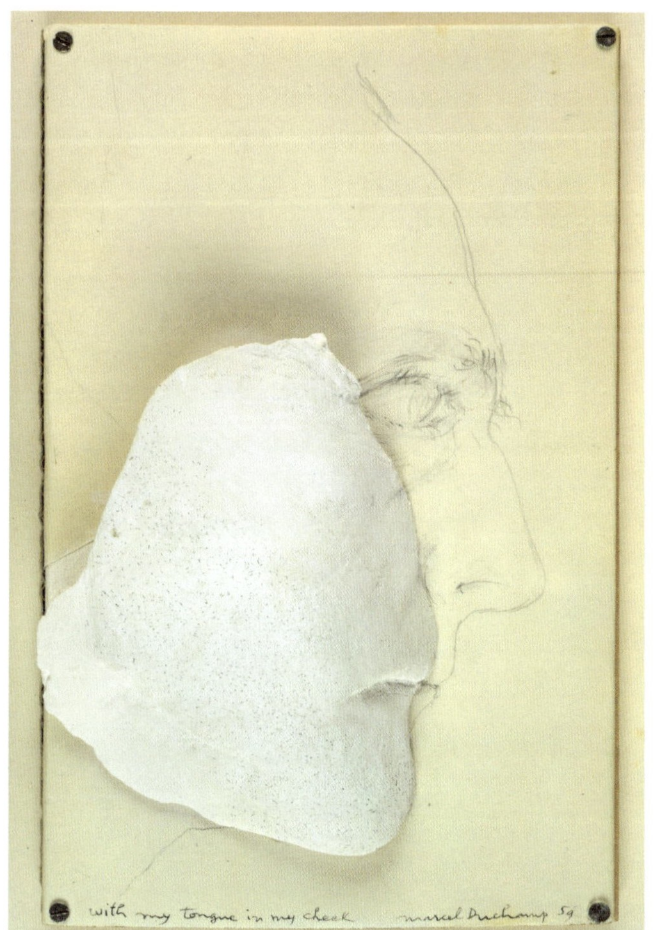

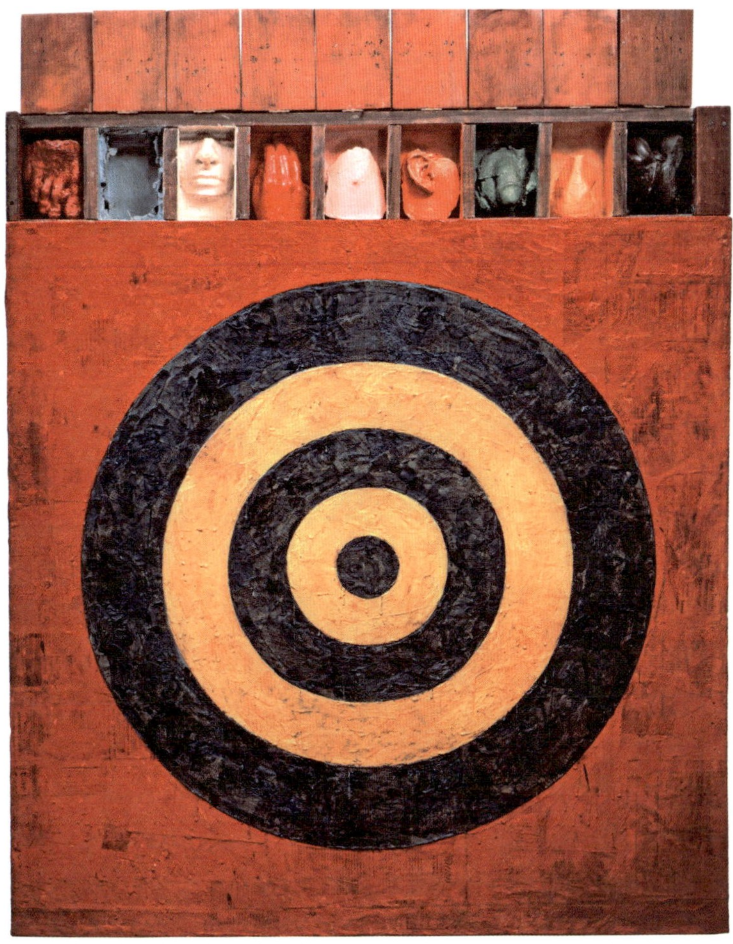

Fig. 37 Marcel Duchamp (American, born France, 1887–1968). *With My Tongue in My Cheek*, 1959.
Plaster, pencil, and paper, mounted on wood; $9\frac{13}{16}$ x $5\frac{7}{8}$ inches (24.9 x 14.9 cm).
Musée National d'Art Moderne, Centre Georges Pompidou, Paris

Fig. 38 Jasper Johns (American, born 1930). *Target with Plaster Casts*, 1955.
Encaustic and collage on canvas with painted plaster cast objects, 51 x 44 x $3\frac{7}{16}$ inches (129.5 x 111.8 x 8.8 cm).
Collection of David Geffen, Los Angeles

In many respects Nauman's approach to Duchamp echoes that of the American artist Hannah Wilke, who famously declared that "to honor Duchamp is to oppose him."[16] In Nauman's 1966 lead sculpture *A Rose Has No Teeth* (fig. 39), the words of the title are engraved in low relief on the convex side of a lead plaque, which was curved to allow it to be affixed to a tree trunk. Like all of his best work, this powerful piece can be understood in a variety of ways, rendering any single interpretation insufficient. One can say, though, that it probably began as a witty response to Morris's 1963 lead sculpture *Litanies*, which overtly referred to Duchamp's cryptic notes for the *Large Glass* (1915–23) by inscribing on a set of twenty-seven keys the words from the "litanies of the chariot" section of the latter's *Green Box* (1923). This dutiful homage is challenged in Nauman's work, whose title he quoted from a passage in Ludwig Wittgenstein's *Philosophical Investigations*.[17] This curious sentence was not, in my opinion, chosen at random, for it puns on the name of Duchamp's salacious feminine alter ego, Rrose Sélavy, as well as on his 1919 piece *Tzanck Check*, an enlarged handmade check for $115 drawn on the fictitious "Teeth's Loan & Trust Company," which Duchamp gave to his dentist, Daniel Tzanck, in payment for dental work.

A Rose Has No Teeth dared to suggest that Duchamp's Dadaist gestures had lost their bite, perhaps through overuse. Nauman clearly felt uncomfortable with the ubiquity of references to the French-born artist's hermetic ideas in the conceptually oriented work of West Coast artists after the landmark Duchamp retrospective exhibition at the Pasadena Art Museum in 1963, which he had not had the opportunity to see firsthand.[18] This sense of overexposure may explain why Nauman added to his 1967 drawing *Untitled (Study after "Wax Impressions of the Right Knees of Five Famous Artists")* (fig. 40) the coda "Do not use Marcel Duchamp," instead proposing the knees of such friends and contemporaries as Samaras, Wiley, Larry Bell, and Leland Bell.

In the same year that Nauman made *A Rose Has No Teeth*, he visited a large Man Ray exhibition at the Los Angeles County Museum of Art and was deeply impressed by the eclectic range of the American artist's work, and by his playful approach to language and artmaking:

> There was a large Man Ray show in Los Angeles, and I went and saw that. I remember thinking there were things I wanted to do and I didn't know how to do them, if I should do them. If they should be performances, if they should be paintings or what. And looking at the Man Ray show relaxed me about some of that, because he seemed very comfortable, how you do it, whether you make a picture, you make a film, or you make a painting. He sort of managed to do all these things.[19]

The 1966 Man Ray retrospective served as a legitimizing force for the youthful Nauman, who was still forging his artistic identity after his recent graduation from the University of California, Davis. The exhibition, which opened on October 26, 1966, had the same vital influence on Nauman that the 1963 Duchamp retrospective had had on West Coast artists like John Baldessari, Chris Burden, Richard Pettibone, and Ed Ruscha: Man Ray's inspirational example helped him to overcome his anxiety and doubt about his preoccupation with creating art

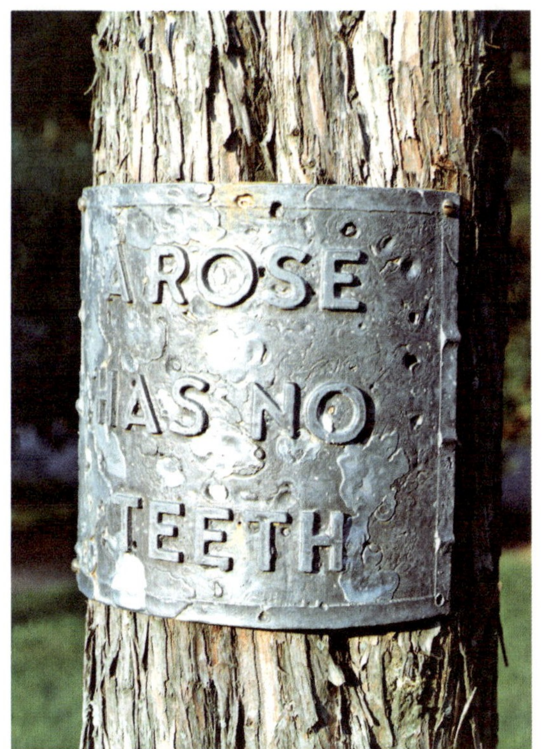

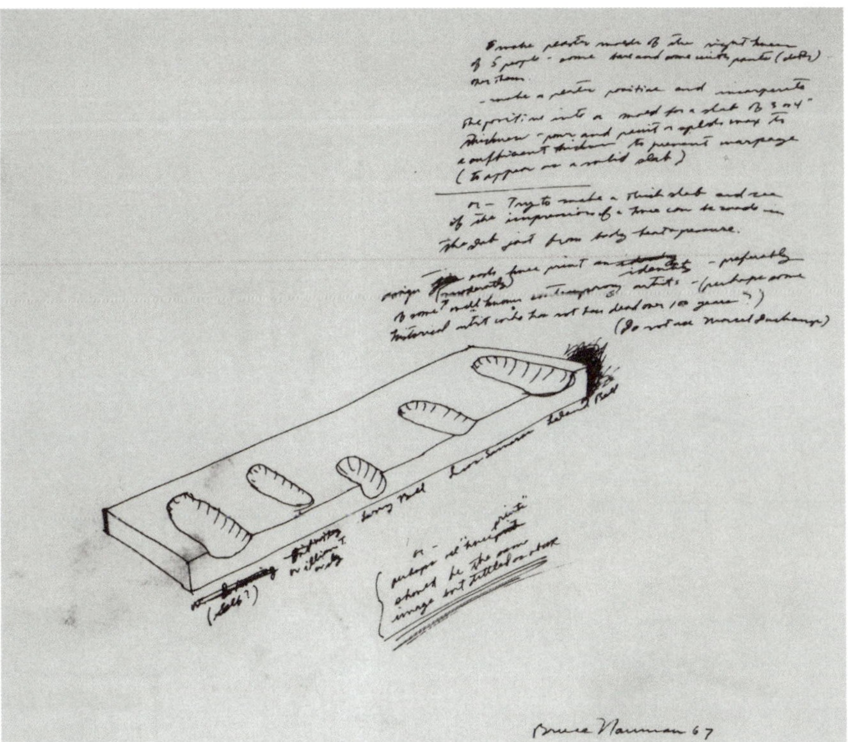

from the people and objects closest to him, including the studio-based activities that he recorded in performances and films. A previously underrecognized and all-too-often unacknowledged source for Nauman's work and ideas,[20] Man Ray was the quintessential studio-based artist. His pragmatic use of everyday materials found in the studio or the local hardware store to construct works of art imbued with personal meaning had a decisive impact on the younger artist, encouraging him to work with whatever medium was available, however unorthodox or improbable, and without worrying about developing a signature style.

The liberating effect of the 1966 exhibition for Nauman came partly from Man Ray's Dadaist rejection of hierarchical attitudes toward materials, a rejection that allowed him to express his ideas in a wide variety of mediums. Fearing that Californian audiences, living in the shadow of the Hollywood film industry, would associate him with commercial photography

Fig. 39 Bruce Nauman. *A Rose Has No Teeth (Lead Tree Plaque)*, 1966.
Lead plaque, $7\frac{1}{2}$ x 8 x $2\frac{3}{16}$ inches (19.1 x 20.4 x 5.6 cm).
Daros Collection, Switzerland

Fig. 40 Bruce Nauman. *Untitled (Study after "Wax Impressions of the Right Knees of Five Famous Artists")*, 1967.
Ink on paper, 19 x 24 inches (48.3 x 61 cm).
Emanuel Hoffmann Foundation, permanent loan to the Öffentliche Kunstsammlung Basel, H 1973.14

rather than the radical experimentation of Dada and Surrealism, Man Ray had insisted that the exhibition's curator, the art critic Jules Langsner, include his oil paintings, aerographs, sculpture, mixed-media objects, chess sets, collages, drawings, watercolors, and books, but no photographic work save for two sets of Rayographs.[21] By ignoring the artist's fashion photography, advertising work, and portraits of the interwar Parisian beau monde, images notable for their ravishing beauty and technical perfection, the kaleidoscopic Los Angeles exhibition, which featured three hundred works of art, presented another Man Ray, a multimedia artist interested in language, especially humorous puns and word games. In doing so it resonated with the concerns of young artists like Nauman, who immediately felt a deep affinity for the freedom and diversity of Man Ray's work and ideas.

The exhibition featured a large number of Man Ray's idiosyncratic objects and assemblages, whose punning titles and economy of means would have a profound impact on Nauman's future work. Man Ray intended these witty and often startling objects (mostly later replicas of originals that had been lost or destroyed by the time of the retrospective) to "amuse, bewilder, annoy, or to inspire reflection."[22] The show included classic examples like *It's Springtime*, of 1961, a jaunty assemblage of two coiled springs that the artist removed from his couch and joined together to form an enchanting work of kinetic art. For another piece, first conceived in 1958, Man Ray coated a long French baguette with cobalt-colored paint and balanced it on a pair of scales to create *Pain Peint* (fig. 41), whose descriptive title refers to the French homophones *pain* (bread) and *peint* (paint). The artist also liked to point out that the repeated refrain of "*pain*" and "*peint*" yields a faithful onomatopoeic representation of the honking sounds of the horns of fire engines, thus adding another level of meaning to the work.[23]

Eschewing the elegant sophistication of Duchamp's many bilingual *jeux de mots*, Man Ray's verbal and visual puns have an abruptness and directness perfectly matching his objects and assemblages, which are characterized by a bold assertiveness and a complete lack of pretension. Although sometimes dismissed as irreverent one-liners, these deceptively simple three-dimensional puns (Man Ray preferred the term "plastic puns") were more often than not the result of a long gestation period in which the artist completely thought through the complex meanings and associations of their titles and individual components.[24] For Nauman, the deadpan humor of these objects and their blunt, descriptive titles were quintessentially American, and far closer to his own sensibility than Duchamp's rarefied linguistic gymnastics. "I like Man Ray better," Nauman would later recall, "there's less 'tied-up-ness' in his work, more unreasonableness."[25]

The impact of Man Ray can be discerned in a number of Nauman's subsequent works, including *From Hand to Mouth* (plate 11), which resonates with Man Ray's literalisms, puns, and other language games in suggesting the breadline existence of the struggling contemporary artist through the idiomatic expression of its title. The artist and critic Coosje van Bruggen likewise suggested a formal relationship between Nauman's series of sculptures, drawings, and photographs entitled *Henry Moore Bound to Fail*, of 1967–70, which show the artist's shirt-clad back, his arms tied with rope, and Man Ray's now-lost assemblage

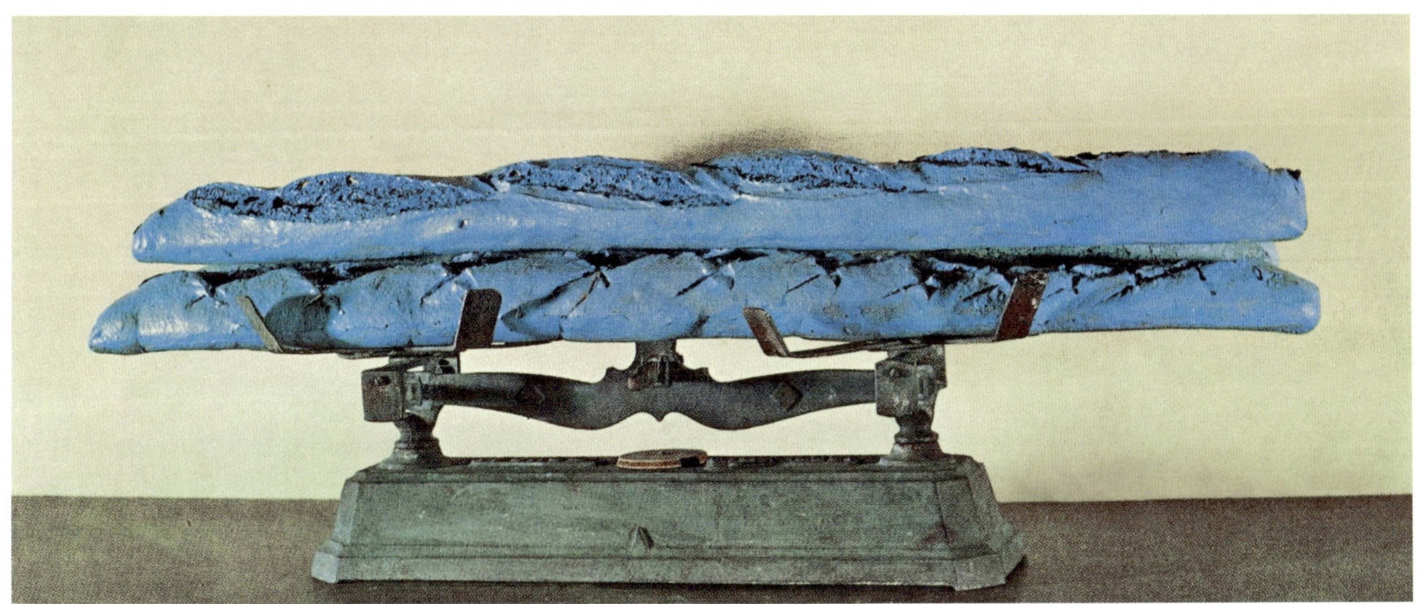

The Enigma of Isidore Ducasse, of 1920, which was reproduced in the Los Angeles exhibition catalogue through a black-and-white photograph.[26] Man Ray had indeed used the effect of cloth over a form tied with rope in this work, an homage to Ducasse, the precocious, Uruguayan-born French poet who wrote under the pseudonym "Comte de Lautréamont." Man Ray's piece consisted of a mysterious object, thought to be a sewing machine in honor of Ducasse's famous phrase "as beautiful . . . as the chance juxtaposition of a sewing machine and an umbrella on a dissecting table," wrapped under an army blanket and secured with ropes.[27]

Light Trap for Henry Moore, No. 1 and *No. 2* (see fig. 45), a pair of black-and-white photographs from 1967, whose zigzagging lines Nauman created by swinging an electric torch in his darkened studio, are also reminiscent of some of Man Ray's Rayographs, fifty-four of which were on display in the Los Angeles exhibition. Imitating the cross-contour drawing style of the British sculptor's drawings of people sheltering in the London Underground during the Blitz, Nauman's looping spirals of light coalesce to create a sculptural form vaguely reminiscent of one of Moore's seated figures, as well as of one-half of Nauman's two-part plaster *Mold for a Modernized Slant Step*, of 1966. Seen in conjunction with *Henry Moore Bound to Fail*, these photographs suggest that Nauman sensed an affinity between Man Ray and Henry Moore, two elder statesmen of modern art whose reputations were then in decline but whose contributions would be valued by future, more open-minded generations of artists and critics.[28]

Fig. 41 Man Ray (American, 1890–1976). *Pain Peint,* 1964.
Baguette with cobalt-colored paint, mounted on scales; length 29 1/2 inches (74.9 cm).
From Los Angeles County Museum of Art, *Man Ray 1966*, exh. cat. (Berlin: Brüder Hartmann, 1966), repro. p. 60

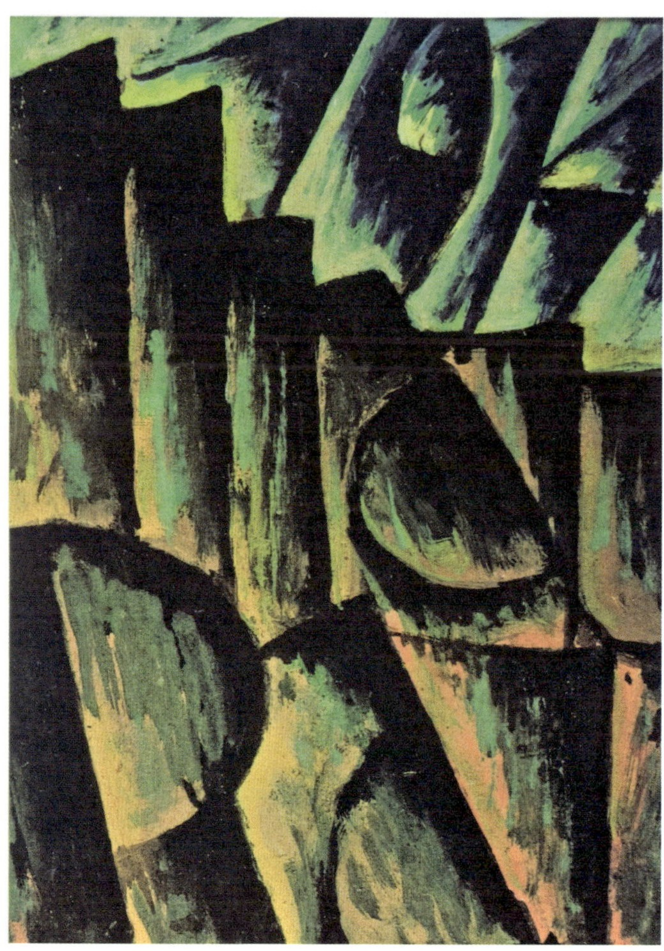

My Last Name Exaggerated Fourteen Times Vertically (see fig. 55), which Nauman created in pale-purple neon in 1967, and another neon piece from the following year, *My Name As Though It Were Written on the Surface of the Moon* (plate 15), can also be related to a work in the Man Ray retrospective. In Nauman's works, the handwritten letters of his Christian name and surname are pulled out of proportion, absurdly elongated in the former and stretched horizontally in the latter, to the point where the signature is virtually indecipherable. A precursor to these distorted visualizations of the artist's name appears in Man Ray's painting *Man Ray 1914* (fig. 42)—a punning disavowal of the idea of a signature style, prominently reproduced in the Los Angeles catalogue—which looks at first glance like a Cubist landscape. A closer inspection reveals that the roughly parallel, slanting forms of the seemingly abstract composition are constructed from the attenuated capital letters of the artist's name and the separate numbers of the painting's year of execution.

Fig. 42 Man Ray (American, 1890–1976). *Man Ray 1914.*
Oil on sketch block, 4 7/8 x 6 13/16 inches (12.3 x 17.3 cm).

Finally, almost every image in the portfolio *Eleven Color Photographs*, which Nauman made with the photographer Jack Fulton in 1966–67 but did not publish until 1970, contains references to Man Ray's literal representation of puns, words, letters, and figures of speech (see fig. 46). (The exception is *Self-Portrait as a Fountain* [fig. 29], which refers to the famous porcelain urinal that Duchamp selected as a readymade and titled *Fountain* in 1917.) Man Ray, like Duchamp, valued cerebral invention over technical proficiency. His puns and word games undoubtedly inspired the younger artist's interest in linguistic experiments, which had also been stimulated by Wittgenstein's language games, and no doubt encouraged Nauman's decision to incorporate anagrams, jokes, palindromes, puns, and rebuses in his neons and drawings. The visceral, often brutal subject matter of these works is far removed from Man Ray's playful whimsicality, but their origins lie in the older artist's adept use of language and his legendary wit, which was often tinged with irony and the occasional drop of acid.

Nauman's intense and sustained engagement with the studio emerges from this account as one of the central themes of his production. As the site of his most profound explorations of artistic meaning, the studio provides a useful framework for understanding his multifarious and ultimately unclassifiable output, since so much of his pioneering work in installation art, sculpture, film, video, neon, photography, and performance can be read as a personalized projection of the artist's private space. Ironically, Nauman's interest in the conceptual and metaphorical meaning of the studio coincided with the French artist Daniel Buren's searing rejection of the privileged, ivory-tower model of the artist's private working space as the exclusive place where art was conceived and made.[29] Buren called instead for art to be made directly in the street, as in his own works, in which he painted and pasted alternating white and colored stripes in a wide variety of public and private locations, such as commercial buildings, the sides of trains, and the sails of boats.

For Buren, the contemporary artist's studio was a kind of depot, where art was produced, stored, and, if all went well, distributed. Since Courbet, he believed, the studio had become a social nexus in which the artist interacted with art dealers, collectors, museum curators, and other arbiters of taste, whose endorsement was crucial to releasing his or her works of art from their purgatory—that is, the environment in which they were made. According to Buren, the work of art "thus falls victim to a mortal paradox from which it cannot escape," since its display in the pristine, white-walled, and spotlit galleries of museums and art galleries is diametrically opposed to the artist's studio, where we generally find a range of completed works, works in progress, and abandoned works, along with the accumulations of furniture, tools, and detritus.[30] The ambiance of the artist's studio, which led to the work being produced in the first place, was lost when a painting or sculpture entered the immaculate spaces of the museum or art gallery, which concealed the mundane and somewhat banal reality of the work's initial production.

Nauman's work, however, has always survived the shift from his working environment in the studio to the museum or gallery, a shift that Buren feared would compromise art's integrity and impact. After more than forty years of intense investigations into the nature of art in relation to language, perception, phenomenology, and psychology, Nauman resolutely retains the raw immediacy of the work as it was first conceived precisely because he uses what he has at hand in the corners and interstices of the studio, including his own, ever-present body, as the subject matter and substance of his continuously inventive art. Instead of transforming these materials into aesthetically beautiful or morally uplifting works of art, Nauman preserves the relationship between the work and its place of production, as well as the imprint of his own thought processes. Whether a sanctuary, prison, cage, theater, or laboratory, the studio remains the crucible in which his defiant and excoriating vision of humanity is molded.

1
Nauman, quoted in Michael Auping, "A Thousand Words: Bruce Nauman Talks about *Mapping the Studio*," *Artforum* 40, no. 7 (March 2002): 121.

2
Nauman may have seen another *Corridor* drawing by Samaras, dated December 9, 1966, in the *American Sculpture of the Sixties* exhibition that opened at the Los Angeles County Museum of Art in April 1967. The drawing, which was also reproduced in the catalogue, showed a series of conjoined corridors made of glass mirrors and crystal spheres, measuring nearly eight feet in length. See Maurice Tuchman, ed., *American Sculpture of the Sixties*, exh. cat. (Los Angeles: Los Angeles County Museum of Art, 1967), p. 184.

3
See Michael Peppiatt and Alice Bellony-Rewald, *Imagination's Chamber: Artists and Their Studios* (Boston: Little, Brown, 1982), p. 71.

4
See Martin S. James, "Mondrian and the Dutch Symbolists," *Art Journal* 23, no. 2 (Winter 1963–64): 110.

5
See Jon Wood, *Close Encounters: The Sculptor's Studio in the Age of the Camera*, exh. cat. (Leeds: Henry Moore Institute, 2001), p. 13. In Constantin Brancusi's photographs of his studio at 8, impasse Ronsin, Paris—emblematic of this shift from portraiture to the studio itself—the aesthetic purity of individual sculptures is enhanced by their placement amid a cluttered array of other works, many of them incomplete, and of tools, in a working environment that denotes the protean creativity of the artist.

6
On the impact and legacy of Alexander Liberman's book see Mary Bergstein, "*The Artist in His Studio*: Photography, Art, and the Masculine Mystique," *Oxford Art Journal* 18, no. 2 (1995): 45–58.

7
Alexander Liberman, "Introduction," in Liberman, *The Artist in His Studio* (New York: The Viking Press, 1960), n.p.

8
See John Richardson, "Picasso's Ateliers and Other Recent Works," *The Burlington Magazine* 99, no. 651 (June 1957): 186. Nauman would also have been aware of Hans Namuth's famous photographs of Jackson Pollock performing shamanistically in his own studio.

9
Nauman, quoted in Brenda Richardson, *Bruce Nauman: Neons*, exh. cat. (Baltimore: The Baltimore Museum of Art, 1982), p. 20.

10
Nauman, quoted in Ian Wallace and Russell Keziere, "Bruce Nauman Interviewed," October 1978, in Nauman, *Please Pay Attention Please: Bruce Nauman's Words: Writings and Interviews*, ed. Janet Kraynak (Cambridge, Mass.: MIT Press, 2005), p. 194.

11
See Michele De Angelus, "Interview with Bruce Nauman," May 1980, in ibid., pp. 244–45.

12
Nauman, quoted in Jane Livingston, "Bruce Nauman," in Livingston and Marcia Tucker, eds., *Bruce Nauman: Work from 1965 to 1972*, exh. cat. (Los Angeles: Los Angeles County Museum of Art, 1972), p. 26.

13
See, for example, Robert Pincus-Witten, "Bruce Nauman: Another Kind of Reasoning," *Artforum* 10, no. 6 (February 1972): 32.

14
Duchamp uttered his famous statement that "the great artist of tomorrow will go underground" at the Philadelphia Museum College of Art in 1961, during an artists' panel titled "Where Do We Go from Here?" He delighted the audience with an assault on the rampant commercialism of the art market, which he said had turned art into "a commodity like soap or securities." According to Duchamp, "Material speculation leads art to a massive dilution, a lowering of taste into the mist of mediocrity," with the only hope being an "ascetic revolution" (a delightful pun on aesthetics and his adopted persona of what he elsewhere called a "lewd monk," working alone in the studio with a minimum of social obligations) that would allow the artist to work outside the gallery system in a kind of hermitlike seclusion. See John Canaday, "Whither Art?" *New York Times*, March 26, 1961, Section X, p. 15.

15
Nauman, "Bruce Nauman: Notes and Projects," in Marcia Tucker, "PheNAUMANology," *Artforum* 9, no. 4 (December 1970): 44.

16
Hannah Wilke, "I Object: Memoirs of a Sugar Giver," quoted in Dieter Daniels, ed., *Übrigens Sterben Immer die Anderen: Marcel Duchamp und die Avantgarde seit 1950*, exh. cat. (Cologne: Museum Ludwig, 1988), p. 269.

17
Ludwig Wittgenstein, *Philosophical Investigations*, trans. G.E.M. Anscombe (New York: Macmillan, 1953), p. 221. The text reads, "'A new-born child has no teeth'—'A goose has no teeth'—'A rose has no teeth.'—This last at any rate—one would like to say—is obviously true! It is even surer than that a goose has none.—And yet it is none so clear. For where should a rose's teeth have been?"

18
On the ripple effect of Duchamp's 1963 retrospective on the work of West Coast artists see Robert L. Pincus, "'Quality Material . . . ': Duchamp Disseminated in the Sixties and Seventies," in Bonnie Clearwater, ed., *West Coast Duchamp*, exh. cat. (Miami Beach: Grassfield Press in association with the Shoshana Wayne Gallery, Santa Monica, 1991), pp. 87–101.

19
Nauman in conversation with Coosje van Bruggen, October 23, 1985, in *Bruce Nauman: Drawings, 1965–1986*, exh. cat. (Basel: Kunstmuseum Basel, 1986), p. 35 n. 13.

20
A rare exception is Constance M. Lewallen's superb essay on Nauman's early work, in which she connects Nauman's "inability to stick with one medium or direction" to Man Ray's protean output. Lewallen also links the older artist's workmanlike approach to "a particularly American work ethic that [Nauman] absorbed not only from his family, but also from his socialist-leaning art teachers at the University of Wisconsin." See Lewallen, "A Rose Has No Teeth," in Lewallen, *A Rose Has No Teeth: Bruce Nauman in the 1960s*, exh. cat. (Berkeley: University of California Press, Berkeley Art Museum, and Pacific Film Archive, 2007), p. 63.
21
See Carl I. Belz, "A Man Ray Retrospective in Los Angeles," *Artforum* 5, no. 4 (December 1966): 22–23.
22
Man Ray, "Objects of My Affection," in Man Ray, *Objects of My Affection*, exh. cat. (New York: Julien Levy Gallery, 1945), n.p.
23
See Arturo Schwarz, *Man Ray: The Rigour of Imagination* (New York: Rizzoli, 1977), p. 199.
24
See Brian O'Doherty, "Light on an Individual: Man Ray," *New York Times*, May 5, 1963, Section X, p. 15.
25
Nauman, quoted in Livingston, "Bruce Nauman," p. 11. Nauman's comment here was perhaps informed by Ron Padgett's review of Man Ray's retrospective exhibition at the Los Angeles County Museum of Art, in which the American poet declared that "Duchamp, for all his blinding intelligence, lacks the playful meanness that makes Man Ray's work the gratuitous, unpredictable thing it is. Man Ray would have taken a fiendish pleasure in inventing the xylophone; the slightly crude 'off' note is one he enjoys hitting." Padgett, "Artist Accompanies Himself with His Rays," *Art News* 65, no. 7 (November 1966): 80.
26
See Coosje van Bruggen, *Bruce Nauman* (New York: Rizzoli, 1988), p. 111.
27
Comte de Lautréamont (Isidore Ducasse), *Maldoror and Poems*, trans. Paul Knight (London: Penguin Books, 1978), p. 217.
28
Most critics failed to share Nauman's enthusiasm for the Man Ray retrospective; indeed, at the time it was widely regarded as an embarrassing failure. On the negative, often hostile reception of the exhibition see Neil Baldwin, *Man Ray: American Artist* (New York: Clarkson N. Potter, 1988), p. 335.
29
See Daniel Buren, "Fonction de l'atelier," 1971, in *Ecrits* (Bordeaux: CAPC–Musée d'art contemporain, 1991), 1:195–205.
30
Daniel Buren, "The Function of the Studio," trans. Thomas Repensek, *October* 10 (Autumn 1979): 53.

Spaces

Marco De Michelis

The artist is the origin of the work. The work is the origin of the artist.
Martin Heidegger, *The Origin of the Work of Art*, 1936[1]

I am the space where I am.
Noël Arnaud, *L'État d'ébauche*, 1950[2]

What Art May Be

A completely typical feature of the dazzling start to Bruce Nauman's career is his anomalous position in the context of the American art of the late 1960s: marginal in relation to that art's geographic center, New York, yet a recognized if incompletely assimilated protagonist in the international art scene. The fate of this artist seems to have been settled during his formative years, well before his move to the lonely tablelands of New Mexico. In the years immediately following his first solo exhibition—at the Nicholas Wilder Gallery, Los Angeles, in May 1966, while he was still a graduate student at the University of California, Davis—Nauman participated in nearly all of the crucial exhibitions that marked the appearance of the American Post-Minimalist generation and, more generally, the international dissemination of Conceptual art. These years, between 1966 and 1969, were truly extraordinary for art (as for much else), seeing the shaping of the first Earthworks; the emergence of such Conceptualist manifestos as Sol LeWitt's thirty-five "Sentences on Conceptual Art";[3] and the proposal of formulas such as "Eccentric abstraction," "Antiform," "Process art," "Body art," and "Arte Povera" to describe often disjointed accumulations of works "in which the idea is paramount and the material form is secondary, lightweight, ephemeral, cheap, unpretentious and/or 'dematerialized.'"[4] The art community that came together in downtown Manhattan was exploring ways to abandon the traditional art spaces of galleries and museums. There was also an interest in politics, which were dominated during those years by student protests and opposition to the Vietnam War.

While Nauman's work was appearing in exhibitions, he himself was living in relative isolation, first, after graduating from UC Davis in the summer of 1966, in San Francisco; then in Mill Valley, where he sublet the house of William T. Wiley, a former teacher of his at the university;

and then, beginning in 1969, in Pasadena, north of Los Angeles, before moving to New Mexico in 1979.[5] At this point he knew the New York art scene well, but he was part of a distinct California community that seemed to disdain market success, preferring to live on art school teaching jobs or other kinds of work rather than on sales in East Coast galleries. As Nauman has remembered, "It was against the rules to go to New York."[6]

In 1967, on the wall of his first San Francisco studio, a former grocery store, Nauman hung a circular piece of neon spelling out the words *The True Artist Helps the World by Revealing Mystic Truths* (plate 22). The phrase quite closely anticipates the first of LeWitt's thirty-five sentences, written nearly three years later: "Conceptual artists are mystics rather than rationalists." The use of neon, which would remain one of Nauman's favorite mediums in later decades, coincided with experiments by other artists, such as Dan Flavin, Jasper Johns, Joseph Kosuth, and Martial Raysse, during the same period,[7] but Nauman in this work seems to have been using the popular technology of the neon sign—remnants of which remained in his studio space from its original commercial use—to send a message about the significance and role of the work of art.

The various phrases that Nauman has used to describe his work in the silent solitude of his studio in the mid-1960s include the formulation "investigating the possibilities of what art may be."[8] He was exploring "the structure of the discipline," interrogating its meaning.[9] During his time at UC Davis, he had already abandoned a plan to become a painter, the discipline with which he had begun as an artist. The art he would interrogate was instead an art "without technique." Its meaning grew simply from the presence of the artist in his studio.

The sources on which Nauman drew often came in some way from outside traditional art practices. He was a passionate reader of modern writers such as Samuel Beckett, Vladimir Nabokov, and Alain Robbe-Grillet, and of texts such as Ludwig Wittgenstein's *Philosophical Investigations.* ("I have always read a lot," Nauman has said; "I read in chunks and will read almost everything.")[10] Having studied music when he was younger, he was interested in American minimalist composers such as Steve Reich, Philip Glass, and, above all, La Monte Young. And he followed the new American dance of these years, as developed by Meredith Monk, Yvonne Rainer, and the group of choreographers gathered around Anna Halprin and her husband, Lawrence, who, although professionally a landscape architect, was equally involved in experiments that would change the face of dance.

For Nauman, Marcel Duchamp was a figure in an unspecified setting; Man Ray took more precise form when Nauman saw an exhibition of his work in Los Angeles; his only information about Joseph Beuys came from a conversation with the German curator Kasper König during a studio visit. Johns and Willem de Kooning, Dada and Surrealism, were essential reference points but were remote in space and time. Nauman was not without information on contemporary art, both internationally and, rather more so, on the American East Coast. But he filtered it through intimately personal interrogations that were still without an answer or, we might say, without a "theory."

Gestalt Therapy

Over twenty years ago, Jean-Christophe Ammann stressed the "existential dimension" of Nauman's work—its ability on occasion to investigate an essential relationship between subject and background, as if the work itself were the result of an "investigation."[11] For Joan Simon, meanwhile, Nauman's research is truly "experimental" in character, suggesting a process involving the question "Where to start and how to continue."[12] The "background" of Nauman's activity, of course, was the space of the studio, largely empty, due to a lack of financial means, and at a moment when the artist had a lot of time at his disposal, due to a lack of commitments. In these conditions, Nauman has recalled, "I was forced to examine myself and what I was doing there."[13]

If Nauman's San Francisco studio was empty in 1966, it would soon be filled with various works of art—sculptures in fiberglass and other materials, filmed performances, photographs, neon pieces, drawings, installations. The only permanent presence was that of the young artist, convinced "that if I was in the studio, whatever I was doing was art."[14] In establishing this relationship between the studio space and the artist searching for an answer to the question of what artmaking might be, Nauman was expressing a desire for reunification, a desire to regain the integrity of his very existence in space.

Nauman's approach here was essentially phenomenological, although he has never included Maurice Merleau-Ponty, for example, among the many authors he read during those years. But he does recall reading a book that would have a deep influence on his work: *Gestalt Therapy*, published in 1951 by Frederick S. Perls, Ralph F. Hefferline, and Paul Goodman.[15] Here Perls and his collaborators advanced the now-classic theories of Gestalt psychology as a therapeutic tool capable of knitting together the fragmented individual, the "dualism of his person, of his thinking, of his language,"[16] the polarization—between body and soul, culture and civilization, intellectual and manual labor, individual and society—so characteristic of the very idea of modernity.

For the Gestalt therapist, "Gestalt formation" is determined by the ability to establish significant relationships among isolated elements—in Perls's words to "make a triangle out of them,"[17] in other words to recompose the interplay in which figure stands out from ground. "In health," Perls writes, "the relation between figure and ground is a process of permanent but meaningful emerging and receding. Thus the interplay of figure and background becomes the center of the theory as presented in this book: attention, concentration, interest, concern, excitement and grace are representative of healthy figure-ground formation, while confusion, boredom, fixations, anxiety, amnesias, stagnation and self-consciousness are indicative of figure-ground formation which is disturbed."[18] We might describe this disturbed condition as that of people who perceive themselves as existing outside themselves, cut off from their own experience of the world, which they view as alienated observers. To remedy it, *Gestalt Therapy* proposes exercises—experiments—meant to "expand or, better, heighten awareness of what you are doing and how you are doing it."[19] These exercises are based on the premise that the individual and his or her environment "are not independent entities, but together . . . constitute a functioning, mutually influencing, total system."[20]

Some of the exercises call for meticulous description of the context in which one finds oneself—that is, for a precise awareness of one's own existence in a place. (Perls records a patient's enthusiastic exclamation: "I feel so peculiar. The world is there, really there! And I have eyes, real eyes!")[21] Others have to do with equilibrium and the idea of "The Opposite," and ask the patient to imagine that events are occurring "as in reverse-motion moving picture film" or with "the picture upside down."[22] One crucial group of exercises articulates the development of a "Technique of Awareness":

> Now I am aware that I am lying on the couch . . . . Now I am aware of hesitating, of asking myself what to do first . . . . Now I feel lost again. I am remembering the advice to stick to the surface. Now I am aware that I am lying with my legs crossed . . . . Concentrate on your body sensation as a whole. Let your attention wander through every part of your body.[23]

Nauman seems to have understood the significance and structure of these Gestalt practices perfectly; some of his performative procedures and sculptural experiments seem to repeat the book's instructions almost literally. At the same time, though, they overturn Perls's therapeutic intent, instead heightening, taking possession of, the experience and awareness of fragmentation and duality. Nauman's experiments suggest no solutions, make no attempt at the recomposition of harmony. Rather, they posit an irresolvable condition of tension and unease.

When, in sculptures and drawings, Nauman repeatedly establishes an unresolved relationship between inside and outside, his goal is not to produce clarity but "to create a confusion between the inside and outside of a piece."[24] His list of "things you could do to a straight bar: bend it, fold it, twist it,"[25] constitutes an orderly sequence of "exercises" producing a fragility of equilibrium, like that of his sculptures in materials (rubber, cloth) that cannot maintain their shape unless they are suspended, hung on the wall, or simply laid flat on the floor. His rough structures in fiberglass similarly seem to stand precariously against the wall. If the modern sculpture of the early decades of the twentieth century lost the stable pedestal that separated it from the ground, here (but also in contemporary works by Richard Serra and Robert Morris, Eva Hesse and Joel Shapiro) it seems deprived even of permanence of form and autonomy in space.

Other works operate as prosthetic appendices of the human body, but instead of increasing its functionality in space, they force it into an unstable equilibrium. Think of *Slant Step*, the strange, inscrutably appealing step- or stoollike object that Nauman and Wiley casually rescued from a Mill Valley junk shop in 1965 and used in a group exhibition of Bay Area artists and poets the following year. Because the slant step slants, it is unusable, a theme that Nauman picked up in *Device to Stand In* (1966; fig. 43), on which the position of the human body could only be difficult and unstable. In many works the artist's body undergoes manipu-

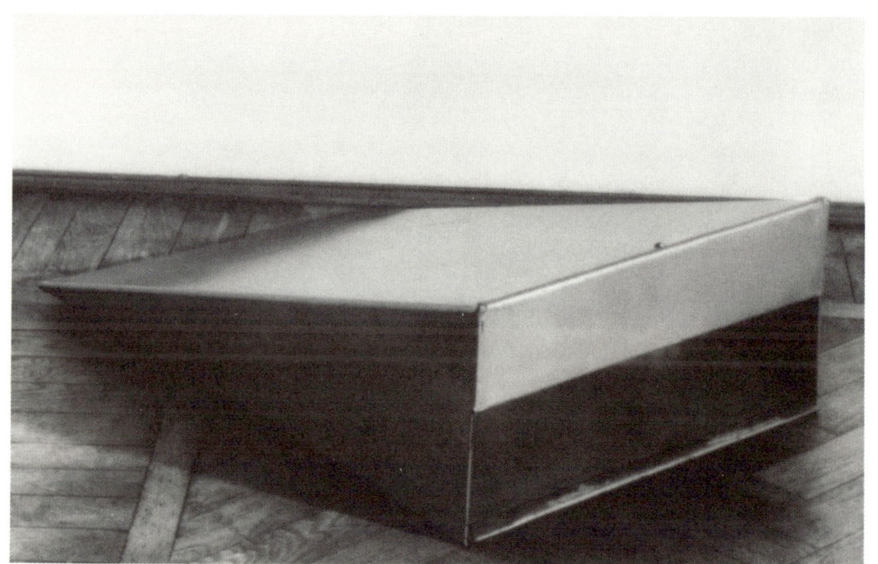

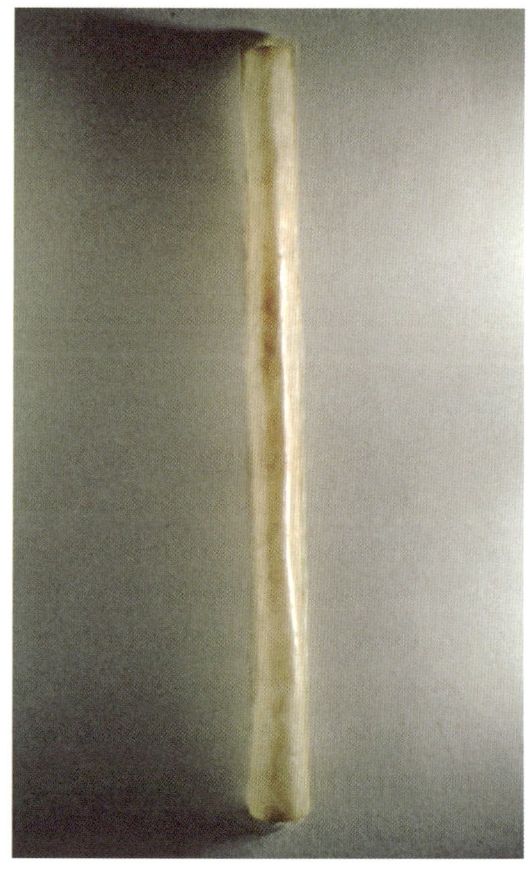

lations and metamorphoses, the face becoming unrecognizable, the frame distorted or expanded into space, the proportions irreparably altered (*Six Inches of My Knee Extended to Six Feet*, 1967, fig. 44; *Storage Capsule for the Right Rear Quarter of My Body*, 1966). Elsewhere fantastic transformations turn the artist's body into the traditional subject of public sculpture, as in the self-portraits (see figs. 29 and 53) that make him into a fountain, as if to illustrate another language work that he set in the window of his San Francisco studio/store, the announcement that *The True Artist Is an Amazing Luminous Fountain* (plate 26).

In *From Hand to Mouth* (1967; plate 11) the body becomes a mutilated appendage that extends from the mouth, down along the arm, to the hand. Its identity is so indefinable that for some time there was uncertainty as to whether this wax cast derived from the artist himself

Fig. 43 Bruce Nauman. *Device to Stand In,* 1966.
Lacquered steel, 8 3/4 x 27 1/4 x 17 1/4 inches (22.2 x 69.2 x 43.8 cm).
Solomon R. Guggenheim Museum, New York. Panza Collection, Extended Loan, L264.93

Fig. 44 Bruce Nauman. *Six Inches of My Knee Extended to Six Feet,* 1967.
Fiberglass, 68 1/2 x 5 11/16 x 3 7/8 inches (174 x 14.6 x 9.8 cm).
Whitney Museum of American Art, New York. Partial and promised gift of Robert A. M. Stern, New York, 91.115

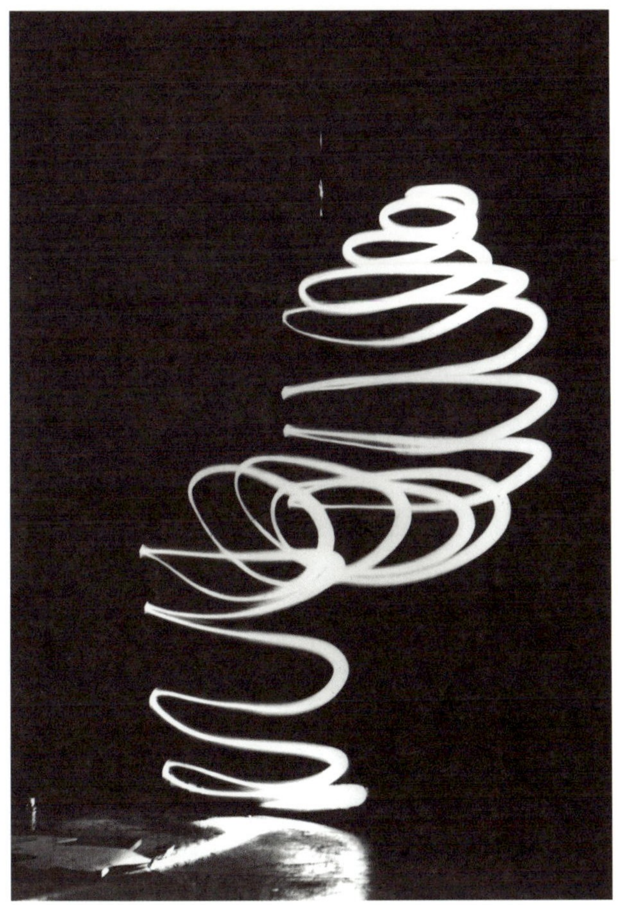

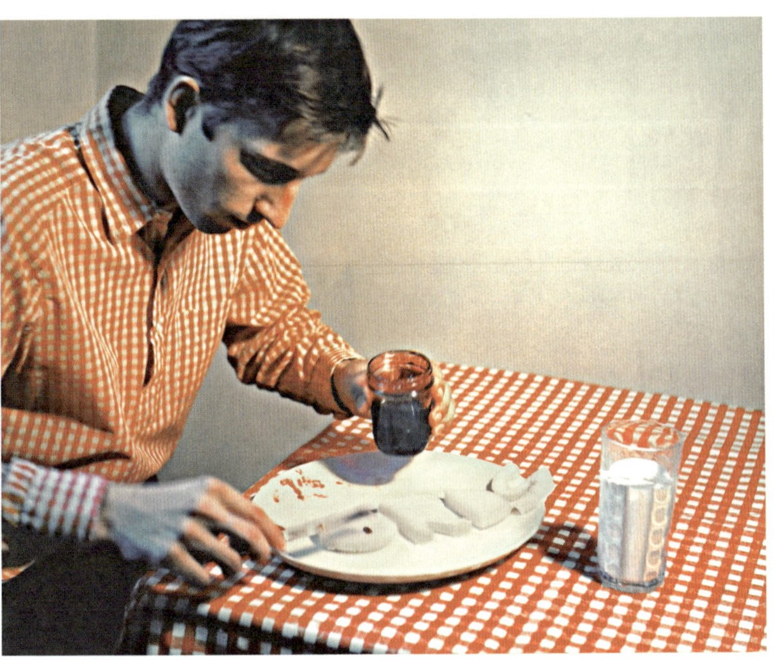

or, as it finally turned out, from his then-wife, Judy. Two photographs from the same year seem still more extreme, as the artist's body apparently dissolves into a luminous, immaterial trace that envelops and erases it (*Light Trap for Henry Moore, No. 1* and *No. 2*; fig. 45). If the goal of Gestalt therapy is the recomposition of an orderly relationship between self and environment, Nauman instead experiments with the cancellation of personal identity, expanding the letters of his name to the point where they are illegible (*My Last Name Exaggerated Fourteen Times Vertically*, 1967; fig. 55; *My Name As Though It Were Written on the Surface of the Moon*, 1968; plate 15), or documenting, in a photograph, their bizarre transformation into food being eaten by the subject himself (*Eating My Words*, 1966–67/1970; fig. 46).

Fig. 45 Bruce Nauman. *Light Trap for Henry Moore, No. 2*, 1967.
Photograph, 71 5/8 x 40 1/8 inches (181.9 x 101.9 cm).
Raussmüller Collection, Schaffhausen, Switzerland

Fig. 46 Bruce Nauman. *Eating My Words*, from the portfolio *Eleven Color Photographs;* 1966–67/1970/2007.
Ink-jet print exhibition copy (originally chromogenic development print). Edition 8/8.
Image: 19 3/8 x 23 3/16 inches (49.2 x 60.5 cm).
Museum of Contemporary Art, Chicago. Gerald S. Elliott Collection, 1994.11.j

The space in which Nauman lives and works is never made to look domestic; one cannot apply to it Gaston Bachelard's description of the house, which "shelters daydreaming . . . protects the dreamer . . . allows one to dream in peace."[26] Far from a nest, a refuge in which to find protection from the outside world, it is rather an enigmatic laboratory for transforming the secret experience of anxiety—"being frustrated and angry"[27]—into a conscious "investigative activity"[28] exploring the artist's own condition.

Living Sculptures

In 1965, at UC Davis, Nauman had done a performance (repeated and documented in the video *Wall-Floor Positions* of 1969) in which he assumed a series of consecutive positions described in words that can immediately be related to those he used to describe his sculptural manipulations. "Bend it, fold it, twist it," was here transformed into "Start off standing against the wall, then away from the wall, then bend over, and then you could bend over and touch the floor, and then lie down, roll over, and stand up."[29] Over the course of an hour, the artist assumed twenty-eight different physical positions in relation to the wall and floor of the room, holding each for about a minute, and following arbitrary but carefully respected rules. In this way his body was transformed into a kind of living sculpture, used and manipulated "as a piece of material."[30] The work reveals for the first time the indifference to the usual expressive media that would remain characteristic of Nauman's art in the years to come.

One could say that the many sixteen-millimeter films that Nauman shot in his studio, making himself the protagonist, document this painful, futile effort to establish a harmonious unity between figure and ground. The exercises to which he subjected himself suggest a disenchanted interpretation of the practices of Gestalt therapy. The artist is shown, for example, bouncing two balls alternately between the ceiling and the floor; running continuously around the perimeter of the room, timing his movements to the beat of a metronome; and playing the same note steadily on a violin while walking in and out of the camera frame, trusting the proof of the action's process to its insistent sound. Rather than progress, these actions repeat; there is no narrative structure, only the attempt to keep a constant rhythm until it is interrupted by chance, error, or the arbitrary decision of the artist. As a result, experiments apparently intended to encourage the individual to "take possession" of space by mapping its boundaries are paradoxically thwarted by their potentially infinite temporal extension, further prolonged in 1969, when the art dealer Leo Castelli offered Nauman the use of a video camera that allowed him to record actions continuously for up to sixty minutes. Meanwhile the attempt to turn the simplest movements into dance shows affinities with parallel experiments by dancers such as Merce Cunningham or Monk (whom Nauman met in San Francisco, then collaborated with in a performance at the Whitney Museum of American Art, New York, in 1969).

Spaces

Nauman confronted the problem of the studio space in the 1966 work *Flour Arrangements* (fig. 47), in which, after emptying the room of objects, he used it for a series of impermanent configurations that Benjamin H. D. Buchloh has described as the first "process sculptures."[31] Over the course of a month, Nauman intermittently modeled a large pile of flour into

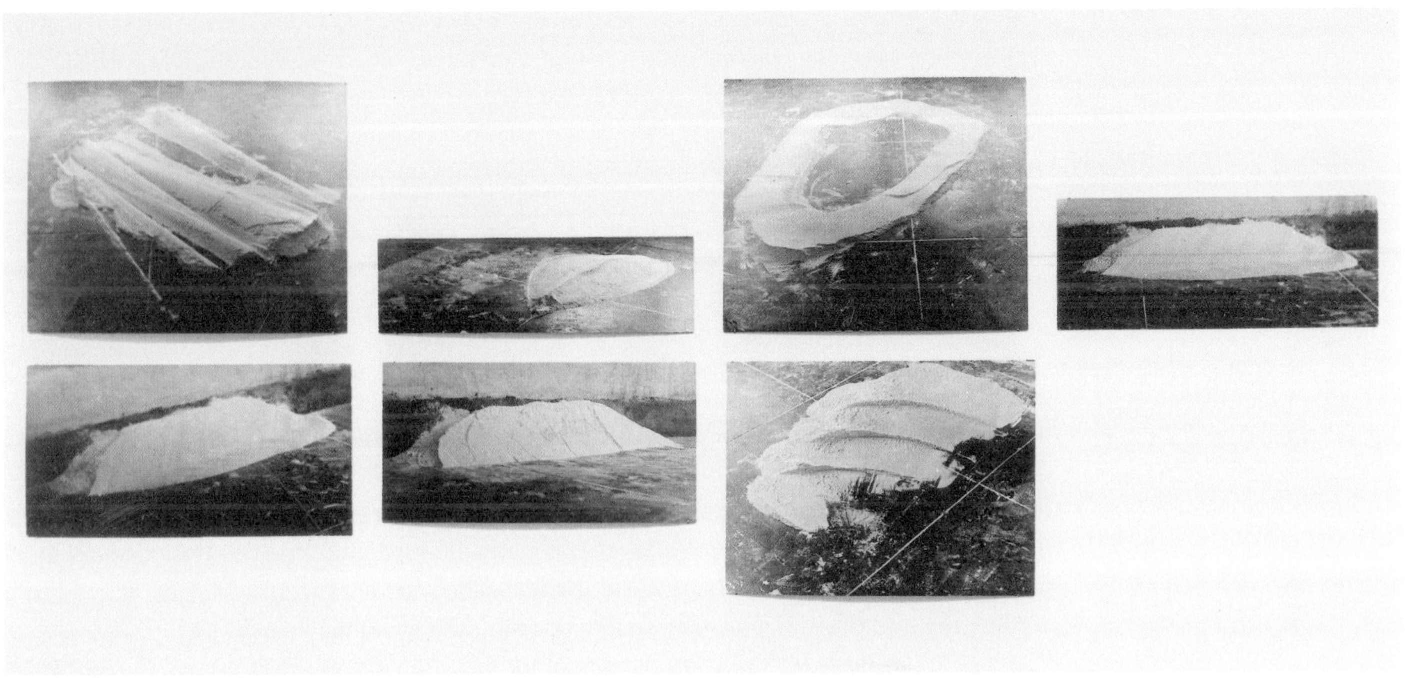

different shapes. Besides carrying the precariousness of the sculptures in fiberglass and other materials to a new extreme, the work involved a refusal to construct static objects, replacing them with the more abstract, residual possibility of documenting the various phases of the work in photographs. The subject of sculpture becomes less the multiplicity of the forms created than the programmatic process of the action carried out: the transformation of the empty studio space into the background for an action that the artist repeats daily, and that is certified only by the photographic, day-by-day documentation of what has occurred.

A crucial aspect of Nauman's early short films and photographic works is an element I call "Dionysian," thinking of Friedrich Nietzsche's description of space, in *The Birth of Tragedy*, as a force field "generated by the dynamism of bodily movement."[32] For Nietzsche, the "overflow of primordial delight" pushes the artist to become, through his body in space, a work of art. The coincidence between the nineteenth-century German philosopher and the young American artist is not misleading. The point is not to claim a direct dependence of the latter on the former, which has never been documented, but to recognize the decisive centrality of the notion of "space" in Nauman's work.

Fig. 47 Bruce Nauman. *Flour Arrangements,* 1966.
Seven color photographs; 19 1/8 x 23 5/8 inches (48.6 x 60 cm), 10 x 23 13/16 inches (25.4 x 60.5 cm), 19 3/16 x 22 11/16 inches (48.7 x 57.6 cm), 11 1/8 x 23 7/16 inches (28.3 x 59.5 cm), 13 3/16 x 23 7/8 inches (33.5 x 60.6 cm), 12 3/16 x 23 5/16 inches (31 x 59.1 cm), 17 11/16 x 23 5/16 inches (45 x 59.1 cm).
Raussmüller Collection, Schaffhausen, Switzerland

"Space" is a word that is anything but neutral. It conveys complex meanings, strongly rooted in the very notion of modernity.[33] The idea that the void within a building or around the modeled volume of a statue constitutes a problem had never been formulated before the modern era; it starts to occupy a central position in the history and philosophy of art only at the end of the nineteenth century. Not until Constantin Brancusi's somehow "architectural" arrangements of his sculptures in his Paris studio did the focus of sculpture shift from the "solid" of plastic modeling to the space around it, as in the work of such artists as Naum Gabo, Alexander Calder, and László Moholy-Nagy.

Today Nauman's space continues to provide answers to questions initially posed in the late nineteenth century, when art historians such as the Germans August Schmarsow and Heinrich Wölfflin, using the theories of empathy developed by Robert Vischer and Wilhelm Worringer as a starting point, proposed an idea of space as an emanation of the presence of the body, as a "construct" that takes shape through the movement of the body and, more, through the gaze of the individual who perceives it, assigning it meaning and interpreting it as a three-dimensional, "introflexed" projection of the observing body.[34] This is where we find the theoretical foundation of the modern concept of space as a "property of the mind, part of the apparatus through which we perceive the world."[35]

Talking to Simon in 1987, Nauman explained *A Cast of the Space under My Chair* (1965–68; fig. 48), one of his most important and enigmatic works, by quoting de Kooning: "When you paint a chair, you should paint the space between the rungs, not the chair itself."[36] The transfer of attention from the "positive" volume of the object, sculptural or otherwise, to the "negative," immaterial volume surrounding it and defining it constitutes a fundamentally important change in perspective. (This truly Gestalt-like shift from figure to environment is still more easily recognizable in Nauman's *Shelf Sinking into the Wall* of 1966, where the space below the shelf, reproduced in a cast, becomes detached from its matrix and ends up indecorously massed on the floor, dragged down by gravity.) The volume of space under the chair, made mysteriously solid, again by casting, seems almost archaic in its immobile materiality and is recognizable only with effort, despite its absolute realism.

On examination, *A Cast of the Space under My Chair* recalls a fundamental problem posited as early as 1893 by the German sculptor Adolf Hildebrand, who sought to transfer the new understanding of space, originally emerging in architecture, to the visual arts and in particular to sculpture. For Hildebrand—who was well acquainted with the work of Wölfflin, Schmarsow, and Vischer, and with Worringer's and Konrad Fiedler's reflections on empathy and vision—space was the principal subject of the work of art, and the basis for the viewer's experience of it. Within a perspective rooted in Immanuel Kant's *Critique of Pure Reason*, which had affirmed the mental character of space, Hildebrand recognized an opening for the visual arts finally to be freed from the ancient task of imitating nature, the yoke of mimesis. Space did not represent external reality, its characteristics and physical properties, but was an autonomous construction of the mind, a projection of the physical, subjective experience of vision. For Hildebrand, artistic form could exist only when it was perceived in a space reflecting the

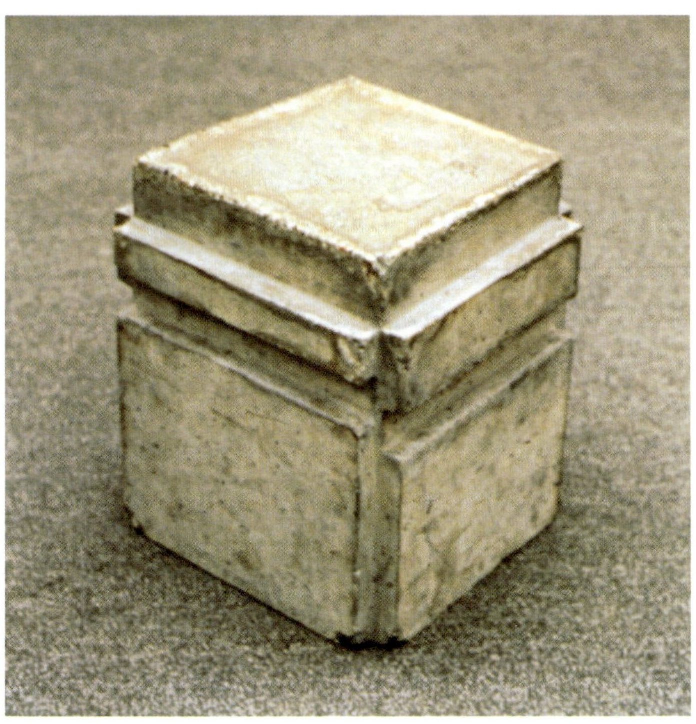

kinesthetic activity of our imagination. Then we first have to imagine it three-dimensionally as a void filled in part by the individual volumes of objects and in part by the air . . . . Just as the boundary or form of an object indicates its volume, it is also possible to compose objects in such a way that they evoke the idea of a volume of air bounded by them. The boundary of an object is, strictly speaking, also the boundary of the body of air surrounding it.[37]

Walking In

In the early 1970s, in two extraordinary essays that are among the timeliest contributions to Nauman studies, Marcia Tucker proposed a phenomenological interpretation of the artist's work. For Tucker, Nauman "does not represent or interpret phenomena, such as sound, light, movement, or temperature, but uses them as . . . basic material."[38] Thus the actual physical, corporeal experience of the work lies at the center of his interest. If this was to some degree already clear in the works in which the artist himself was the protagonist, it would become crucial in the installations that, beginning in 1969, directly involved the physical experience of the viewer.

Fig. 48 Bruce Nauman. *A Cast of the Space under My Chair,* 1965–68.
Concrete, 17 11/16 x 15 3/8 x 14 5/8 inches (45 x 39 x 37 cm).
Kröller-Müller Foundation, Otterlo, The Netherlands, formerly in the Visser collection. Purchased with support from the Mondriaan Foundation

The previous year, Nauman had built a narrow corridor, no wider than twenty inches, in his studio. In the video *Walk with Contrapposto* (1968; fig. 32) he traversed this space, barely big enough to hold him, using a walk that exaggerated the oscillation of his hips. In 1969 this corridor reappeared in the exhibition *Anti-Illusion: Procedures/Materials* at the Whitney, this time as a sculptural object that visitors could enter, repeating in some way the artist's earlier experience (fig. 49). Nauman himself has described the oneiric quality of the work ("It was about being in a long corridor and there was a room at the end of the corridor . . . . I had the dream many times and I kind of figured it must be a part of myself I hadn't identified. It seemed important to objectify myself"),[39] and the claustrophobia induced by the corridor's extreme narrowness. In this way he transferred his own experience to many potential subjects—if only implicitly, since he gave no instruction or explanation to the corridor's visitors, who in turn assumed the role of "performer," their own perceptual experience becoming one with the work of art.

At the same time, the visitors' margin of freedom was limited by the corridor's specific character. Nauman was not interested in giving them the same freedom he had had in inventing the work; he was concerned not to stimulate a general perceptual experience in and of itself but to reproduce the particular condition that he himself had wanted to experience. "I wasn't interested and I didn't want to present situations where people could have too much freedom to invent what they thought was going on," he has said. "I wanted it to be my idea, and I did not want the people to invent the art. The corridor was specific enough. Whatever ways you could use it were so limited that people were bound to have more or less the same experiences I had."[40] In response to the remark that these installations have a certain intrinsic perversity, he peremptorily said of the viewer: "He can do only what I want him to do. I mistrust audience participation."[41] In this way the work asserted its experimental nature in a way that allowed no misunderstanding, to the point where it presumed the possibility of repeating its effects, confirming its results, with other subjects, in the manner of modern scientific practice.

Nauman's central interest was not—and is not—the experiential event but the experience of unease, the challenge to individual identity and to the boundaries between inside and outside, public and private, the dilemma or question that might produce a condition of tension and might require not just awareness but a certain degree of physical involvement. All of his architectural installations propose this condition. The corridors, which Nauman has repeated in many variations over the years, are like traps into which visitors slip without suspecting the consequences, only to find themselves in situations that elude univocal interpretations. Unexpected sounds pulsate on the ear; walls narrow until the body is almost immobilized; distant mirrors reflect the body but cut off the head; visitors see themselves in television monitors from behind, simultaneously advancing toward the end of the corridor and growing distant in the video image; or they see the corridor empty at the same time that they are experiencing it as literally crowded with the body that has penetrated it. The multiplication and superimposition of contradictory information are central aspects of these works, and produce a "tension of not being able to put them together."[42]

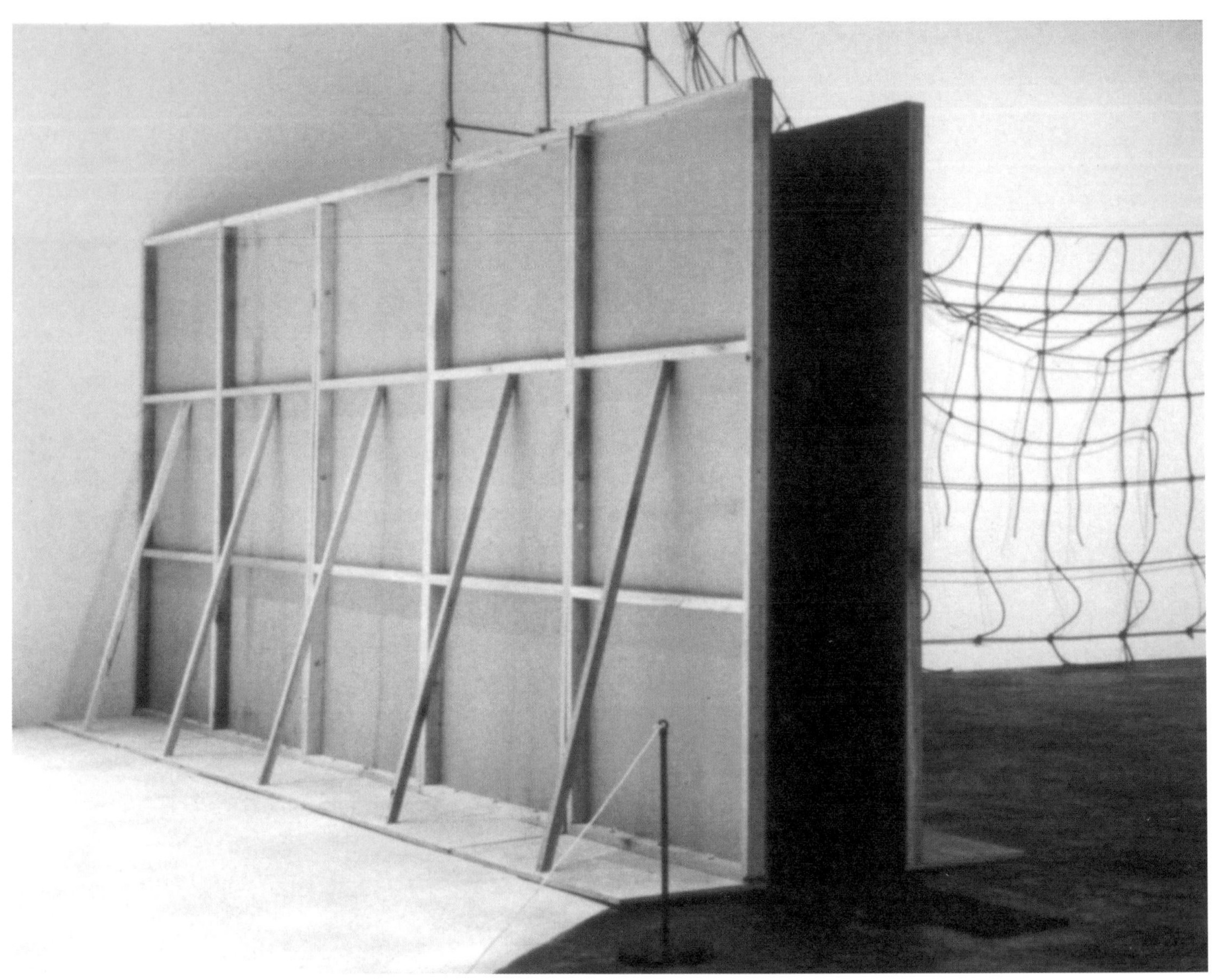

Fig. 49 Bruce Nauman. Installation view of *Performance Corridor*, 1969. From the exhibition *Anti-Illusion: Procedures/Materials*, Whitney Museum of American Art, New York, May 19–July 6, 1969. Wallboard and wood, 96 x 240 x 20 inches (243.8 x 609.6 x 50.8 cm). Solomon R. Guggenheim Museum, New York. Panza Collection, Extended Loan, L264.93

Mental Architectures

In the 1970s Nauman exhibited a number of "models" for large constructions, mostly circular tunnels, labyrinthine underground spaces, or deep depressions dug into the ground like upside-down pyramids. These schemes, which the models reduced to a 1:40 scale,[43] Nauman considered "extensions of the different corridor pieces."[44] On a monumental level, and in a more abstract and conceptual way (since the visitor could not physically enter the models but had to imagine what entering them would feel like), they were meant to reproduce the tension between outside and inside, closed and open, beginning and end, that he had sought since making his first full-scale architectural environments, and were to be physically negotiable by the individual who would "inhabit" them.

In a certain way the role of Nauman's drawings seems conceptually similar to that of the models. These drawings are never just "plans," two-dimensional renderings intended to be used by others to realize what the artist has imagined, as architectural drawings are. Instead, Nauman's drawings seek to prefigure and describe the effect that the idea, if brought to fruition, would determine. Michael Auping, quoting Douglas Huebler, has described them as "mental sculptures."[45] Some resemble diagrams superimposing the dynamic function of time on spatial organization, as, for example, in the studies for the video *Slow Angle Walk (Beckett Walk)* (1968; fig. 50), which, like choreographic notations, meticulously delineate the complex sequence of movements that the artist would repeat for the camera. Elsewhere the spatial arrangement of the elements overlaps with studies of the invasive effects of colored neon light, the intricate paths of images bouncing from mirror to mirror or from video monitor to video monitor, the possible displacements and shifts of the viewer's body, or the careful planning of different viewpoints and their effects. At root, these works seem governed more by the practices of dance and theater than by those of architecture.

The conceptual complexity of all of these works resides in their deliberate overlaps of contradictory information, which multiply their meanings and preclude any uniform perception, whether emotional, psychological, or physiological. The models for underground tunnels can be interpreted as portents of the "walled-in tragedy" that Bachelard recognized in the dark, secret spaces of cellars—"walls that have the entire earth behind them"[46]—but they are also simply large sculptures in the orthogonal space of the gallery or museum. The viewer is forced to oscillate between imagining what it might be like actually to penetrate the works' viscera, opaque and isolated from the world, were they built at full scale, and observing the real effects of the sculptural volumes in the exhibition space.

The desire to create "uncomfortable spaces and shapes" is an explicit constant in Nauman's work, a tool for triggering a cognitive experience that begins with a condition of unease.[47] This state is a sudden reminder that art is only marginally concerned with "how to provide or make beautiful things";[48] rather, as Nauman had learned from the genius of Wittgenstein, it is about "how to go about thinking about things."[49] The triangular spaces ("I find triangles really uncomfortable, disconcerting kinds of space"),[50] underground tunnels, corridors so narrow as to be almost impassable, and the colored, shadowless light that sometimes fills

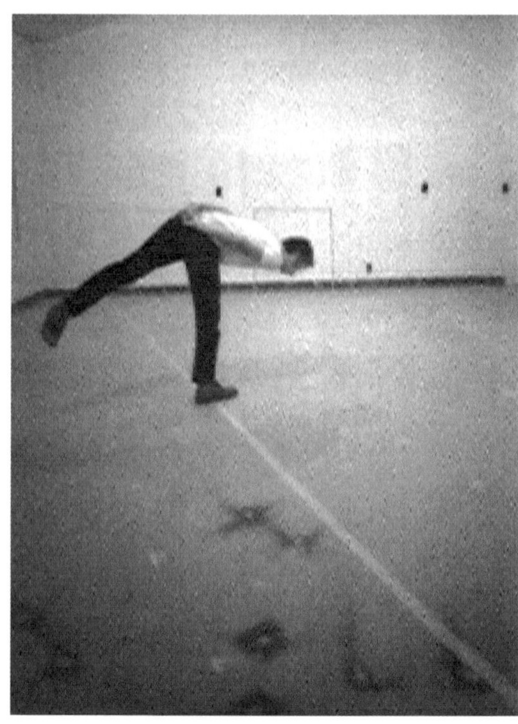

them have this function: to arouse attention or awareness and look for a response to the sensations that have been stirred up.

Crucial works such as *Double Steel Cage Piece* (1974; plate 3), a chain-link cage that the visitor can enter—the theme here is the ambiguity of a space that is simultaneously enclosed and transparent—seem to raise questions about not just the individual but a general condition of human existence. This is equally apparent in *South American Triangle* (1981; fig. 51), one of Nauman's few works revealing a direct relationship to historical events, in this case torture and violence in Latin America. Nauman has spoken of both of these works in terms of a personal involvement so profound as to call into question the possibility of continuing in the direction they opened up: "I didn't do anything like that for a long time after because I was so scared to really focus on these loaded subjects."[51] And, he said, "It stopped my work for a long time because the image was really strong and so far from earlier work."[52]

This kind of unease seems a decisive quality of Nauman's art beginning in his earliest work, where he tested his body with actions that involved extreme mental attention and demanding physical strains. His art always speaks of the artist's own anxiety: a rage and dismay at the human condition that come from the profound layers of his soul. In the end, this is what

Fig. 50 Bruce Nauman. *Slow Angle Walk (Beckett Walk)*, 1968.
Videotape (black-and-white) and sound; 60 minutes

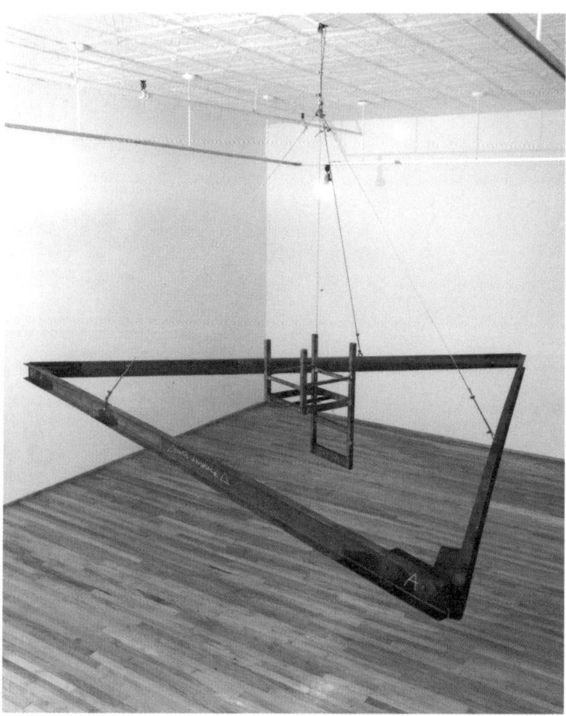

legitimizes his claim to ask others—the public—to share his experience and travel his path. The response to that invitation is not always positive; as Nauman himself has recognized, some of the situations he has created are intolerable, leading the authoritative interpreter and acute observer Arthur Danto, for example, to refuse the imperative "do what you see" that seemed to him to be proposed and imposed by Nauman's traveling retrospective in 1995, which the critic saw at the Museum of Modern Art, New York. For Danto, the most dramatic installations in that exhibition reproposed the astute emotional manipulations of the artists of the Baroque, with results that were "peremptory, invasive, aggressive," even repellent, rather than constituting an anguished reflection on the human condition.[53]

Tucker correctly observed that the overlap between the role of the viewer and that of the performer—the ambivalence between "the sensor and the sensed"[54]—recalls a fundamental motif in Merleau-Ponty's writing on phenomenology: the dialectical interchange between individuals and the world they occupy, the ambiguity in that world's "being at once lived from the inside and observed from the outside." What Nauman does is try to prompt an alteration in the ways in which we perceive the world in which he lives. But if, Tucker observes,

Fig. 51 Bruce Nauman. *South American Triangle*, 1981.
Steel, cast iron, and wire; 39 x 169 x 169 inches (99.1 x 429.3 x 429.3 cm), suspended 60 inches (152.4 cm) above the floor.
Hirshhorn Museum and Sculpture Garden, Smithsonian Institution, Washington, D.C.
Holenia Purchase Fund, 1991

"what we know of the world is the sum of our perceptions, and our physical, emotional, and intellectual reactions to our environment, then to effectively manipulate these factors is to effect a virtual change in that world."[55]

Sound Spaces

Days and *Giorni*—Bruce Nauman's most recent works, presented on the occasion of the 2009 Venice Biennale and discussed elsewhere in this catalogue—have their origins in the beginnings of his career, revealing a deep continuity in his work. In fact their roots trace back to the early 1960s, when Nauman still thought he might be a musician and was exploring piano, guitar, and bass; when he was studying the dissolution of classical structures in Beethoven's late work and in Schönberg's subsequent "invention" of the twelve-tone system; and when, a little later, he encountered the music of John Cage and the work of the musical minimalists Reich, Glass, and Young. What Nauman discovered here was the replacement of temporal structure with a continuous flow, subtly variable and vibrant, without beginning or end. There were parallels in the ordinary, everyday, yet precise dance movements of Cunningham and Monk, the dramatic constructions of Beckett, and the literary structures that Robbe-Grillet described as follows: "Instead of having to deal with a series of scenes which are connected by causal links, one has the impression that the same scene is constantly repeating itself, but with variations."[56]

A Nauman installation of 1968 was simply an empty room inside which a recorded voice steadily mumbled the peremptory order, "Get out of my mind, get out of this room" (checklist 20). Visual experience was replaced by sound, a sound involving both the placement of the body in space—the experience of visitors-listeners in a room they were invited to leave—and a more general, anxious, broken condition of existence in the world, a separation of the figure/mind from the space/background inhabited by the body. Leaving the room, complying with the order, might have seemed an easy solution; much less feasible, however, was the injunction to remove oneself from a reality as immaterial as that of the mind. It was precisely this duality between space and idea, a duality difficult to reconcile, that gave the work the character of an "experiential sculpture."[57]

In *Sound Breaking Wall* (fig. 52), an installation at the Sonnabend gallery, Paris, in 1969, almost imperceptible whispers and sighs, alternating with noisy laughs and thuds, emerged from a series of small speakers hidden in the wall. The difficulty in finding the sources of the sound, and anticipating it in time, produced the condition of "threatening" uncertainty so frequent in Nauman's work. The next year, 1970, brought an even more disquieting work in the Sperone gallery in Turin: touching one wall, the visitor produced a sound that was dislocated onto a different one.

In Venice forty years later, Nauman is creating a double installation, distinguished by the use of two languages, Italian and English, and by the work's placement in two buildings in different parts of the city. In each installation, fourteen speakers repeat the names of the seven days of the week, in different sequences. The regular passage of time is altered both

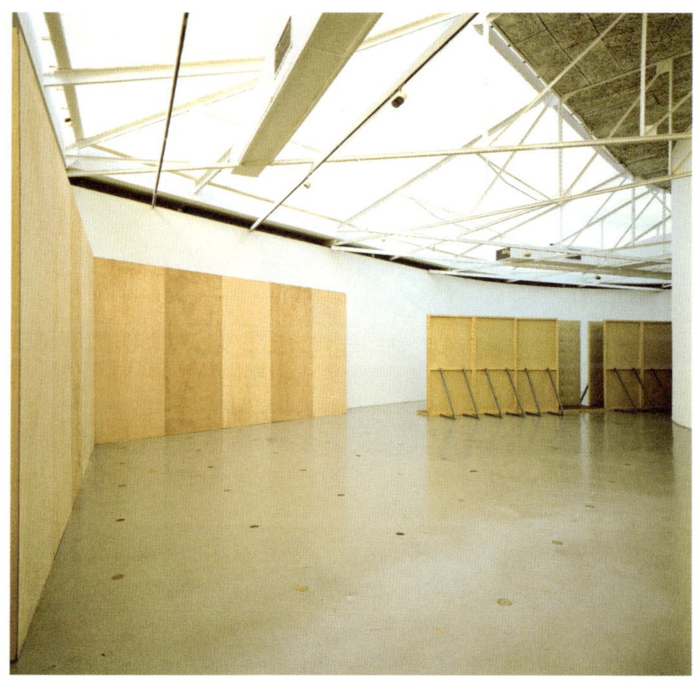

by the modification of the sequence of the days and by the only roughly equal rhythms of the different voices reciting them. Visitors alternate constantly between listening to an individual voice, when they are near a particular speaker, and listening to a "symphony" of superimposed but imperfectly synchronized voices as they move toward the center of the room. The placement of the body in space, then, transforms the regularity of each reading—the regularity of passing time, and of the endlessly repeating weekly cycle—into a barely intelligible babble, in a time deprived of its transparent linearity. Parts and whole merge, and only awareness of the position of the individual figure in a context indicates a possible yet inevitably precarious order. With the passing of the years, the Nauman anxiety seems to have lost some of its early violence and frustration; it no longer announces the fluctuating coexistence of good and evil, life and death, virtue and vice. Yet a subtle trace remains—it still excavates abysses of unease. Has time stopped? We barely sense it.

Translated from Italian by Marguerite Shore

Fig. 52 Bruce Nauman. *Sound Breaking Wall,* 1969.
Wallboard, tape, and speakers; 108 x 288 inches (274.3 x 731.5 cm)
Solomon R. Guggenheim Museum, New York. Panza Collection Gift, 1992. 92.4163

1
Martin Heidegger, *L'origine dell'opera d'arte*, trans. I. De Gennaro and G. Zaccaria (1936; Milan: Christian Marinotti, 2000), p. 3.
2
Noël Arnaud, quoted in Gaston Bachelard, *The Poetics of Space* (1958; Eng. trans., Boston: Beacon Press, 1969), p. 137.
3
Sol LeWitt, "Sentences on Conceptual Art," *0–9*, no. 5 (January 1969).
4
Lucy R. Lippard, *Six Years: The Dematerialization of the Art Object from 1966 to 1972* (Berkeley: University of California Press, 1973), p. vii.
5
For a chronology of Nauman's life in the years 1964–69 see Elizabeth Allison Ferrel, "Chronology," in Constance M. Lewallen, *A Rose Has No Teeth: Bruce Nauman in the 1960s*, exh. cat. (Berkeley: University of California Press, Berkeley Art Museum, and Pacific Film Archive, 2007), pp. 193–213.
6
Nauman, quoted in Michele de Angelus, "Interview with Bruce Nauman," 1980, in Nauman, *Please Pay Attention Please: Bruce Nauman's Words: Writings and Interviews*, ed. Janet Kraynak (Cambridge, Mass.: MIT Press, 2005), p. 238. This interview, Nauman's longest and most revealing, was granted in the context of the California Oral History Project, Archives of American Art, Smithsonian Institution, Washington, D.C., 1980. Nauman is an artist of few words; unlike some of his contemporaries, he is little inclined to theoretical elaboration. Interviews such as this one, however, have been released over the years and are essential tools for interpreting his ideas and intentions.
7
See Coosje van Bruggen, *Bruce Nauman* (New York: Rizzoli, 1988), p. 15.
8
Nauman, quoted in ibid., p. 7.
9
Nauman, quoted in de Angelus, "Interview with Bruce Nauman," p. 285.
10
Nauman, quoted in Christopher Cordes, "Talking with Bruce Nauman: An Interview," 1989, in Nauman, *Please Pay Attention Please*, p. 285.
11
Jean-Christophe Ammann, "Wittgenstein and Nauman," in *Bruce Nauman*, exh. cat. (London: Whitechapel Art Gallery, 1986), pp. 21–29.
12
Joan Simon, "Nauman Variations," in ibid., p. 11.
13
Nauman, quoted in Willoughby Sharp, "Two Interviews," 1970, in Robert C. Morgan, ed., *Bruce Nauman* (Baltimore and London: Johns Hopkins University Press, 2002), p. 237.
14
Nauman, quoted in Joan Simon, "Breaking the Silence: An Interview with Bruce Nauman," 1987, in Nauman, *Please Pay Attention Please*, pp. 322–23.
15
See Lorraine Sciarra, "Bruce Nauman," 1972, in ibid., p. 166. The book is Frederick S. Perls, Ralph F. Hefferline, and Paul Goodman, *Gestalt Therapy: Excitement and Growth in the Human Personality* (New York: The Julian Press, 1951).
16
Perls, Hefferline, and Goodman, *Gestalt Therapy*, p. viii.
17
Ibid., p. ix.
18
Ibid.
19
Ibid., p. 39.
20
Ibid., p. 73.
21
Ibid., p. 41.
22
Ibid., p. 47.
23
Ibid., pp. 84–86.
24
Nauman, quoted in Sharp, "Two Interviews," p. 237.
25
Ibid., p. 242.
26
Bachelard, *The Poetics of Space*, p. 6.
27
Nauman, quoted in de Angelus, "Interview with Bruce Nauman," p. 239.
28
Nauman, quoted in Ian Wallace and Russel Keziere, "Bruce Nauman Interviewed," 1978, in Nauman, *Please Pay Attention Please*, p. 188.
29
Nauman, quoted in Sciarra, "Bruce Nauman," p. 161.
30
Nauman, quoted in Sharp, "Two Interviews," p. 242.
31
Benjamin H. D. Buchloh, "Process Sculpture and Film in Richard Serra's Work," in Buchloh, *Neo-Avantgarde and Culture Industry: Essays on European and American Art from 1955 to 1975* (Cambridge, Mass.: MIT Press, 2000), p. 414.
32
Friedrich Nietzsche, *The Birth of Tragedy* (1872; London: Penguin, 1993), p. 141.
33
See Adrian Forty, "Space," in *Words and Buildings: A Vocabulary of Modern Architecture* (New York: Thames & Hudson, 2000), pp. 256–75.
34
On August Schmarsow, Robert Vischer, and Wilhelm Worringer see Harry F. Maligrave and E. Ikonomou, eds., *Empathy, Form, and Space* (Santa Monica: The Getty Center, 1994).

35
Forty, "Space," p. 356.
36
See Simon, "Breaking the Silence," p. 324.
37
Adolf Hildebrand, "The Problem of Form in the Fine Arts," in Maligrave and Ikonomou, eds., *Empathy, Form, and Space*, p. 239.
38
Marcia Tucker, "PheNAUMANology," *Artforum* 9, no. 4 (December 1970): 38–44. Reprinted in Morgan, ed., *Bruce Nauman*, pp. 21–27. The second essay is Tucker, "Bruce Nauman," in Jane Livingston and Tucker, *Bruce Nauman: Work from 1965 to 1972*, exh. cat. (Los Angeles: Los Angeles County Museum of Art, 1972), pp. 31–48.
39
Nauman, quoted in Amei Wallach, "Artist of the Showdown," in Morgan, ed., *Bruce Nauman*, pp. 36–42. Originally published in *Newsday*, January 8, 1989.
40
Nauman, quoted in van Bruggen, *Bruce Nauman*, p. 18.
41
Nauman, quoted in Sharp, "Two Interviews," p. 235.
42
Nauman, quoted in de Angelus, "Interview with Bruce Nauman," p. 265.
43
The 1:40 value appears in Wallace and Keziere, "Bruce Nauman Interviewed," p. 186. In de Angelus, "Interview with Bruce Nauman," p. 276, Nauman speaks of a 1:12 scale for his tunnel models.
44
Nauman, quoted in de Angelus, p. 278.
45
Michael Auping, "Projection and Displacement," in *Bruce Nauman: Drawing for Installations* (New York: Sperone Westwater, 2008), pp. 7–12. See also *Bruce Nauman: Drawings; Zeichnungen, 1965–1986* (Basel: Museum für Gegenwartskunst, 1986).
46
Bachelard, *The Poetics of Space*, p. 20.
47
Nauman, quoted in Bob Smith, "Bruce Nauman Interview," in Nauman, *Please Pay Attention Please*, p. 298.
48
Nauman, quoted in Simon, "Breaking the Silence," p. 332.
49
Nauman, quoted in Sharp, "Two Interviews," p. 245. Nauman's familiarity with Ludwig Wittgenstein's *Philosophical Investigations* is well-known. See, e.g., Ammann, "Wittgenstein and Nauman," and Robert Storr, "Beyond Words," in Kathy Halbreich and Neil Benezra, *Bruce Nauman* (Minneapolis: Walker Art Center, 1994), pp. 47–66.
50
Nauman, quoted in Simon, "Breaking the Silence," p. 332.
51
Nauman, quoted in Smith, "Bruce Nauman Interview," p. 299.
52
Ibid., p. 300.
53
Arthur C. Danto, "Bruce Nauman," in Morgan, ed., *Bruce Nauman*, p. 150. The article was originally published in *The Nation*, May 8, 1995.
54
Tucker, "PheNAUMANology," p. 23.
55
Ibid., p. 27.
56
Alain Robbe-Grillet, quoted in Ingrid Schaffner, "Bruce Nauman through Samuel Beckett," in ibid., p. 168.
57
Janet Kraynak, "Bruce Nauman's Words," in Nauman, *Please Pay Attention Please*, p. 1.

Analogy as Art: The Infinite Trajectories of Bruce Nauman

Erica F. Battle

One way I worked was by using the tension between two kinds of information that don't quite line up—it's not just the object that you contemplate and experience; it's the object in connection with some other piece of information that you have to deal with.

Bruce Nauman[1]

Analogy : Topology

In *Bruce Nauman: Topological Gardens,* analogies abound. Within the attempt to tackle Nauman's forty-year career with a curatorial strategy, any desire for a single line of continuity soon gives way, thankfully, to the realization that his oeuvre is an unmappable universe. Nauman's practice prohibits modernist medium specificity and denies strict chronology its conventional weight. In fact, a common characteristic of the critical writing on Nauman throughout the decades is an opening proclamation similar to my own—that his is a career of deviation, aberration, and disparity.[2]

The simplest response to this predicament is to say that Nauman continues to ask diverse questions—of the world and of himself as an artist—through equally diverse approaches, using an economy of mediums that is at once of great material breadth and conceptual restraint. Nauman's art has taught us to eschew the linear path in favor of circles, diagrammatic labyrinths, and—in topological terms—a mapping out of a network of fixed points amid the oscillation of an evolving artistic practice. By its very nature, *Topological Gardens* asserts that navigating Nauman's art throughout its chronology and varying forms is a matter of finding topoi to guide us through both.

Yet the idea of assigning a single topos to represent Nauman is also problematic; a commitment to a definite leitmotif can only be so generous. What is needed is a paradigm that allows for both continuity and elasticity—such as the three themes selected for this exhibition. These "threads," as Carlos Basualdo calls them in his essay here, weave in and out, up and down, through the positive and negative spaces of Nauman's work and through a fourth presence in the show: the topography of Venice. These themes that deal in dualities—Fountains and Neons, Heads and Hands, Sound and Space—are themselves analogically defined.

Analogical thinking, which some consider to be at the core of cognitive reasoning,[3] offers an intriguing method of examining Nauman's art that often emanates from the tension between pragmatic meanings and semantic possibilities, whether his works deal specifically with language or confuse viewers' expectation through their physical reality. In her 1988 book on Nauman, Coosje van Bruggen describes many of his early sculptures, such as *From Hand to Mouth* (1967; plate 11), as "formal analogies."[4] So too do Nauman's early text pieces show a propensity toward analogical language. As noted by Michael Auping, the "type of messaging in which Nauman engaged in the late 1960s, addressing directly or obliquely the subjects/analogies laid out in *Codification*, sometimes forged and often tested the relationship between words, forms, and their meanings."[5] In that text piece of 1966, Nauman even wrote the phrase "Analogic and digital codification," confusing analogy and analogue in wordplay.[6]

Further, Nauman's well-known coming-of-age story, which tells of a decisive moment during his junior year at the University of Wisconsin–Madison, when he shifted his studies from structural mathematics to art, points to a formative capacity for thinking in parallels. Even once the academic switch was made, Nauman retained his interest in mathematics and once cited a math professor, an algebraic topologist, as an enduring influence on him.[7] Both direct mathematical concepts (such as proofs, permutations, and skew lines) and their metaphoric applications surface continuously in Nauman's artistic process.[8] He brought with him to art an undeniable satisfaction in problem-solving, which persists from his early experiments in film and video through his subsequent forty years of practice.

The analogous relationships that can be traced in multiple parallel lines through Nauman's works in sculpture, installation, performance, neon, and sound across the decades are the focus and connective tissue of *Topological Gardens*. Here we locate our version of Nauman's logic that the tension that drives his work is not derived from an object or experience in isolation, but that "it's the object in connection with some other piece of information that you have to deal with."[9] The "other pieces of information" that we propose are the three threads thematically linking the works in the exhibition, along with the geographical and social contours of Venice. Comprising three sites stretched over the city's interlocking islands—the U.S. Pavilion, in the southeastern heart of the Giardini; the Università Iuav di Venezia, at Tolentini, near Piazzale Roma, to the northwest; and between these two, the Exhibition Spaces at Università Ca' Foscari, at a critical bend of the Grand Canal—the exhibition posits physical routes that embrace the city as a holistic space. Possible juxtapositions between individual works of art at the same sites and larger connections that cut across the exhibition's geography allow for an interpretation, experience, and cognition of Nauman's art that are distinctly entwined with the experience of Venice. The fountains and neons in Nauman's work, for example, relate analogically to the fountains and shop signs in the city's public spaces.

A rudimentary analogy starts with an assumption (the source), which is followed by another information set (the target). Although based on a necessarily dualistic mode of comparison, analogies imply not purely oppositional thinking but continuous *lines* of thinking that range from the obvious and fixed to the oblique and infinite. The structure of the exhibition in its three locations is similarly unbounded; the conceptual threads that run through Nauman's works are not presented as contained corollaries exclusive to each site. Like a Venn diagram of three translucent circles in which the possibility of isolating one theme is checked by points of intersection in various combinations, the show operates in the gray areas in which Nauman's art thrives, and which visitors are left not to resolve but to encounter and navigate for themselves.

Repetition, permutation, redrafting, rethinking. These are keys to Nauman's practice. For this reason, we position *Topological Gardens* as just one permutation of a universe that remains open to the potential for alternate axiomatic readings. Thus we posit that although the works selected necessarily reach beyond themselves—acting, like all of Nauman's works, as signifiers for whole paths and possible tangents in the interpretation of his practice—something particularly enlightening in the topological model of space and the analogical method of comprehension saves us from the paradoxical attempt to close the loop. Fountains and Neons, Heads and Hands, Sound and Space, are therefore not closed conditions but open categories. They are the fixed points where we can start, but the trajectories are infinite.

Fountains : Neons

A quintessential moment in which early modernism met its contemporary counterpart is Nauman's entrée into fashioning himself as a fountain in the photograph *Self-Portrait as a Fountain* (1966–67/1970; see fig. 29). As Michael Taylor notes in his essay in this book, Nauman created the image—and likely the series of works following that take up the notion of the fountain—in inevitable relation to Marcel Duchamp's iconic urinal of 1917. Yet the metaphor relating the fountain to the artist/producer stems from a longer history, from the most academic to innovative of artists, as from Ingres to Pablo Picasso. The persistence of this imagery is partly due to the expectation that the artist possesses the godly capacity to create—endlessly. The awareness of the artist that he is both capable of and responsible for the regeneration of inspiration has repeatedly found its expression in water—whether flowing from a jug, a fountain, or a stream. Some of these representations themselves were expected to achieve untainted purity and academic perfection, as one finds in Ingres's *La Source* (1856; Musée d'Orsay, Paris).

In *Self-Portrait as a Fountain* and in the black-and-white photograph *The Artist as a Fountain* that soon followed (1966–67; fig. 53), however, Nauman exposes the watery metaphor as a loaded expectation, here irreverently embodied by the artist himself posing as "the source." Spurting water with pursed lips and showing off a naked torso, or posing as a fountain in a garden, Nauman presents himself as the artist at both his most ambitious and his most sacrilegious. By employing his body as a fountain, Nauman eclipses the distance allowed by his predecessors between themselves and their florid metaphors (or unsightly urinals); his body enacts his equivocal relationship to the expectations laid out by society, art historical and otherwise. Perhaps this was why, in 1968, *Self-Portrait as a Fountain* was chosen to

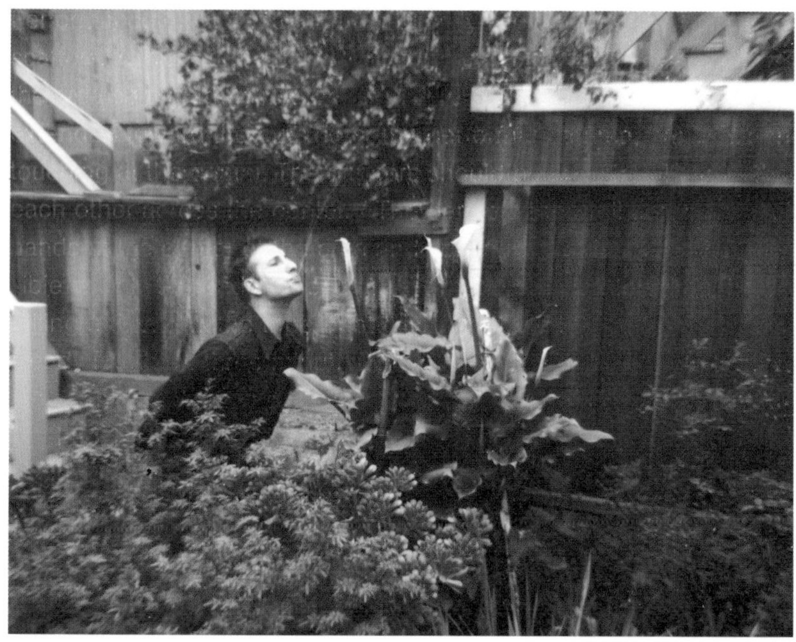

encapsulate Nauman's announcement of himself to the New York art world, as it was featured on the postcard sent out by the Leo Castelli Gallery for his first one-man show there. On the reverse was an equally undisguised handwritten entreaty: "Please Come to the opening of Bruce Nauman's show on Saturday, Jan. 27."[10]

The topos of the fountain intermittently occupied Nauman's art for the three early years from 1966 through 1968, although the questions about the role of the artist embedded in these fountain-related works can be said to underlie much of his subsequent "output." (In the 1990s and mid-2000s, too, he would revisit the motif explicitly by creating functional sculptural fountains composed in other shapes.) Pausing over the works hung together in that inaugural 1968 show at Castelli, we see that on one wall the fountain-based works were joined by works in an incredible variety of media (fig. 54). In *Neon Templates of the Left Half of My Body Taken at Ten-Inch Intervals* (1966; fig. 13), *The True Artist Is an Amazing Luminous Fountain (Window or Wall Shade)* (1966), and *Self-Portrait as a Fountain* (fig. 29), Nauman reiterates analogical investigations of the self. Made after *Self-Portrait as a Fountain*, the semitransparent Mylar sign, rose in hue, that constitutes *The True Artist Is an Amazing Luminous Fountain (Window or Wall Shade)* transfers the fountain theme to the method of sign-making. The 1966 study for this work, *The True Artist Is an Amazing Luminous Fountain (Design for Around the Edge of a Window or Wall of*

Fig. 53 Bruce Nauman. *The Artist as a Fountain*, 1966–67. Black-and-white photograph, 8 x 10 inches (20.3 x 24.5 cm). The National Gallery of Art, Washington, D.C.

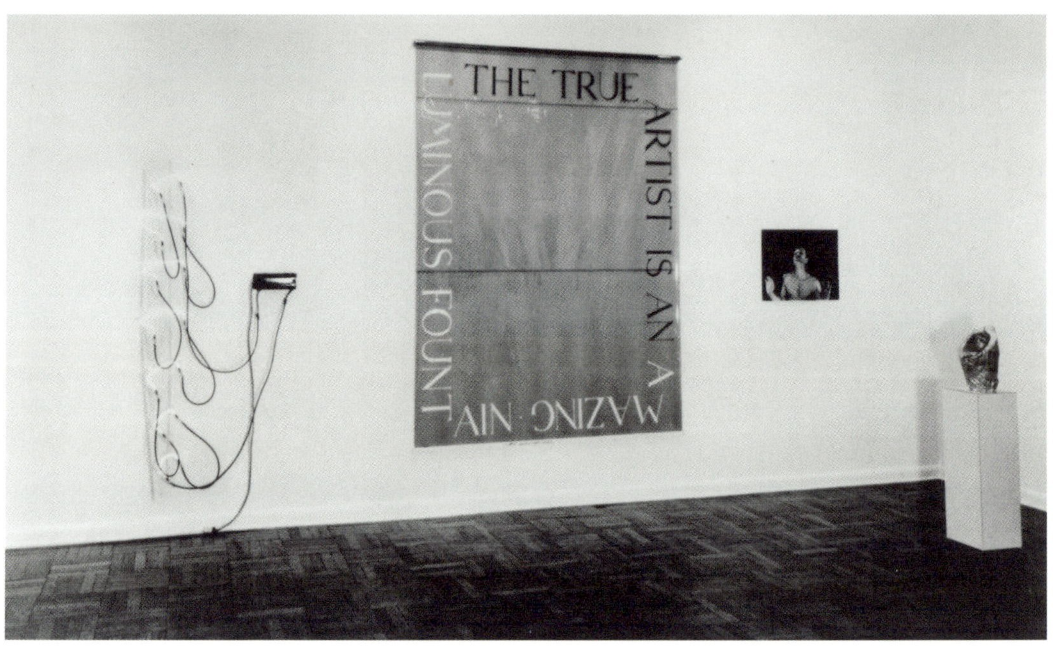

These Proportions), marks the first moment that Nauman put his ambitious and ambivalent artist's statement into writing, invoking the fountain motif along with the words "luminous" and "true artist."

Whereas these terms resonated with both a concern over and a critique of Nauman's intellectual role as an artist, many of his early neons signified impressions of other aspects of his selfhood—whether bodily, in *Neon Templates*, or nominally, in *My Last Name Exaggerated Fourteen Times Vertically* (1967; fig. 55). Both of these were included in the Castelli exhibition, as was the composite photograph *My Name As Though It Were Written on the Surface of the Moon: Bbbbbbbbbbrrrrrrrrrruuuuuuuuuucccccccccceeeeeeeeee* (1967; fig. 56), which would later inspire another name-based neon sign. Of these early incarnations connecting selfhood with object-making, Marcia Tucker wrote in 1970, "This concern with physical self is not simple artistic egocentrism, but use of the body to transform intimate subjectivity into objective demonstration."[11] According to our analogous logic, that "objective demonstration" would connect the fountains—bodily animated and otherwise—directly to the neons invoking the artist's name; both gestures efface the gap between the artist's selfhood and his objects. Although Nauman's name-based neons seem to brandish an authorial concern, any suspicion of seriousness is quickly belied by the sense of humor surrounding a joke about a young artist out to "make a name" for himself. Perhaps in reaction to the expectation of a "signature style," Nauman attenuated his name in neon, whether

Fig. 54 Bruce Nauman. Installation view from *Bruce Nauman*, Leo Castelli Gallery, New York, January 27–February 17, 1968

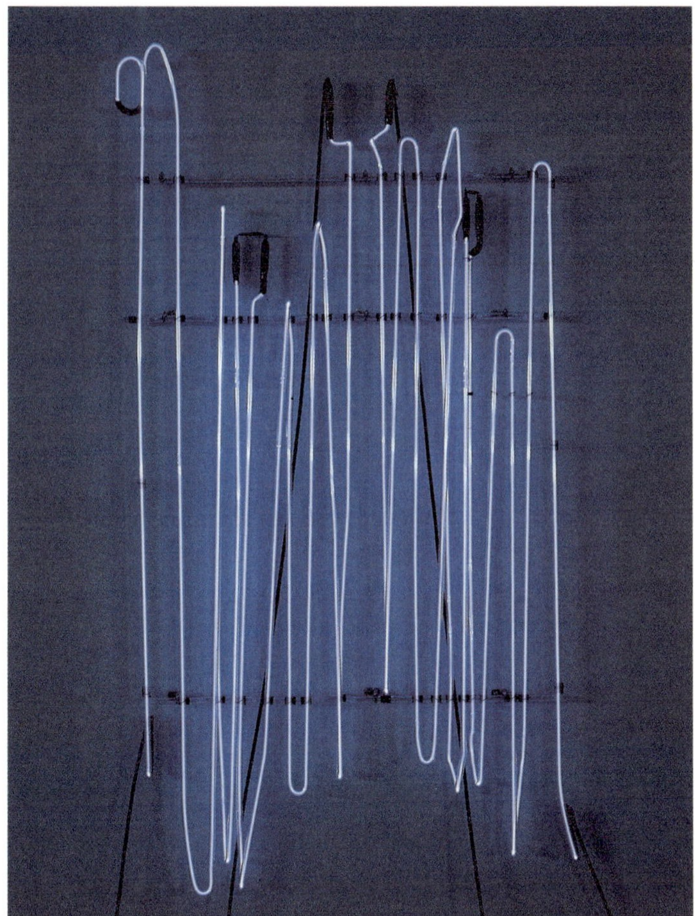

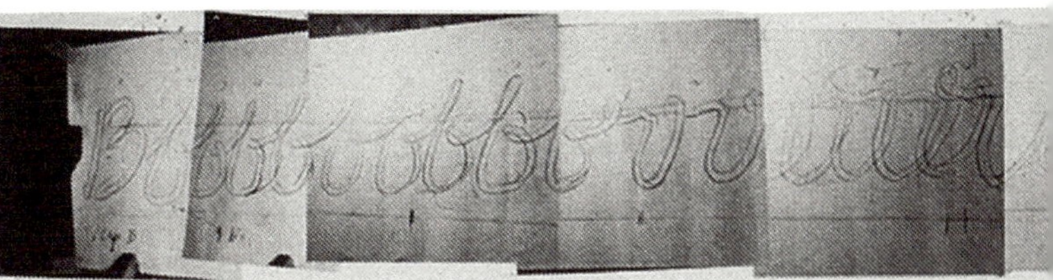

Fig. 55 Bruce Nauman. *My Last Name Exaggerated Fourteen Times Vertically,* 1967.
Neon tubing with clear glass tubing suspension frame, 63 x 33 x 2 inches (160 x 83.8 x 5.1 cm).
Glenstone

Fig. 56 Bruce Nauman. *My Name As Though It Were Written on the Surface of the Moon: Bbbbbbbbbbrrrrrrrrrruuuuuuuuuucccccccccceeeeeeeeee,* 1967.
Fifteen black-and-white photographs and tape; 13 x 138 inches (33 x 350.5 cm).
Private collection

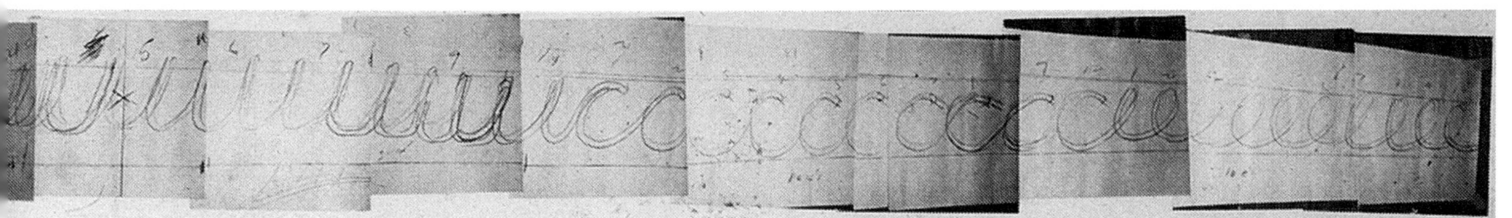

by elongating the lines visually constituting his last name into parabolas of cool violet in *My Last Name Exaggerated Fourteen Times Vertically* or by repeating the letters of his first name to engender the skewed perspective of the hot blue-white *My Name As Though It Were Written on the Surface of the Moon* (1968; plate 15).

Much of Nauman's early neon production was closely linked to sign-making, as evidenced by *The True Artist Is an Amazing Luminous Fountain (Window or Wall Shade)*, which presaged the iconic neon sign he would fabricate a year later for his San Francisco storefront studio, the spiraling *The True Artist Helps the World by Revealing Mystic Truths (Window or Wall Sign)* of 1967 (plate 22). Here, however, Nauman playfully subtracts the phrase "is an amazing luminous fountain" from the statement, relying instead upon the resplendent neon sign to index the sentence's previous incarnations. Yet he inserted additional phrases equally daunting: "helps the world" and "mystic truths." Nauman displayed *The True Artist Helps the World by Revealing Mystic Truths (Window or Wall Sign)* in the window of his studio, a former grocery store, facing the street, giving passersby the opportunity to distinguish his artist's statement from other neons populating the urban landscape—if they paid attention. In *Topological Gardens*, the humming sign is hung backward to the visitor who has entered the U.S. Pavilion, echoing its original installation as a sign facing the street, appearing in reverse to those who had access to Nauman's studio.

The U.S. Pavilion's entrance is also marked by a second encounter connecting fountains and neons. Curving over the entrance, *Untitled (The True Artist Is an Amazing Luminous Fountain)* (plate 26) occupies the interstitial space of the threshold between the outside and the inside of the building. The work is another sign, originally executed in store-bought Upson board letters in 1968. In Venice it is spelled out in commercially available cast-aluminum letters that Nauman chose for this particular context. These works—as well as the window-shade version of *The True Artist Is an Amazing Luminous Fountain* that preceded them—reveal Nauman's early interest in making art that responded directly to architectural cues in particular spaces.

Ideal for drawing attention to a message only to undermine it, neon signs proved a perfect platform for Nauman's formal, linguistic, humorous, and provocative investigations. The viability of marketing ideas instead of products—or ideas as products of the artist—interested Nauman, though any linkage of his use of neon to Pop art's commandeering of a commercial language is thwarted by his subverted and subversive content. Playing with anagrammatic

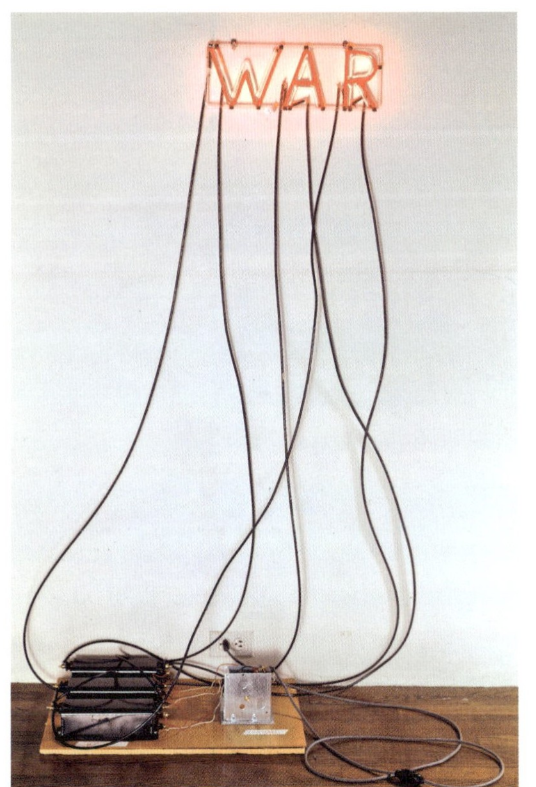

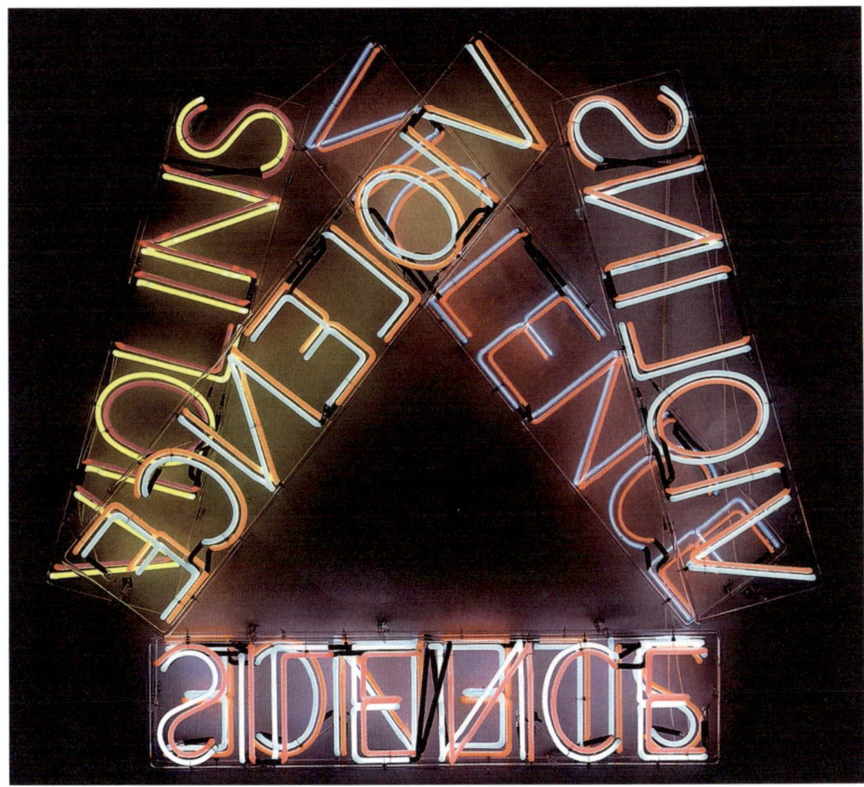

■ **Fig. 57** Bruce Nauman. *Raw War,* 1970.
Red and orange glass tubing, with clear glass suspension frame, transformer, and flashing mechanism;
6 1/2 x 17 1/8 x 2 1/2 inches (16.5 x 43.5 x 6 cm).
The Baltimore Museum of Art. Gift of Leo Castelli, New York. BMA 1982.148

■■ **Fig. 58** Bruce Nauman. *Violins Violence Silence,* 1981–82.
Neon tubing with clear glass tubing suspension frame, height approximately 48 inches (121.9 cm).
Collection Camille O. Hoffmann, Chicago

language, *None Sing Neon Sign* of 1970 (plate 16) reflects on its own embodiment as an art object. Other word-based neons, such as *Raw War* from the same year (fig. 57), use palindromes to drum up political language as the letters flash to reveal the connection between the two words. As analogical reasoning exercises, Nauman's word-based neons require the viewer to make the lingering, sometimes stinging connection. In 1982, at the Baltimore Museum of Art, the curator Brenda Richardson organized a show focused solely on the neons, for which Nauman created the permanent large-scale installation *Violins Violence Silence* as well as a smaller, wall-hanging version of the work (fig. 58).[12] In both, forward and backward neon versions of the title words are superimposed and subject to flashing sequences that complicate the implied meaning of the assonant phrase, whose interpretations could range from a child's rhyming game to an allusion to the myth of Nero fiddling while Rome burned.

Violins Violence Silence paved the way for Nauman's neons to become large-scale public installations such as *Vices and Virtues* (plate 27), whose dates of execution, 1983–88, reflect the work's proposal, initial rejection, and final realization for the Stuart Collection at the University of California, San Diego. Essentially a roster of the proverbial seven virtues and seven vices, the work could hardly be more laconic; yet the proposal found resistance due to the polemical interpretations of these words by theater staff, community officials, and journalists.[13] In letters stretching seven feet high, *Vices and Virtues* was ultimately installed at the university's Charles Lee Powell Laboratory.

Vices and Virtues has been remade for *Topological Gardens*, rescaled to the size of the exterior frieze that occupies the entire perimeter of the neoclassical U.S. Pavilion. As a set of information derived from common cultural knowledge, the vices and virtues are paired up and superimposed, "Anger," for example, fusing with "Fortitude," giving the piece its interpretive hinge. A timed flashing sequence lights the virtues in clockwise order and the vices counterclockwise, yielding seemingly endless permutations of meaning. Every once in a while, all of the words light up and assert themselves in a few spectacular flashes. In this moment Nauman seems to be assessing the human condition, and concluding that we are capable not only of select vices and virtues individually but of simultaneously embodying, enacting, and inspiring these fourteen characteristics at any given time.

Heads : Hands

To arrive at the next thematic trajectory of *Topological Gardens* is to see the impossibility of extracting one thread from the others: this section on Heads and Hands will start with neons and end with fountains. In the 1980s, when Nauman's neon production reached its zenith, he was making neon signs comprising electrified bodies or their component parts—heads, hands, male genitalia, and stick figures, sometimes engaged in violent and/or sexual acts. Lit up in bright colors, tortuous and tortured heads poke and are poked in the eyes, as in *Double Poke in the Eye II* (1985; plate 4), or feast on one another's noses, as in *Eating Buggers (Version II)* (1985; plate 5). Nauman often drew the contours of the neon bodies from his own shadow, accounting for their eerily swollen and cartoon-like features, which, robbed of all specificity, allow for the interplay between the comedic and the grotesque. As

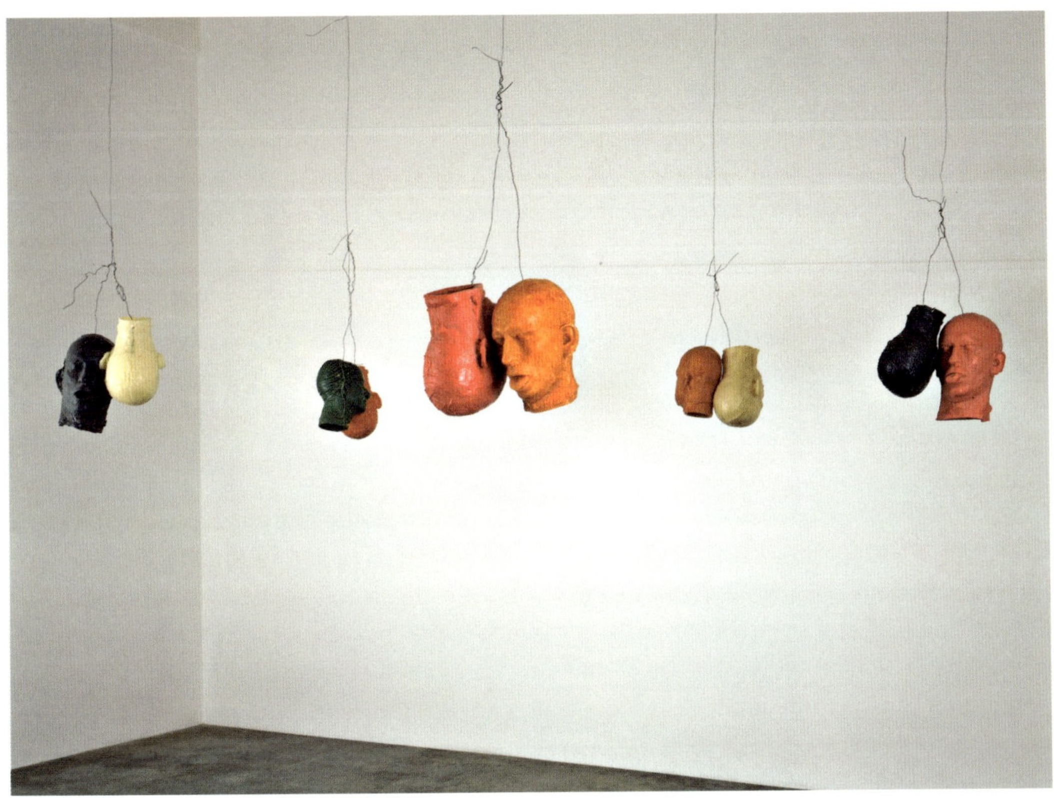

kinetic neons, *Double Poke in the Eye II* and *Eating Buggers (Version II)* flash to illustrate systematic eating or poking in an uncanny stop-motion flux. Such untoward behavior is paradoxically countered by the clean lines and sterile surfaces of the aluminum boxes that hide much of the works' electrical apparatuses. (Many of Nauman's word-based neons, on the other hand, allow wires and transformers to hang out and down in wayward fashion.)

Asked to account for his shift from thinking about math to making objects, Nauman once replied, "Art allowed me room for both my mind and my hands to work."[14] Many of Nauman's works feature an analogical relationship in which heads, hands, or both act as signifiers for thinking and making, so that the mental and physical acts of creation are as continuous as the topological surfaces of the body. Heads and hands have figured as both subjects of his works and signifiers of this idea throughout Nauman's career, and they appear throughout the exhibition in many permutations and in a variety of media. Separated or together, they act as compelling distillations of the act of making art and the complexities of thought and communication.

Fig. 59 Bruce Nauman. *Ten Heads Circle/In and Out,* 1990.
Wax and wire; diameter 96 inches (243.8 cm), heads approximately 12 x 9 x 6 inches (30.5 x 22.9 x 15.2 cm) each, suspended 56 1/2 to 60 inches (143.5 to 152.4 cm) above the floor

In *Human Sexual Experience* (1985; plate 14), flashing neon lights make explicit the purpose with which the forefinger of one hand inserts itself into the hole of the other. This provocative movement can be directly associated with the sculpture *Untitled (Hand Circle)* (1996; plate 25), whose soldered bronze hands gesture likewise, while also making witty reference to heads—the heads of its viewers; the sculpture is hung at eye level, as if threatening to poke them in the eye. These works are joined at the Exhibition Spaces at Università Ca' Foscari by *Untitled (#358)* of 1986 (plate 23), a suspended foamcore-and-cardboard construction of Nauman's own head and various limbs curiously tacked together with wooden pieces and store-bought binder clips. *Untitled (#358)* further reflects the artist's playful use of his shadow, here embodied in a foamcore template that he traced to create some of the figurative neons of the same period. Suspended like *Untitled (Hand Circle)*, its joints and limbs are confounded by the dissection and recomposition of its original form. It hangs like a precedent to Nauman's later suspended carousels, animals with rearranged limbs, heads hanging from baling wire, and hovering resin-head fountains.

Nauman intends many of his sculptural works to be encountered at eye level, activating a kind of one-to-one ratio of experience that feeds into the confrontational aspect of his work. In this way he controls the interaction between the viewer's body and his sculptures, as in his various permutations of heads that hang from the ceiling by wire. In *Four Pairs of Heads (Wax)* of 1991 (plate 10), the pairs of heads, truncated at the neck, hang far enough apart for the viewer to circumnavigate them, two dangling from a horizontal rebar that suggests puppeteering. Unlike the candy-colored heads in the closely related works of 1990 *Ten Heads Circle/Up and Down* and *Ten Heads Circle/In and Out* (fig. 59), *Four Pairs of Heads (Wax)* dangles heads that are predominantly skin-colored with blood-red slabs of wax affixed to their hollow craniums, whose brain cavities are eerily visible. Each pair is bound together by wire that chafes and cuts into the wax, evoking a brutality that serves to help in the realization that not only are these heads that hang, but they are *hanging heads*. Perhaps this is why, when a series of Nauman's heads was shown at the Castelli gallery in 1990, a critic dubbed him "Master of the Morbid Fragment."[15] In *Hanging Head for Leo* (1990; plate 13) the head is incarnated in bronze, like an impending pendulum.

Nauman allows traces of the casting process by which he makes the wax heads to remain clearly visible, as he did in the cast sculptures of his MFA years in the mid-1960s. An observable seam connects the front and back of each head; at times, a breathing plug remains in the mouth, evoking the physical difficulty endured by the sitter. In some heads whose mouths hang open, Nauman has inserted a cast of his own tongue.[16] As in a death mask, the eyes are always closed. When the heads are not hanging, they suffer nuisances like those in neons such as *Double Poke in the Eye II* and *Eating Buggers (Version II)*—tongues poke into eyes, tongues lick heads, inverted noses interlock, heads fuse together. In *Five Pink Heads in the Corner* of 1992 (plate 8), Nauman stacks the heads facing the wall, denying the viewer the usual focus of visual information—their faces. Through their purposeful relegation to the corner, they enact shame; in the Pavilion, their ignominy is analogously connected to the heads that sway on wire (as in "hanging your head").

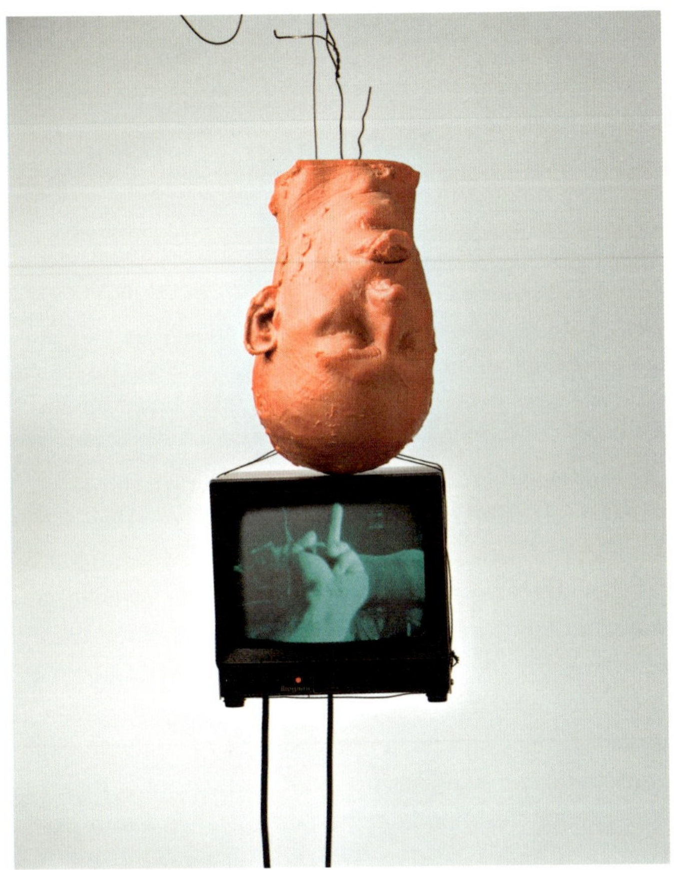

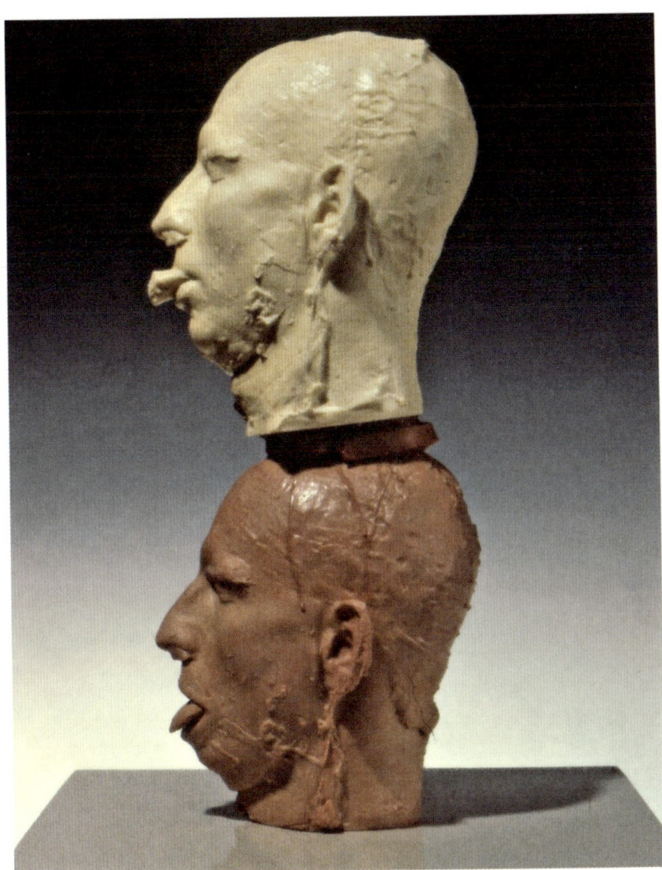

In the late 1980s and early 1990s the motif of stacked heads persisted in other wax sculptures and also was transferred to video. *Perfect Balance (Pink Andrew with Plug Hanging with TV)* (1989; fig. 60) comprises a wax head balancing atop a suspended video monitor that shows a hand giving the finger. The wax heads stacked like the ominous beginning to a totem pole in works such as *Andrew Head/Andrew Head Stacked* (1990; fig. 61) start to find corollaries in video works of the mid-1990s such as *Think*, *Work* (fig. 62), and *Jump*, in which Nauman's own head features on pairs of stacked monitors. In *Think* of 1993 (plate 20), Nauman records himself jumping up and down, his head appearing and reappearing in the static frame of the video camera as he shouts the work's monosyllabic title.

Fig. 60 Bruce Nauman. *Perfect Balance (Pink Andrew with Plug Hanging with TV)*, 1989.
Wax head, black-and-white video monitor, U-matic player, and U-matic tape; height approximately 75 inches (190.5 cm) overall; head 11 7/16 x 9 7/8 x 6 11/16 inches (29 x 25 x 17 cm).
Museum für Moderne Kunst, Frankfurt. Inv. No. 1989/7.1-2

Fig. 61 Bruce Nauman. *Andrew Head/Andrew Head Stacked*, 1990.
Wax, 22 x 8 x 9 inches (55.9 x 20.3 x 22.7 cm).
Private collection

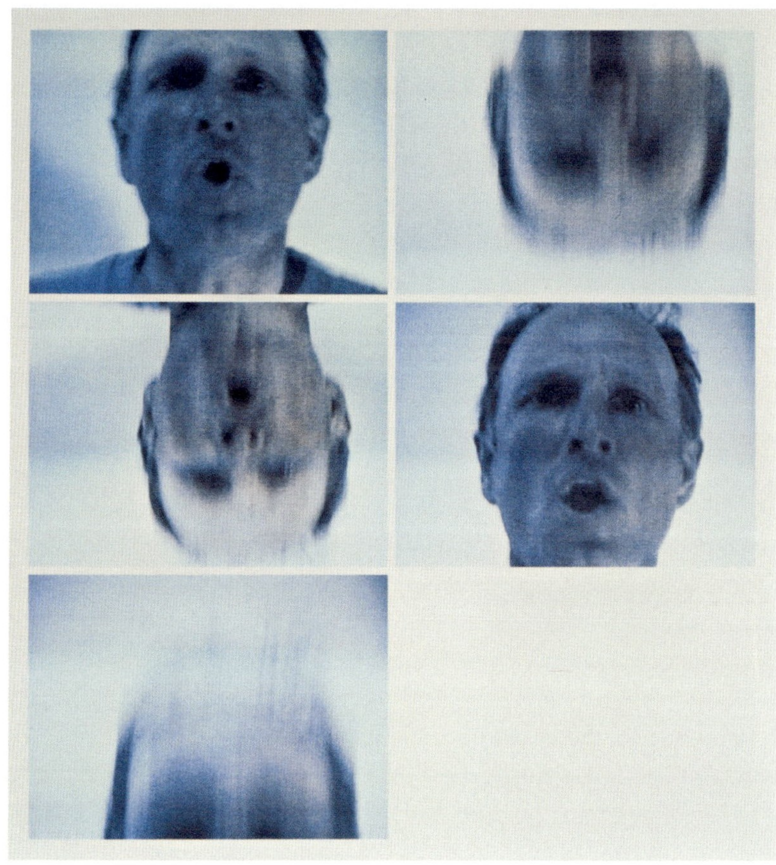

One monitor captures his kinetic motion right-side up, the other upside down; the aggressive, insistent, and out-of-breath injunctions to "Think! Think! Think!" are unsynchronized, creating a cacophony, so that Nauman's pragmatic command is immediately countered by the impossibility of taking a moment to think within range of this broken-record speech act. *Think* and other videos in the "Raw Materials" series recall Nauman's studio films in that they were made in his studio and capture deceptively simple actions. Perhaps, in videos such as *Think*, Nauman was asking himself the same fundamental question he had pondered while sitting in his studio in 1967: how to think up art.

While *Think* greets visitors, and students, at the Iuav site at Tolentini, two double-stacked video-monitor works from the same period appear at the U.S. Pavilion.[17] In the lower video channel of *Coffee Spilled and Balloon Dog* of 1993 (plate 2), a magician uses his trademark dexterity to create a dog from a clear balloon. Wearing black but for his face and hands,

Fig. 62 Bruce Nauman. Video stills from *Work*, 1994.
Two video discs, two video disc players, two monitors, steel cart, color, and sound.
Froehlich Collection, Stuttgart

and standing against a dark background, his body largely disappears, his head becoming as disembodied as those hanging in the adjacent room. His hands, curtailed at the cuffs, resonate with the topological gestures of works found elsewhere in the Pavilion, such as *Fifteen Pairs of Hands* (1996; plate 7), in which sandblasted bronze casts of Nauman's hands perform permutations of infinitely interpretable gestures. On the upper screen, a coffee cup repeatedly falls in slow motion to crash into the pristine surface of a white tablecloth. While the comparison of spilling coffee and creating a balloon dog is an easily interpreted analogy between destroying and creating with one's hands, both the coffee cup and the balloon are topological figures. Just as a coffee cup is topologically congruous with a donut (as Basualdo notes in his essay here, recalling Nauman's early sculptures of the coffee cup and its saucer), so too is a balloon a topological paradigm: it can change shape without accruing matter or losing its essence.

In *Washing Hands Normal* (1996; plate 28) Nauman films himself washing his hands with a vigor exceeding that necessary to achieve cleanliness. Acting out the motions of the topological surfaces seen in *Fifteen Pairs of Hands, Washing Hands Normal* also likens the sound of the sink's constant flow to a fountain. In the opposite wing of the U.S. Pavilion, the spring is realized in two functioning fountains, *Three Heads Fountain (Three Andrews)* (see fig. 26) and *Three Heads Fountain (Juliet, Andrew, Rinde)* (plate 21), both of 2005. Hanging in clusters of three, the resin heads are punctured in various spots to spurt water from the eyes and ears as well as the mouth. Spit, sprayed, and dribbled, the water falls into a basin made of the most raw and unceremonious of materials—a wood frame and pond liner. Here Nauman deposes any classical or metaphorical notion of the source and replaces it with a pun: these are, quite literally, fountainheads. As such, they cycle us back to the beginning.

Sound : Space

Nauman's suspended sculptures linger in overlaps among the exhibition's proposed categories. In *Hanging Carousel (George Skins a Fox)* of 1988 (plate 12), for example, the visual motif of hands lures us back into Heads and Hands, while the contraption of the rotating carousel pushes us forward into Sound and Space. This third analogical passage of *Topological Gardens* is a seemingly dematerialized pairing, concerned more with the mode of art than with its subject. Yet sound and space are integral to Nauman's formal concerns, and he has harnessed them like blunt-force objects. In an often-quoted moment, he compared the desired effect of his work to "getting hit in the face with a baseball bat. Or better, like getting hit in the back of the neck. You never see it coming; it just knocks you down."[18] It is in his works that manipulate sound and space as tools for inescapable experience in which this drama habitually plays out.

Hanging Carousel (George Skins a Fox) manifests a confrontational impulse similar to that of the hanging heads. Here, polyurethane animal forms used in taxidermy are strung to the ends of steel fulcrums reaching in four directions by wires wrapped around their inanimate necks. Rotating both clockwise and counterclockwise on a timed motor, the carousel destroys any carnival association with its melancholic churning. At the center, a suspended monitor broadcasts video footage of Nauman's former neighbor, George Stumpff, flaying a fox. Stumpff's striking skill relates back to the theme of hands; skinning a fox is a manual act of both destruction (killing, flaying) and creation (making something new, as implied by the taxidermy forms). The polyurethane forms, which Nauman started to use in the 1980s in collages, carousels, and sculptures, are strangely inchoate figures without their finish of skins. As a whole, the sculpture seems to intimate the possibility of interaction, but its arms, like some labored windmill, are too threatening to get too close.

Flaying is also invoked in the installation *Flayed Earth Flayed Self (Skin Sink)* of 1973 (plate 9), in which Nauman used masking tape to divide floor and walls into six sections in a pinwheel pattern. Originally published as a small booklet for Nicholas Wilder Gallery, Los Angeles, an accompanying text alludes to the peeling and uncovering of earth and self in an effort to become unbounded in the face of compression. Several blank pages precede and follow the text in the booklet, as if to suggest the potential of negative space to become positively charged in the infinite universe.[19] Nauman's use of masking tape to map, contain, and implode floor space is inherently linked to earlier mappings of his studio, as in *Dance or Exercise on the Perimeter of a Square (Square Dance)* of 1967–68, in which he allows the structure of a square of masking tape mapped on the floor of Wiley's studio to guide, limit, and direct his movements to a metronome (fig. 63). After making *Flayed Earth Flayed Self (Skin Sink),* Nauman crafted the concentric circles of *Cones Cojones* (1973–75; fig. 64), which according to an accompanying collage of text evoke conical sections, one inside the other, projecting outward from the center of the earth. In both works the visitor is meant to stand at the center to feel, through the kinesthesia implied by their texts, the forces of nature that propel space to undergo the topological motions of expansion and contraction.

The *Flayed Earth* text includes wordplay that seems to foretell another spatial dimension of Nauman's work that brings us back to a discussion of objects that hang: "Suspension of belief, suspension of an object/object of suspension—to hang."[20] Suspension oddly empowers Nauman's hanging heads, monitors, sculptures, and carousels; it is within an early series of models of tunnels, passageways, and trenches, constructed mostly out of plaster, that suspension starts coming into play. In *Model for Trench and Four Buried Passages* of 1977 (fig. 65), for example, concentric rings of plaster and fiberglass ensnare the floor and hang from the ceiling at eye level, obscuring the sight of the sculpture in full. Nauman once said that these models were meant to be experienced with the knowledge that they could potentially be made at full scale; when viewing them, "you'd have this other information that if it were built the spaces would be ten feet high so that you could enter."[21] In *Topological Gardens, Smoke Rings (Model for Underground Tunnels)* of 1979–80 (plate 18) comprises two floor-bound plaster models whose impossible tunnels have a crucial flaw: there is no entrance or exit.

Games of access and denial are experiential motifs in many of Nauman's works in which space is conjugated into corridors, sealed rooms, capsules, and isolation chambers, whose interiors are often captured by surveillance cameras. Nauman has remarked that the models

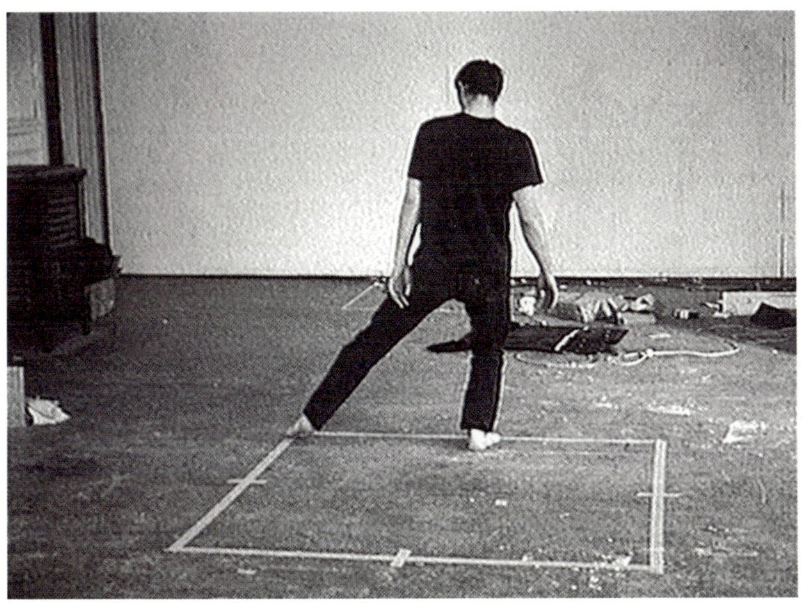

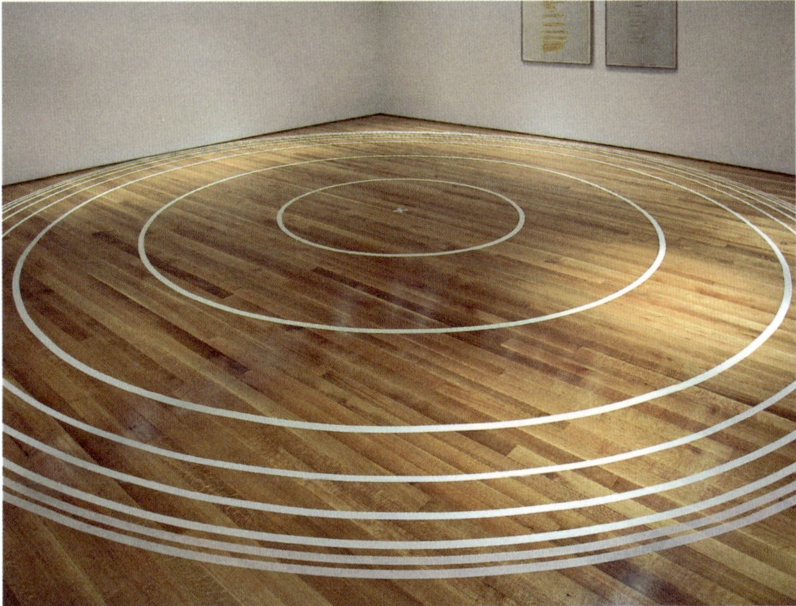

Fig. 63 Bruce Nauman. Film still from *Dance or Exercise on the Perimeter of a Square (Square Dance)*, 1967–68.
Sixteen-millimeter film (black-and-white) and sound; 10 minutes

Fig. 64 Bruce Nauman. Installation view of *Cones Cojones*, 1973–75. From the exhibition *Bruce Nauman: Drawings for Installations*, Sperone Westwater, New York, February 19–March 29, 2008.
Installation: masking tape; diameter of largest circle 480 inches (1219.2 cm). Text: typewriting, paper, and tape on paper; two sheets: 39 15/16 x 25 15/16 inches (101.4 x 65.9 cm) each.
The Museum of Modern Art, New York. Acquired through the generosity of Donald L. Bryant, Jr., Kathy and Richard S. Fuld, Jr., and Marlene Hess and James D. Zirin, 2008

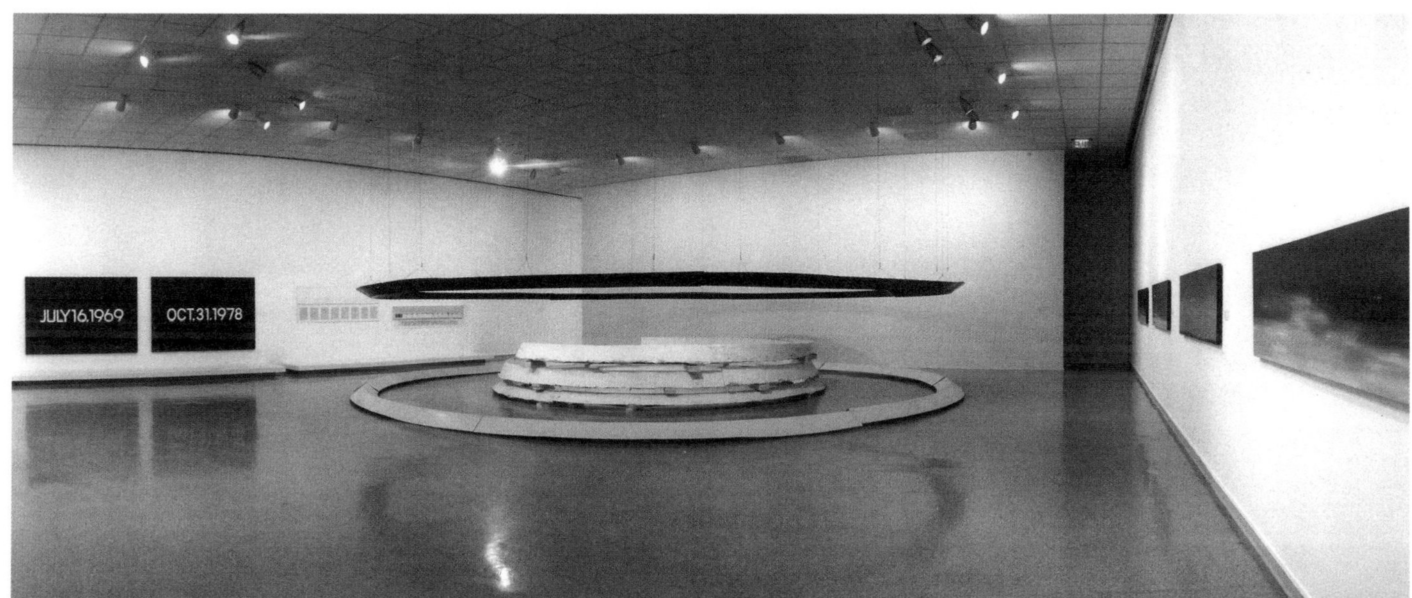

for underground tunnels, and works that similarly complicate normalized spatial relationships, are related to the social dimension of space:

> I guess one of the more important parts of a lot of the work had to do with the difference between private space and public space, and how it's psychologically different to be in a room with a bunch of people by yourself . . . . For instance if you're in a space and then other people enter, then your apprehension of the space changes, or the way you function in the space and how you locate yourself in the space, where you don't know the people . . . . So that one of the main things that I had thought about was to deal with trying to find the edge, to enforce the tension between that sort of transformation, between your space and having to share it, socially.[22]

Given their vested interest in socialization, Nauman's corridor works, and sculptural environments like *Double Steel Cage Piece* (1974; plate 3), are strikingly antisocial; they are designed not to encourage interaction but to enforce the awkwardness of public expectation when the individual is put on display. As Marco De Michelis further details in his essay in this book, they perform the classic bait-and-switch of psychological experiments in deception: one enters one of Nauman's narrow corridors out of curiosity and perhaps audacity, but once inside, the option of movement is immediately restricted. In *Double Steel Cage Piece*,

Fig. 65 Bruce Nauman. *Model for Trench and Four Buried Passages,* 1977.
Plaster, fiberglass, and wire; height 65 inches (165.1 cm), diameter of outer circle 360 inches (914.4 cm), diameter of inner circle 192 inches (487.7 cm).
Collection of Jay Chiat, New York

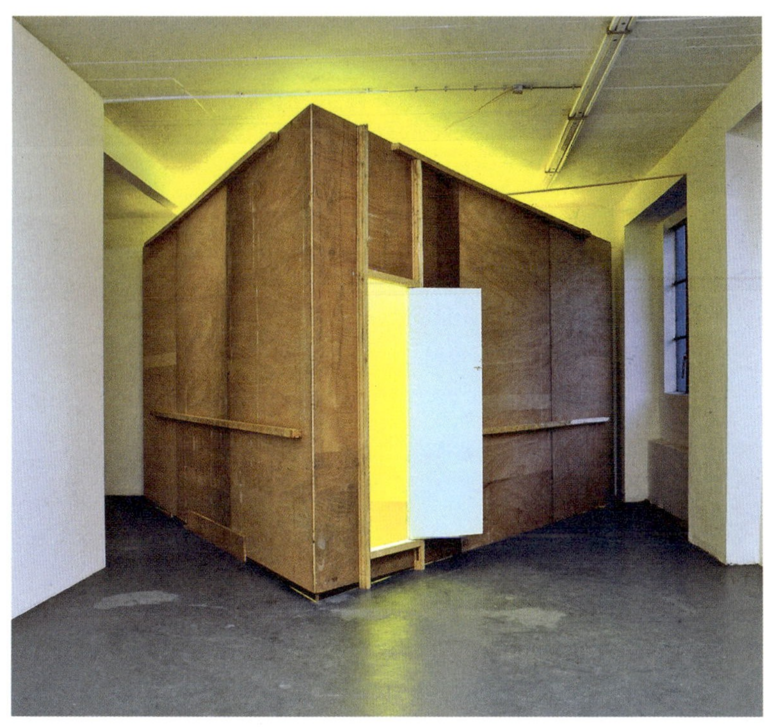

the bold spirit who enters the steel-mesh structure spontaneously becomes part of the object and is on view to others in the room, so that any presumed autonomy is inverted into imposed subjectivity.

Nauman's interest in granting or denying access to space is analogous to his decisions to supply or obstruct information. In *Audio Video Piece for London, Ontario* (1969–70; plate 1), for example, a surveillance camera oscillates on its side in a room adjacent to but sealed off from the viewer; what appears on the monitor is essentially a space void of content, its meaning galvanized by its isolation. Nauman therefore turns a contained and inaccessible space, though patently void, into an object of desire. Here, as in *Double Steel Cage Piece*, which also possesses a sealed interior room, Nauman has raised the status of emptiness.

When Nauman does grant access, he often tests the psychological and physical endurance of his unknowing participant. In the 1970s, working out of his interest in phenomenology, he began to construct purposefully uncomfortable experiences through corridors and environments that used bright lights in jarring colors, as in *Green Light Corridor* of 1970 or *Yellow Room (Triangular)* of 1973 (fig. 66). This effect is exemplified in *Topological Gardens* by *Pink and Yellow Light Corridor (Variable Lights)* of 1972 (plate 17), with its strata of pink and

Fig. 66 Bruce Nauman. *Yellow Room (Triangular)*, 1973.
Wallboard, plywood, and yellow fluorescent lights; 120 x 177 x 157 inches (304.8 x 449.6 x 398.8 cm).
Solomon R. Guggenheim Museum, New York. Panza Collection, 1991

yellow fluorescent lights stretching across one arcade of the Tolentini Cloister at Università Iuav. The lights are programmed so that, in the same moment, the pink fluorescents fluctuate from 100% to 30% power while the yellows go from 30% to 100%, and vice versa. This vacillating light casts a disquieting aura over the space's entire architecture.

In sound and video works that seem innocuous to the senses, the duration, endless looping, and sheer volume of the sound that Nauman harnesses often make watching or experiencing an act of endurance. In *End of the World* (1996; plate 6), the music emanating from lap steel and pedal steel guitars is at first gentle, even nostalgic, evoking some abstract notion of the West; but over time, the audio from all three projections stirs up and cloys the senses. Nauman produces similar effects with sound as a corollary to space in works using both audio tracks and constructed environments, such as *Get Out of My Mind, Get Out of This Room* (1968; checklist 20), that play one against the other. Here, a tight, square room is specially constructed with hidden speakers that powerfully project Nauman's voice, whispering and raspy, shaping the repeated command "Get out of my mind, get out of this room," into an ominous force. While the architecture allows entry, the audio demands expulsion. Many of Nauman's environments, sound pieces, and video installations present similar paradoxes of experience, in which, as Janet Kraynak has commented, participation "emerges as an oppressive concept that is at the *expense* of the viewer."[23] Many of the works on view at Iuav tap into this aspect of Nauman's art, in which the information given by the artist conflicts with the sensorial and psychological response of the viewer.

Get Out of My Mind, Get Out of This Room is one of the five audio tracks that Nauman grouped in a compilation dubbed *Studio Aids II* (1967–68; checklist 21). Variously alluding to or replicating the sound of the actions of Nauman's studio-based films and videos, the other four tracks—*Violin Tuned D.E.A.D.*, *Rolling on the Studio Floor*, *Jumping*, and *Walking in the Studio*—play one after the other as a sound installation in Iuav's entryway.[24] Nauman's use and reuse of the muffled sounds of rolling, jumping, and walking present strategies similar to his approach to drawing; as he has said: "I do drawings to work the pieces out, to figure out how to proceed. Then sometimes I make a drawing after the piece is finished to explain to myself what is really there."[25] As drawings are drafted, notated, and retraced, sometimes after the realization of the installation they figure, sound can be permutated, conjugated, reused, and rerecorded.

Nauman has resumed this notion in recent works, including his multiple variations of *Mapping the Studio I (Fat Chance John Cage)* of 2001 (fig. 31). Of the several incarnations of the first seven-channel projection, the single-channel *Sound for Mapping the Studio Model (The Video)* (2001; plate 19) particularly demonstrates Nauman's penchant for returning to a subject to take it to another level of editorial manipulation. *Sound for Mapping the Studio Model (The Video)* was created out of the same night-vision surveillance-camera footage as *Mapping the Studio I*, but the tapes were reedited to piece together the most action-filled moments in the video and notable atmospheric sounds on the audio tracks—which, however, are not in sync. The disconnect between the visual and the auditory information that results

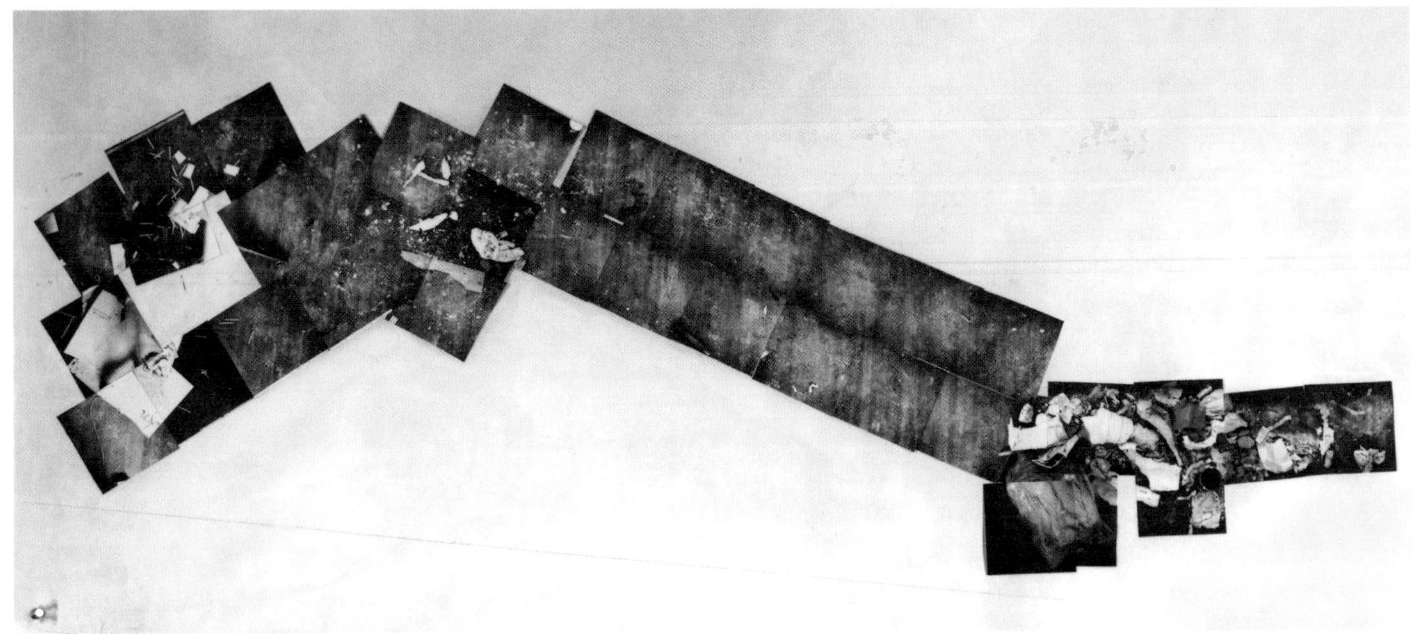

reveals how reliant the one is on the other; the video feels like an exercise in dissociation and suspension. Nauman's penchant for recycling sounds and images is in this instance inextricably connected to the space of the studio, a continual source for the raw stuff of much of his art. Referring to earlier studio-based works like *Composite Photo of Two Messes on the Studio Floor* (1967; fig. 67), Coosje van Bruggen wrote in 1988 that this resourcefulness "was also a kind of artistic economy—he didn't want to leave any idea or material unused."[26] As a platform for examining what exactly it means to make art, the studio has supplied the subject, structure, space, and sounds that figure again and again in Nauman's work. Known for being an intensely private person, Nauman positions his studio as the space in which he can choose to overlap with the rest of the world; though it is an inner sanctum, its internal workings are turned into the fabric of his art.

Nauman's latest works, *Days* and *Giorni* (checklist 16 and 25), also operate as products of both the structure of the studio and the mutation of sounds. For these works Nauman wrote scripts jumbling the order of the days of the week, in English and Italian, respectively. The scripts were then performed by hired speakers for around twelve minutes at a time. Nauman programmed the resulting audio to feed into seven pairs of directional speakers mounted with binder clips to steel cables that hang from the ceiling and are weighted to the floor. Further discussed elsewhere in this book, *Days* and *Giorni* create a kind of sound

Fig. 67 Bruce Nauman. *Composite Photo of Two Messes on the Studio Floor*, 1967.
Gelatin silver print, 40 1/2 x 123 inches (102.9 x 312.4 cm).
The Museum of Modern Art, New York. Gift of Philip Johnson (505.1984)

corridor in which the voices shift in and out of focus, disembodied save for the flat, square audio speakers. Like the word-based *Vices and Virtues* (plate 27) before them, the new sound installations are composed of the simplest, most culturally ingrained information set, but through their programmatic sequencing they orchestrate the days of the week into a concerto of undulating voices, dissolving the visitors' concern for pragmatic meanings. Instead they must resign themselves to the sensuousness of sound saturating space.

Nauman : Venice

In this account of *Topological Gardens*, the end point coexists with an early moment. Just as *Giorni* was recorded in Venice as a second iteration of *Days*, linking the making of the work to the circumstances of realizing the exhibition, *Untitled* was remade in February 2009 in the precise spot in the Exhibition Spaces at Ca' Foscari in which it is installed in the show (fig. 68). Nauman originally composed the instructions for performance that comprise *Untitled* as a proposal for the Tokyo Biennial of 1970. Though he did not attend, he recalls Sol LeWitt describing the recorded performance as it was shown in Japan. A perennial predicament of performance pieces, the ephemerality of *Untitled*, until now a one-time installation, left us two fixed sources from which to interpolate: Nauman's original written instructions, and a facsimile of a drawing that roughed out the positions of dancers, marks on the floor made with tape, and the imagined construction of a scaffold from which to record the performance. We also had the greatest ammunition: the artist's willingness to entertain the idea of revisiting, remaking, restaging, and reproducing *Untitled*, not only in the exhibition but in the city itself. Thus Venice emerges as the show's fourth conceptual category, less as a topos in its own right than as an embedded enabler; the analogical relationship between Venice and Nauman projects into the preceding trajectories of Fountains and Neons, Heads and Hands, Sound and Space, threading them together through space and experience.

For those who have combed through Nauman's instruction-based performance pieces of the late 1960s and early 1970s, the phrase "Hire a dancer" is a familiar directive. The hiring of professionals whose movements are then recorded echoes throughout Nauman's career, exemplified in the exhibition by the musicians in *End of the World* (plate 6), the magician in *Coffee Spilled and Balloon Dog* (plate 2), and George Stumpff in *Hanging Carousel (George Skins a Fox)* (plate 12). Following the spirit of this division of labor, we hired dance students of Iuav to participate in the re-creation of *Untitled*.

Nauman's instructions for the performance are strict and to the point (see text with plate 24): hands touching, two prone dancers rotate their bodies in a single straight line, rolling in a circle over a surface that has been marked in a starburst pattern contained in a square (plate 24). At first static as the dancers move, the camera then rotates with them, making them appear to be rolling in place as the starburst moves beneath them. A reverse rotation of the camera follows, stemming from a practical matter: the need to unravel its electrical cord. *Hanging Carousel (George Skins a Fox)* shares this logic, rotating first clockwise, then counterclockwise, to disentangle the monitor's power cords; thus the spatial movements of

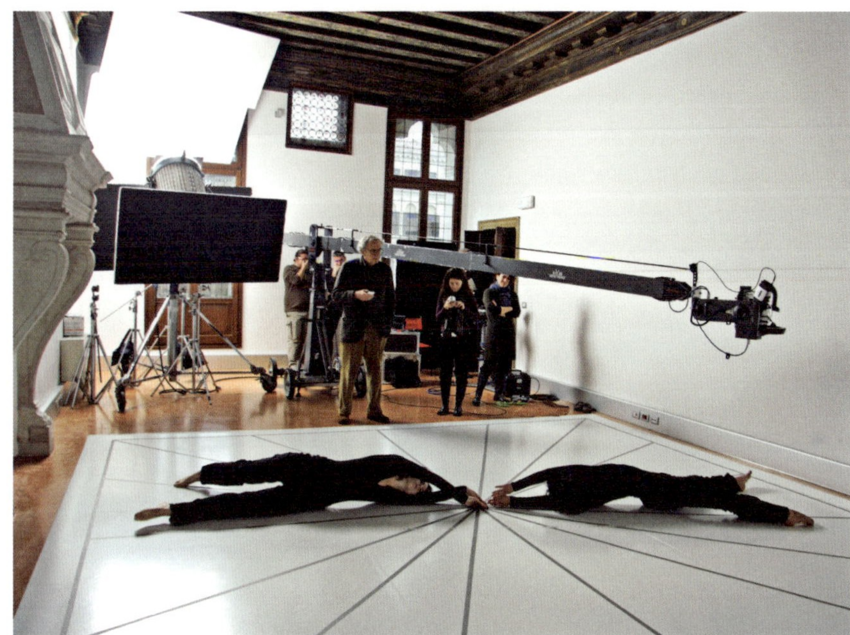

both of these pieces are determined by the tension between the concept that drives it and the physical realities that impose restrictions on it—just as *Double Steel Cage Piece* (plate 3) both beckons its participants and inflicts a bodily compression on them.

Rolling on the floor and keeping one's body in line with that of another dancer, all while performing a circular movement, is itself an empirically difficult action even when enacted by skilled dancers striving for exactitude. Many of Nauman's performance pieces similarly imply a type of quixotic endurance, whether they ask dancers to perform redundant tasks over a long period or simply require repetitive movements to the inevitable point of exhaustion. Nauman often takes this fact into account in his instructions, which at times are posed more as feasibility studies.[27] He once remarked that in setting up the situations for his performances, films, and videos: "What I always wanted to be careful about was to have the structure include enough tensions in either random error or getting tired and making a mistake . . . . that there always was some structure programmed into the event . . . . I think the pieces that were successful were successful for those reasons, and the pieces that weren't successful failed to be because they didn't have enough structure built into them."[28]

In *Untitled* this structural tension plays out over time. The dancers start their clockwork movement over the starburst in complete fidelity to the instructions. Touching at the center, their hands are axes for steering their motions, and their interlocking grasps recall the

Fig. 68 Dancers roll in a circular motion over a mat marked with tape during the production of Bruce Nauman, *Untitled*, 1970/2009, filmed at the Exhibition Spaces at Università Ca' Foscari, February 2009.

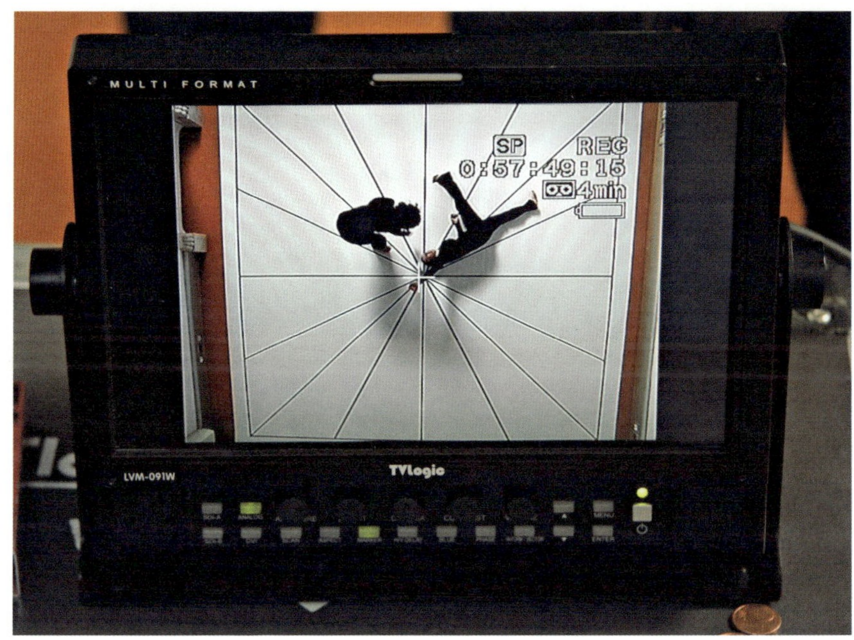

topological hands that surface elsewhere in the exhibition. In calculated measures, they cycle over the pattern of gaffer's tape, and suddenly the camera that is suspended over them starts to turn too, following their timing to create an illusion of movement under their bodies. Watching the dancers course over the bright white mat marked in tape, we realize that they are essentially performing over a drawing. Their movements and the dance between them and the camera are remarkably consistent; the tension that Nauman has carefully built in is so far present less in the performance than in our minds, as we realize the potential for failure, and ask of the dancers, "How much longer can they go?" The intermittent rotation of the camera also puts their movements into perspective: asked to hold a straight line across the screen, they are steady at moments, faltering at others. Finally, over the course of thirty-two minutes, the physical demands of precision start a predicted course toward exhaustion. The dancers' hands detach, and the line of their bodies ruptures into odd angles. In the recording of the performance, it is evident that the dancers share a moral commitment; both press on, neither wanting to be the first to stop (figs. 69 and 70). In this way they share Nauman's sensibility that the question is never why, but how, and for how long.

All the while, the orange terrazzo floor and the stone foot of an original fireplace—preexisting features of this room in the Exhibition Spaces of Ca' Foscari—cycle in and out of the frame. To film *Untitled* in the same location where it was to be exhibited to the public proved important

Fig. 69 The view captured by the camera suspended above the dance surface during the production of Bruce Nauman, *Untitled*, 1970/2009, filmed at the Exhibition Spaces at Università Ca' Foscari, February 2009.

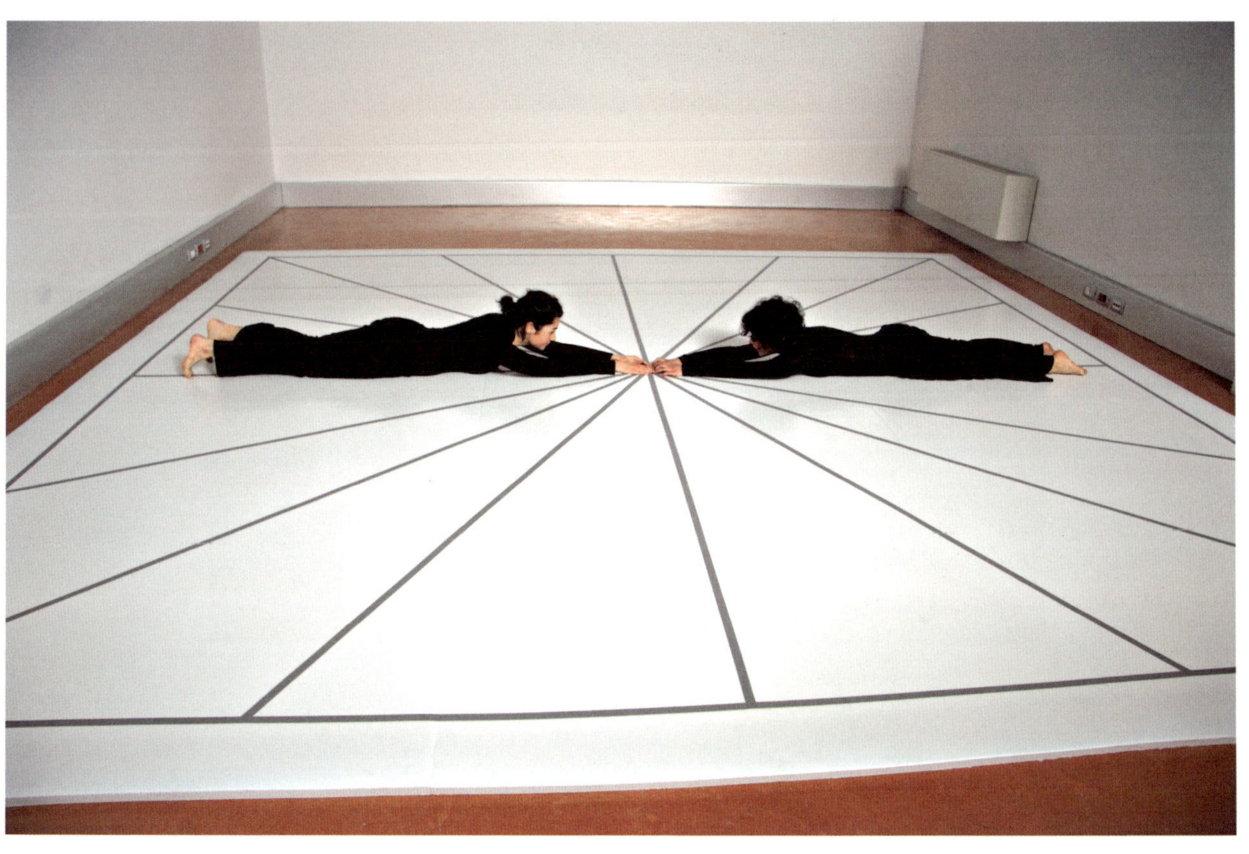

Fig. 70 The dancers prepare to start the performance during the production of Bruce Nauman, *Untitled*, 1970/2009, filmed at the Exhibition Spaces at Università Ca' Foscari, February 2009.

to Nauman, as it was in other examples of his instructions for performance.[29] In this desire for spatial consistency, the distance between live performance and its recorded counterpart is collapsed, as if not to privilege one over the other.

As a conflation of the 1970s and the first decade of the twenty-first century, *Untitled* of 1970/2009 typifies the synchronicity that drives *Topological Gardens*, which finds in Nauman's works from across four decades, in place of chronology, a "style of cognition"[30] that analogically links the topoi in his practice. The analogical charting of Fountains and Neons, Heads and Hands, and Sound and Space shapes the exhibition and drives this particular reading of Nauman's work. Defined in part by the vacillating category of Venice, these points of entry are intended not to designate a path or design a reaction but to open up Nauman's art to the field of experience. Our interpretation is inevitably subject to further extrapolation—by the public, by the reader, and by the artist as he continues to work.

In this way our analogical logic accounts for possibilities of substitution, comparison, and reinvention—a redrafting of the source assumptions on the path to new variations. Nauman invites this type of cyclical thinking, in which the conclusion is ephemeral, replaced by a new task at hand, a new form of the problem, but always a reiteration of the essentials of art—think, work, make. An excerpt from Nauman's text for *Flayed Earth* (plate 9) seems to acknowledge that he must stand ever ready:

I HAVE QUICK HANDS MY MIND IS ALERT
I HOLD MY BODY READY FOR INSPIRATION
ANTICIPATION ANY SIGN RESPIRATION
ANY SIGH I THINK NEITHER AHEAD NOR
BEHIND READY BUT NOT WAITING NOT
ON GUARD NOT PREPARED.[31]

Ever the artist/fountain, Nauman perpetually stands on the brink, ready to proceed to the next incarnation along the infinite trajectories of his art.

1
Bruce Nauman, quoted in Coosje van Bruggen, *Bruce Nauman* (New York: Rizzoli, 1988), p. 108. Throughout this chapter of her book, van Bruggen excerpts quotations from her conversations with the artist that took place in June 1985 and April 1986.
2
See Jane Livingston and Marcia Tucker, eds., *Bruce Nauman: Work from 1965 to 1972*, exh. cat. (Los Angeles: Los Angeles County Museum of Art, 1972), p. 10; Neal Benezra, "Surveying Nauman," in Neal Benezra and Kathy Halbreich, eds., *Bruce Nauman: Exhibition Catalogue and Catalogue Raisonné* (Minneapolis: Walker Art Center, 1994), p. 16; and Christine Hoffman, "Denk Dank (Think-Thank)," in Susan Cross, ed., *Bruce Nauman: Theaters of Experience*, exh. cat. (New York: Guggenheim Museum Publications, 2003), p. 54.
3
Researching analogical reasoning made it clear that this type of logic finds applications in multiple fields of study including law, education, political science, mathematics, and linguistics. Example-based cognition strategies such as analogies allow for a mode of comparative thinking that can contribute to building principles of learning and larger arguments germane to a myriad of disciplines. Articles testifying to this diversity that also contain appropriate and accessible definitions of analogical reasoning for their respective subjects include: Emily Sherwin, "A Defense of Analogical Reasoning in Law," *University of Chicago Law Review* 66, no. 4 (Autumn 1999): 1179–97; Marijke Breuning, "The Role of Analogies and Abstract Reasoning in Decision-Making: Evidence from the Debate over Truman's Proposal for Development Assistance," *International Studies Quarterly* 47, no. 2 (June 2003): 229–45; and Lyn D. English and Patrick V. Sharry, "Analogical Reasoning and the Development of Algebraic Abstraction," *Educational Studies in Mathematics* 30, no. 2 (March 1996): 135–57.
4
Van Bruggen, *Bruce Nauman*, p. 109.
5
Michael Auping, "Metacommunicator," in *Raw Materials*, exh. cat. (London: Tate Publishing, 2004), p. 9.
6
See Nauman, *Please Pay Attention Please: Bruce Nauman's Words: Writings and Interviews*, ed. Janet Kraynak (Cambridge, Mass.: MIT Press, 2002), p. 49.
7
Nauman, quoted in Michele de Angelus, "Interview with Bruce Nauman," 1980, in ibid., p. 213: "I think that I maybe knew a little bit about mathematics, I had a really good feeling about—not practical mathematics, but about understanding the structure of mathematics, a lot of interest in it, so I continued to do that. It had to do with the way it was taught, I think. I had a very small class for a couple of years and a particularly good instructor who was an algebraic topologist and presented things very well."
8
See Nauman, "Notes and Projects," *Artforum* 9, no. 4 (December 1970): 44. Reprinted in Nauman, *Please Pay Attention Please*, p. 58.
9
Nauman, quoted in van Bruggen, *Bruce Nauman*, p. 108.
10
See Susan Brundage, ed., *Bruce Nauman 25 Years Leo Castelli* (New York: Rizzoli, 1994), n.p.
11
Marcia Tucker, "PheNAUMANology," *Artforum* 9, no. 4 (December 1970): 38–44. Reprinted in Robert C. Morgan, ed., *Bruce Nauman* (Baltimore and London: John Hopkins University Press, 2002), p. 23.
12
See Brenda Richardson, *Bruce Nauman: Neons*, exh. cat. (Baltimore: Baltimore Museum of Art, 1982), p. 92.
13
For an insightful firsthand account of the five-year journey of *Vices and Virtues* from conception to fruition, see Mary Livingston Beebe, *Landmarks: Sculpture Commissions for the Stuart Collection at the University of California, San Diego* (New York: Rizzoli, 2001), pp. 128–41.
14
Nauman, quoted in van Bruggen, *Bruce Nauman*, p. 7.
15
Adam Gopnik, "Bits and Pieces," *The New Yorker*, May 14, 1990.
16
See Benezra and Halbreich, eds., *Nauman*, no. 397, which also describes this particular casting process.
17
In *Topological Gardens*, the stackable cube monitors originally used by Nauman for these works have been replaced by flat screens mounted to the wall in a stacked formation. The decision to use flat-screen monitors was made by both the curatorial team and the Nauman studio for this particular context, and as such points to Nauman's attitude toward migrating technology as an acceptable progression in the display of his art amid fast-changing equipment standards.
18
Nauman, quoted in Ingrid Schaffner, "Circling Oblivion/Bruce Nauman through Samuel Beckett," in Morgan, ed., *Bruce Nauman*, p. 163.
19
See Nauman, *Flayed Earth Flayed Self (Skin Sink)* (Los Angeles: Wilder Gallery, 1973), n.p.
20
Ibid.
21
Nauman, quoted in de Angelus, "Interview with Bruce Nauman," p. 278.
22
Ibid., p. 278.
23
Nauman, quoted in Janet Kraynak, "Dependent Participation," *Grey Room*, no. 10 (Winter 2003): 24.
24
Although *Get Out of My Mind, Get Out of This Room* was originally included as one of the five tracks that comprised *Studio Aids II*, it has since become a sound installation in its own right, and for *Topological Gardens*, the artist and the curatorial team decided to separate them into two distinct experiences at Iuav.

25
Nauman, quoted in Auping, "Projection and Displacement," in *Bruce Nauman: Drawings for Installations* (New York: Sperone Westwater, 2008), p. 7.
26
See van Bruggen, "Sounddance," 1988, in Morgan, ed., *Bruce Nauman*, p. 48.
27
In an untitled piece from 1969, Nauman instructs a dancer to perform for thirty minutes each day of the exhibition with the following caveat: "I add this extra note of caution: I have worked on the exercise and it is difficult. Do not make the mistake of hiring someone not physically and mentally equipped to undertake this problem." Quoted in Nauman, *Please Pay Attention Please*, p. 53.
28
Nauman, quoted in de Angelus, "Interview with Bruce Nauman," pp. 247–48.
29
See, e.g., the text for an untitled work of 1969 in Nauman, *Please Pay Attention Please*, p. 51. Kraynak's book also includes a number of instructions for performance pieces containing the words "hire a dancer," or notations regarding the potential for becoming too tired to continue.
30
De Angelus uses this apt phrase in "Interview with Bruce Nauman," p. 268.
31
Nauman, *Flayed Earth Flayed Self (Skin Sink)*, n.p.

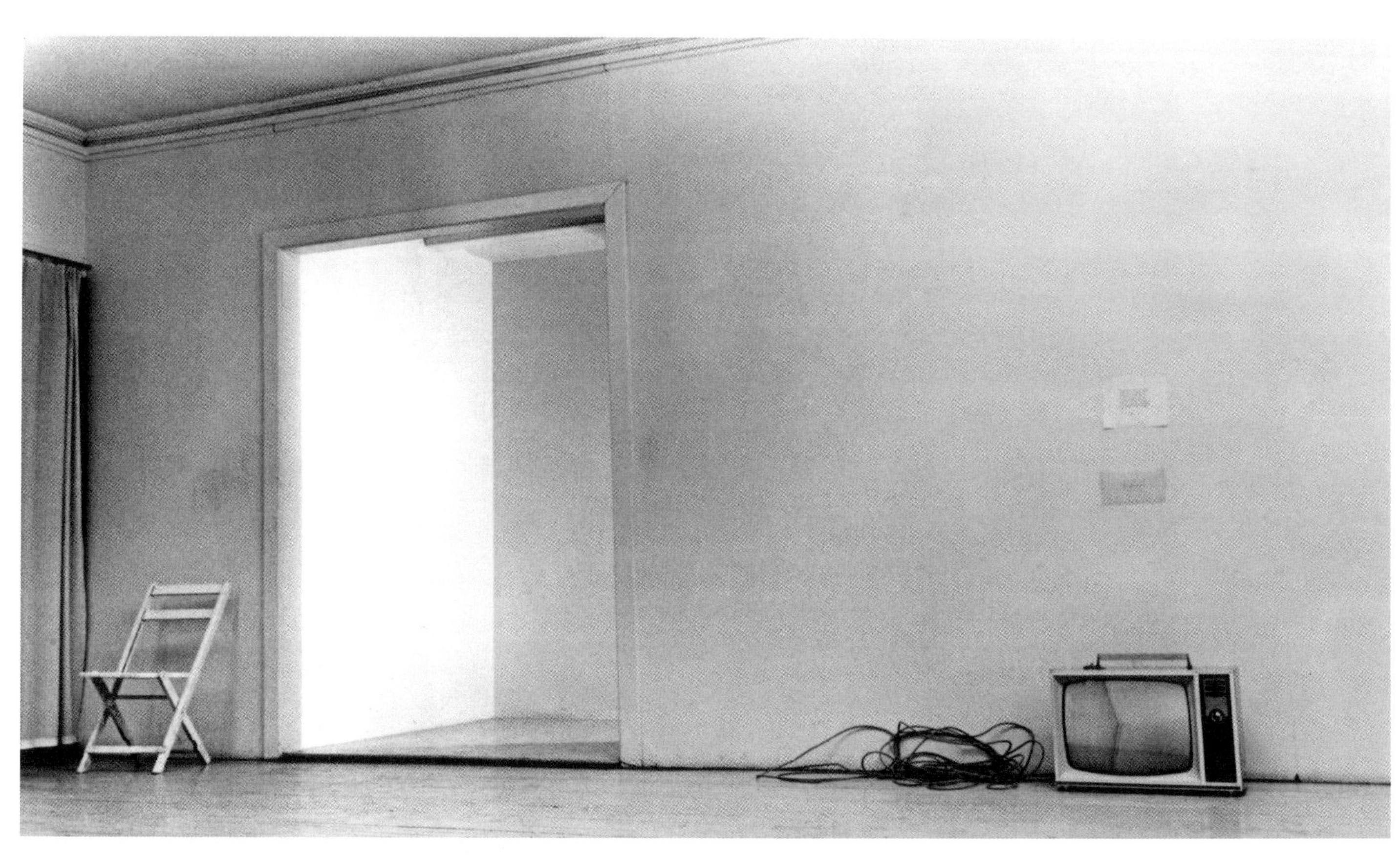

 Plate 1 *Audio Video Piece for London, Ontario*, 1969–70. Collection Donald Young, Chicago

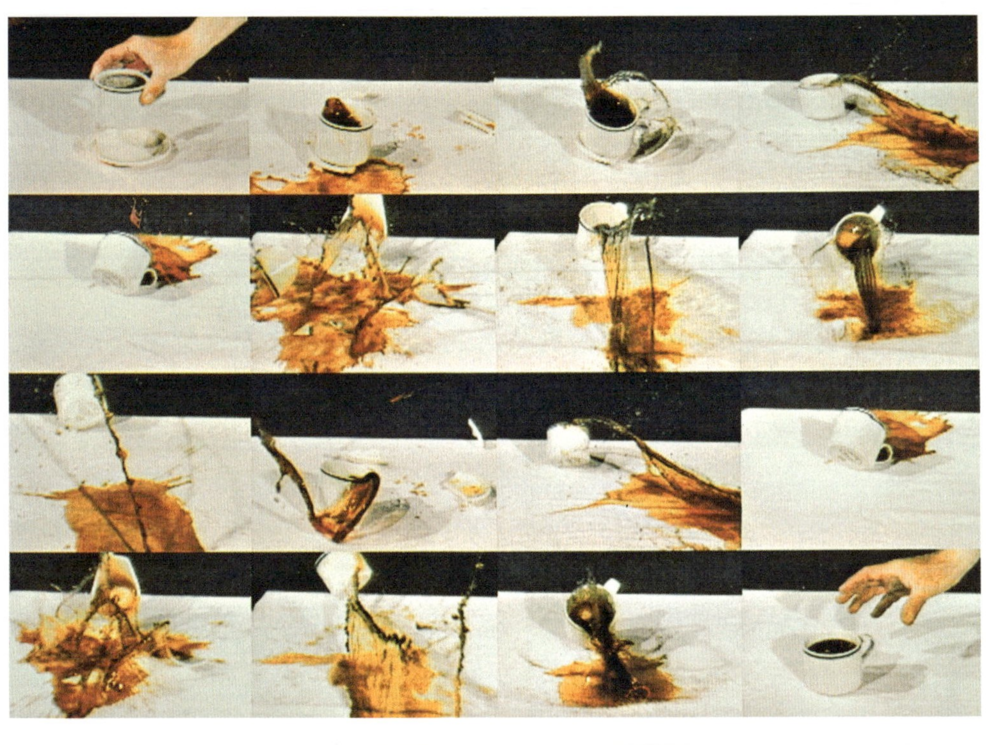

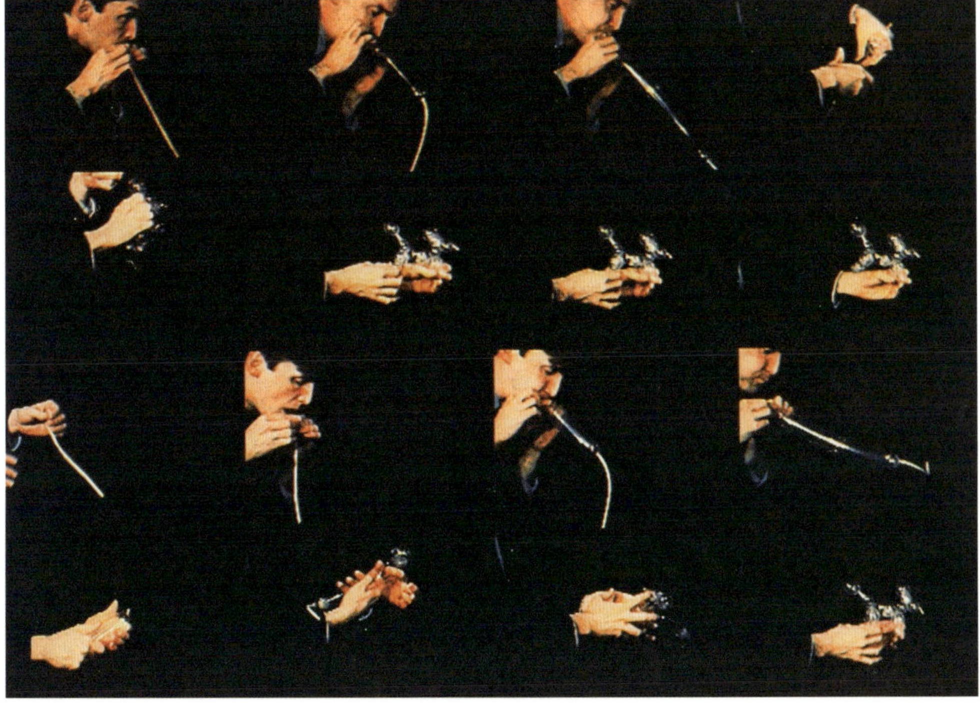

Plate 2 Video stills from *Coffee Spilled and Balloon Dog*, 1993. Staatliche Museen zu Berlin, Nationalgalerie, Sammlung Marx

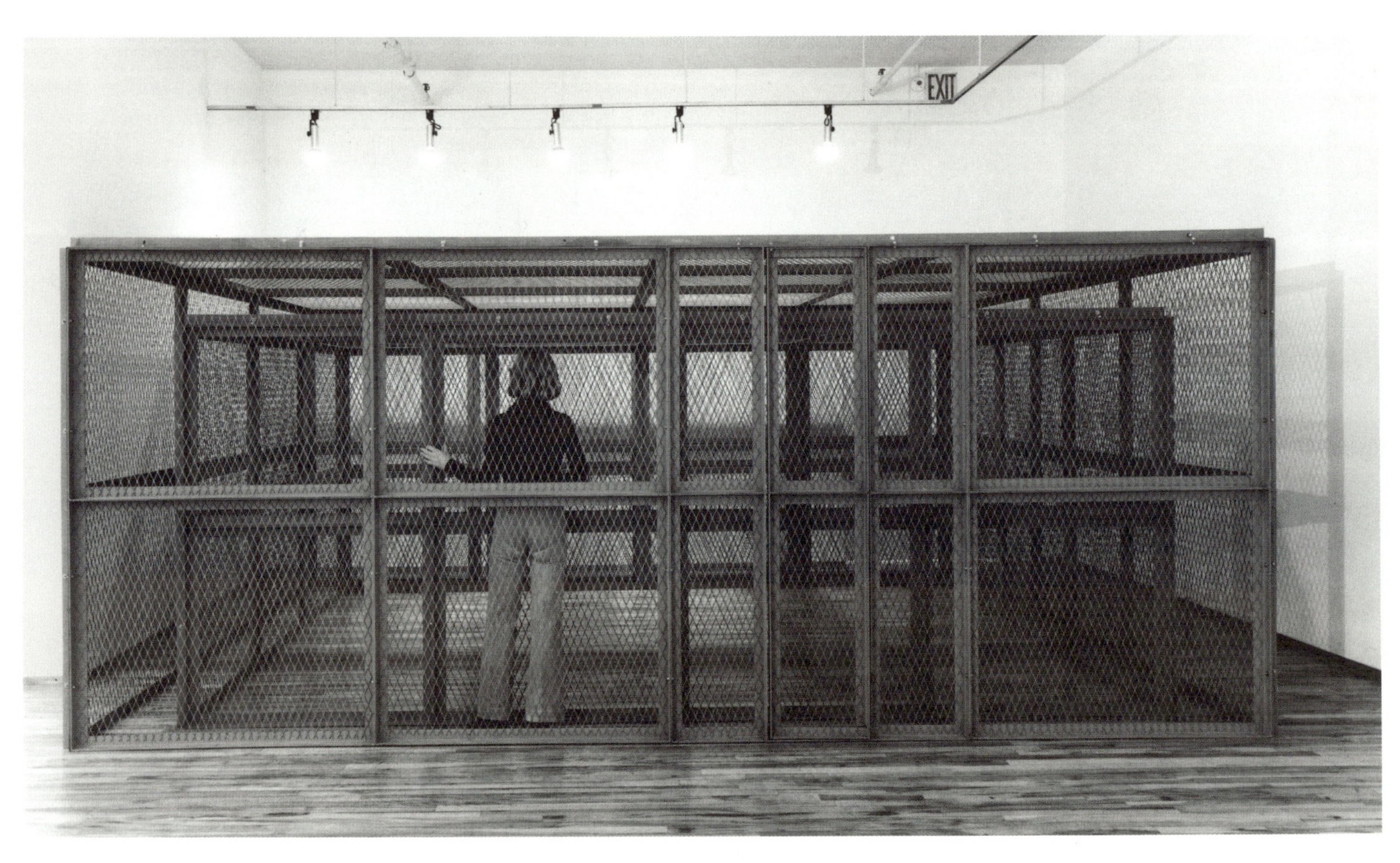

Plate 3 *Double Steel Cage Piece*, 1974. Museum Boijmans Van Beuningen, Rotterdam.
Purchase 1980

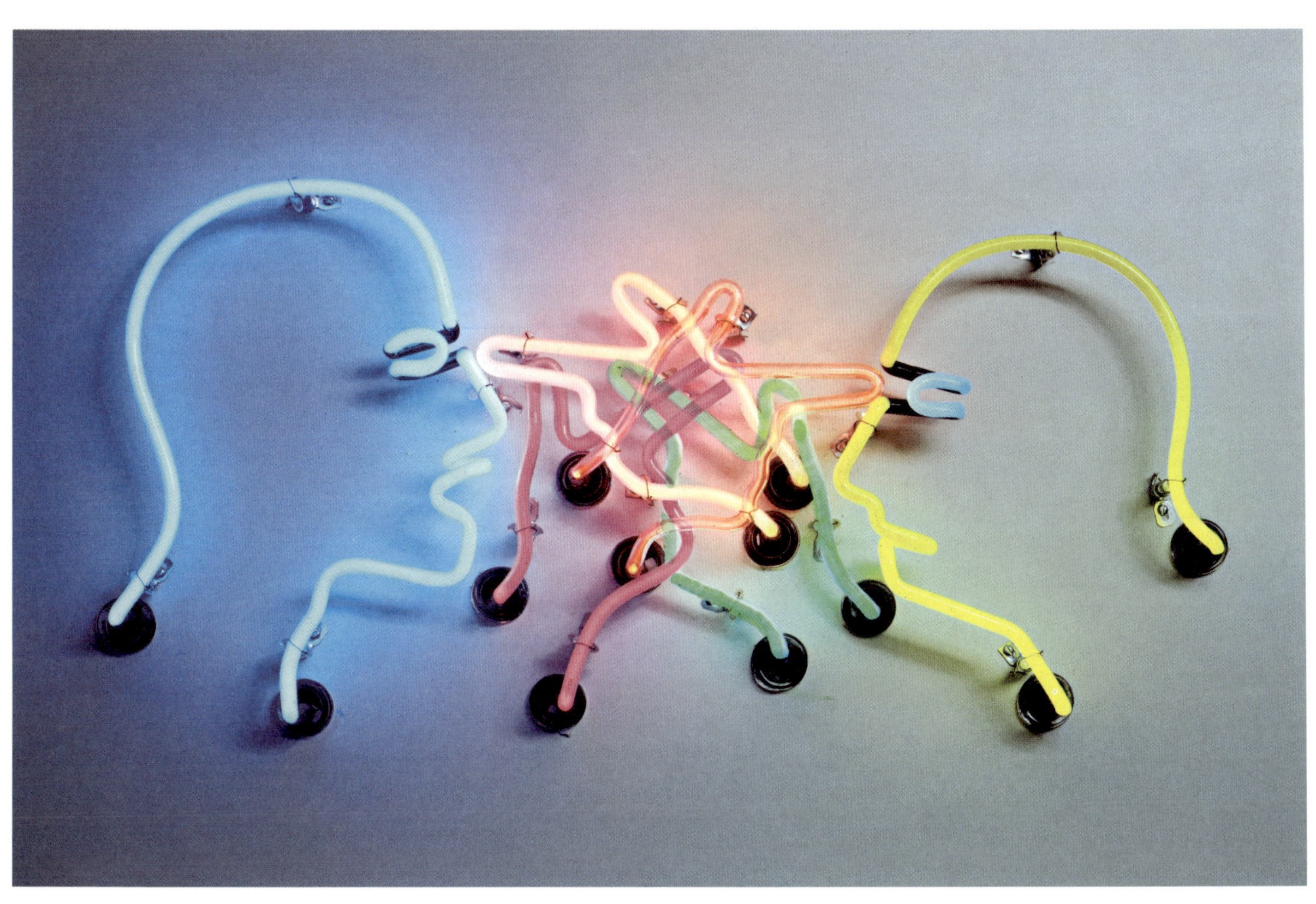

Plate 4 *Double Poke in the Eye II*, 1985. CIAC: Colección Isabel y Agustín Coppel

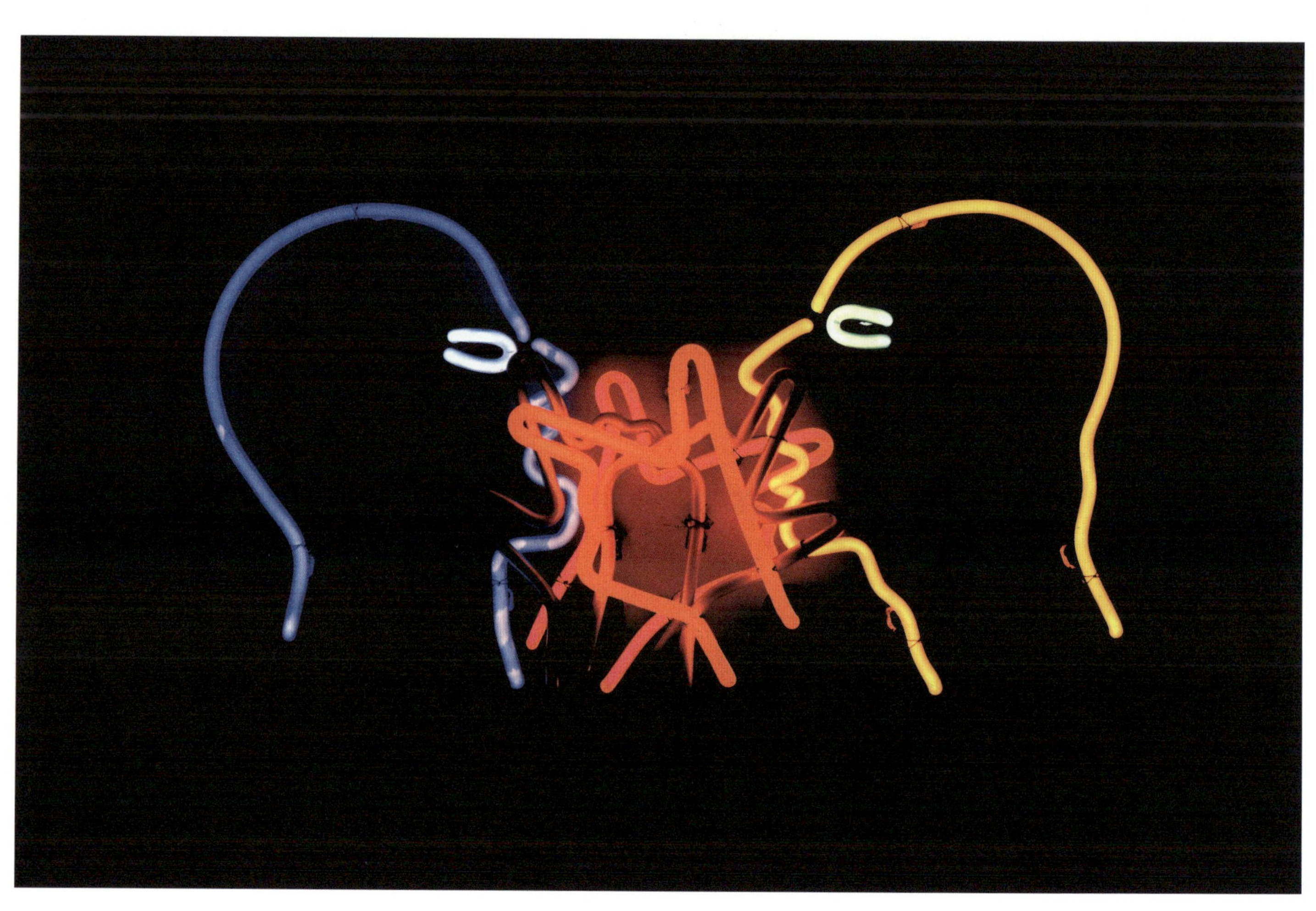

Plate 5 *Eating Buggers (Version II)*, 1985. Private collection. Courtesy Hauser & Wirth, Zurich and London

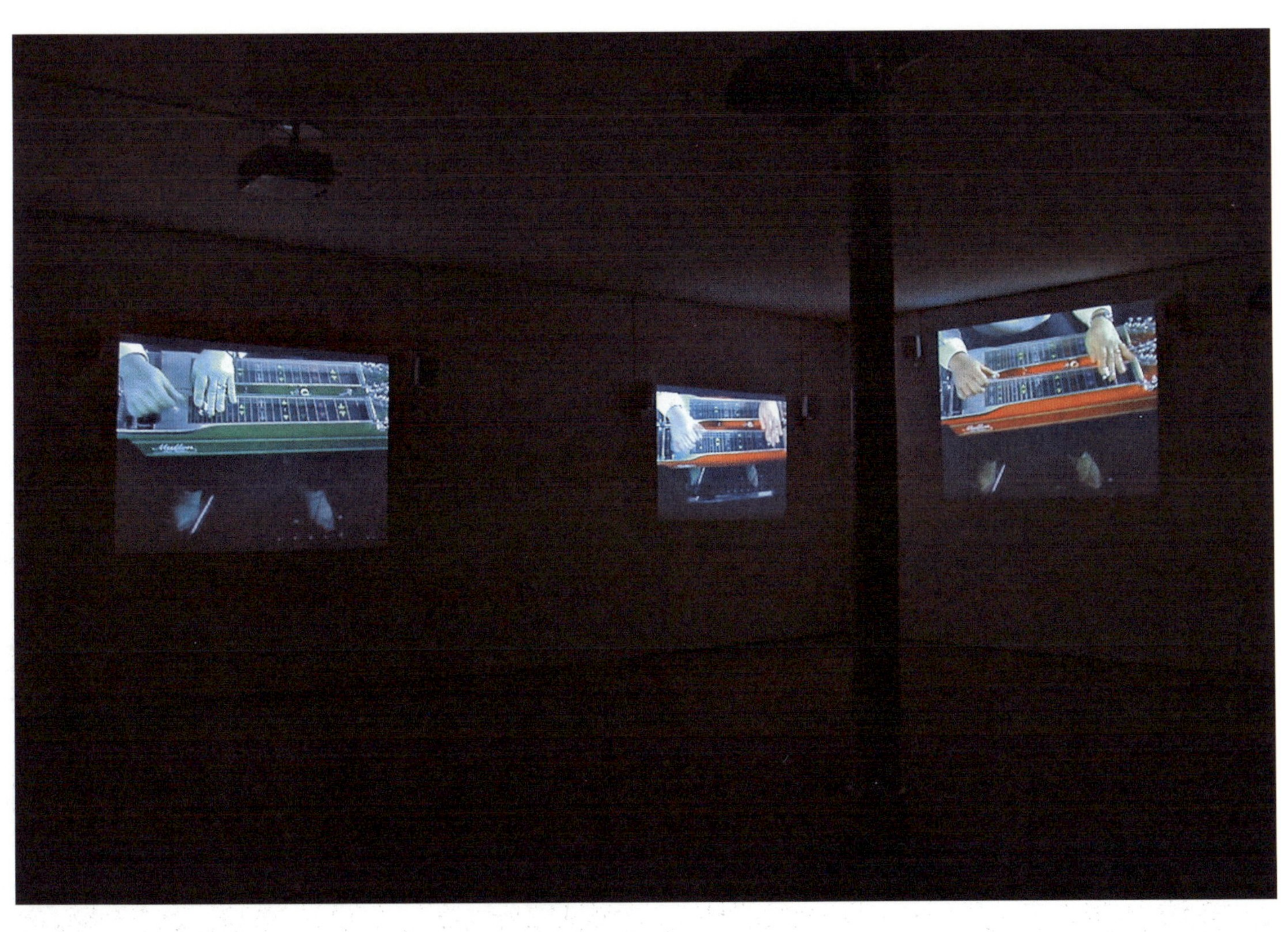

Plate 6 *End of the World*, 1996. Emanuel Hoffmann Foundation, permanent loan to the Öffentliche Kunstsammlung Basel

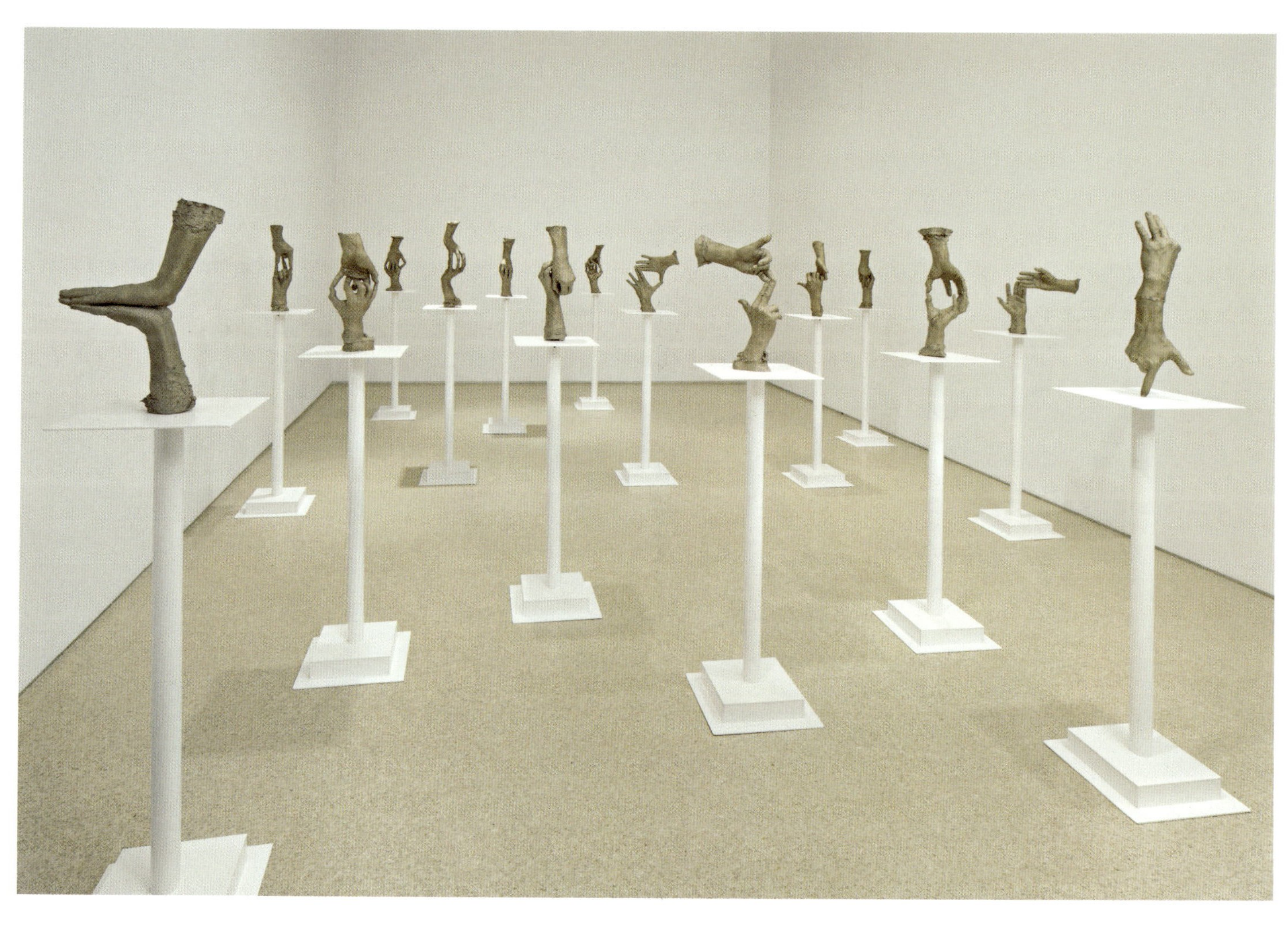

 Plate 7 *Fifteen Pairs of Hands*, 1996. Courtesy the artist and Sperone Westwater, New York

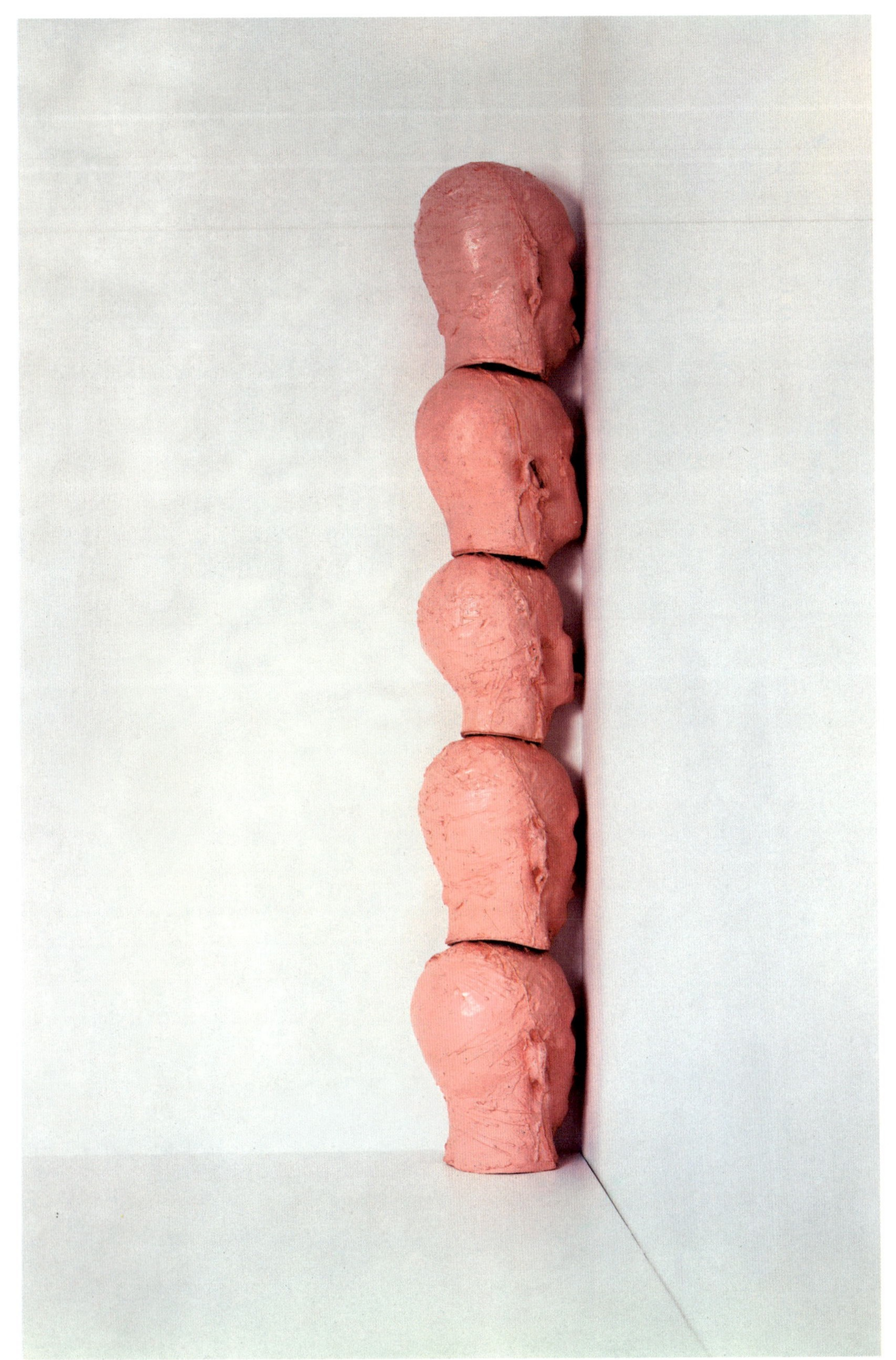

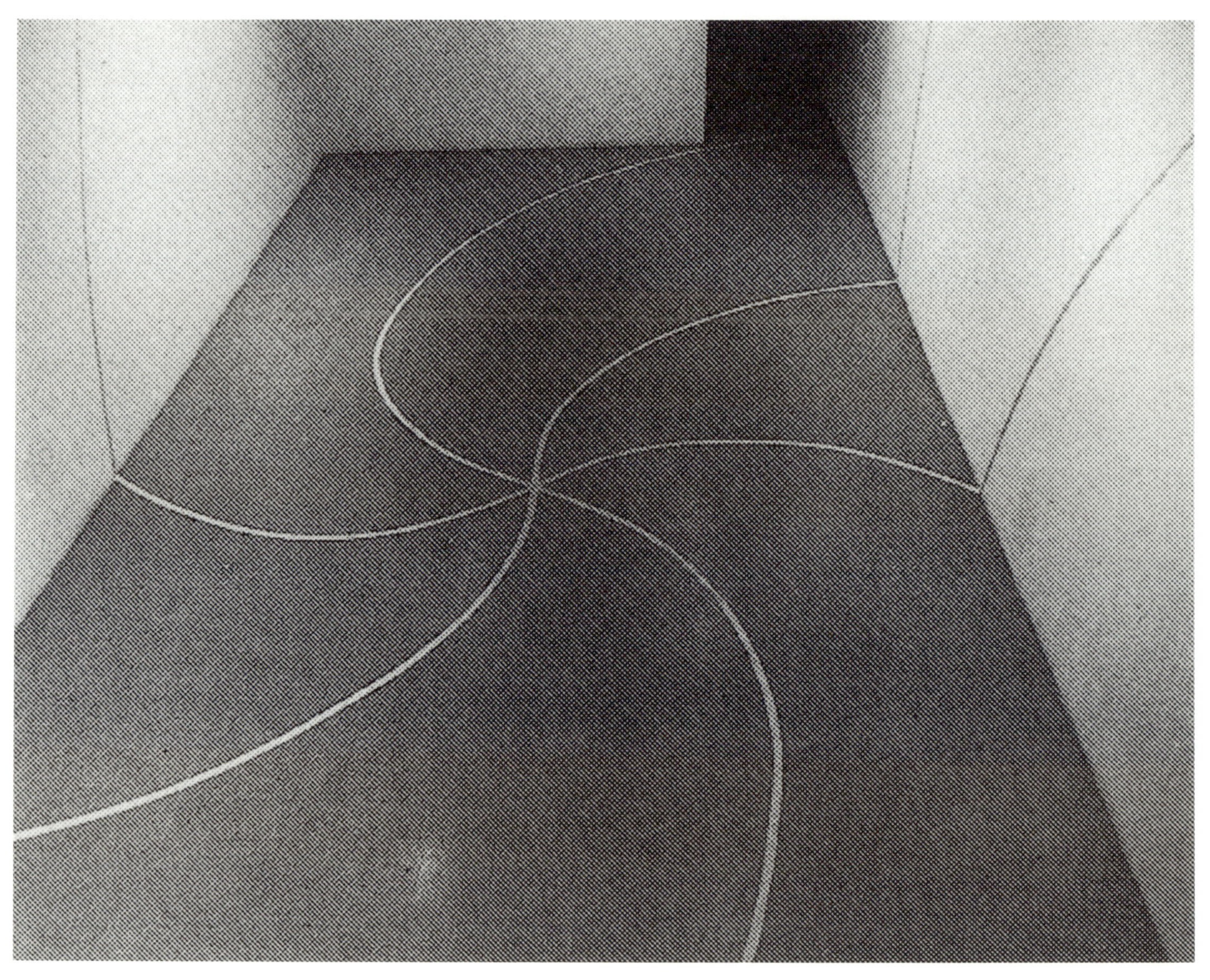

Plate 8 *Five Pink Heads in the Corner*, 1992. Friedrich Christian Flick Collection

Plate 9 *Flayed Earth Flayed Self (Skin Sink)*, 1973. Friedrich Christian Flick Collection

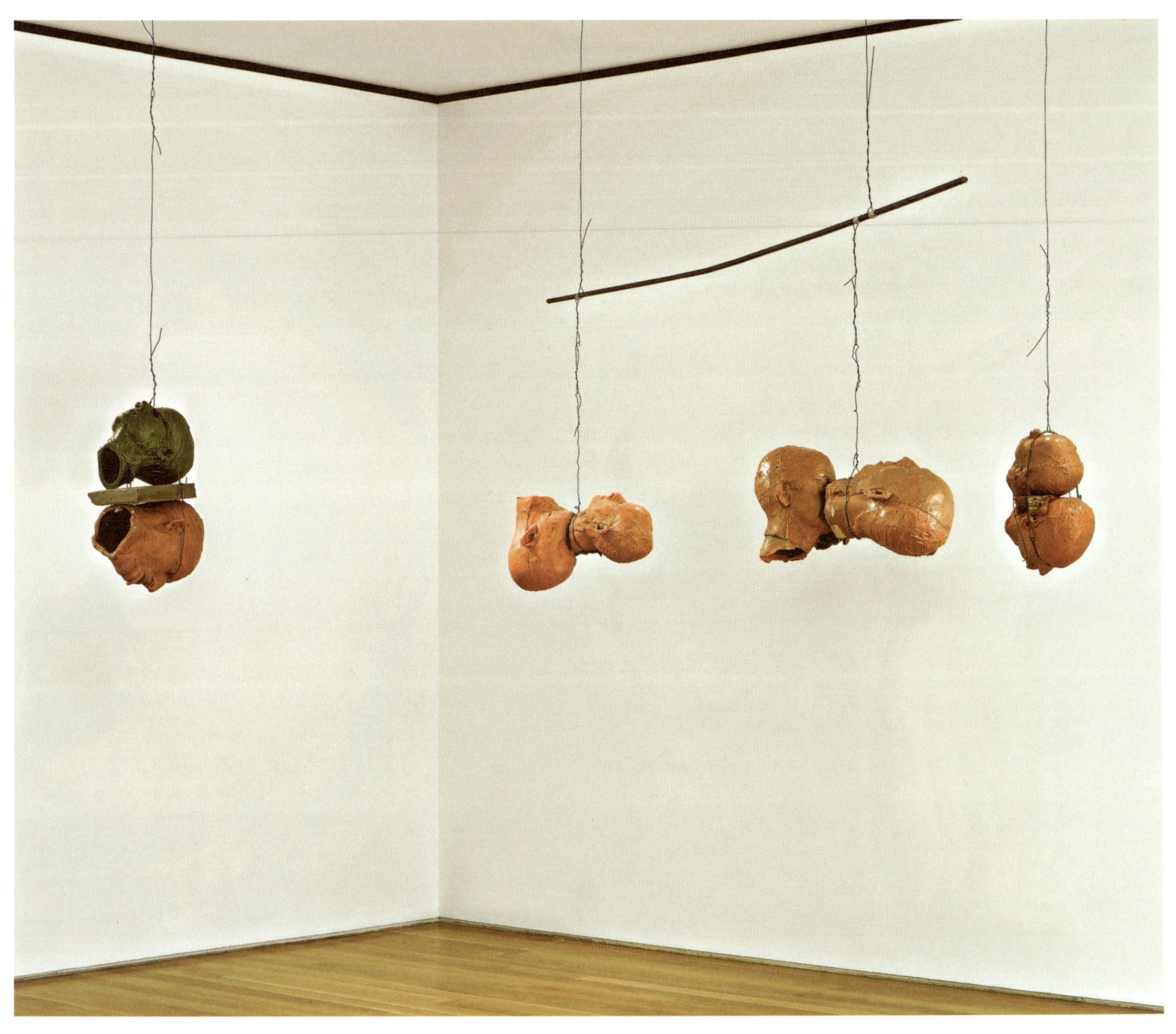

Plate 10 *Four Pairs of Heads (Wax)*, 1991. Courtesy the artist

Plate 11 *From Hand to Mouth*, 1967. Hirshhorn Museum and Sculpture Garden, Smithsonian Institution, Washington, D.C. Joseph H. Hirshhorn Purchase Fund, Holenia Purchase Fund, in memory of Joseph H. Hirshhorn, and Museum Purchase, 1993. HMSG93.6

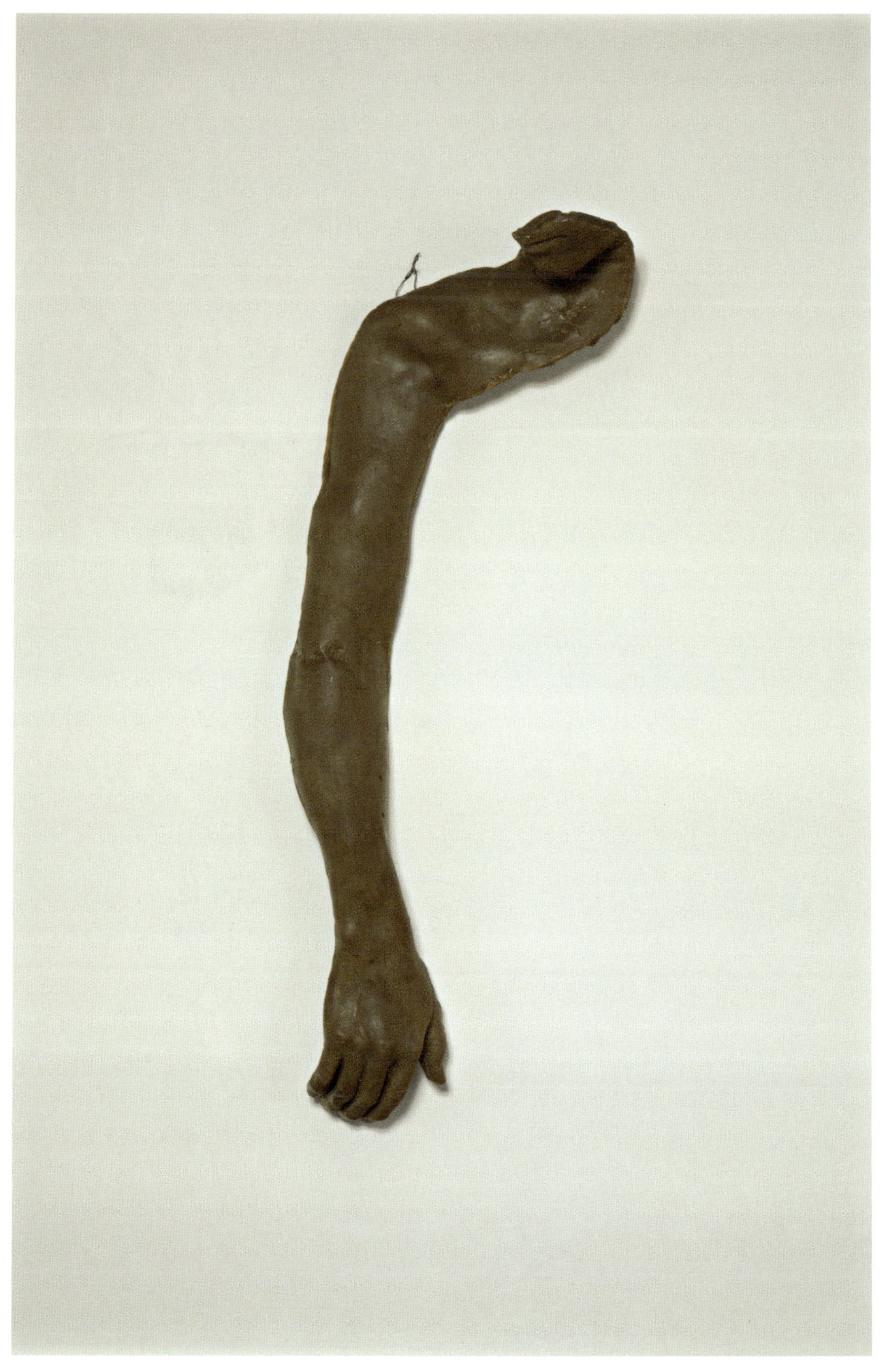

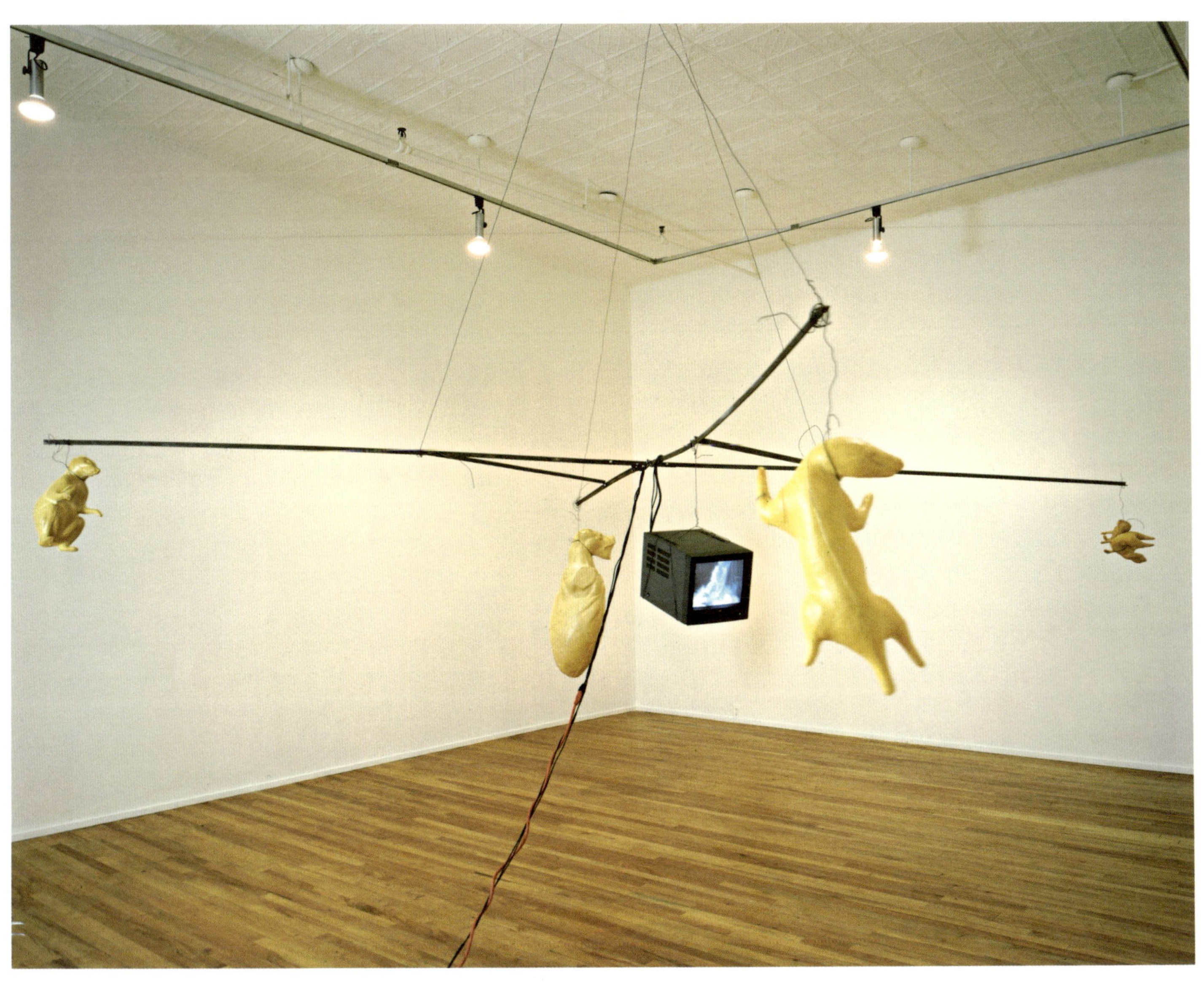

Plate 12 *Hanging Carousel (George Skins a Fox)*, 1988. Museum of Contemporary Art, Chicago. Gerald S. Elliott Collection, 1995.76

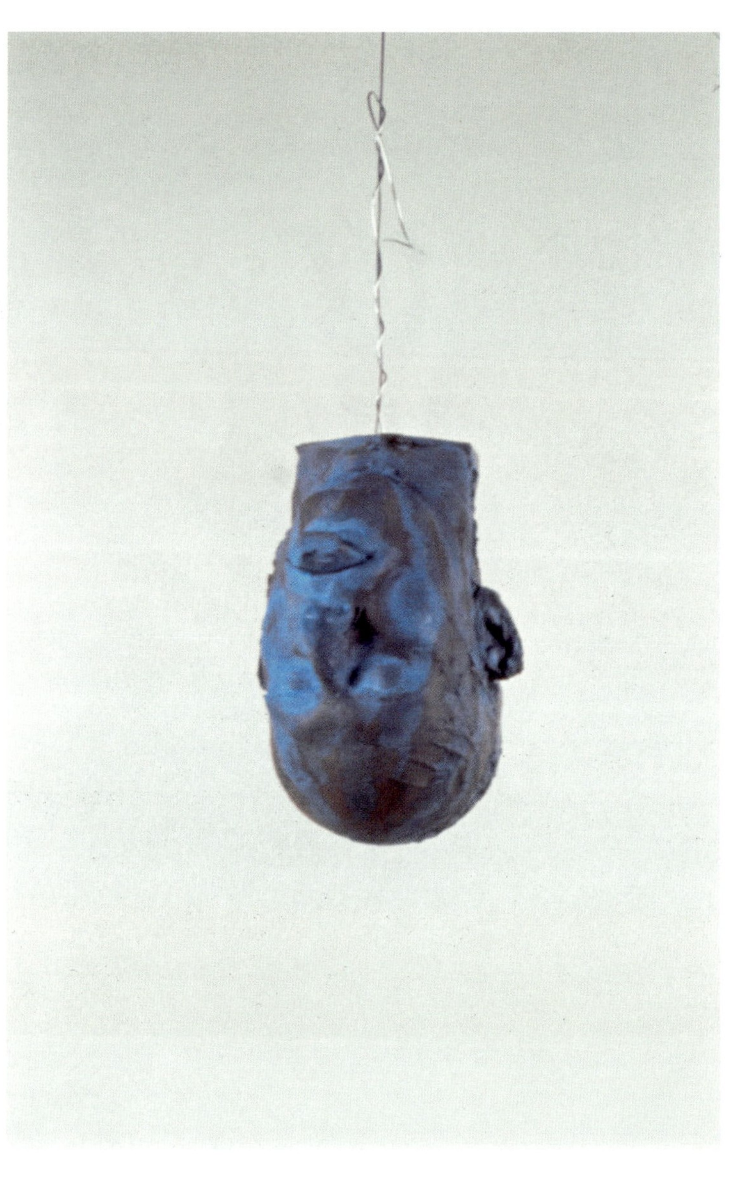

 Plate 13 *Hanging Head for Leo*, 1990. Collection Rachel and Jean-Pierre Lehmann

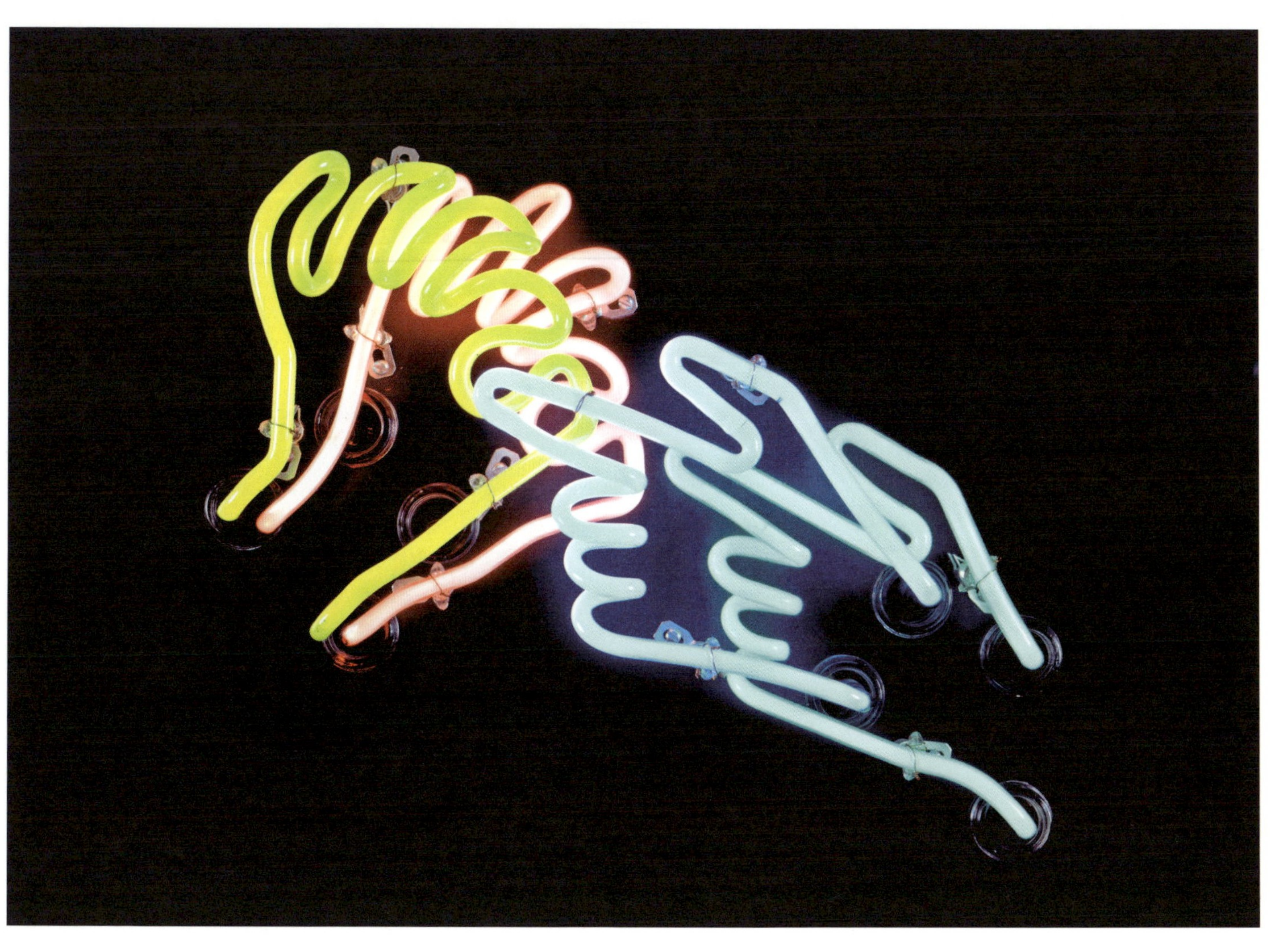

Plate 14 *Human Sexual Experience*, 1985. Marc and Livia Straus Family Collection

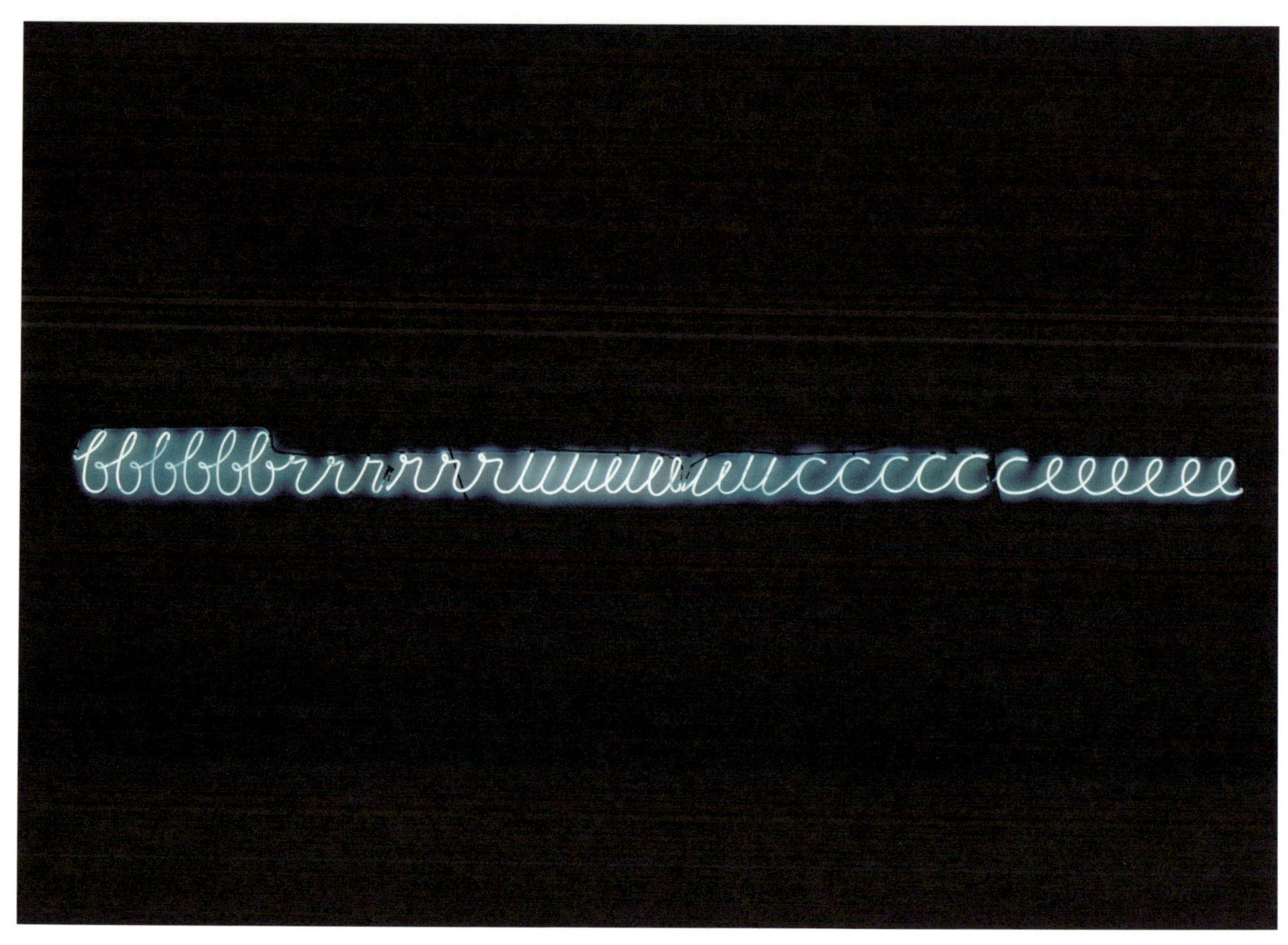

Plate 15 *My Name As Though It Were Written on the Surface of the Moon*, 1968.
Stedelijk Museum, Amsterdam

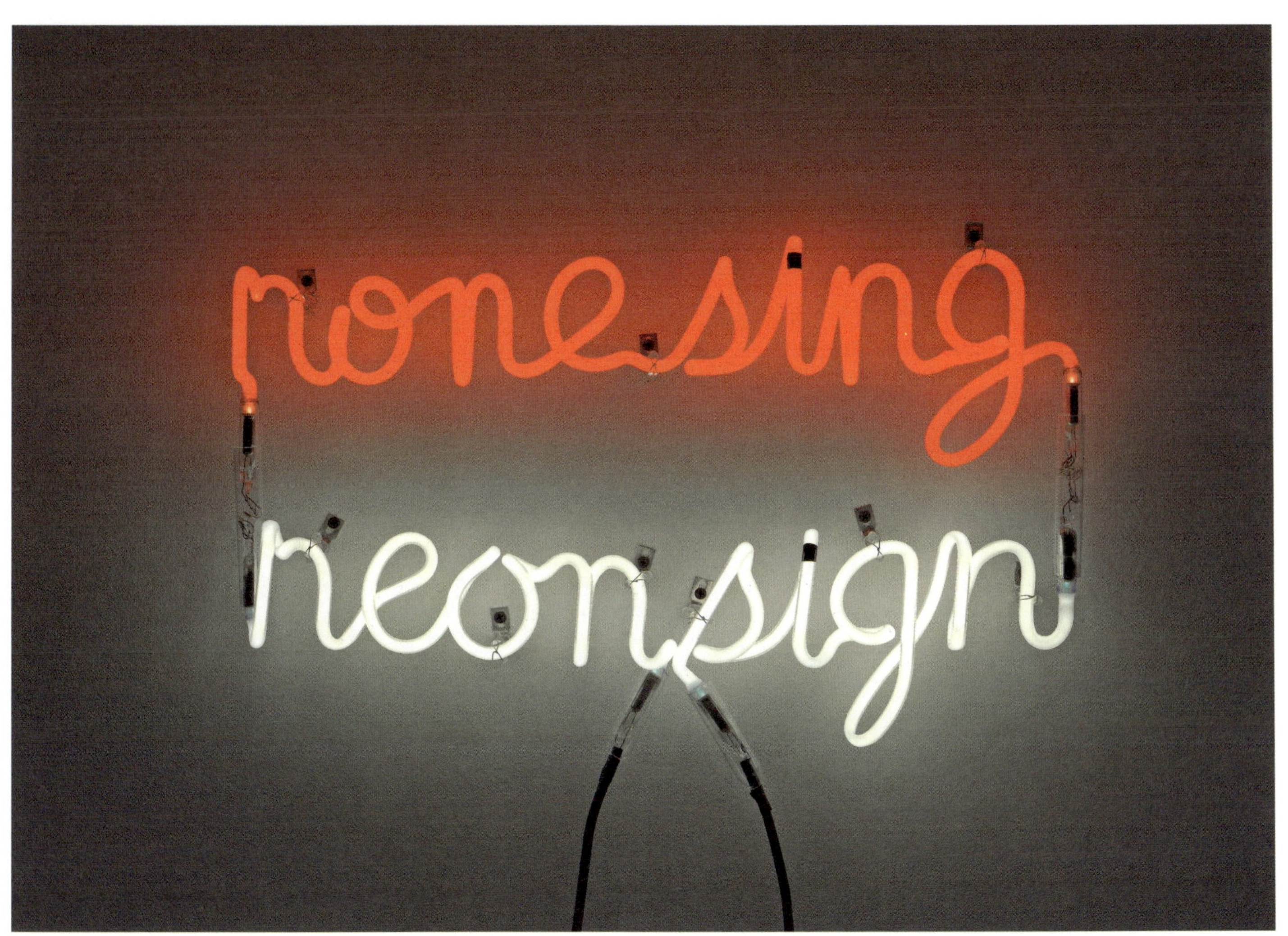

Plate 16 *None Sing Neon Sign*, 1970. Solomon R. Guggenheim Museum, New York. Panza Collection, 1991. 91.3825

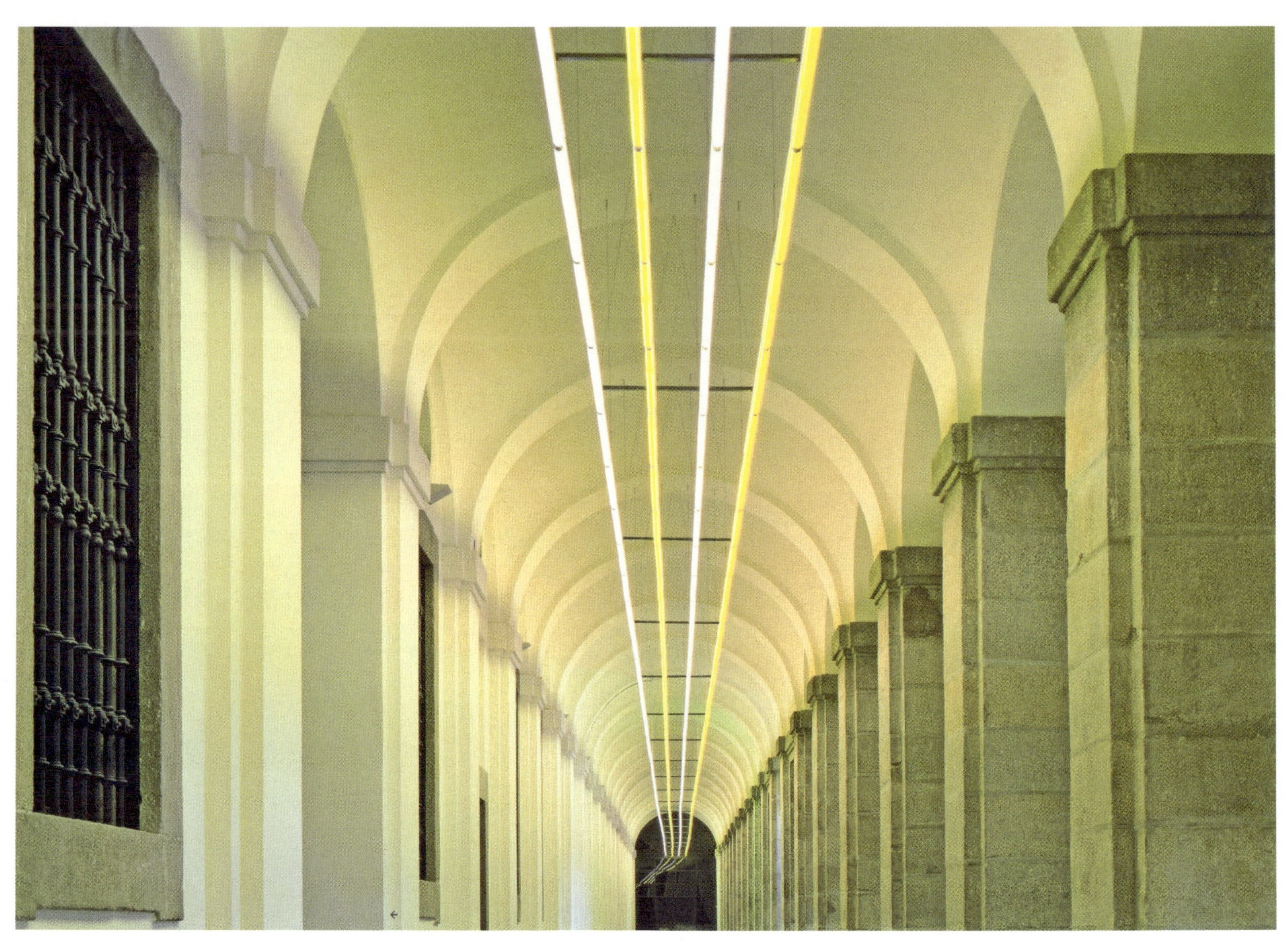

Plate 17 *Pink and Yellow Light Corridor (Variable Lights)*, 1972. Solomon R. Guggenheim Museum, New York. Panza Collection, 1991. 91.3828

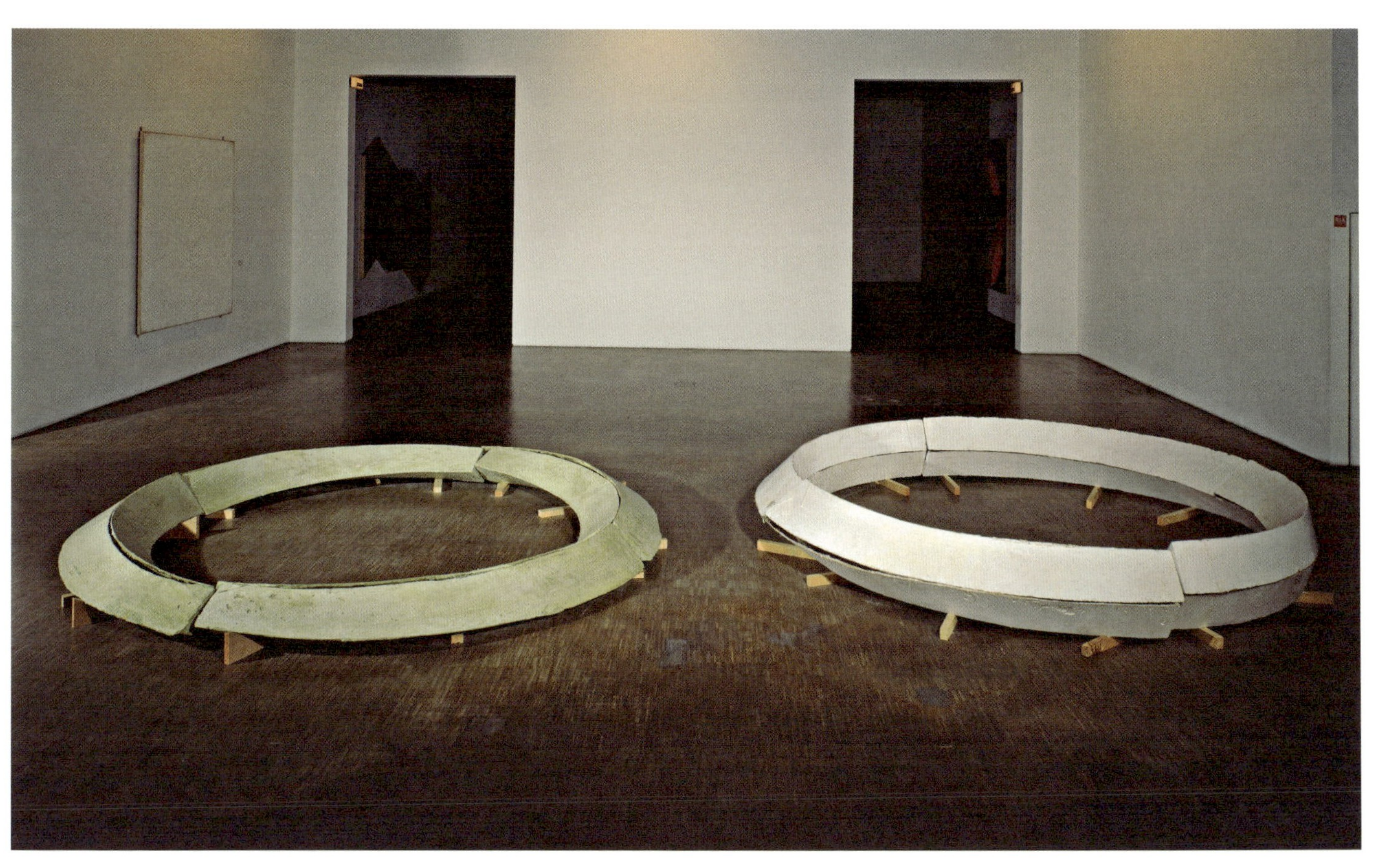

Plate 18 *Smoke Rings (Model for Underground Tunnels)*, 1979–80. Centre Georges Pompidou, National Museum of Modern Art – Center for Industrial Creation, Paris. Purchased 1985. AM1985-140

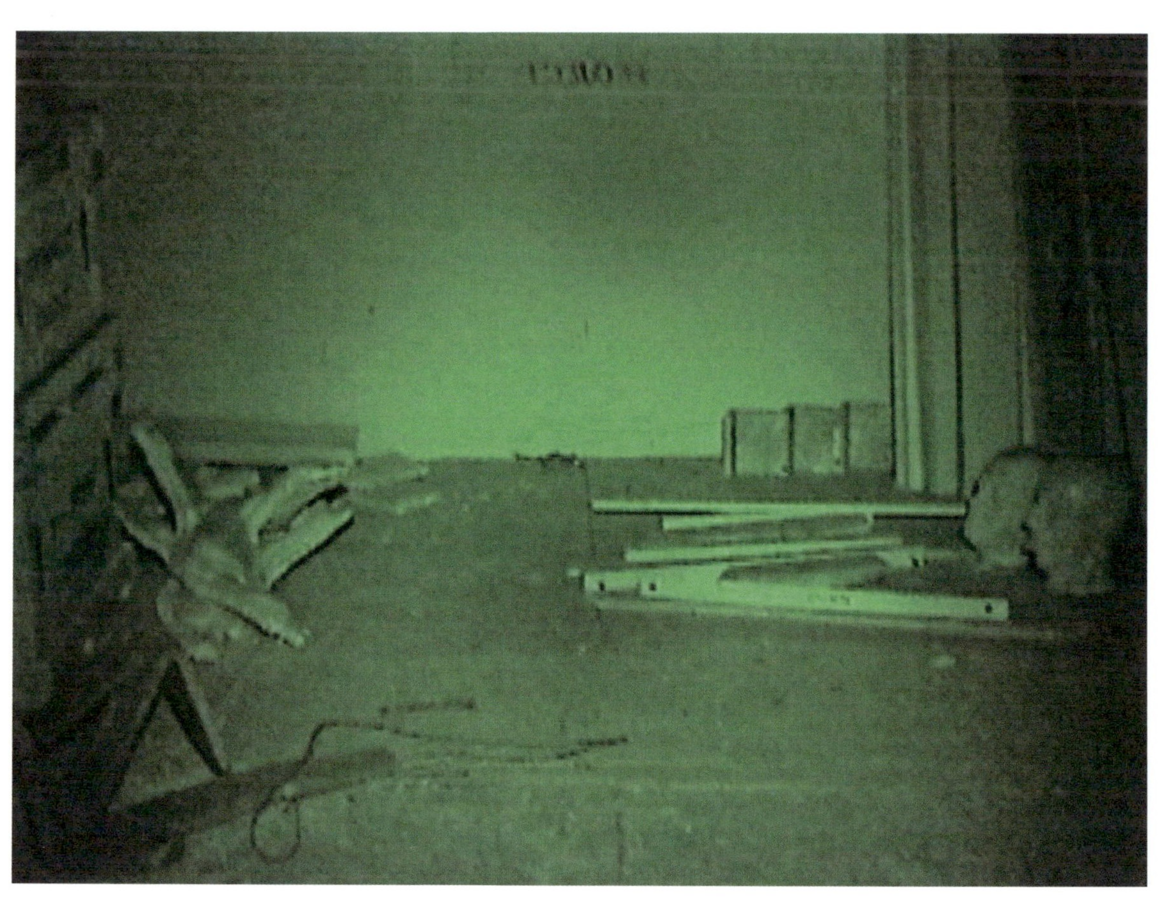

Plate 19 Video still from *Sound for Mapping the Studio Model (The Video)*, 2001. CIAC: Colección Isabel y Agustín Coppel

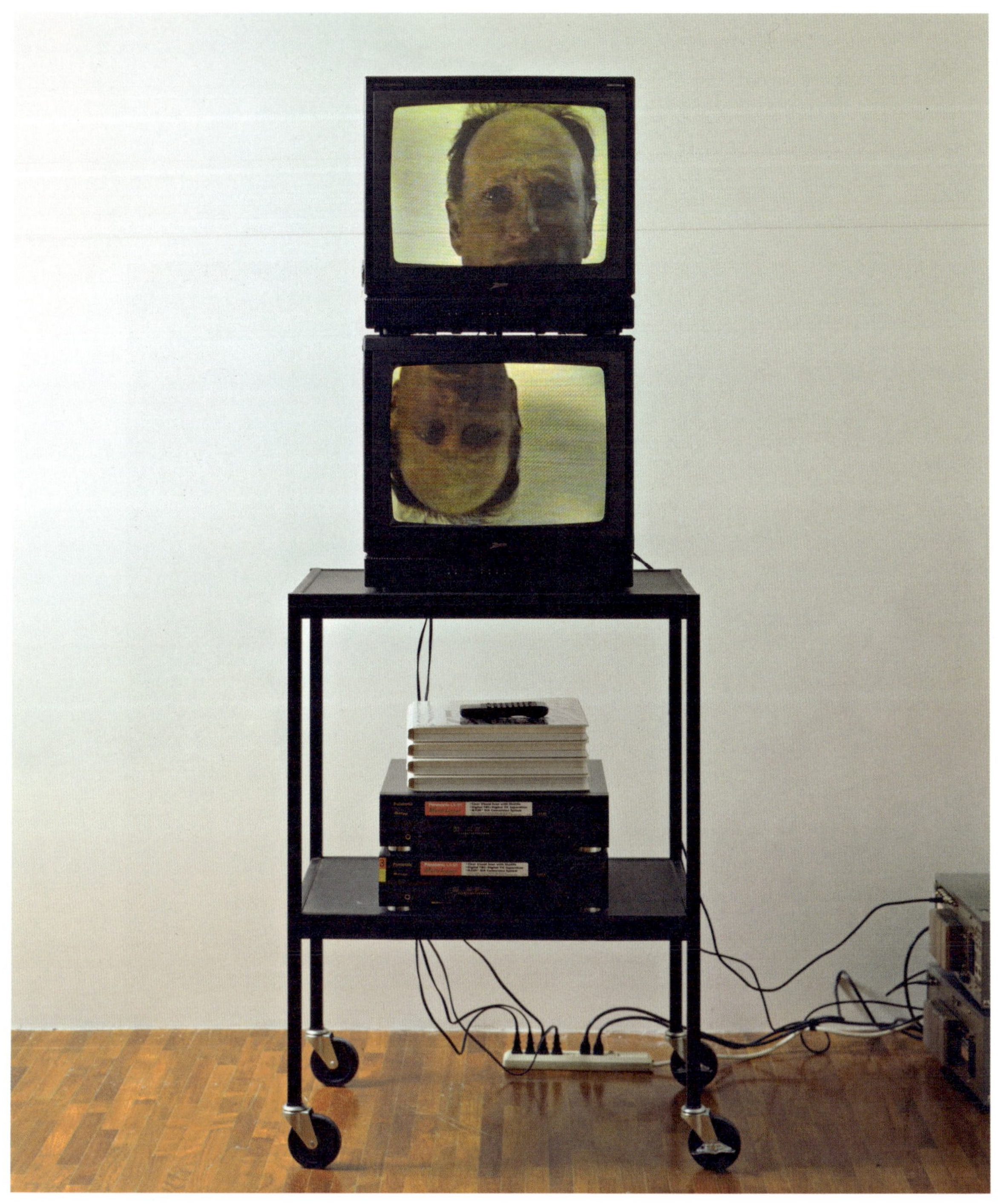

Plate 20 *Think*, 1993. The Museum of Modern Art, New York. Gift of Werner and Elaine Dannheisser, 1996

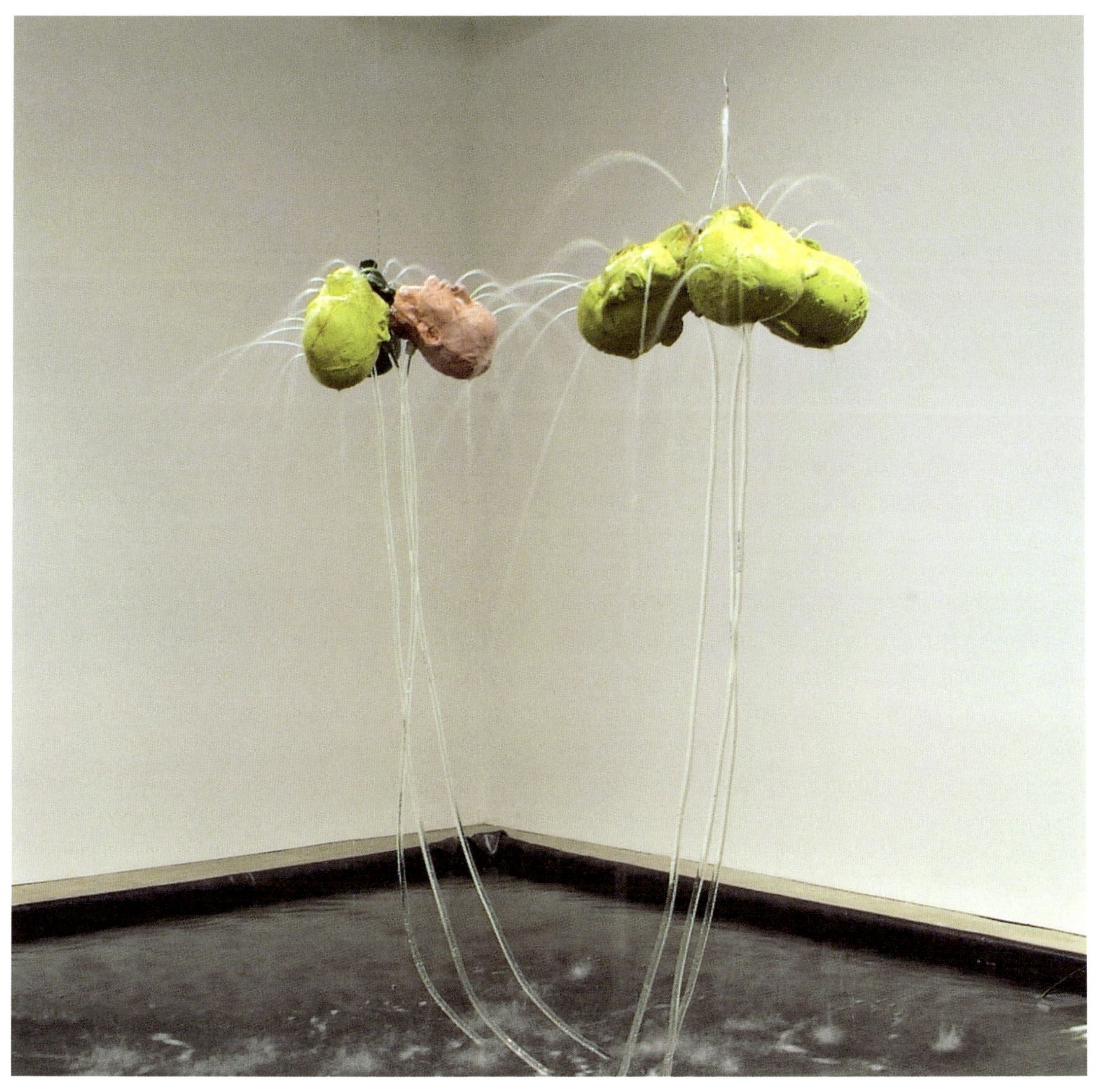

Plate 21 Left: *Three Heads Fountain (Juliet, Andrew, Rinde)*, 2005. Private collection, Madrid. Courtesy Donald Young Gallery, Chicago. Right: *Three Heads Fountain (Three Andrews)*, 2005. François Pinault Foundation

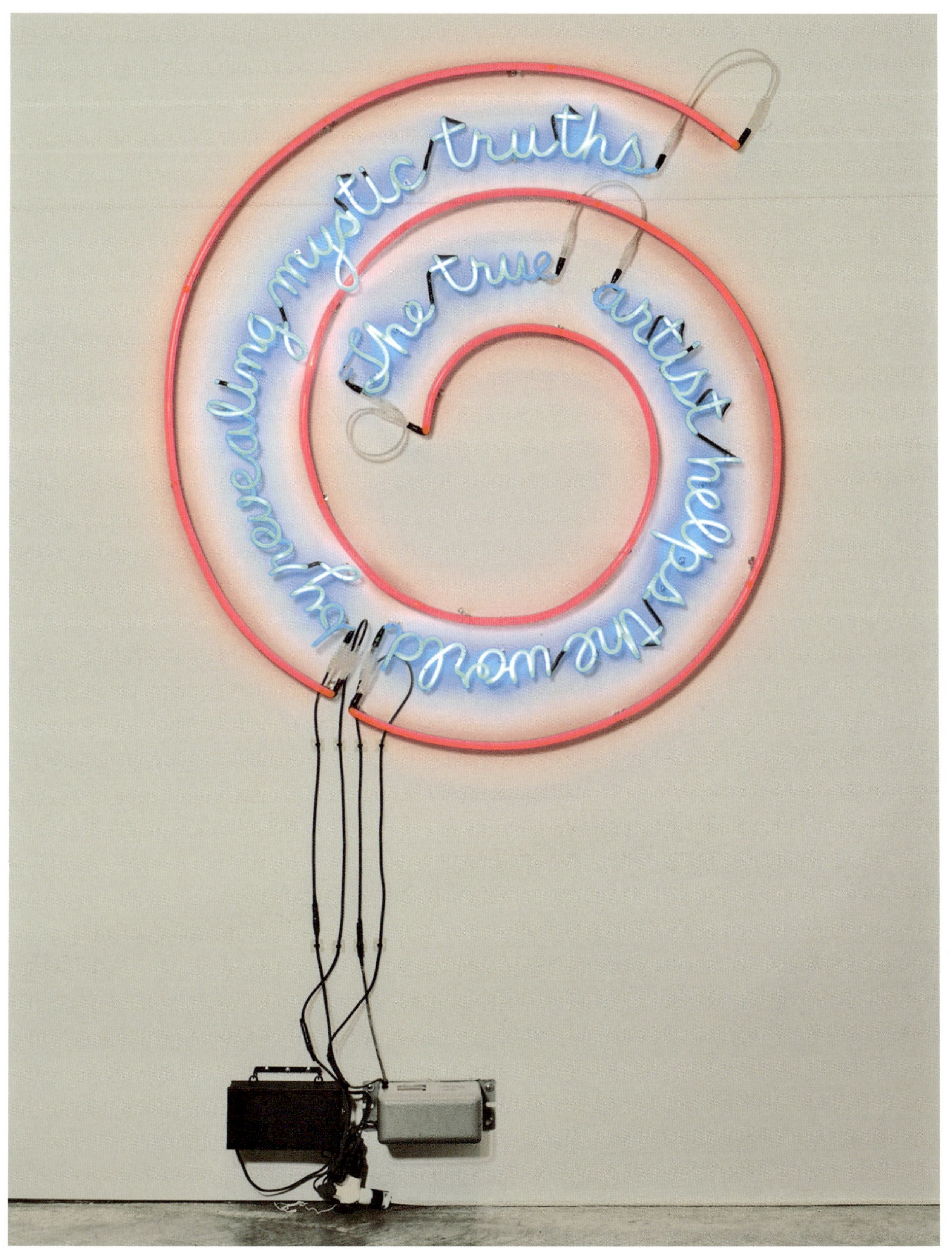
The true artist helps the world by revealing mystic truths

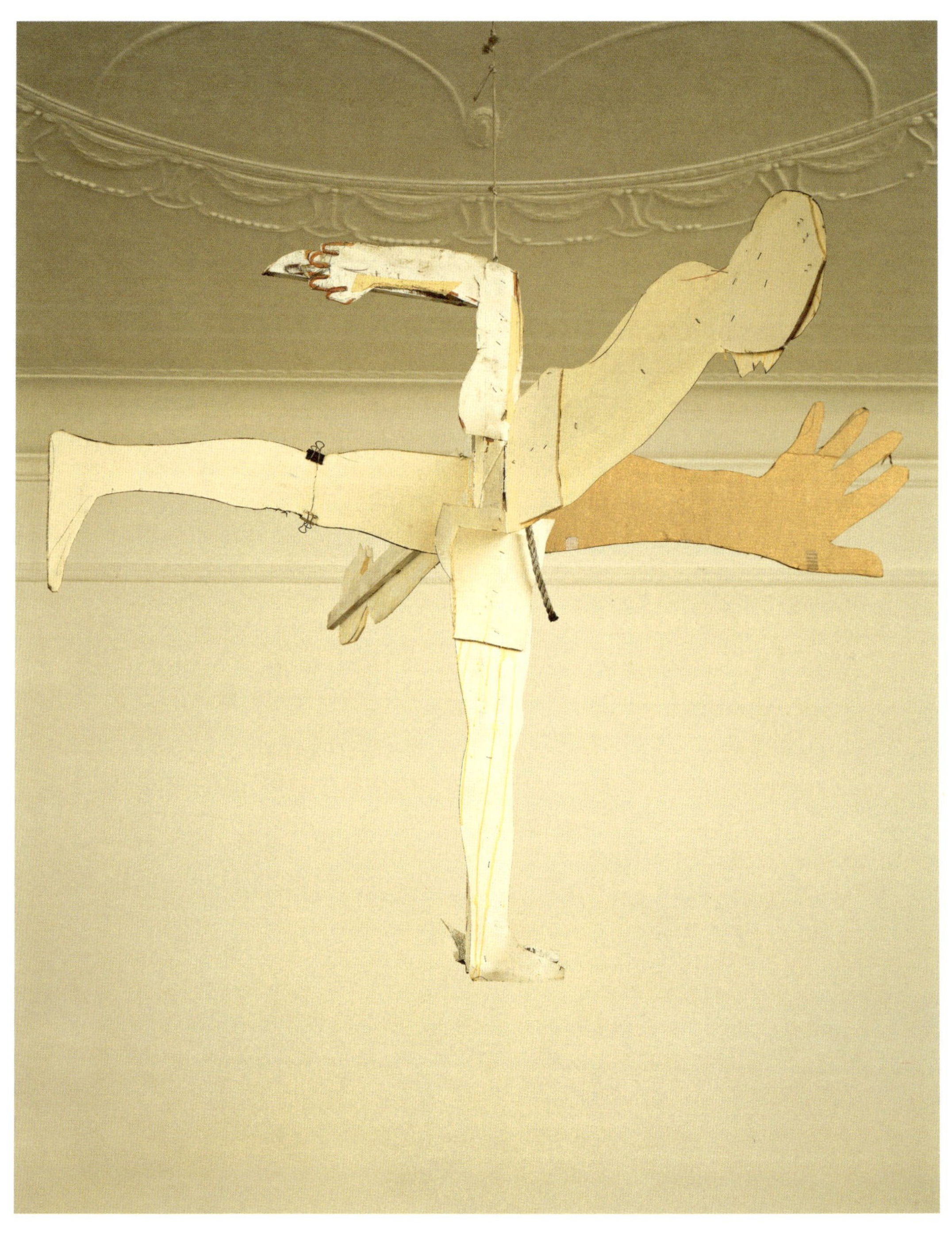

Plate 22 *The True Artist Helps the World by Revealing Mystic Truths (Window or Wall Sign)*, 1967. Philadelphia Museum of Art. Purchased with the generous support of The Annenberg Fund for Major Acquisitions, the Henry P. McIlhenny Fund, the bequest (by exchange) of Henrietta Meyers Miller, the gift (by exchange) of Philip L. Goodwin, and funds contributed by Edna Andrade, 2007-44-1

Plate 23 *Untitled (#358)*, 1986. Collection Dorothee and Konrad Fischer

Performance must be taped from directly over the center of the area so you must build a scaffold over the area that will hold the cameraman or devise a mirror arrangement above the area so that the cameraman may remain on the floor. / The dancers lie with their feet extended toward the outside of the performance area, hands extended overhead and touching at the center. The dancers should be in a straight line—that is, exactly opposite each other across the center. / The dancers then roll around in a circle, keeping their hands at the center of the area and continue to roll at a moderate speed as long as possible or until the end of the tape. / With the area centered on the screen and the dancers rolling a circle on the taped pattern, videotape the performance with the camera held steady for about three minutes. For the next three minutes, the cameraman must rotate the camera at the same speed as the dancers are revolving so that they appear to be in a fixed position and the floor turning under them. Again hold the camera steady for three minutes and then again rotate the camera for about three minutes, this time in the opposite direction to unwind the camera cords. Continue alternating until the dancers must stop or the tape is finished. The recording must be continuous.

Bruce Nauman, 1970.

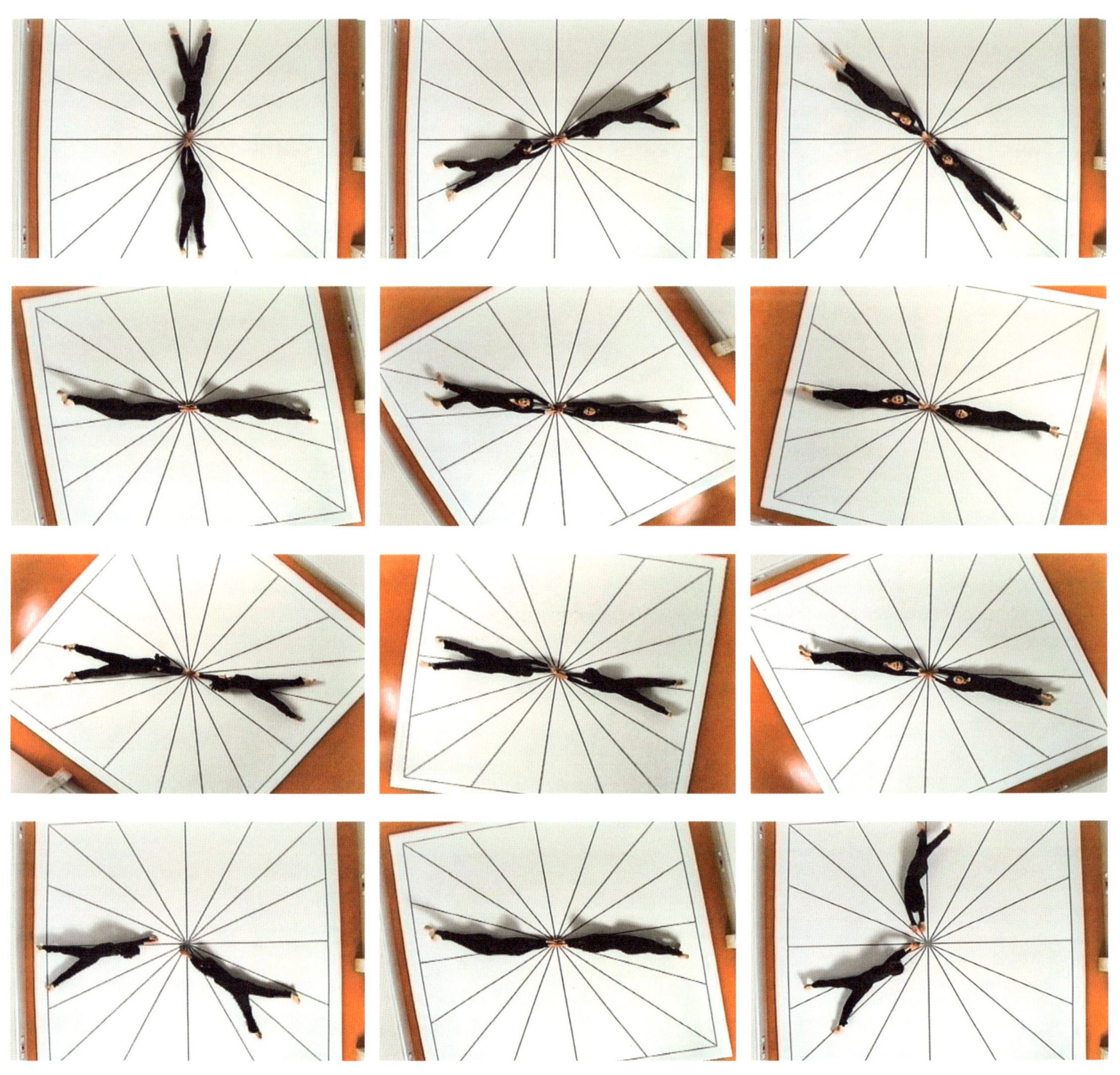

 Plate 24 *Untitled*, 1970/2009. Courtesy Sperone Westwater, New York

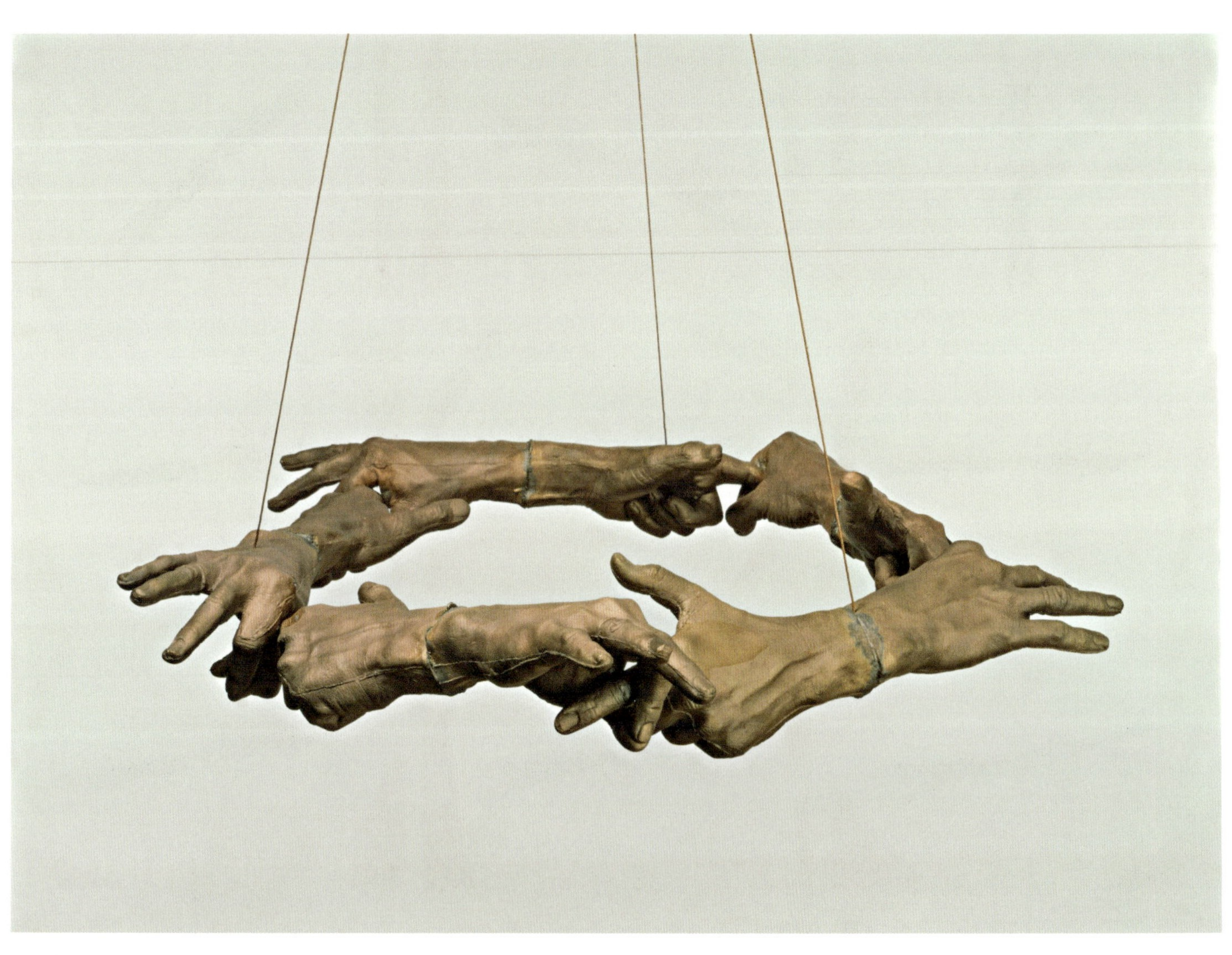

Plate 25 *Untitled (Hand Circle)*, 1996. Indianapolis Museum of Art. Henry F. and Katherine DeBoest Memorial Fund and Mr. and Mrs. Richard Crane Fund, 1996.248

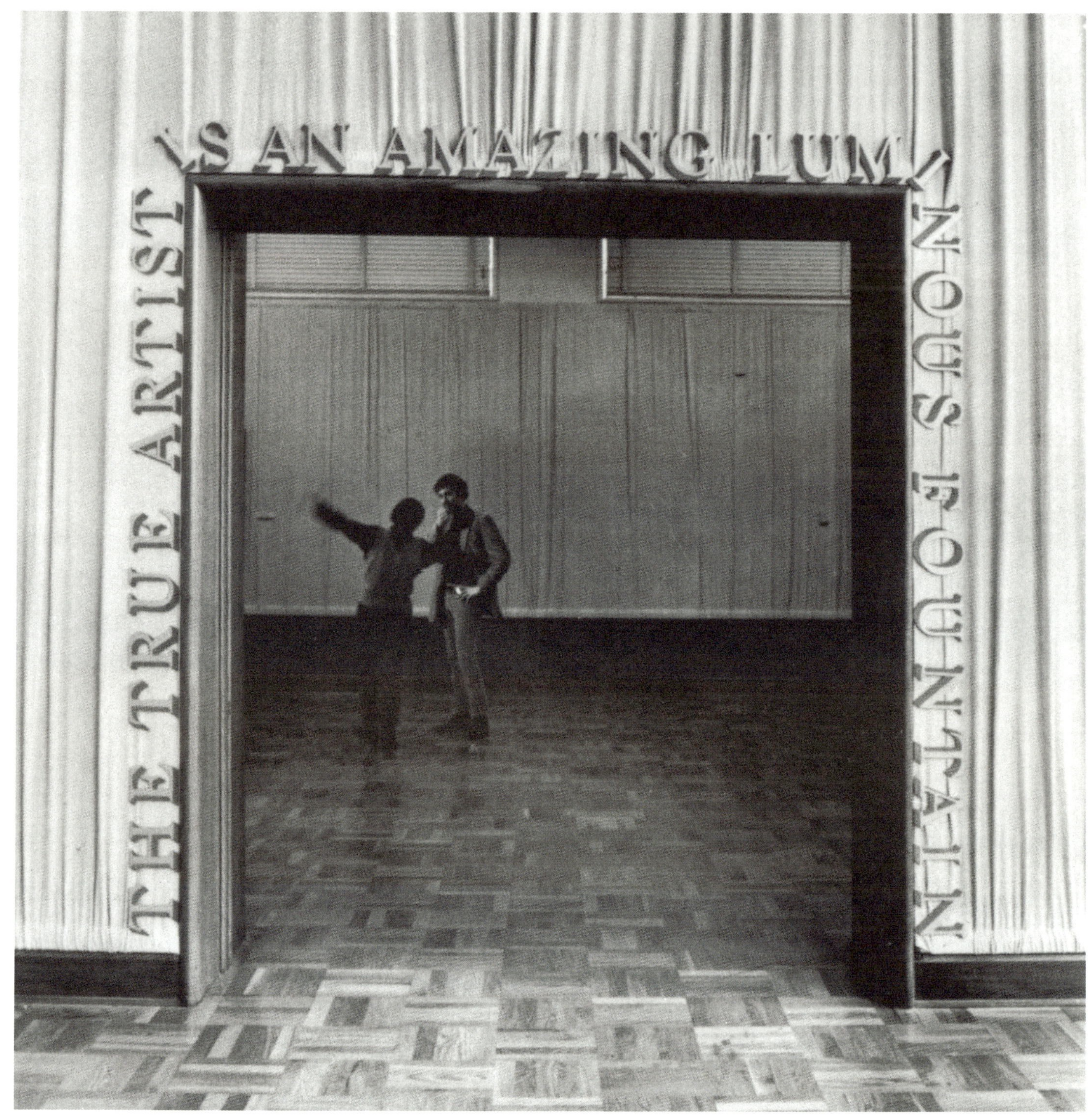

 Plate 26 *Untitled (The True Artist Is an Amazing Luminous Fountain)*, 1968. Courtesy the artist

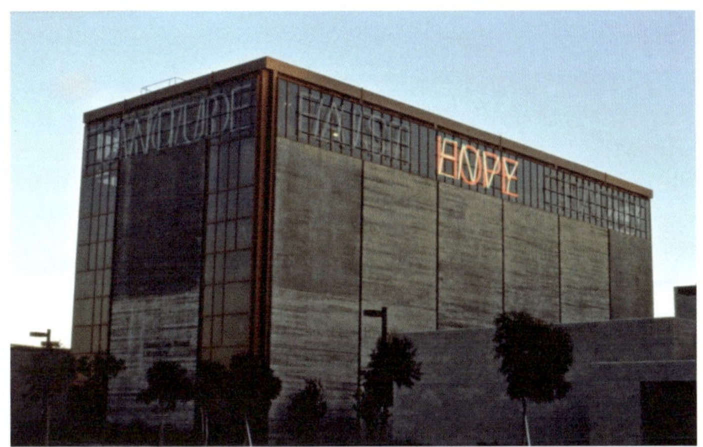

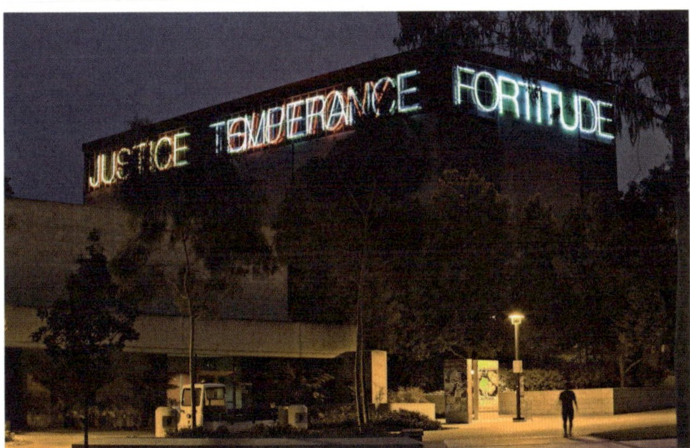

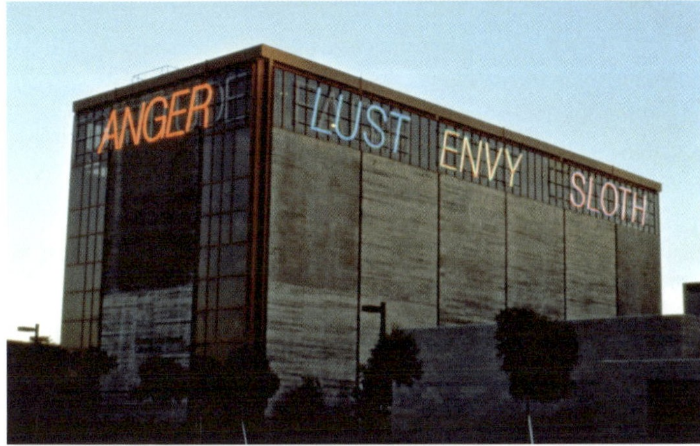

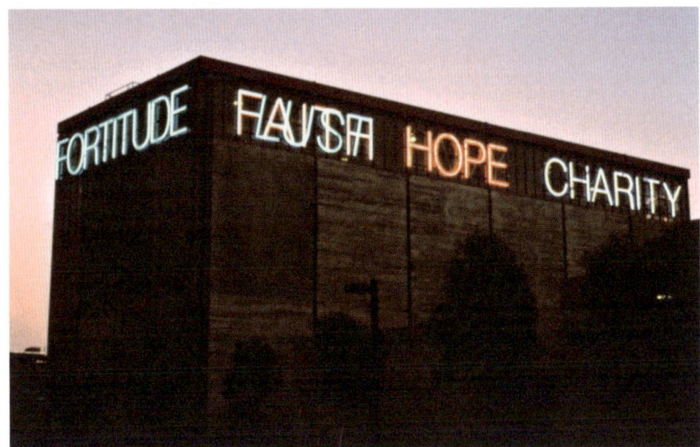

Plate 27 *Vices and Virtues*, 1983–88. Stuart Collection at the University of California, San Diego

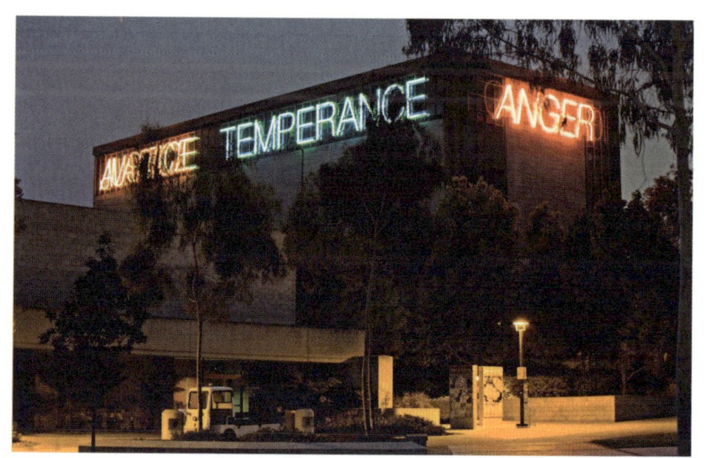
TEMPERANCE
ANGER
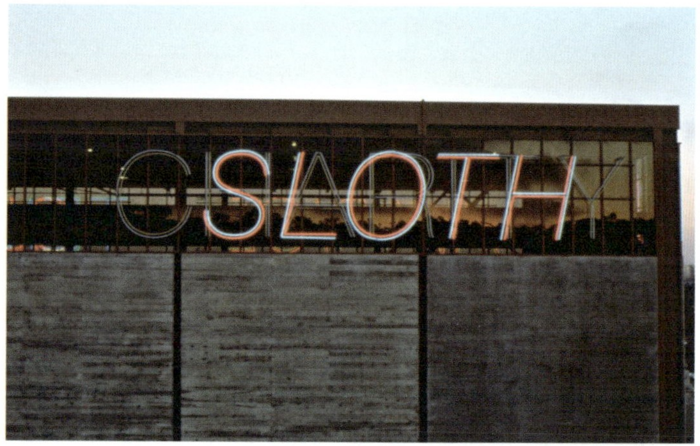
SLOTH
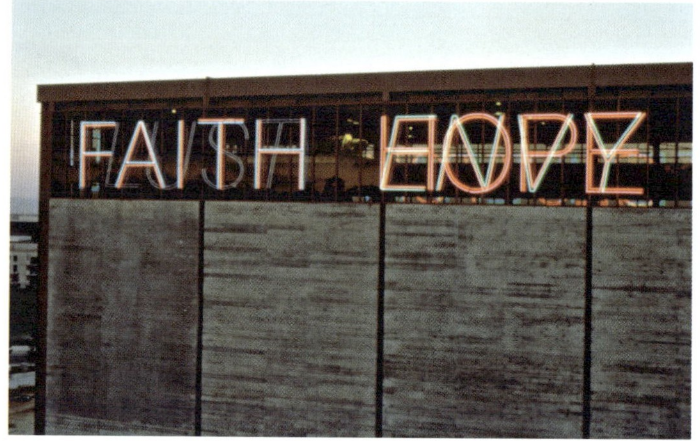
FAITH
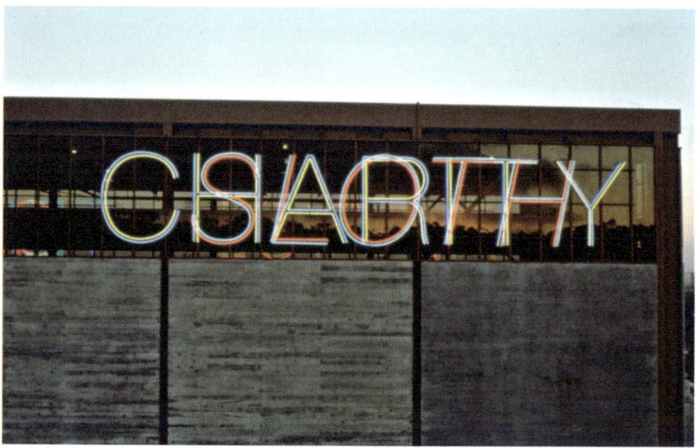

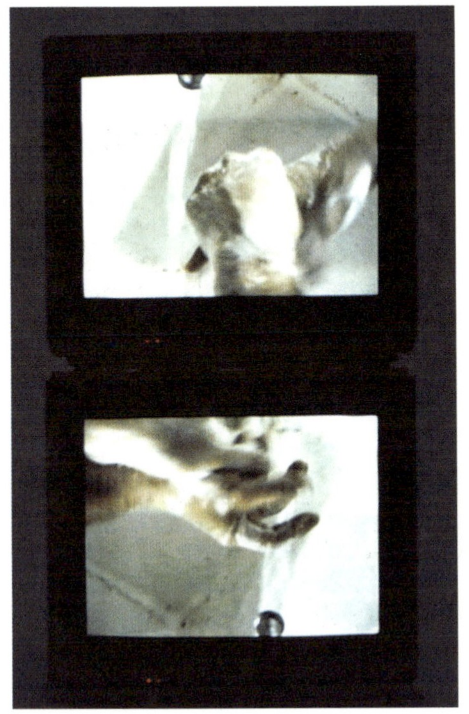
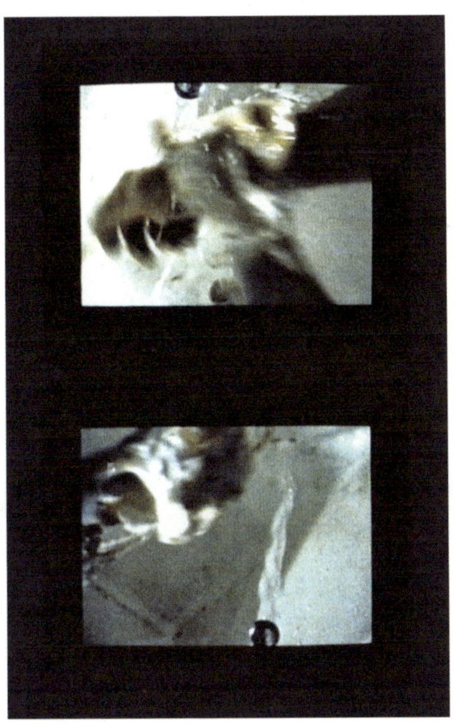
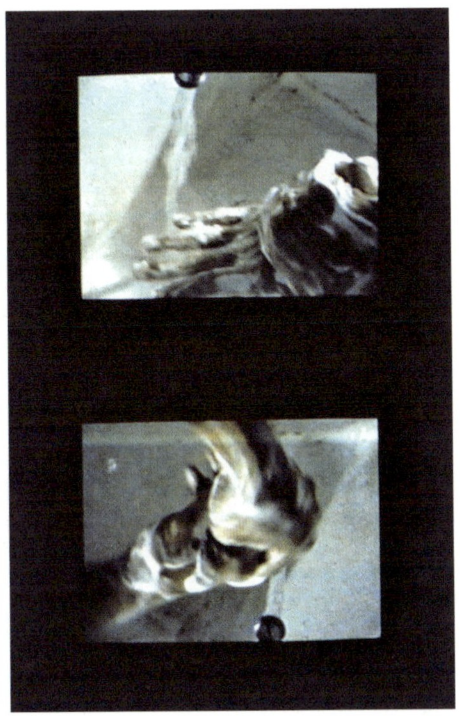

Plate 28 Video stills from *Washing Hands Normal,* 1996. ARTIST ROOMS: Tate and National Galleries of Scotland. Acquired jointly through the d'Offay Donation with assistance from the National Heritage Memorial Fund and The Art Fund, 2008

Days/Giorni

The scripts that appear in this section, in which the days of the week are subjected to a series of permutations, were written by Bruce Nauman for his most recent sound installations, *Days* and *Giorni*. Nauman wrote two subtly varying scripts in English for *Days* that were then translated into Italian for *Giorni*. Each of the two versions was read aloud by participants and recorded as audio tracks for the individual works.

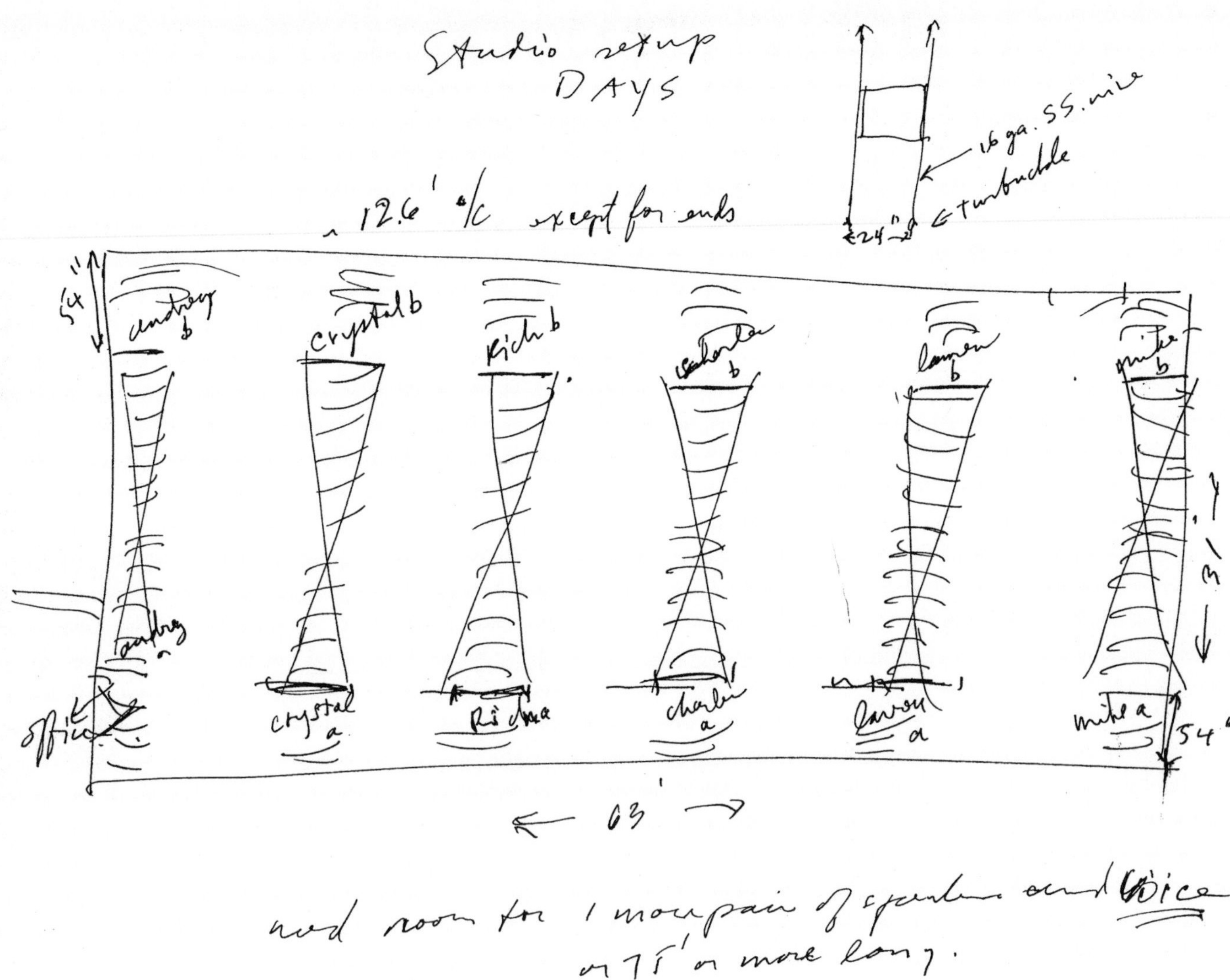

Bruce Nauman. *Untitled*, 2008. Ink on paper, 8 x 10 inches (20.3 x 25.4 cm). Courtesy the artist

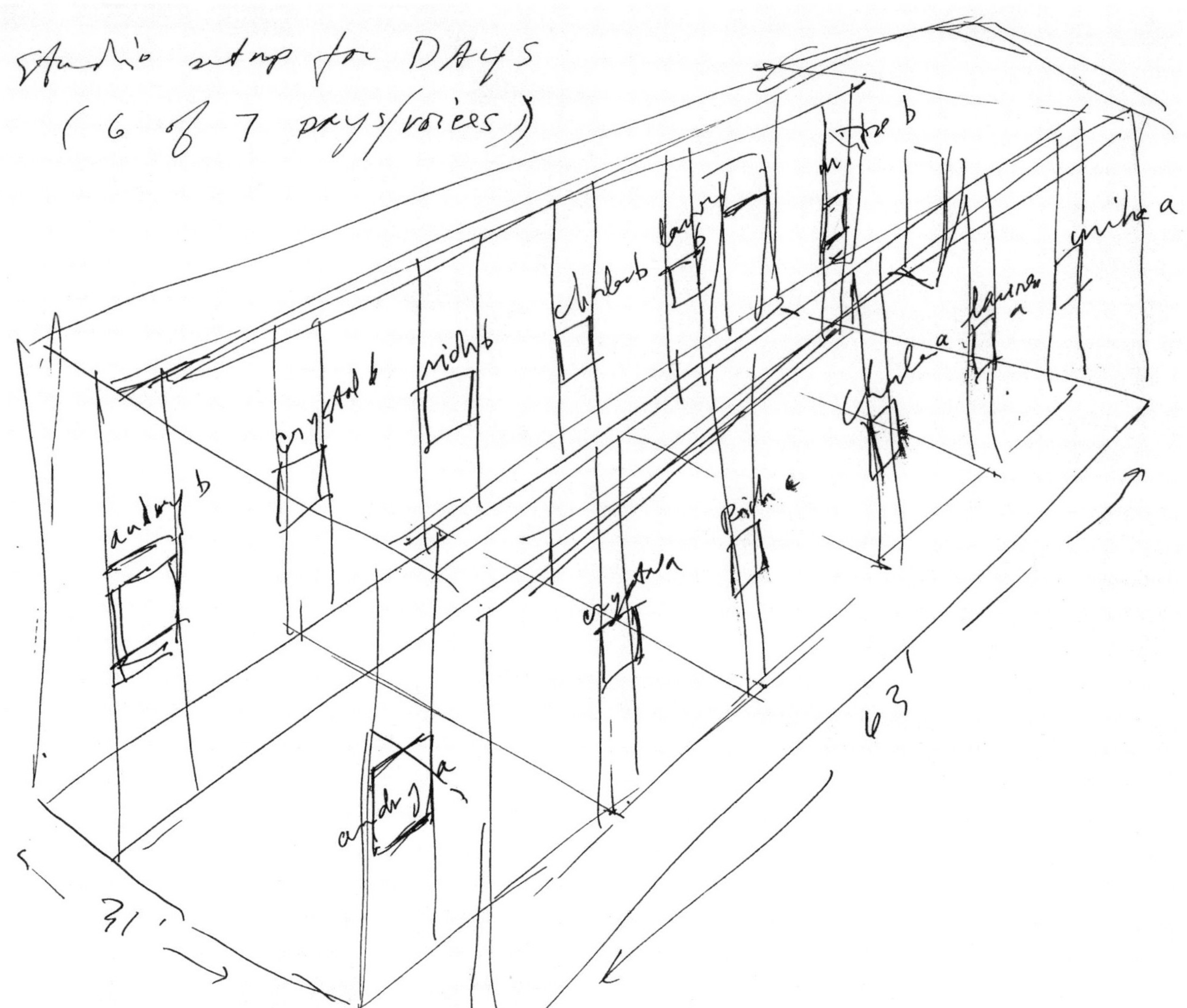

147 Bruce Nauman. *Untitled,* 2008. Ink on paper, 8 x 10 inches (20.3 x 25.4 cm). Courtesy the artist

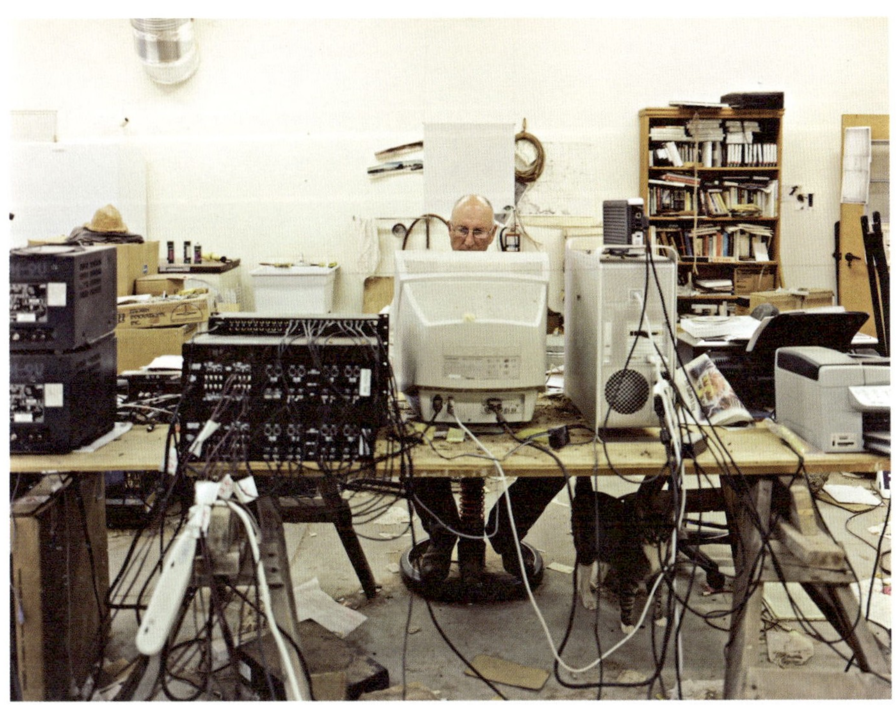

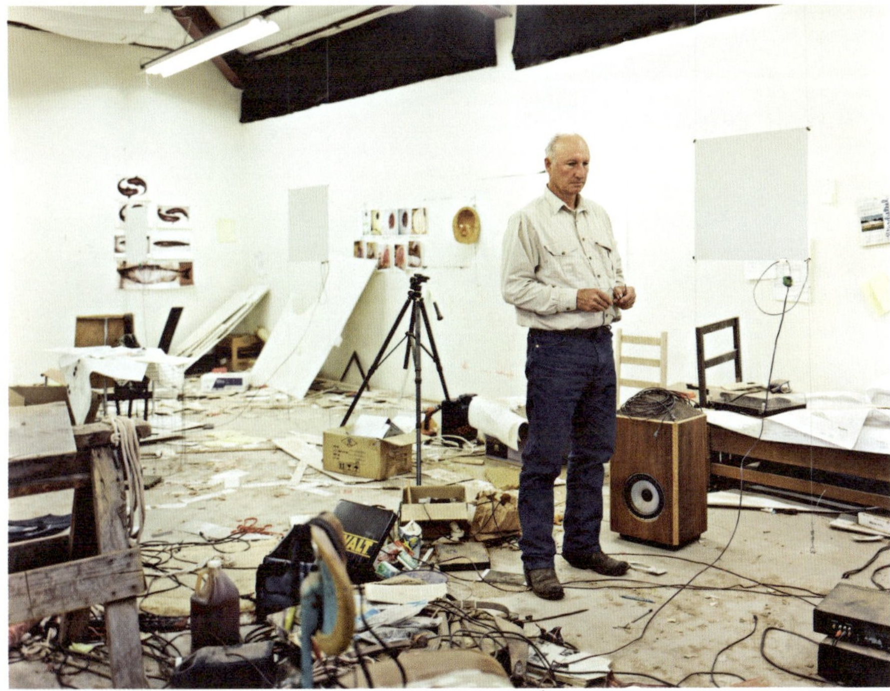

Bruce Nauman in his New Mexico studio; the flat, square speakers that comprise the installation of *Days* and *Giorni* hang behind him.

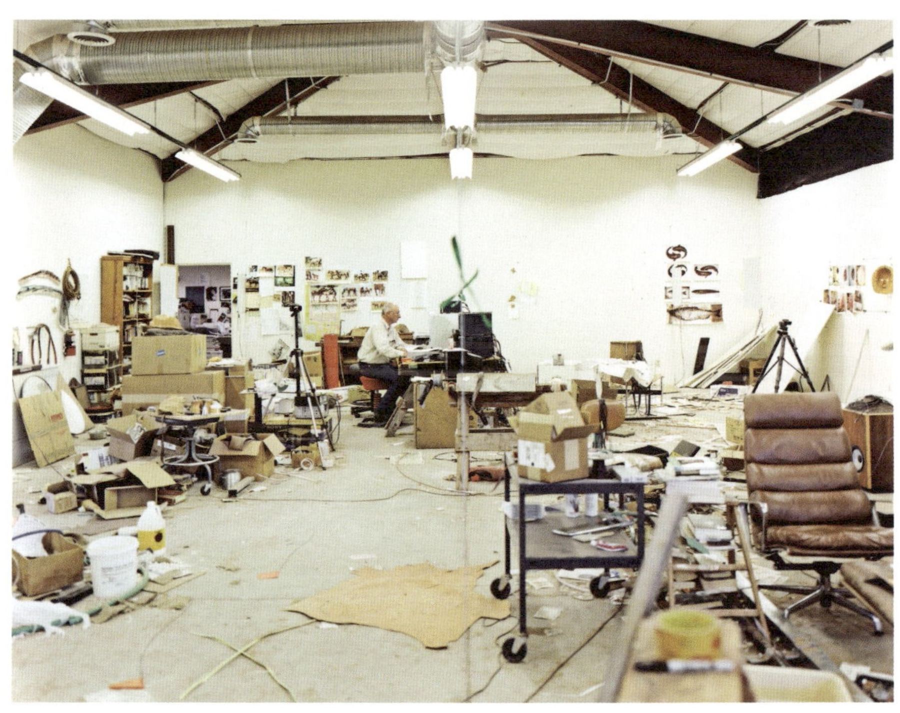

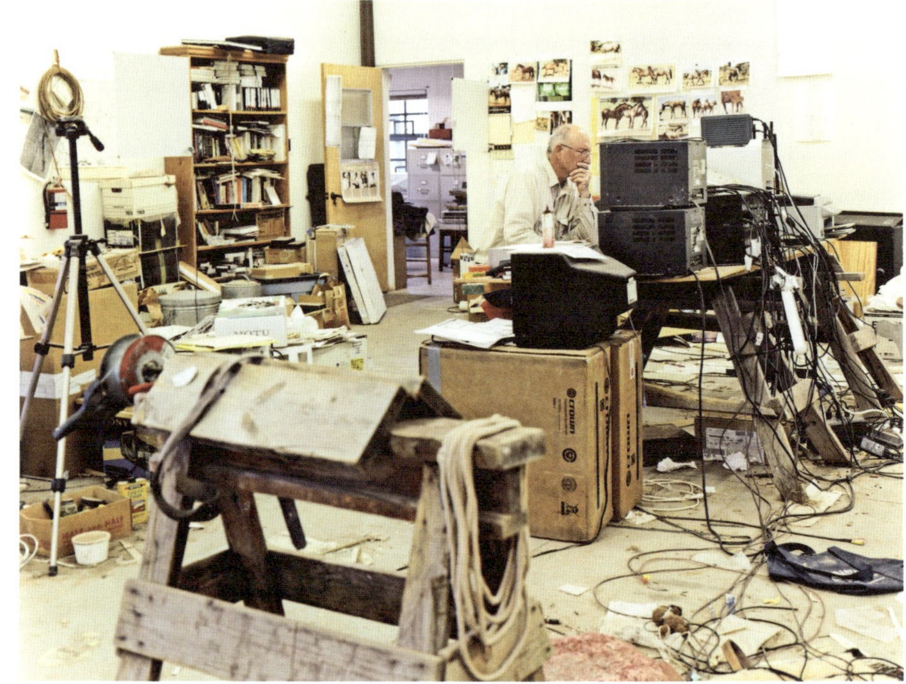

149 Bruce Nauman works in his studio in northern New Mexico.

Sunday
Monday
Tuesday
Wednesday
Thursday
Friday
Saturday

7/6

Sunday
Monday
Tuesday
Wednesday
Thursday
Friday

Sunday
Monday
Tuesday
Wednesday
Thursday
Saturday

Sunday
Monday
Tuesday
Wednesday
Friday
Saturday

Sunday
Monday
Tuesday
Thursday
Friday
Saturday

Sunday
Monday
Wednesday
Thursday
Friday

Saturday

Sunday
Tuesday
Wednesday
Thursday
Friday
Saturday

Monday
Tuesday
Wednesday
Thursday
Friday
Saturday

7/5

Sunday
Monday
Tuesday
Wednesday
Thursday

Sunday
Monday
Tuesday
Wednesday
Friday

Sunday
Monday
Tuesday
Thursday
Friday

Sunday
Monday
Wednesday
Thursday
Friday

Sunday

Tuesday
Wednesday
Thursday
Friday

Monday
Tuesday
Wednesday
Thursday
Friday

Sunday
Monday
Tuesday
Wednesday
Saturday

Sunday
Monday
Tuesday
Thursday
Saturday

Sunday
Monday
Wednesday
Thursday
Saturday

Sunday
Tuesday
Wednesday
Thursday
Saturday

Monday
Tuesday
Wednesday
Thursday
Saturday

Sunday
Monday

Tuesday
Friday
Saturday

Sunday
Monday
Wednesday
Friday
Saturday

Sunday
Tuesday
Wednesday
Friday
Saturday

Monday
Tuesday
Wednesday
Friday
Saturday

Sunday
Monday
Thursday
Friday
Saturday

Sunday
Tuesday
Thursday
Friday
Saturday

Monday
Tuesday
Thursday
Friday
Saturday

Sunday
Wednesday
Thursday

Friday
Saturday

Monday
Wednesday
Thursday
Friday
Saturday

Sunday
Monday
Tuesday
Wednesday
Thursday

7/4

Tuesday
Wednesday
Thursday
Friday

Monday
Wednesday
Thursday
Friday

Monday
Tuesday
Thursday
Friday

Monday
Tuesday
Wednesday
Friday

Monday
Tuesday
Wednesday
Thursday

Tuesday

Wednesday
Thursday
Saturday

Monday
Wednesday
Thursday
Saturday

Monday
Tuesday
Thursday
Saturday

Monday
Tuesday
Wednesday
Friday

Tuesday
Wednesday
Friday
Saturday

Monday
Wednesday
Friday
Saturday

Monday
Tuesday
Friday
Saturday

Tuesday
Thursday
Friday
Saturday

Monday
Thursday
Friday
Saturday

Wednesday
Thursday
Friday
Saturday

Sunday
Wednesday
Thursday
Friday

Sunday
Tuesday
Thursday
Friday

Sunday
Tuesday
Wednesday
Friday

Sunday
Tuesday
Wednesday
Thursday

Sunday
Wednesday
Thursday
Saturday

Sunday
Tuesday
Thursday
Saturday

Sunday
Tuesday
Wednesday
Saturday

Sunday
Wednesday
Friday

Saturday

Sunday
Tuesday
Friday
Saturday

Sunday
Thursday
Friday
Saturday

Sunday
Monday
Thursday
Friday

Sunday
Monday
Wednesday
Friday

Sunday
Monday
Wednesday
Thursday

Sunday
Monday
Thursday
Saturday

Sunday
Monday
Wednesday
Saturday

Sunday
Monday
Friday
Saturday

Sunday

Monday
Tuesday
Friday

Sunday
Monday
Tuesday
Saturday

Sunday
Monday
Tuesday
Wednesday

Sunday
Monday
Tuesday
Thursday

7/3

Saturday
Sunday
Monday

Saturday
Sunday
Tuesday

Saturday
Sunday
Wednesday

Saturday
Sunday
Thursday

Saturday
Sunday
Friday

Friday
Sunday

Monday

Friday
Sunday
Tuesday

Friday
Sunday
Wednesday

Friday
Sunday
Thursday

Thursday
Sunday
Monday

Thursday
Sunday
Tuesday

Thursday
Sunday
Wednesday

Wednesday
Sunday
Monday

Wednesday
Sunday
Tuesday

Tuesday
Sunday
Monday

Saturday
Monday
Tuesday

Saturday

Monday
Wednesday

Saturday
Monday
Thursday

Saturday
Monday
Friday

Friday
Monday
Tuesday

Friday
Monday
Wednesday

Friday
Monday
Thursday

Thursday
Monday
Tuesday

Thursday
Monday
Wednesday

Wednesday
Monday
Tuesday

Saturday
Tuesday
Wednesday

Saturday
Tuesday
Thursday

Saturday
Tuesday
Friday

Friday
Tuesday
Wednesday

Friday
Tuesday
Thursday

Thursday
Tuesday
Wednesday

Saturday
Wednesday
Thursday

Saturday
Wednesday
Friday

Saturday
Thursday
Friday

Friday
Wednesday
Thursday

7/2

Saturday
Friday

Saturday
Thursday

Saturday
Wednesday

Saturday
Tuesday

Saturday
Monday

Saturday
Sunday

Friday
Thursday

Friday
Wednesday

Friday
Tuesday

Friday
Monday

Friday
Sunday

Thursday
Wednesday

Thursday
Tuesday

Thursday
Monday

Thursday
Sunday

Wednesday
Tuesday

Wednesday
Monday

Wednesday

Sunday

Tuesday
Monday

Tuesday
Sunday

Monday
Sunday

7/1 – same as 7/7

Sunday

Monday

Tuesday

Wednesday

Thursday

Friday

Saturday

seven a time
Sunday
Monday
Tuesday
Wednesday
Thursday
Friday
Saturday

six a time
Sunday
Monday
Tuesday
Wednesday
Thursday
Friday

Sunday
Monday
Tuesday
Wednesday
Thursday
Saturday

Sunday
Monday
Tuesday
Wednesday
Friday
Saturday

Sunday
Monday
Tuesday
Thursday
Friday
Saturday

Sunday
Monday
Wednesday
Thursday
Friday
Saturday

Sunday
Tuesday
Wednesday
Thursday
Friday
Saturday

Monday
Tuesday
Wednesday
Thursday
Friday
Saturday

five a time
Sunday
Monday
Tuesday
Wednesday
Thursday

Sunday
Monday
Tuesday
Wednesday
Friday

Sunday
Monday
Tuesday
Wednesday
Saturday

Sunday
Monday
Tuesday
Thursday
Friday

Sunday
Monday
Tuesday
Thursday
Saturday

Sunday
Monday
Tuesday
Friday
Saturday

Sunday
Monday
Wednesday
Thursday
Friday

Sunday
Monday
Wednesday
Thursday
Saturday

Sunday
Monday
Wednesday
Friday
Saturday

Sunday
Monday
Thursday
Friday
Saturday

Sunday
Tuesday
Wednesday
Thursday
Friday

Sunday
Tuesday
Wednesday
Thursday
Saturday

Sunday
Tuesday
Wednesday
Friday
Saturday

Sunday
Tuesday
Thursday
Friday
Saturday

Sunday
Wednesday
Thursday
Friday
Saturday

Monday
Tuesday
Wednesday
Thursday
Friday

Monday
Tuesday
Wednesday
Thursday
Saturday

Monday
Tuesday
Wednesday
Friday
Saturday

Monday
Tuesday
Thursday
Friday

Saturday

Monday
Wednesday
Thursday
Friday
Saturday

Tuesday
Wednesday
Thursday
Friday
Saturday

four a time

Sunday
Monday
Tuesday
Wednesday

Sunday
Monday
Tuesday
Thursday

Sunday
Monday
Tuesday
Friday

Sunday
Monday
Tuesday
Saturday

Sunday
Monday
Wednesday
Thursday

Sunday
Monday
Wednesday
Friday

Sunday
Monday
Wednesday
Saturday

Sunday
Monday
Thursday
Friday

Sunday
Monday
Thursday
Saturday

Sunday
Monday
Friday
Saturday

Sunday
Tuesday
Wednesday
Thursday

Sunday
Tuesday
Wednesday
Friday

Sunday
Tuesday
Wednesday
Saturday

Sunday
Tuesday
Thursday
Friday

Sunday
Tuesday
Thursday
Saturday

Sunday
Tuesday
Friday
Saturday

Sunday
Wednesday
Thursday
Friday

Sunday
Wednesday
Thursday
Saturday

Sunday
Wednesday
Friday
Saturday

Sunday
Thursday
Friday
Saturday

Monday
Tuesday
Wednesday
Thursday

Monday
Tuesday
Wednesday
Friday

Monday
Tuesday
Wednesday
Saturday

Monday
Tuesday
Thursday
Friday

Monday
Tuesday
Thursday
Saturday

Monday
Tuesday
Friday
Saturday

Monday
Wednesday
Thursday
Friday

Monday
Wednesday
Thursday
Saturday

Monday
Wednesday
Friday
Saturday

Monday
Thursday
Friday
Saturday

Tuesday
Wednesday
Thursday
Friday

Tuesday
Wednesday
Thursday

Saturday

Tuesday
Wednesday
Friday
Saturday

Tuesday
Thursday
Friday
Saturday

Wednesday
Thursday
Friday
Saturday

three a time

Sunday
Monday
Tuesday

Sunday
Monday
Wednesday

Sunday
Monday
Thursday

Sunday
Monday
Friday

Sunday
Monday
Saturday

Sunday
Tuesday
Wednesday

Sunday
Tuesday
Thursday

Sunday
Tuesday
Friday

Sunday
Tuesday
Saturday

Sunday
Wednesday
Thursday

Sunday
Wednesday
Friday

Sunday
Wednesday
Saturday

Sunday
Thursday
Friday

Sunday
Thursday
Saturday

Sunday
Friday
Saturday

Monday
Tuesday
Wednesday

Monday
Tuesday
Thursday

Monday
Tuesday
Friday

Monday
Tuesday
Saturday

Monday
Wednesday
Thursday

Monday
Wednesday
Friday

Monday
Wednesday
Saturday

Monday
Thursday
Friday

Monday
Thursday
Saturday

Monday
Friday
Saturday

Tuesday
Wednesday
Thursday

Tuesday
Wednesday
Friday

Tuesday
Wednesday
Saturday

Tuesday
Thursday
Friday

Tuesday
Thursday
Saturday

Tuesday
Friday
Saturday

Wednesday
Thursday
Friday

Wednesday
Thursday
Saturday

Wednesday
Friday
Saturday

Thursday
Friday
Saturday

two a time

Sunday
Monday

Sunday
Tuesday

Sunday
Wednesday

Sunday
Thursday

Sunday
Friday

Sunday
Saturday

Monday
Tuesday

Monday
Wednesday

Monday
Thursday

Monday
Friday

Monday
Saturday

Tuesday
Wednesday

Tuesday
Thursday

Tuesday
Friday

Tuesday
Saturday

Wednesday
Thursday

Wednesday
Friday

Wednesday
Saturday

Thursday
Friday

Thursday
Saturday

Friday
Saturday

one a time
Sunday

Monday

Tuesday

Wednesday

Thursday

Friday

Saturday

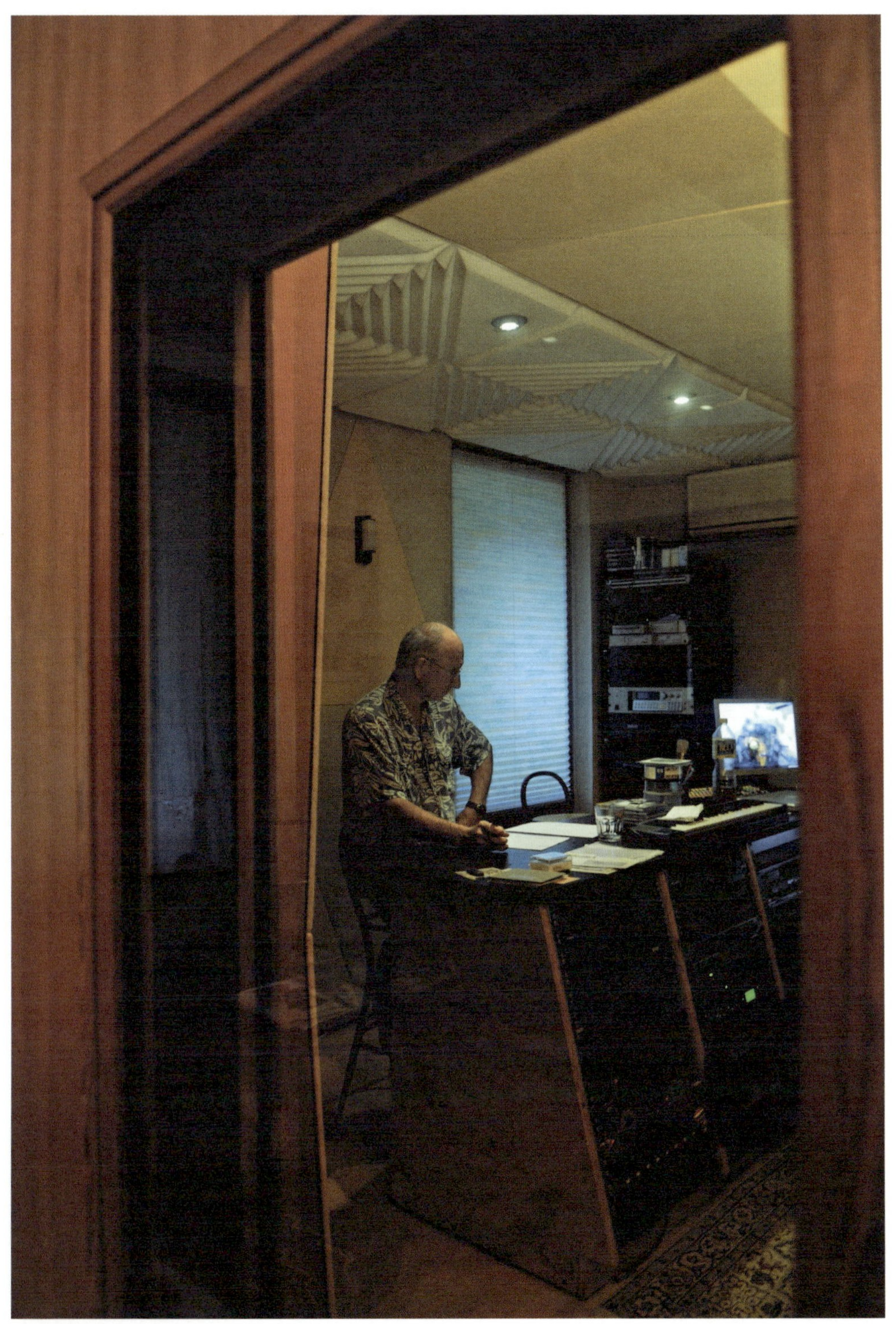

Bruce Nauman during the recording of *Giorni* at Waterland Music Studio, Venice, on June 13, 2008

To Bear, to Endure

Carlos Basualdo

It was rather cold and menacingly wet on the morning of June 13, 2008, another unlikely summer day in Venice. It was still early when we finally arrived—after the inevitable wandering that is so unavoidable a part of the Venetian experience—at the appropriately named Waterland Music Studio, near the Ghetto in Cannaregio, a large neighborhood on the northwest side of the city. We had been walking in a hurry, sorting out tourists on our way out of the Lista de Spagna—the busy pedestrian way that connects Rialto with the train station—and into a much narrower alley that culminated in a gated entrance. We crossed a small wooden bridge, climbed a flight of slippery stone steps, and rang a bell. Beyond the heavy doors a wonderfully Arcadian garden with a pool surprised us, sprawling and almost suburban in its careless deployment of green space. A neat stone path, shining furiously with the rain and peppered with a variety of children's toys, discreetly crossed the garden. We walked past a rusty little tricycle and the washed-out colors of a big plastic ball. A glass door took us into the house, where the studio's owner greeted us in a large room where a checkered Venetian floor competed for attention with lots of hanging clothes and more toys, strollers, even a few stuffed animals. Everything was wet, slightly chaotic, but positively happy. To the right was a set of tall wooden doors; opposite the garden was a flight of stairs; and toward the back, another door, very modest, finally opened into an impeccably equipped professional recording studio—the rarest of finds, one could not help thinking, in the middle of a medieval island.

We were there to record the voices for *Giorni*, the Italian version of *Days*, a sound installation that Bruce Nauman had just completed in his studio in New Mexico. From 9:30 in the morning until around 6 in the evening that day we were visited by a seemingly unending procession of people, including many of my university students, the dean of the School of Art and Design at the Iuav, artists, and some random friends. One at a time, each in turn came into the studio, sat on a bench, and read aloud the Italian translation of two versions of a text containing a list of permutations of the days of the week that Nauman had written for the work. Nauman and the sound technician stood behind a large soundproof window, quietly listening, occasionally giving the performers precise indications. Reading each version of the text took about twenty minutes, so that Nauman spent a little more than half an hour with each of the readers. After the recording was done, each reader would leave the studio and join the rest of us briefly in the room outside, to be paid, sign forms, and sit and chat.

At noon we stopped for a hearty lunch, and toward the end of the day, after the rain eventually stopped, we headed across the Grand Canal for dinner in the home of Massimo Magrí, a professor of film at the school.

We know the days of the week by heart. We are so intimately familiar with their names, and with the order in which they unpretentiously chart the passing of our time, that we forget to think about them as a relatively arbitrary way to measure our lives. They have become, to some extent, an invisible armature to which we have given the power to decide who we see and what we do, where we go and when we rest. Unrecognized as such, they are nevertheless ourselves as much as we exist in time, as much as our use of time is the substance of our thoughts. If Tuesday refused to follow Monday, if Sunday arbitrarily fell in the middle of the week, who would we then be?

Reading Nauman's mutated list of days for the first time felt to me like walking down steep stairs without the help of a handrail. But this time it was not my body that claimed its presence by making me acutely self-conscious of each potentially dangerous movement, but my very consciousness that hesitantly became wary of itself. The same feeling of quiet disorientation seems to have been shared by all of the readers that day in the studio near the Ghetto. As if by an overflowing river that trespasses beyond its bed, they felt subsumed by their own voices. When, occasionally entering the studio, we quietly watched them recording, what we witnessed and heard was the purely expressive substance of their voices, temporarily released from conscious restraint.

In the final installations of both *Days* and *Giorni*, each voice plays through a pair of speakers set facing each other. There are seven pairs of speakers altogether, arranged in two parallel rows, a placement that inevitable reminds us of a corridor. As in *Raw Materials*, Nauman's sound installation in the Turbine Hall of Tate Modern, London, in the fall of 2004, the speakers produce directional sound. The type of speakers used in *Days* are thin, square, off-white, and produce sound in both directions. Ordinary metal clips attach each of them to two floor-to-ceiling steel cables, at eye level, which makes them look like opaque, empty mirrors. When the work is playing, all the voices are heard at the same time, but because the speakers are directional, each of them can also be listened to in isolation. In fact we perceive them less as "voices" than as "people"—people that come to inhabit the room, pushing us from one voice to another, gently forcing us to face those empty mirrors, in which we find reflected a time without sequence or constraint. Each voice, freed from time, seems to be calling us like a blinded siren.

In *Days,* as in many other works of Nauman's, repetition is used to enhance the expressive nature of the individual repeated element. This is clearly unlike the use of repetition in Minimalism, which makes the whole expressive to the detriment of each component. A possible antecedent might be the work of Jasper Johns—the flags, the targets, and most of all the extraordinary series of numbers begun in the mid-1950s. For Johns, too, repetition has the effect of problematizing a supposedly natural order, so that each number is finally liberated from the tyranny of the series and allowed to stand for itself, allowing for a purely subjective viewing experience. By again becoming ciphers, outside the forced logic of an ordering sequence, the individual numbers in Johns's paintings can be subjected to the sheer force of interpretation. Freed from time, the voices in *Days* are likewise allowed to become intimately personal, to such a degree that we end up seeing ourselves reflected in their boundless emotion.

In the English-language *Days,* as in several of Nauman's earlier works, the voices are looped, so that the sequence has neither beginning nor end. A different logic plays out in *Giorni*: one voice opens the sequence, then a second, then the rest of the voices join in, and at the end, two and then finally just one voice is heard. The duration of the resulting cycle is slightly longer than the reading time required by the text. The first voices to be heard are those of two young female students, the last, that of the oldest man in the group. The sequence clearly evokes the passing of time, measured not so much in days as in lives. The female voices that open the sequence vibrate with expectation and sensuality; toward the end, a counterpoint between two male voices declares a more somber mood. Perhaps for the first time in Nauman's long career, the determining factor in the duration of the work seems to be purely subjective. Not surprisingly, this structure makes the work both more musical and more emotional, as if the artist's intentionality were carrying the expressive content of the individual voices even farther.

While *Days* seems to evoke the passage of time itself—time passing, twisting and turning, unraveling inside and over us—*Giorni* hints at the passage of a life, our inexorable life sinking in time. *Days* may have its origins in the experience of the empty artist's studio, where time never stops passing, and its passing takes the form of an endless interrogation of the nature of work and art. *Giorni*, though, belongs to an experience of passion and endurance. *Passione* shares its Latin root with *Patire*, the Italian verb that means to bear and to endure. To bear the passing of time, to endure a passing passion—to live and then disappear—it is passion, this work seems to tell us, in the full sense of the word, that is profoundly experienced in the unending passivity of our protean selves.

-----Forwarded message-----
From: **Susanna Carlisle**
Date: Wed, Nov 26, 2008 at 6:55 PM
Subject: Days
To: Bruce Nauman

Hi Bruce,

Although I saw/heard *Days* a few weeks ago in your studio, my response to your installation has been ricocheting around in my thoughts. Bruce [Hamilton] thought you might be interested in hearing them, so this is what has been playing in my mind.

The voices coming from one speaker in our computer room created a tedium that I felt was what you were originally going for, but when I heard the voices coming from multiple speakers in the spatial arena that you created, my response surprised me. I smiled because I felt the *Days* were finally able to exhale. Having experienced them substantially compressed, I was amazed by the expansive and complex relationships the voices conveyed. I didn't feel tedium at all, but instead a powerful surge of visceral delight. I finally was able to experience the astonishing musicality inherent in each version. For me, the English and Italian have very different tempos, textures, and cultural personas.

Since the voices in the English version were recorded in different places, at different levels, and at different times, I feel each symbolically accentuates the individualist nature of the American spirit. It is much bolder than the Italian version and seems a lamination of the different energies that color our country. Musically it reminds me of John Cage, Steve Reich, and Cecil Taylor—often discordant, but with an underlying structure that is always on the move. The language may have something to do with the edginess. Monday, Tuesday, etc. create a linear American English that is industrious and bold, but lack the elasticity, flexibility, and subtlety of spoken Italian.

Since the Italian voices were all recorded at the same time and in the same place, there seems to be a consistent flow, repetition, and harmony in the sound. It's more about a communal voice—like church choirs or an operatic chorus. It's a bit more civilized than the English version—like the Italian custom of lingering over meals rather than the American breakfast standing up, lunch at the wheel, dinner in front of the TV sensibility. I don't know why I get this hit. I think of spoken Italian as more musical with a more volumetric expression than English. Perhaps having recorded the voices all at once in one place created a more harmonious texture where each voice stretched and sprung back in the same way???

I think that by using a simple vehicle—voices speaking the days of the week—you have woven an extremely complex tapestry of sound that reflects the persona of each particular culture. It's also really important that whoever enters *Days* has the option to listen to individual voices. You have provided us with that space. Yet I think the impact from the piece is from the integration of the whole—definitely greater than the sum of its parts.

Needless to say, *Days* is provocative and very fine! Thanks for giving me the opportunity to get a preview. I know there are others things I thought about, but they have vamoosed for now. If you want further input, please let me know.

Take care, Susanna

domenica
lunedì
martedì
mercoledì
giovedì
venerdì
sabato

7/6

domenica
lunedì
martedì
mercoledì
giovedì
venerdì

domenica
lunedì
martedì
mercoledì
giovedì
sabato

domenica
lunedì
martedì
mercoledì
venerdì
sabato

domenica
lunedì
martedì
giovedì
venerdì
sabato

domenica
lunedì
mercoledì
giovedì
venerdì

sabato

domenica
martedì
mercoledì
giovedì
venerdì
sabato

lunedì
martedì
mercoledì
giovedì
venerdì
sabato

7/5

domenica
lunedì
martedì
mercoledì
giovedì

domenica
lunedì
martedì
mercoledì
venerdì

domenica
lunedì
martedì
giovedì
venerdì

domenica
lunedì
mercoledì
giovedì
venerdì

domenica

martedì
mercoledì
giovedì
venerdì

lunedì
martedì
mercoledì
giovedì
venerdì

domenica
lunedì
martedì
mercoledì
sabato

domenica
lunedì
martedì
giovedì
sabato

domenica
lunedì
mercoledì
giovedì
sabato

domenica
martedì
mercoledì
giovedì
sabato

lunedì
martedì
mercoledì
giovedì
sabato

domenica
lunedì

martedì
venerdì
sabato

domenica
lunedì
mercoledì
venerdì
sabato

domenica
martedì
mercoledì
venerdì
sabato

lunedì
martedì
mercoledì
venerdì
sabato

domenica
lunedì
giovedì
venerdì
sabato

domenica
martedì
giovedì
venerdì
sabato

lunedì
martedì
giovedì
venerdì
sabato

domenica
mercoledì
giovedì

venerdì
sabato

lunedì
mercoledì
giovedì
venerdì
sabato

domenica
lunedì
martedì
mercoledì
giovedì

7/4

martedì
mercoledì
giovedì
venerdì

lunedì
mercoledì
giovedì
venerdì

lunedì
martedì
giovedì
venerdì

lunedì
martedì
mercoledì
venerdì

lunedì
martedì
mercoledì
giovedì

martedì

mercoledì
giovedì
sabato

lunedì
mercoledì
giovedì
sabato

lunedì
martedì
giovedì
sabato

lunedì
martedì
mercoledì
venerdì

martedì
mercoledì
venerdì
sabato

lunedì
mercoledì
venerdì
sabato

lunedì
martedì
venerdì
sabato

martedì
giovedì
venerdì
sabato

lunedì
giovedì
venerdì
sabato

mercoledì
giovedì
venerdì
sabato

domenica
mercoledì
giovedì
venerdì

domenica
martedì
giovedì
venerdì

domenica
martedì
mercoledì
venerdì

domenica
martedì
mercoledì
giovedì

domenica
mercoledì
giovedì
sabato

domenica
martedì
giovedì
sabato

domenica
martedì
mercoledì
sabato

domenica
mercoledì
venerdì

sabato

domenica
martedì
venerdì
sabato

domenica
giovedì
venerdì
sabato

domenica
lunedì
giovedì
venerdì

domenica
lunedì
mercoledì
venerdì

domenica
lunedì
mercoledì
giovedì

domenica
lunedì
giovedì
sabato

domenica
lunedì
mercoledì
sabato

domenica
lunedì
venerdì
sabato

domenica

lunedì
martedì
venerdì

domenica
lunedì
martedì
sabato

domenica
lunedì
martedì
mercoledì

domenica
lunedì
martedì
giovedì

7/3

sabato
domenica
lunedì

sabato
domenica
martedì

sabato
domenica
mercoledì

sabato
domenica
giovedì

sabato
domenica
venerdì

venerdì
domenica

lunedì

venerdì
domenica
martedì

venerdì
domenica
mercoledì

venerdì
domenica
giovedì

giovedì
domenica
lunedì

giovedì
domenica
martedì

giovedì
domenica
mercoledì

mercoledì
domenica
lunedì

mercoledì
domenica
martedì

martedì
domenica
lunedì

sabato
lunedì
martedì

sabato

lunedì
mercoledì

sabato
lunedì
giovedì

sabato
lunedì
venerdì

venerdì
lunedì
martedì

venerdì
lunedì
mercoledì

venerdì
lunedì
giovedì

giovedì
lunedì
martedì

giovedì
lunedì
mercoledì

mercoledì
lunedì
martedì

sabato
martedì
mercoledì

sabato
martedì
giovedì

sabato
martedì
venerdì

venerdì
martedì
mercoledì

venerdì
martedì
giovedì

giovedì
martedì
mercoledì

sabato
mercoledì
giovedì

sabato
mercoledì
venerdì

sabato
giovedì
venerdì

venerdì
mercoledì
giovedì

7/2

sabato
venerdì

sabato
giovedì

sabato
mercoledì

sabato
martedì

sabato
lunedì

sabato
domenica

venerdì
giovedì

venerdì
mercoledì

venerdì
martedì

venerdì
lunedì

venerdì
domenica

giovedì
mercoledì

giovedì
martedì

giovedì
lunedì

giovedì
domenica

mercoledì
martedì

mercoledì
lunedì

mercoledì
domenica

martedì
lunedì

martedì
domenica

lunedì
domenica

7/1 – same as 7/7

domenica

lunedì

martedì

mercoledì

giovedì

venerdì

sabato

domenica
lunedì
martedì
mercoledì
giovedì
venerdì
sabato

7/6

domenica
lunedì
martedì
mercoledì
giovedì
venerdì

domenica
lunedì
martedì
mercoledì
giovedì
sabato

domenica
lunedì
martedì
mercoledì
venerdì
sabato

domenica
lunedì
martedì
giovedì
venerdì
sabato

domenica
lunedì
mercoledì
giovedì
venerdì

sabato

domenica
martedì
mercoledì
giovedì
venerdì
sabato

lunedì
martedì
mercoledì
giovedì
venerdì
sabato

7/5

domenica
lunedì
martedì
mercoledì
giovedì

domenica
lunedì
martedì
mercoledì
venerdì

domenica
lunedì
martedì
mercoledì
sabato

domenica
lunedì
martedì
giovedì
venerdì

domenica

lunedì
martedì
giovedì
sabato

domenica
lunedì
martedì
venerdì
sabato

domenica
lunedì
mercoledì
giovedì
venerdì

domenica
lunedì
mercoledì
giovedì
sabato

domenica
lunedì
mercoledì
venerdì
sabato

domenica
lunedì
giovedì
venerdì
sabato

domenica
martedì
mercoledì
giovedì
venerdì

domenica
martedì

mercoledì
giovedì
sabato

domenica
martedì
mercoledì
venerdì
sabato

domenica
martedì
giovedì
venerdì
sabato

domenica
mercoledì
giovedì
venerdì
sabato

lunedì
martedì
mercoledì
giovedì
venerdì

lunedì
martedì
mercoledì
giovedì
sabato

lunedì
martedì
mercoledì
venerdì
sabato

lunedì
martedì
giovedì

venerdì
sabato

lunedì
mercoledì
giovedì
venerdì
sabato

martedì
mercoledì
giovedì
venerdì
sabato

7/4

domenica
lunedì
martedì
mercoledì

domenica
lunedì
martedì
giovedì

domenica
lunedì
martedì
venerdì

domenica
lunedì
martedì
sabato

domenica
lunedì
mercoledì
giovedì

domenica

lunedì
mercoledì
venerdì

domenica
lunedì
mercoledì
sabato

domenica
lunedì
giovedì
venerdì

domenica
lunedì
giovedì
sabato

domenica
lunedì
venerdì
sabato

domenica
martedì
mercoledì
giovedì

domenica
martedì
mercoledì
venerdì

domenica
martedì
mercoledì
sabato

domenica
martedì
giovedì
venerdì

domenica
martedì
giovedì
sabato

domenica
martedì
venerdì
sabato

domenica
mercoledì
giovedì
venerdì

domenica
mercoledì
giovedì
sabato

domenica
mercoledì
venerdì
sabato

domenica
giovedì
venerdì
sabato

lunedì
martedì
mercoledì
giovedì

lunedì
martedì
mercoledì
venerdì

lunedì
martedì
mercoledì

sabato

lunedì
martedì
giovedì
venerdì

lunedì
martedì
giovedì
sabato

lunedì
martedì
venerdì
sabato

lunedì
mercoledì
giovedì
venerdì

lunedì
mercoledì
giovedì
sabato

lunedì
mercoledì
venerdì
sabato

lunedì
giovedì
venerdì
sabato

martedì
mercoledì
giovedì
venerdì

martedì

mercoledì
giovedì
sabato

martedì
mercoledì
venerdì
sabato

martedì
giovedì
venerdì
sabato

mercoledì
giovedì
venerdì
sabato

7/3

domenica
lunedì
martedì

domenica
lunedì
mercoledì

domenica
lunedì
giovedì

domenica
lunedì
venerdì

domenica
lunedì
sabato

domenica
martedì

mercoledì

domenica
martedì
giovedì

domenica
martedì
venerdì

domenica
martedì
sabato

domenica
mercoledì
giovedì

domenica
mercoledì
venerdì

domenica
mercoledì
sabato

domenica
giovedì
venerdì

domenica
giovedì
sabato

domenica
venerdì
sabato

lunedì
martedì
mercoledì

lunedì

martedì
giovedì

lunedì
martedì
venerdì

lunedì
martedì
sabato

lunedì
mercoledì
giovedì

lunedì
mercoledì
venerdì

lunedì
mercoledì
sabato

lunedì
giovedì
venerdì

lunedì
giovedì
sabato

lunedì
venerdì
sabato

martedì
mercoledì
giovedì

martedì
mercoledì
venerdì

martedì
mercoledì
sabato

martedì
giovedì
venerdì

martedì
giovedì
sabato

martedì
venerdì
sabato

mercoledì
giovedì
venerdì

mercoledì
giovedì
sabato

mercoledì
venerdì
sabato

giovedì
venerdì
sabato

7/2

domenica
lunedì

domenica
martedì

domenica
mercoledì

domenica
giovedì

domenica
venerdì

domenica
sabato

lunedì
martedì

lunedì
mercoledì

lunedì
giovedì

lunedì
venerdì

lunedì
sabato

martedì
mercoledì

martedì
giovedì

martedì
venerdì

martedì
sabato

mercoledì
giovedì

mercoledì
venerdì

mercoledì
sabato

giovedì
venerdì

giovedì
sabato

venerdì
sabato

one a time
domenica

lunedì

martedì

mercoledì

giovedì

venerdì

sabato

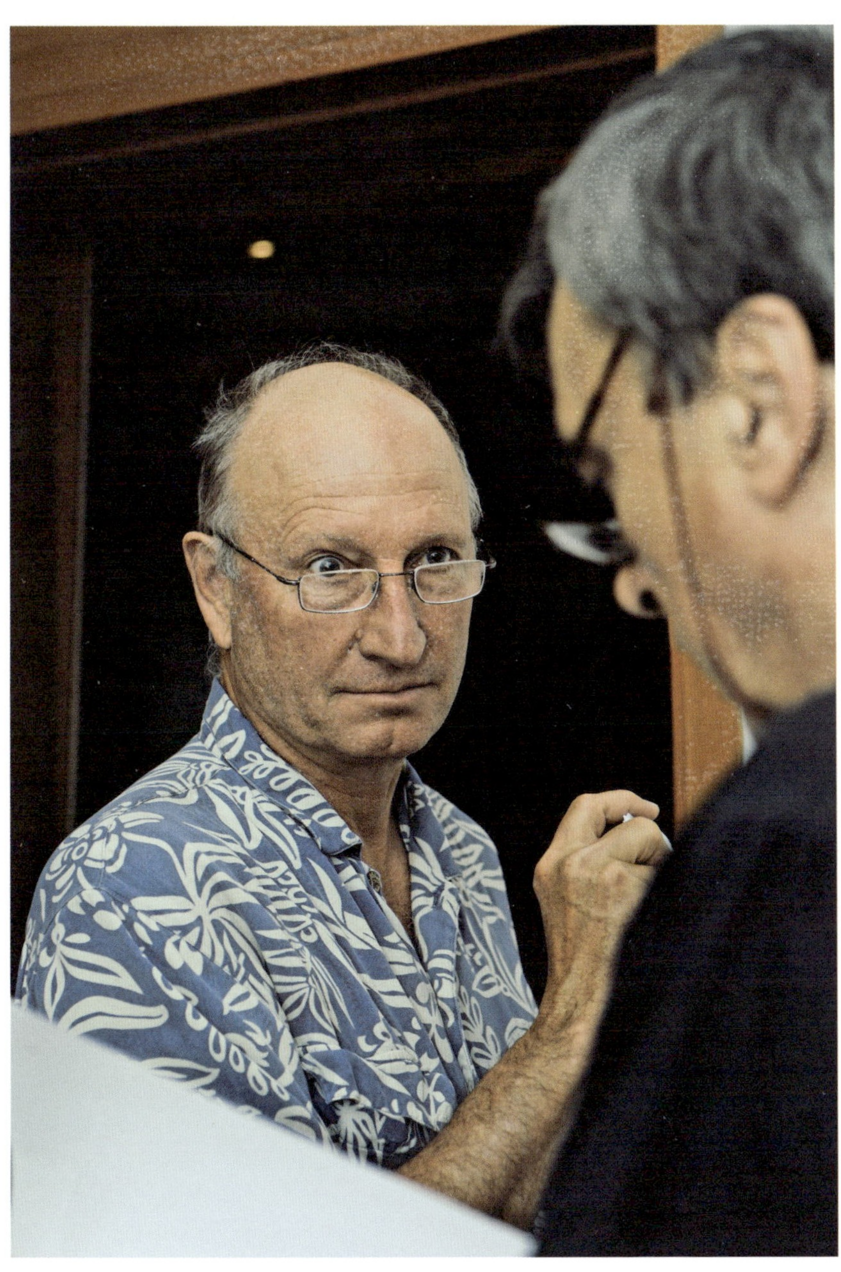

Bruce Nauman and Marco De Michelis review the scripts for *Giorni* at the Waterland Music Studio, Venice, on June 13, 2008.

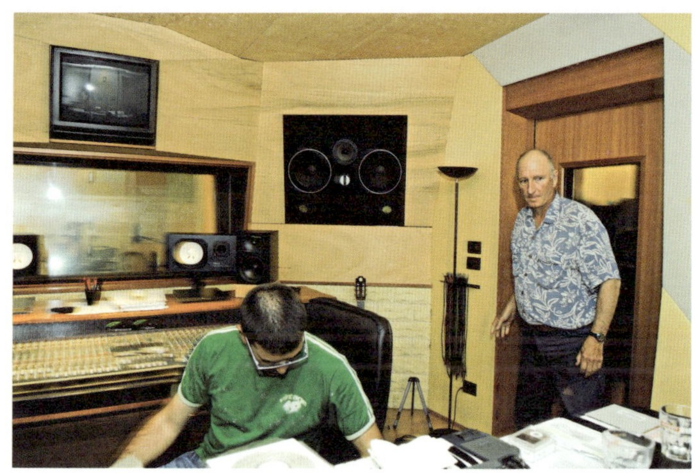

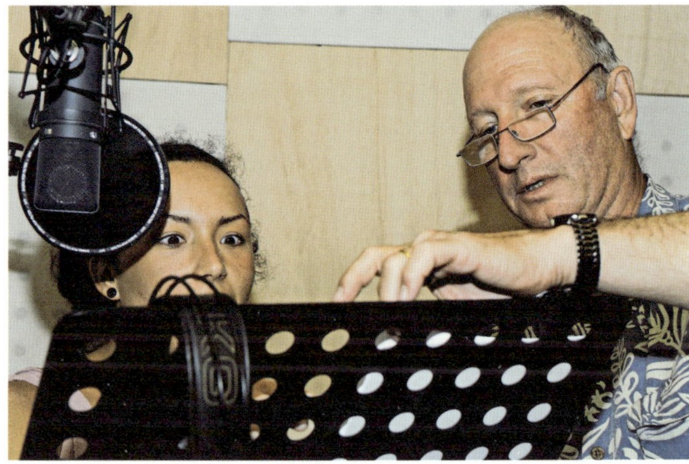

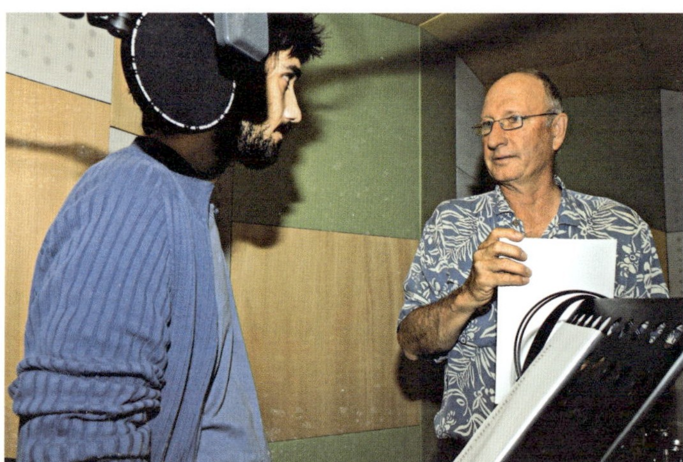

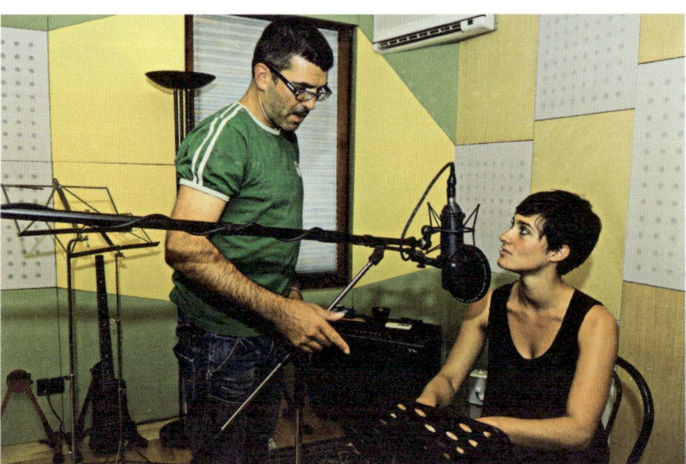

Bruce Nauman and Cristiano Verardo, owner of Waterland Music Studio, prepare to record *Giorni* in Venice on June 13, 2008.

Bruce Nauman and Michele Graglia discuss the recording of *Giorni* at Waterland Music Studio, Venice, on June 13, 2008.

Bruce Nauman and Valentina Barboni discuss the recording of *Giorni* at Waterland Music Studio, Venice, on June 13, 2008.

Cristiano Verardo discusses the recording setup with Claudia Di Lecce on June 13, 2008.

Exhibition Checklist by Site

U.S. Pavilion at the Giardini della Biennale

1
Coffee Spilled and Balloon Dog
1993
Two color video monitors, two video disc players, and two video discs (color, sound)
Dimensions variable
Staatliche Museen zu Berlin, Nationalgalerie, Sammlung Marx
Plate 2

2
Double Poke in the Eye II
1985
Neon tubing on aluminum monolith
24 x 36 x 9 1/4 inches (61 x 91.4 x 23.5 cm)
Artist's proof F of 8 (A-H), edition of 40
CIAC: Colección Isabel y Agustín Coppel
Plate 4

3
Eating Buggers (Version II)
1985
Blue, white, and yellow neon on white metal box
24 1/8 x 36 x 9 1/4 inches (61.3 x 91.4 x 23.5 cm)
Private collection. Courtesy Hauser & Wirth, Zurich and London
Plate 5

4
Fifteen Pairs of Hands
1996
Fifteen white bronze sculptures on painted steel bases
Dimensions variable
Artist's proof
Courtesy the artist and Sperone Westwater, New York
Plate 7

5
Five Pink Heads in the Corner
1992
Epoxy resin and fiberglass
50 x 8 1/2 x 7 1/2 inches (127 x 21.5 x 19 cm)
Friedrich Christian Flick Collection
Plate 8

6
Four Pairs of Heads (Wax)
1991
Wax, resin, rebar, and wire
Dimensions variable
Courtesy the artist
Plate 10

7
From Hand to Mouth
1967
Wax over cloth
28 x 10 1/8 x 4 inches (71.1 x 25.7 x 10.2 cm)
Hirshhorn Museum and Sculpture Garden, Smithsonian Institution, Washington, D.C. Joseph H. Hirshhorn Purchase Fund, Holenia Purchase Fund, in memory of Joseph H. Hirshhorn, and Museum Purchase, 1993. HMSG93.6
Plate 11

8
Hanging Carousel (George Skins a Fox)
1988
Color video installation with steel and polyurethane foam
Diameter 204 inches (518.2 cm); suspended 74 1/2 inches (189.2 cm) above the floor
Museum of Contemporary Art, Chicago. Gerald S. Elliott Collection, 1995.76
Exhibition copy
Plate 12

9
Hanging Head for Leo
1990
Bronze and wire
11 x 9 x 7 inches (27.9 x 22.9 x 17.8 cm)
Collection Rachel and Jean-Pierre Lehmann
Plate 13

10
Three Heads Fountain (Juliet, Andrew, Rinde)
2005
Epoxy resin and fiberglass, wire, clear hoses, immersible pump, rubber-lined basin, water
10 x 21 x 21 inches (25.4 x 53.3 x 53.3 cm)
Private collection, Madrid. Courtesy Donald Young Gallery, Chicago
Plate 21 (left)

11
Three Heads Fountain (Three Andrews)
2005
Epoxy resin and fiberglass, wire, clear hoses, immersible pump, rubber-lined basin, water
10 x 21 x 21 inches (25.4 x 53.3 x 53.3 cm)
François Pinault Foundation
Plate 21 (right)

12
The True Artist Helps the World by Revealing Mystic Truths (Window or Wall Sign)
1967
Neon
59 x 55 x 2 inches (149.9 x 139.7 x 5.1 cm)
Philadelphia Museum of Art. Purchased with the generous support of The Annenberg Fund for Major Acquisitions, the Henry P. McIlhenny Fund, the bequest (by exchange) of Henrietta Meyers Miller, the gift (by exchange) of Philip L. Goodwin, and funds contributed by Edna Andrade, 2007-44-1
Exhibition copy
Plate 22

13
Untitled (The True Artist Is an Amazing Luminous Fountain)
1968
Cast aluminum
Letters 8 inches (20.3 cm) in height, variable widths
Courtesy the artist
Exhibition copy
Plate 26

14
Vices and Virtues
1983–88
Neon and clear glass tubing mounted on aluminum support grid
Letters 84 inches (213.4 cm) in height, variable widths
Stuart Collection at the University of California, San Diego
Exhibition copy
Plate 27

15
Washing Hands Normal
1996
Dual-channel video (color, sound)
ARTIST ROOMS: Tate and National Galleries of Scotland. Acquired jointly through the d'Offay Donation with assistance from the National Heritage Memorial Fund and The Art Fund, 2008
Plate 28

Università Iuav di Venezia at Tolentini

16
Days
2009
Audio (fourteen channels)
Continuous play
One audio source consisting of seven stereo audio files, fourteen speakers, two amplifiers, and additional equipment
Dimensions variable
Courtesy Sperone Westwater, New York

17
End of the World
1996
Video and sound with three laser discs, three laser disc players, three video projectors, three amplifiers, and six speakers
Dimensions variable
Emanuel Hoffmann Foundation, permanent loan to the Öffentliche Kunstsammlung Basel
Plate 6

18
Pink and Yellow Light Corridor (Variable Lights)
1972
Pink and yellow fluorescent lights
Dimensions variable
Solomon R. Guggenheim Museum, New York. Panza Collection, 1991. 91.3828
Plate 17

19
Think
1993
Two color video monitors, two laser disc players (color, sound), and metal table
Dimensions variable
The Museum of Modern Art, New York. Gift of Werner and Elaine Dannheisser, 1996
Plate 20

20
Get Out of My Mind, Get Out of This Room
1968
Audio (stereo sound)
6 minutes, continuous play
One audio source consisting of one audio file, one stereo amplifier, two hidden speakers, and ten-watt clear incandescent light bulb mounted at center of ceiling
Room dimensions: 9 x 12 x 12 feet (2.7 x 3.7 x 3.7 m)
(One of five audio tracks from *Studio Aids II,* 1968)
Collection Jack and Nell Wendler, London. Courtesy Sperone Westwater, New York

21
Studio Aids II
1967–68
Audio (stereo sound), continuous play
One audio source consisting of four audio files of varying duration: *Violin Tuned D.E.A.D.*; *Rolling on the Studio Floor*; *Jumping*; *Walking in the Studio*
Stereo amplifiers and speakers
(Fifth audio track, *Get Out of My Mind, Get Out of This Room,* shown separately)
Dimensions variable
Collection Jack and Nell Wendler, London. Courtesy Sperone Westwater, New York

Exhibition Spaces at Università Ca' Foscari

22
Audio Video Piece for London, Ontario
1969–70
Video camera, oscillating mount, video monitor, CD player, amplifier, and audio CD, repeating continuously
Dimensions variable
Collection Donald Young, Chicago
Plate 1

23
Double Steel Cage Piece
1974
Steel
81 1/16 x 154 5/16 x 204 3/4 inches (206 x 392 x 520 cm)
Museum Boijmans Van Beuningen, Rotterdam. Purchase 1980
Plate 3

24
Flayed Earth Flayed Self (Skin Sink)
1973
Tape and text
Dimensions variable
Friedrich Christian Flick Collection
Plate 9

25
Giorni
2009
Audio (fourteen channels)
14 minutes, 28 seconds; continuous play
One audio source consisting of one audio file, fourteen speakers, two amplifiers, and additional equipment
Dimensions variable
Courtesy Sperone Westwater, New York

26
Human Sexual Experience
1985
Neon tubing on aluminum monolith
17 x 23 x 9 1/2 inches (43.2 x 58.4 x 24.1 cm)
Marc and Livia Straus Family Collection
Exhibition copy
Plate 14

27
My Name As Though It Were Written on the Surface of the Moon
1968
Neon tubing with clear glass tubing suspension frame
11 x 204 x 2 inches (27.9 x 518.2 x 5.1 cm)
Exhibition copy (2005), produced with permission of the artist and the Stedelijk Museum, Amsterdam. The original (1968) is in the collection of the Stedelijk Museum, Amsterdam
Plate 15

28
None Sing Neon Sign
1970
Ruby-red and cool-white neon
13 x 24 1/4 x 1 1/2 inches (33 x 61.6 x 3.8 cm) overall
Solomon R. Guggenheim Museum, New York. Panza Collection, 1991. 91.3825
Plate 16

29
Smoke Rings (Model for Underground Tunnels)
1979–80
Assemblage comprised of two sculptures: the first of eight parts of white plaster, the second of eight parts of green plaster, both resting on wooden mounts
Diameter 133 7/8 inches (340 cm) each assemblage
Centre Georges Pompidou, National Museum of Modern Art – Center for Industrial Creation, Paris. Purchased 1985. AM1985-140
Plate 18

30
Sound for Mapping the Studio Model (The Video)
2001
Single-channel video (color, sound), 1 hour, 1 minute, 20 seconds
Edition 3 of 6
CIAC: Colección Isabel y Agustín Coppel
Plate 19

31
Untitled (#358)
1986
Foamcore, cardboard, wood, rope, and paint
55 1/8 x 68 7/8 x 76 3/4 inches (140 x 175 x 195 cm)
Collection Dorothee and Konrad Fischer
Plate 23

32
Untitled
1970/2009
Video (color, stereo sound), continuous play
One video source, one video projector, one stereo amplifier, two stereo speakers, one video monitor, 15 x 15 foot (4.6 x 4.6 m) rubber mat, tape
Dimensions variable
Courtesy Sperone Westwater, New York
Plate 24

33
Untitled (Hand Circle)
1996
Phosphorus-patinated bronze with wire
Edition 3 of 9
Height 4 3/4 inches (12.1 cm); diameter 27 inches (68.6 cm)
Indianapolis Museum of Art. Henry F. and Katherine DeBoest Memorial Fund and Mr. and Mrs. Richard Crane Fund, 1996.248
Plate 25

Bruce Nauman: A Brief History

Bruce Nauman was born in 1941 in Fort Wayne, Indiana. During his undergraduate schooling at the University of Wisconsin–Madison, Nauman initially studied mathematics and physics before changing his focus to studio art under the tutelage of Italo Scanga, among others. Nauman then pursued an M.F.A. at the University of California, Davis, where faculty artists such as William T. Wiley, Robert Arneson, and Wayne Thiebaud supported his growing desire to investigate art making beyond his earlier abstract paintings. There he experimented with casting objects in fiberglass and polyester resin, leaving their surfaces unrefined to reflect the casting process. While at Davis, Nauman also staged his first two performances, one utilizing a fluorescent tube as an extension of his body as he performed mundane actions, which he would later record on video.

After graduate school, Nauman occupied a storefront studio in San Francisco, where he focused on the act and process of making art by photographing visual puns and daily actions. An old neon beer sign in this former grocery store served as inspiration for Nauman's celebrated neon, *The True Artist Helps the World by Revealing Mystic Truths (Window or Wall Sign)*. At once genuine and ironic, this statement initiated a tongue-in-cheek discourse concerning the role of the artist in society that persists through much of Nauman's work. The Philadelphia Museum of Art recently acquired this iconic work from 1967 for its permanent collection. Nauman later moved to Wiley's studio in Mill Valley, California, where he made various films of himself walking around the space while altering his bodily movement. He began to garner critical attention in 1966 with his first solo show at the Nicholas Wilder Gallery in Los Angeles, as well as his inclusion in Lucy R. Lippard's *Eccentric Abstraction* group exhibition in New York. Nauman's solo debut in New York at the Leo Castelli Gallery in 1968 was soon followed by a one-man exhibition at the Konrad Fischer Galerie in Düsseldorf. In 1972–73, the Los Angeles County Museum of Art and the Whitney Museum of American Art co-organized the first major survey of his work, *Bruce Nauman: Works from 1965–1972*, an exhibition that traveled to Italy, Switzerland, Germany, the Netherlands, and other venues within the United States.

Influenced early on by philosophy and literature—such as Ludwig Wittgenstein's *Philosophical Investigations* and Samuel Beckett's *Molloy*—Nauman's practice constantly tests rational systems of language, spatial and bodily boundaries, duration, and psychology through sculpture, video installations, and constructed environments. In the late 1960s, Nauman continued to work with neon and also began to construct corridors, sometimes filming his performances within them. Larger constructed environments in the early 1970s often included video surveillance cameras and monitors that overlooked and recorded viewers as they entered them. Nauman continued to make large sculptures and installations in the 1970s and early 1980s, mapping space with masking tape or evoking physical or psychological constraints through the creation of passages and tunnels. For a ten-year period during this time Nauman halted his work with video, an art form he would take up again in the mid-1980s with many multi-channel video installations that further explored language and his metaphorical use of labyrinths and the personae of rats and clowns. In the late 1980s he also introduced the iconography of life-sized animals cast in wax that hang suspended in carousel-like formations. The 1990s brought sculptures of human heads and hands in wax and bronze, video installations, and sustained work with neon. In the early twenty-first century, Nauman's video work, sound installations, and sculptures continue themes that have resurfaced throughout his oeuvre since the 1960s.

Museum exhibitions have continued to map Nauman's practice, and notable solo shows include *Bruce Nauman, 1972–1981*, held at the Rijksmuseum Kröller-Müller, Otterlo, in the Netherlands and at the Staatliche Kunsthalle, Baden-Baden, in West Germany in 1981; a survey organized by the Walker Art Center, Minneapolis, that traveled in 1993–95 to Madrid, Los Angeles, Washington, D.C., and New York; and, in 2006–7, an exhibition of his early work, *A Rose Has No Teeth*, that traveled to the University of California, Berkeley Art Museum, Castello di Rivoli Museo d'Arte Contemporanea in Turin, Italy, and the Menil Collection in Houston. Among the prestigious group shows that have included Nauman are the Venice Biennale in 1978, 1980, 1999, and 2007, as well as several Documenta exhibitions (1972, 1977, 1982, and 1992). Garnering multiple awards throughout his career for his exceptionally wide-ranging and conceptually challenging practice, Nauman has received the Wexner Prize in 1994, the Leone d'oro (The Golden Lion) along with Louise Bourgeois at the 48th Venice Biennale in 1999, and the Praemium Imperiale for Visual Arts in 2004 in Japan. He holds honorary Doctor of Fine Arts degrees from the San Francisco Art Institute and the California Institute of the Arts. In 1979, Nauman moved to New Mexico where he continues to work and live along with his wife, the painter Susan Rothenberg.

Traduzione italiana
Elena Cimenti

Una chiave di lettura per la comprensione delle sequenze

Bruce Nauman: Topological Gardens propone tre punti di partenza, o "sequenze", per accedere e sperimentare i quarant'anni dell'opera di Bruce Nauman: Teste e Mani; Suono e Spazio; Fontane e Neon. Tali sequenze sono ampiamente discusse nei saggi di Carlos Basualdo e di Erica F. Battle, contenuti in questo catalogo. Dal momento che tali ricorrenti sequenze si possono ritrovare in molti lavori artistici di Nauman, la lista delle opere in mostra punta verso una selezione più ampia possibile di opere che ininterrottamente hanno fatto parte del nostro processo di pensiero. Con l'intento di presentare in modo chiaro al lettore tali categorie sperimentali, che non hanno né un ordine né una gerarchia, abbiamo deciso di assegnare un colore-codice a tutte le immagini delle opere di Nauman, sia facenti parte della mostra sia presenti nel catalogo. Si noti che, potenzialmente, potrebbero essere sviluppate altre sequenze durante l'interpretazione dell'opera di Nauman e che tali principi organizzativi non dovrebbero essere considerati esclusivi o esaurienti, ma strategicamente utili per gli scopi di questa mostra.

- Teste e Mani
- Suono e Spazio
- Fontane e Neon

Sedi espositive

Comprendendo tre sedi espositive (Padiglione degli Stati Uniti d'America ai Giardini della Biennale, Università Iuav di Venezia ai Tolentini e Ca' Foscari Esposizioni dell'Università Ca' Foscari), *Bruce Nauman: Topological Gardens* richiede ai visitatori di attraversare Venezia, facendo divenire il tessuto urbano parte integrante del loro sperimentare la mostra e l'opera di Bruce Nauman. Le icone che compaiono affianco alle didascalie nella sezione dedicata alle tavole all'interno del presente catalogo, indicano la locazione dei diversi lavori dell'artista nelle differenti sedi che li ospitano.

- Padiglione degli Stati Uniti d'America ai Giardini della Biennale
- Università Iuav di Venezia ai Tolentini
- Ca' Foscari Esposizioni dell'Università Ca' Foscari

Bruce Nauman: Topological Gardens

Carlos Basualdo

Non capisco nulla di questa "città", dove tutto viaggia tranne i piccioni.

Marcel Duchamp, cartolina a Jacques Doucet, Venezia, 23 maggio 1926

1. Dita e buchi

Venezia sembra obsoleta e, almeno in termini di struttura urbana, l'impressione non è del tutto sbagliata. La mappa topografica della città tracciata da Bernardo e Gaetano Combatti nel 1847, e aggiornata otto anni più tardi, mostra poche differenze significative con la mappa attuale (fig. 1). Nel secolo e mezzo che ha visto le capitali europee espandersi clamorosamente in dimensioni e numero degli abitanti, Venezia è rimasta quasi identica dal punto di vista fisico, mentre la sua popolazione in realtà è diminuita. Oggi il viaggiatore ritorna in città con la stessa sicurezza di un amante che va a rileggere le vecchie lettere nascoste in un baule. Non solo ponti, chiese e *campi* saranno ancora lì, ma probabilmente anche la macelleria, la libreria nascosta, la gelateria. È una città che non si incontra ma si riscopre all'infinito, e persino la sensazione di perdersi nei suoi stretti passaggi e gli scorci incredibilmente belli, eppure penosamente indistinguibili, diventano un sogno ad occhi aperti, una parte attesa dell'esperienza della visita. Lo stesso visitatore che reagisce con eccitazione al continuo cambiamento dei paesaggi di Mexico City o di New York, arriva ad aborrire qualsiasi modifica della laguna. Venezia dovrebbe rimanere com'è, a infondata garanzia di una nostra improbabile immutabilità. Se dovesse cambiare, potremmo perdere la memoria.

Prima che Venezia avesse una memoria, tuttavia, il suo paesaggio era caotico quanto può esserlo una vita che inizia. La tradizione sostiene che la prima fondazione della città avvenne sull'isola di Rivoaltus (Rialto) nel 421 d.C., grazie ai cittadini della vicina Padova in fuga dall'esercito di Attila. La mappa più antica tuttora esistente della città, una proiezione ortografica di Paolino da Venezia che risale al 1346 e appare nella *Chronologia Magna*, un manoscritto miniato trecentesco, rivela un territorio informe e frammentato, che fa pensare all'espressione ansiosa sul volto di un sommozzatore che emerge dall'acqua boccheggiando (fig. 2). Il Canal Grande è chiaramente visibile, come anche il Canale della Giudecca, ma la città resta un insieme disordinato di appezzamenti di terra, privo di struttura. Fin dalla tuttora incredibile veduta dall'alto, miracolosamente disegnata da Jacopo de' Barbari nel 1500, e prima pianta della città ad essere stampata, siamo cresciuti con l'abitudine ad immaginare una Venezia inclinata, appoggiata con grazia su un fianco (fig. 3). La città viene letta da ovest a est, e da sinistra a destra, come una pagina intessuta in modo fantastico. La più antica *Chronologia Magna*, tuttavia, la rappresenta invece eretta, rovesciata, l'est che punta al sommo della pagina, l'ovest al fondo, forse orientata in modo da permettere ai suoi governanti di immaginare che la geografia sia un segno del destino e che il loro ducato potrà prevalere sul proprio passato e avanzare verso il centro dell'Europa. Sembra che la terra esitante sia meno importante per il cartografo delle strisce ondulate, più scure, che indicano le vie d'acqua tra Venezia e la terraferma, quest'ultima rappresentata sulla sezione superiore della mappa, occupata, tra l'altro, anche da due colonne di testo. L'acqua definisce la terra, quasi a offrire insieme forma e nutrimento. Invece di ritrarre una città inerte, ideale, la mappa parla degli infiniti negoziati tra rive e maree che costituiscono la vera sostanza di Venezia, in cui nulla è mai rimasto immobile. Venezia sembra ergersi come un idolo di fango, circondato dalle diramazioni acquatiche di un albero in espansione, i frammenti che aderiscono alle radici esitanti, pronte a perdere o guadagnare un lembo di terra. E in realtà, nei trecento anni successivi la città continuerà a intrecciare una danza di avido desiderio nel fluido abbraccio della laguna, acquisendo territorio e solidità, muovendosi senza sosta verso la sua struttura attuale.

La Venezia instabile, impantanata nei suoi ormeggi, esiste ancora oggi. Non è evidente, elude l'osservazione superficiale, ma si può nonostante tutto percepire, e coloro che si trovano a camminare lungo le strade della città senza l'aiuto di mappe o della tranquillizzante regolarità dei vaporetti, sono destinati a scoprirlo: andare da un luogo all'altro si dimostra sempre più difficile del previsto, persino più difficile di ieri o della notte scorsa. Come un sipario di velluto, la città tiene chiusi i propri lembi con zelo lento e indifferente, e poi, all'improvviso, li apre in fretta. La distanza tra i luoghi è determinata dall'umore di chi cammina, più che da una qualsiasi unità di misura oggettiva avulsa dalle circostanze e dagli eventi fortuiti che si verificano lungo il percorso. Nella mente, la città si espande e si contrae costantemente, come una mano avida che si stringe per afferrare, o un corpo disteso che reagisce con fremiti percettibili al tocco fuggevole delle correnti d'acqua sotterranee. Camminiamo guidati dalle maree e dai fiumi che percepiamo scorrere sotto terra, ma la loro direzione continua a cambiare e lo stesso fanno i nostri passi, per cui ci perdiamo in una moltitudine di pensieri, vedute e impressioni mutevoli, finché ci avviciniamo ad una destinazione inaspettata che nondimeno riconosciamo come fosse intenzionale, semplicemente perché si trova lì, in attesa del nostro arrivo. Ne deduciamo, dunque, che la città non è l'ampia rete di meraviglie ritratta dalla maggior parte delle raffigurazioni, ma un traguardo in movimento su cui proiettiamo incessantemente le nostre emozioni, la mutevole esperienza di noi stessi.

***

Molti dizionari definiscono il termine topologia aridamente, come branca della matematica che studia le caratteristiche qualitative dello spazio. La topologia non si occupa di misure o distanze, ma della *struttura* dello spazio, e del modo in cui lo spazio funziona. La *Encyclopædia Britannica* la definisce come lo studio matematico delle proprietà di un oggetto geometrico che non cambia a seguito di deformazioni causate da torsioni, allungamenti o compressioni, ma non da rotture. Una sfera è topologicamente equivalente a un cubo della stessa dimensione relativa, perchè se fossero fatti, ad esempio, di creta modellabile, ognuno dei due potrebbe essere deformato nell'altro senza essere rotto. Una sfera, invece, non è equivalente a una ciambella, perché per inserire il buco si dovrebbe romperla. I concetti e i metodi topologici stanno alla base di gran parte della matematica moderna, e l'approccio topologico ha chiarito importanti concetti strutturali in molte delle sue branche. Si dice generalmente che un esperto di topologia non sa distinguere una tazza di caffè da una ciambella, dato che una può essere trasformata nell'altra con una semplice deformazione. La struttura urbana di Venezia, ad esempio, si potrebbe capire meglio servendosi della topologia più che di una mappa, dato che il linguaggio rappresentativo di quest'ultima è limitato al linguaggio astratto e semplificato della bidimensionalità. Una veduta aerea di Venezia come quella di de' Barbari, che mette in risalto la morfologia del tessuto urbano, può essere definita topologica rispetto a una proiezione ortografica, in cui le forme degli edifici e le relazioni tra parti diverse della città vengono sacrificate per rispettare misure e dimensioni. È interessante notare che, dopo la prima suggestiva mappa di Paolino, siano dovute passare intere generazioni prima che le proiezioni ortografiche di Venezia divenissero la norma, sostituendo poco alla volta, a partire dall'affermarsi dell'Illuminismo, le vedute aeree. Venezia sembra richiedere una topologia emozionale più che una mappa, una topologia che può corrispondere all'opera di un artista.

Come scrive Joan Simon nel breve ma esaustivo saggio pubblicato a proposito di *Fingers and Holes*, le stampe che Bruce Nauman produce nel 1994, il tema delle mani ricorre nella produzione dell'artista fin da quando a metà degli anni sessanta lascia intenzionalmente le proprie impronte digitali sulla superficie delle prime sculture in fibra di vetro. In *Fingers and Holes*, una serie di otto stampe, Nauman stabilisce quello che sembra essere un vocabolario di gesti, come se fosse deciso a gettare le basi di un linguaggio segreto, senza parole. Solo ad una immagine si può attribuire un preciso significato sessuale: l'indice e il pollice di una mano formano un cerchio che l'indice dell'altra mano penetra famelicamente (fig. 7). Questa configurazione era già apparsa nel piccolo neon giallo e verde *Human Sexual Experience* del 1985 (plate 14), e la stampa in cui riappare, la più grande della serie, sembra essere stata ottenuta ripetendo in sequenza ininterrotta il disegno originale, seguendo il perimetro di un cerchio immaginario (fig. 5). Due anni dopo, la forma curiosa creata da questa ripetizione viene fusa in bronzo in *Untitled (Hand Circle)* del 1996 (tav. 25). Sei stampe della serie *Fingers and Holes* rappresentano due mani, destra e sinistra, disegnate in modo schematico ma preciso, le cui dita si toccano in varie posizioni (figs. 6–11). In una stampa vediamo, invece, due serie di mani, come a rappresentare due momenti diversi dello stesso gesto (fig. 12). Nauman riferisce a Simon che "All'inizio la serie non era incentrata sui buchi" ma che poi, dopo aver capito "cosa stava succedendo", aveva iniziato a pensare alla topologia, una materia studiata durante i corsi di matematica frequentati inizialmente alla University of Wisconsin a Madison. Casualmente, anche Jasper Johns, altro artista nella cui produzione artistica le mani occupano un ruolo rilevante, almeno a partire dalle serie di stampe *Skin* dei primi anni sessanta, che mappano bidimensionalmente la superficie della sua faccia e delle mani, in molti dipinti si occupa della mappatura concettuale di uno spazio topologico paradossale.

Nauman esplora la presenza scultorea dello spazio vuoto fin dagli inizi della sua carriera artistica. Se *Neon Templates of the Left Half of My Body Taken at Ten-Inch Intervals* del 1966 (fig. 13) è un esempio precoce di questa insistenza, già l'opera dello stesso anno *Platform Made Up of the Space Between Two Rectilinear Boxes on the Floor* mette in evidenza quanto lo spazio vuoto acquisti una chiara manifestazione fisica (fig. 14). In entrambi i casi i titoli sono descrizioni precise del processo implicato nella concezione e nell'esecuzione delle sculture. Solo un anno più tardi, Nauman utilizza la tecnica chiamata *moulage* per prendere il calco in cera verde, porosa e delicata, di una parte del corpo di Judy, all'epoca sua moglie, che risale dall'estremità della mano destra lungo il braccio fino al collo, al mento, e infine alla bocca. Il titolo dell'opera, *From Hand to Mouth* (tav. 11), rende tangibile un modo di dire e così facendo riesce a creare una relazione tra due parti del corpo che continueranno ad essere presenti in tutta la produzione artistica di Nauman, sia astratta che concreta. La misteriosa presenza, in un certo qual modo inquietante, di un frammento staccato dal corpo sembra tuttavia richiamare insistentemente l'attenzione sull'assenza dell'intero. In quest'opera, con maggior forza che in *Neon Templates* o in *Platform Made Up of the Space*, Nauman collega indissolubilmente una presenza frammentaria ad un'assensa in modo tale da creare un continuum che sbroglia i limiti tra un corpo scultoreo e il suo contesto fisico.

Nell'analizzare l'operazione formale in atto nelle stampe *Fingers and Holes*, Simon si serve ulteriormente della topologia suggerendo che un fondamento logico di questo tipo potrebbe essere presente in opere simili di Nauman. Anche Michael Auping nel saggio per il catalogo della mostra *Raw Materials*, tenutasi alla Tate Modern di Londra nel 2005, parla di come Nauman si interessasse alla topologia quando ancora studiava matematica. Nell'analisi di Auping la topologia è funzionale a spiegare il modo in cui Nauman si muove tra diversi mezzi espressivi e discipline nella sua produzione artistica, "rigirando un'idea della forma senza strapparla". Eric de Bruyn, infine, nel suo *Topological Pathways of Post-Minimalism* descrive il modo in cui Dan Graham arriva a servirsi della topologia come modello critico, dopo aver visto una scultura senza titolo in gomma di Nauman degli anni 1965–66, e dopo aver assistito ad una delle prime performance dell'artista, una variazione del video *Bouncing in a Corner* del 1968–69, in occasione della mostra *Anti-Illusion*, tenutasi nel 1969 al Whitney Museum of American Art di New York.

E' possibile rappresentare Venezia formando con la mano destra una U orizzontale, e inserendo la sinistra a pugno in modo da lasciare tra le mani uno spazio sinuoso che evoca le sconcertanti curve del Canal Grande. Simultaneamente, un simile gesto può essere riscontrato in una delle sculture che fa parte dell'opera *Fifteen Pairs of Hands* (1996, fig. 15). La capacità mimetica di un paio di mani sembra esprimere la complesità del luogo in un modo che le mappe non riescono a eguagliare. Solo le prime mappe, in cui il contorno delle isole risulta principalmente dalla demarcazione delle vie d'acqua circostanti (schema che maggiormente stava a cuore ai fruitori originali delle mappe, utile ad identificare i percorsi navigabili in città e nei dintorni), esprimono in modo altrettanto efficace la natura topologica dello spazio urbano. Parlando delle vedute di Venezia dall'alto (nelle quali il punto di vista si trova chiaramente localizzato nel Bacino di San Marco) Egle Trincanato sottolinea l'intenzione dei cartografi di attribuire pari importanza alla città edificata e all'acqua che la circonda, come a dichiarare tacitamente, ma decisamente, che a Venezia non si dovrebbero fare distinzioni tra terra e acqua. Il Canal Grande divide e allo stesso tempo unisce con grazia la terra che si affaccia sulle sue rive. La fluidità di Venezia è fugace come un gesto, e sembra implicare allo stesso modo una promessa di significato che non mantiene. I "buchi" che Nauman infine identifica tra le dita, non come spazio vuoto ma come sostanza autentica di cui si compongono i gesti, corrispondono esattamente, in termini topologici, alla profonda instabilità che ancora articola la nostra attuale esperienza di Venezia. Allo stesso modo in cui Venezia ci fa pensare all'aspetto topologico dell'opera di Nauman, l'esperienza dell'opera di Nauman ci permette di capire la città: sembra che corrispondano inevitabilmente l'una all'altra, come due mani.

2. Giardini topologici

L'estate a Venezia è svogliata, e questo si nota ancor più ai Giardini di Castello, posti quasi all'estremità orientale dell'isola. Qui, negli anni in cui non si svolge la mostra, l'erba cresce liberamente tra le porte e le finestre sbarrate dei padiglioni della Biennale. Nella lunga e tortuosa storia dell'arcipelago, i Giardini Pubblici sono un'addizione recente e spettacolare. Nel 1797 la Repubblica veneziana, già indebolita, soccombe davanti alle truppe di Napoleone. La fine non giunge in seguito a una sanguinosa battaglia, ma è il risultato inverosimile di una votazione, cui seguono le dimissioni dell'ultimo doge, Ludovico Manin, una serie di eventi alquanto vergognosi che sarebbe pesata su quell' importante famiglia veneziana per generazioni. Tra il 1805 e il 1814, Venezia fa ancora parte del crescente impero di Napoleone; è in questo periodo che vengono creati i primi giardini pubblici, uno dei molti difficili cambiamenti che la città e i cittadini si trovano ad affrontare in quell'epoca. L'architetto veneziano Giannantonio Selva, incaricato di disegnare i nuovi giardini nell'ambito dei progetti napoleonici di espansione dell'isola, segue rigidi ideali neoclassici, che mal si adattano ad una città che rimane loro profondamente estranea, sotto qualsiasi aspetto. La veduta panoramica di Venezia di Giorgio Fossati, del 1743, ultimo documento originale che testimonia l'aspetto di Venezia prima della caduta della Repubblica, nello spazio in cui dovevano estendersi i nuovi giardini mostra un gruppo di edifici densamente abitato (fig.16). Tra il 1808 e il 1812, case, chiese e conventi sono rasi al suolo e i canali vengono interrati per fare spazio al parco bucolico, che all'inizio era disposto in lunghi sentieri e aiuole simmetriche.

I veneziani all'inizio trovano poco utili i nuovi giardini pubblici. Al visitatore Venezia sembra una città di pietra, mattoni e malta; pochi alberi sparsi languono qua e là in alcuni dei *campi* più ampi, un dubbio sollievo per cani e bambini, ma certo non sufficiente a modificare il carattere di una città che sembra essere stata creata per negare la natura. Dietro mura e portoni, tuttavia, Venezia dispiega spudoratamente erba e alberi, e rivela una comunione asimmetrica ma intensa proprio con quella natura che la sua fondazione sembra negare. Ampie parti del sestriere di Dorsoduro in realtà sono state utilizzate per secoli come frutteti, come anche l'estremità orientale del sestriere di Castello, proprio dove sarebbero stati creati i giardini pubblici, a fianco di alcune tra le chiese più antiche della città. Considerati dal nostro punto di vista, si può dire che i giardini a Venezia fossero soprattutto "privati": alcuni di essi rimangono silenziosi e segreti ancora oggi, accessibili solamente ai proprietari. Ancor più importante, è il fatto che è difficile imporre i concetti astratti di "pubblico" e "privato" alla struttura urbana ingarbugliata di una città che sembra ignorarli sfacciatamente, come se la distinzione fosse grossolana e volgare. Fin dagli inizi Piazza San Marco ha svolto un ruolo cerimoniale ma anche funzionale, e i molti *campi*, in realtà poli magnetici attorno ai quali si organizza la vita della città, erano e sono fruiti nei modi più complessi e affascinanti, diventando in momenti diversi, o allo stesso tempo, mercati, luoghi d'incontro, palcoscenici, *campi* gioco, estensioni dei salotti nei quali persone di ogni età si incontrano per caso o di proposito. È facile immaginare che questi spazi aperti fossero un tempo ancora più profondamente integrati nella vita sociale degli abitanti della città, le cui vite si svolgevano all'aperto, nelle piazze in cui potevano essere se stessi e allo stesso tempo recitare il proprio ruolo nel più ampio palcoscenico della vita nella Repubblica. Con l'affermarsi del moderno concetto di pubblico e privato arriva anche la rigida suddivisione delle attività quotidiane. I Giardini Pubblici fanno parte di quel progetto, che la struttura urbana di Venezia contraddice: in una città topologica non c'è spazio per isolare le forme dai loro usi possibili.

Il fatto che la città all'inizio non abbia saputo cosa farsene del luogo di svago appena creato, posto poco oltre le passate glorie dell'Arsenale, più vicino delle altre zone della città alle sponde protettive della lunga isola del Lido, può essere un segno della profonda resistenza di Venezia all'organizzazione razionale della vita imposta dalla pesante cappa delle leggi napoleoniche. Solo dopo più di mezzo secolo, nel 1887, in seguito all'Unità d'Italia, quando si cerca un luogo per ospitare la *Esposizione Nazionale Artistica di Venezia*, i giardini trovano finalmente la loro destinazione: esporre. Il successo di tale evento coglie Venezia di sorpresa, e incoraggia la costituzione di una presenza più duratura e stabile a Venezia, la Biennale, inizialmente concepita per attirare visitatori, educare le masse e stimolare un mercato artistico che si muoveva in modo stentato. Nel 1895, Mario de Maria progetta la prima sede della mostra, il Palazzo delle Esposizioni, noto come Padiglione Italia e recentemente ribattezzato con il nome di Palazzo delle Esposizioni. Da allora la Biennale ha raggiunto fama internazionale, si è svolta quasi senza interruzioni ed ha avuto un impatto profondo e duraturo sulla vita della città.

Quando nel 1907 il Belgio costruisce il proprio padiglione nazionale sul territorio dei Giardini, la Biennale non fa che seguire un percorso iniziato nel 1867 a Parigi, quando la *Exposition Universelle* utilizza per la prima volta edifici separati per l'esposizione dei prodotti delle diverse nazioni. Allora, all'apice del colonialismo, la paradossale solidità dei padiglioni temporanei vuole rappresentare il potere dello stato-nazione, e il legame indissolubile tra la sua cultura e la sua identità, concepita soprattutto in termini etnici. Ciascun padiglione costituisce un monumento all'articolazione di corpi, idee, e razza su cui si fonda il moderno concetto di stato-nazione. I Giardini vengono presto costellati di edifici di questo tipo: una mappa dei giardini che risale al 1910 mostra anche il padiglione inglese e quello bavarese, ora padiglione tedesco. Entro il 1932, due anni dopo la costruzione del padiglione degli Stati Uniti, anche Ungheria, Spagna, Olanda, Unione Sovietica, Cecoslovacchia e Danimarca seguono le fila delle nazioni presenti sui terrapieni dove erano sorti gli antichi orti della Serenissima Repubblica. L'aumento dei padiglioni nazionali ai Giardini si può ben evidenziare paragonando le piante topografiche del 1920 e del 1934 pubblicate nel catalogo della Biennale (fig. 17; fig. 18).

***

Nauman ha parlato ripetutamente della propria passione per le cabine telefoniche. Al loro interno, afferma, sei esposto e isolato allo stesso tempo, in uno spazio personale che non ti protegge dall'essere visibile a tutti. In questo collegamento paradossale, che si potrebbe descrivere meglio nel linguaggio della topologia, Nauman trova elementi che danno vita a molte delle sculture, dei video, e delle installazioni di maggior successo, a partire dalle prime sculture create in ceramica, presenti nel catalogo ragionato e datate 1965. Della prima, intitolata *Cup and Saucer Falling Over* (fig. 19) si può forse dire che ricorda *The Horse* (1914; fig. 20) di Raymond Duchamp-Villon, ma l'opera rappresenta anche il tentativo di riprodurre tempo e movimento grazie a un sistema di piani intersecanti che compongono un volume virtuale. *Cup Merging with Its Saucer* (fig. 21) è simile, ma in questo caso il movimento non sembra originato da un'azione esterna; la tazza, invece, si sfalda letteralmente nel piattino, ed entrambi gli oggetti sono stretti in un ampio gesto a spirale. Nel secondo oggetto l'interno della tazza diviene il piattino che la racchiude, nel primo sia la tazza che il piattino si dissolvono nella rappresentazione concreta della loro caduta. Come nella cabina telefonica, la condizione di possibilità che permette l'esperienza soggettiva dell'interno viene paradossalmente determinata dall'esposizione del soggetto. Come nel caso di tazza e piattino, o di dita e buchi, quello che emerge risulta non dalla separazione da ciò che sta all'interno, o da un taglio netto, ma da un dispiegamento, uno srotolamento, una momentanea liberazione che non raggiunge mai stabilità o equilibrio. Come afferma Nauman in un'intervista concessa a Ian Wallace e Russell Keziere nel 1979: "Voglio usare la polarità investigativa che esiste nella tensione tra spazio pubblico e privato, e usarla per creare un margine"; un limitare l'esperienza, si potebbe aggiungere, in cui si vuole che anche i confini tra oggetto e osservatore siano dissolti.

Nauman esplora questa logica topologica in una serie di operazioni, alcune precisamente oblique, altre estremamente letterali. In *Flayed Earth Flayed Skin (Skin Sink)* del 1973 (tav. 9), l'artista lascia che il pubblico occupi il centro che si va metaforicamente "spellando" di una stanza segnata da sei linee radianti di nastro coprente, che partono dal centro del pavimento fino a salire sulle pareti, dividendo lo spazio in sei sezioni uguali. Al centro della stanza l'osservatore isolato trova il centro del proprio corpo, che nell'immaginazione si curva finché la sua superficie è tappezzata sulle pareti rientranti, "stirandosi ed espandendosi" finché la stanza diviene il sé disincarnato. Entrando in *Double Steel Cage Piece* (1974; tav. 3), l'osservatore, ora sedotto a partecipare attivamente all'opera, cammina di lato verso l'interno, il corpo compresso tra due reti d'acciaio che lasciano spazio appena sufficiente a muoversi solo in quella posizione, lontano dall'entrata della gabbia, lungo il perimetro claustrofobico, mentre l'interno vuoto resta inaccessibile ma visualmente a portata di mano. Il nucleo interno e la struttura fisica dell'opera sono rivelati chiaramente, per cui il visitatore può immaginarsi al suo interno, mentre per trovare una via d'uscita dovrà disfare la struttura nella propria mente, erodendo allo stesso tempo la certezza di avere una propria identità distinta.

Un'operazione simile ha luogo nell'opera *Piano Phase,* scritta dal compositore Steve Reich nel 1967: due pianisti ripetono costantemente un certo schema, ma uno accelera gradualmente il ritmo, lentamente, fino a trovarsi a precedere l'altro. Per suonare il pezzo si richiede, nota Reich, un ascolto attento del pezzo, più che la lettura dello spartito musicale. L'esecuzione dell'opera richiede ai musicisti di immergersi profondamente nella sua struttura, ascoltandola e ricordandola mentre suonano. L'opera mette in atto la memoria come condizione vitale della possibilità di agire. L'opera di Nauman insiste ad evocare e distorcere la memoria, che sta alla base del nostro senso dell'io, fondendo esperienza e ambiente in un moto verso la scoperta impermanente di un io topologico.

3. Prospettiva forzata

Nel 1927, Antonio Maraini, scultore italiano, critico d'arte e diplomatico di professione, viene nominato segretario generale della Biennale di Venezia, posizione che ricoprirà per quasi un quarto di secolo. Sotto la guida di Maraini, la Biennale si lega strettamente alla politica culturale dello stato fascista ed ha come sua missione la promozione dell'"Arte Italiana", concepita in modo totalizzante e unificante. Le prime Biennali sono state molto diverse l'uno dall'altra. A pochi anni dall'unificazione, l'Italia era ancora una federazione di regioni abbastanza distinte, con dialetti, storia e cultura proprie; la Biennale, dunque, inizialmente rispecchia queste differenze, assegnando ad ogni regione una sala del Palazzo delle Esposizioni, e consentendo ad ognuna di esporre le proprie caratteristiche di eccellenza a fianco delle altre, in un gesto inteso a migliorare conoscenza e comprensione reciproca. L'approccio fascista è piuttosto l'opposto: le differenze locali sono inglobate sotto il vessillo di un'unica identità nazionale, e la Biennale diviene l'istituzione incaricata ufficialmente di portare a termine questo compito nel campo delle arti visive.

Il palcoscenico di questa trasformazione demiurgica è il Palazzo delle Esposizioni, ribattezzato Padiglione Italia (fig. 22). Le nazioni che all'inizio avevano esposto nell'edificio di fianco alle regioni italiane, ora iniziano il processo migratorio, dalla coesistenza cosmopolita nelle stanze del Palazzo alle casette sparse nel paesaggio bucolico degli ex giardini pubblici. Nel 1927, quando Maraini diventa direttore della Biennale, nei Giardini si trovano solo nove padiglioni nazionali, che entro il 1934 diventano quindici. Mentre il Padiglione Italia diviene il contenitore di una certa idea di ciò che l'arte italiana potrebbe o dovrebbe essere (un significante dell'identità di una penisola forgiata da poco) ai padiglioni nazionali, sotto Maraini, viene richiesto di diventare gli araldi delle rispettive culture e genti, e il compito dell'arte diviene quello di chiarificare e distillare le identità nazionali. Maraini persegue il fine politico attraverso un attento processo di selezione, assegnando solo un ruolo marginale ai Futuristi, ad esempio, e mettendo invece in rilievo una forma di realismo più conservatrice e romantica. Egli, inoltre, rende esplicito il nuovo ruolo del Padiglione Italia modificandone l'aspetto architettonico con una nuova facciata (che il padiglione conserva ancora) e una sequenza semplificata di stanze interne organizzate su un asse narrativo in modo da rendere evidente l'itinerario del visitatore, e sovradeterminare il significato delle opere d'arte esposte (fig. 23). Forse non è una coincidenza, ma sembra esserci una corrispondenza tra l'obiettivo di Maraini di trasformare in un unicum coerente il labirinto di stanze del Palazzo delle Esposizioni, cresciuto in modo caotico nei primi decenni della Biennale, e i piani di Napoleone di trasformare la complessa struttura urbana di Venezia in una città moderna e leggibile. Maraini riesce a raggiungere il proprio presumibile scopo con le ultime due edizioni della Biennale che si svolgono sotto la sua supervisione, nel 1940 e 1942. Il massimo livello di controllo sul contenuto della mostra esposta nel Padiglione Italia, che viene supportato dall'architettura e dall'organizzazione del percorso della mostra in modo che rimanga fortemente impresso nel visitatore, coincide paradossalmente con la disintegrazione del regime politico che rendeva auspicabile tale obiettivo. La coesistenza di politica e arte sotto il tetto della Biennale di Venezia non avrebbe potuto avere un pedigree più dubbio: si tratta dell'eredità diretta del progetto colonialista che nell'Ottocento promuove le esposizioni universali in Inghilterra e in Francia, un lascito che si manifesta nella costruzione del primo padigline nazionale, quello del Belgio, nel momento di massima espansione coloniale del Paese. Sotto Maraini questo contenuto già discutibile viene ulteriormente contaminato dalle tendenze autoritarie di un progetto culturale provatamente fascista, inteso a correggere l'indesiderabile varietà della cultura italiana dopo poco tempo dall'unificazione del Paese. Solo la più cieca determinazione rende possibile immaginare che l'arte possa rappresentare l'identità di una nazione, in quanto massima espressione culturale di uno specifico gruppo etnico.

Nulla può essere più lontano da questo concetto della realtà pluralista e incostante cambiamento che ha sempre caratterizzato il territorio degli Stati Uniti. Il Padiglione degli Stati Uniti viene progettato nel 1929 dagli architetti William Adams Delano e Chester Holmes Aldrich, famosi per i palazzetti e i club neo-georgiani costruiti a New York (fig. 24). I due architetti scelgono un progetto in stile neoclassico, all'epoca quasi la norma negli Stati Uniti per gli edifici a destinazione culturale; l'irregolare edificio neoclassico del Philadelphia Museum of Art, ad esempio, viene costruito più o meno nello stesso periodo. Progettato con tale impronta neoclassica, il Padiglione degli Stati Uniti fa una figura piuttosto bizzarra in compagnia di architetture più innovative, come il padiglione dell'Austria, opera di Josef Hoffmann, del 1934, il padiglione dell'Olanda di Gerrit Rietveld, del 1954, il padiglione del Venezuela di Carlo Scarpa, del 1956, e il bel padiglione della Finlandia, disegnato da Alvar Aalto nel 1956.

Il Padiglione degli Stati Uniti ha ospitato la partecipazione americana alla Biennale quasi ininterrotamente a partire dal 1930, con poche eccezioni, soprattutto per la Biennale del 1942, quando il mondo era in guerra. Solo in un paio di occasioni le mostre degli Stati Uniti si sono estese in città, all'esterno del padiglione. Nel 1964, ad esempio, quando Robert Rauschenberg vince, come tutti sanno, un controverso Gran Premio per la pittura, la mostra che rappresenta gli Stati Uniti, organizzata da Alan Solomon, è in realtà una mostra collettiva composta di due parti, esposta sia all'interno del Padiglione sia all'interno del Consolato degli Stati Uniti, chiuso recentemente, situato nell'edificio adiacente a Palazzo Venier dei Leoni, che ospita la Peggy Guggenheim Collection. Nel 1990, quando per la prima volta gli Stati Uniti vincono il Leone d'Oro con la personale di Jenny Holzer, la mostra del Padiglione viene integrata da proiezioni all'aperto tenute al Lido, nonostante il commissario Michael Auping aveva pensato ad un'occupazione ancor più estesa della città. Crediamo che mai prima del 2009 la mostra degli Stati Uniti sia stata concepita concettualmente e programmaticamente per estendersi oltre i confini fisici e ideologici dei padiglioni nazionali, e stabilire consonanze più profonde tra l'opera dell'artista esposto, il tessuto urbano di Venezia e la struttura sociale, etnica e culturale della nazione che si suppone rappresenti. Esporre opere come quelle di Nauman, artista che ha sistematicamente esplorato ed eroso i confini tra pubblico e privato, in una città in cui questi confini sono stati, e sono ancora, oggetto di trattativa, inequivocabilmente richiede un insolito approccio alla mostra stessa.

4. Vizi e Virtú

Il punto di partenza per la definizione di *Bruce Nauman: Topological Gardens* è stato il chiedersi se una mostra, grazie alla propria struttura, possa aiutare il visitatore a entrare in relazione sia con le opere presentate che con il contesto in cui sono esposte. Nel caso di una mostra che cerca dall'inizio di realizzare il compito impossibile di rappresentare una Nazione, la sfida è riconoscerne in modo produttivo questa impossibilità, integrandola nella logica della mostra. Immaginare che una nazione possa essere rappresentata dall'opera di un unico artista, sia pure un'opera con la complessità dell'arte di Nauman, è difficile quanto immaginare che sia possibile organizzare un'unica mostra che presenti in modo esemplare ed esaustivo la totalità della produzione artistica di Nauman. Una mostra che si può immaginare, tuttavia, è quella la cui struttura le permetta una relazione attiva sia con il soggetto che con il contesto. Cercando di produrre una mostra di tale genere, abbiamo usato il modello della topologia per proporre un modo specifico, legato al contesto, che possa permettere di avvicinarsi all'opera di Nauman, ma anche di interpretare la struttura urbana della città in cui la mostra si svolge. La mostra, permettendo al pubblico di usare la propria esperienza della città per entrare in relazione con l'opera dall'artista e viceversa, si propone di mettere in discussione le basi ideologiche dei padiglioni nazionali che la circondano. La nozione di topologia, quindi, è utilizzata in questo ambito per stabilire connessioni, per curiosare in territori apparentemente separati, in modo che la loro mutua risonanza generi una relazione più intensa tra essi e il pubblico.

Incorporando due sedi esterne ai Giardini e all'edificio di Delano e Aldrich, Il Padiglione degli Stati Uniti immaginato in *Bruce Nauman: Topological Gardens* è legato dal punto di vista estetico, più che da quello territoriale, alla città di Venezia, alla sua storia, ai suoi abitanti e all'uso reale dei suoi spazi. L'interno restaurato di un palazzo gotico sul Canal Grande, che ospitava gli uffici amministrativi dell'Università Ca' Foscari, e il chiostro e l'aula magna, in origine un refettorio, dell'Università Iuav, nell'ex convento adiacente alla chiesa dei Tolentini, sono esempi del palinsesto di spazi pubblici e privati di cui si compone il tessuto di Venezia (fig. 25, 27, 28, 30). In questo senso, la loro presenza come sedi espositive è intesa ad amplificare le contraddizioni tra la creazione dei Giardini nell'Ottocento e il successivo utilizzo come sede di un'esposizione ancora strettamente associata ad un progetto politico ed economico ben definito. Insieme, le tre sedi di *Topological Gardens* compongono una specie di frase che analizza sintatticamente esempi di instabilità strutturale tra pubblico e privato che caratterizza il tessuto urbano di Venezia.

Se le tre sedi della mostra sono chiamate a porsi come manifestazione visibile della natura topologica della struttura urbana di Venezia, le tre sequenze concettuali, intorno alle quali la mostra è stata concepita, vogliono, dunque, fare in modo che il visitatore immagini la logica topologica nell'opera di Nauman. Ancora una volta, ciascuna sequenza è organizzata come una frase, in cui le opere sostituiscono le parole, o come i gruppi di note in uno spartito musicale. Le sequenze non sono destinate a esaurire le possibilità di una qualsiasi specifica operazione artistica, ma a indicarne la direzionalità, ad additare un persorso più che seguirlo fino in fondo. Una sequenza non è una raccolta di prove, ma la manifestazione di una possibilità estetica.

Le sequenze operano in modo semplice. Innanzitutto, ciascuna sequenza funziona semplicemente come collegamento tra due termini. Anche se ne sono state identificate tre, ne avremmo potuto trovare di più: dalla mano alla testa, dallo spazio al suono, dalle fontane ai neon. Tali elementi hanno chiaramente ruoli diversi, ma non è importante che i termini collegati da una sequenza appartengano allo stesso ordine di cose: questi termini esistono solo come esempi provvisori delle polarità che le sequenze rappresentano. Le sequenze non sono esaustive e non pretendono né hanno l'intenzione di vincolare la sempre sorprendente indefinitezza della produzione artistica di Nauman: sono delle categorie aperte. Non si esclude, poi, che gli elementi di una sequenza possano far parte di un'altra: un'opera come *Three Heads Fountain (Three Andrews)* (2005; fig. 26), ad esempio, può esistere in molti di questi parametri concettuali, o più esattamente, tra loro. Le sequenze costituiscono percorsi immaginari in evoluzione tra le singole opere, e accompagnano visivamente, esperienzialmente, e concettualmente il visitatore da un termine all'altro, come se fossero collegati metonimicamente. Più esattamente, la relazione tra gli elementi di una sequenza si può definire topologica, nel senso che sembra sempre possibile immaginare un passaggio da un'opera all'altra con allungamenti e torsioni, riduzioni e contrazioni, per citare ancora le parole usate da Nauman nel testo che accompagna *Flayed Earth Flayed Self (Skin Sink)* del 1973 (tav. 9). Il fatto che le trasformazioni del corpo visibili in Mani e Teste sembrino imitare le transizioni presenti in Suono e Spazio, e che entrambe riprendano i passaggi da immagine a linguaggio illustrati nella sequenza che va da Fontane a Neon, testimonia la coerenza della produzione artistica di Nauman nel tempo e nei diversi mezzi espressivi.

Nella traiettoria dalla mano alla testa si incontra per prima la bocca. Eppure se *From Hand to Mouth* (1967; tav. 11) segna l'inizio della prima sequenza, è solo perchè la sua superficie verdastra, ricca di dettagli e associazioni vagamente macabre, evoca precisamente la totalità del corpo che il processo di calco ha sottratto. La delicata mano con le dita tese non afferra nulla. Le cinque dita si moltiplicano nei gesti di *Fifteen Pairs of Hands* (1996; tav. 7), che rendono tridimensionale il movimento iniziato dalle stampe *Fingers and Holes* già citate (figs. 5-12). La relazione tra le due opere può fungere da esempio del passaggio da un termine della sequenza all'altro. Una delle sculture in bronzo che fanno parte di *Fifteen Pairs of Hands* (1996; fig. 4) è formata da due mani saldate ai polsi in modo da puntare in direzioni opposte. I loro gesti assomigliano a quelli delle mani al neon di *Human Sexual Experience* (1985; tav. 14), che ora però sono rivolti nella direzione opposta: l'indice di una mano, invece di entrare nel buco creato da indice e pollice dell'altra, indica la base, mentre l'altra mano, rovesciata, sembra segnalare che tutto va bene. I gesti, isolati e ricombinati, cambiano significato. Fatto ancora più importante, l'impermanenza del significato sembra estendersi anche ad altre paia di mani, come se tutte e quindici le paia costituissero le parole di una frase incomprensibile. La forma promette significato solo come pura promessa, sempre disattesa, mentre il significato viene rivelato come accidente della forma.

Mani e teste si moltiplicano in serie differenti. *Untitled* (1970/2009: tav. 24) inizia come performance di due danzatori, le cui dita si toccano appena, un contatto sottile che li aiuta a definire lo spazio tracciato dal movimento circolare dei corpi sulla superficie segnata sul pavimento. La loro performance viene filmata, e la registrazione video dei loro movimenti che si dipanano, cerchio infinito di corpi che si avvolgono in una spirale, viene mostrata nella stessa stanza in cui ha avuto luogo. Le mani che gesticolano in silenzio, costantemente in movimento, sono le uniche protagoniste di *Washing Hands Normal* (1996; tav. 28), mentre in *Coffee Spilled and Balloon Dog* (1993; tav. 2), le mani si muovono al rallentatore rovesciando caffè o allungando e piegando un palloncino gonfiabile per creare un cane. Il piegarsi e riaprirsi sia delle mani che dell'oggetto manipolato anticipa i gesti di *Fifteen Pairs of Hands*, "avvitando, svitando". Nel frattempo, compaiono teste di cera (*Four Pairs of Heads [Wax]*, 1991; tav. 10); teste di bronzo (*Hanging Head for Leo,* 1990, tav. 13), o in neon (*Double Poke in the Eye II* e *Eating Buggers*, entrambe del 1985, rispettivamente tav. 4 e 5). Teste silenziose sono installate con la faccia rivolta ad un muro bianco in un angolo della stanza, (*Five Pink Heads in the Corner* del 1992, tav. 8), teste urlanti saltano su schermi video (*Think* del 1993; tav. 20), e quando troviamo teste che pendono mature da tubi di plastica, sputando e spruzzando acqua, abbiamo superato una soglia e entriamo nella vasca di una fontana (le opere *Three Heads Fountain* del 2005; tav. 21, fig. 26).

La sequenza che porta da Suono a Spazio potrebbe iniziare nel vuoto dello studio dell'artista, in cui Nauman ha "trascorso un sacco di tempo ... cercando di riconsiderare, o considerare, il perchè, la ragione per cui sei un artista, e cosa fai", come l'artista racconta a a Michele de Angelus nel 1980. Uno studio vuoto in cui l'assensa di qualcuno che lavora è tutto quel che c'è da vedere nel video *Sound for Mapping the Studio Model (The Video)* (2001; tav. 19), in cui l'opera d'arte viene creata, dunque, anche se non si vede alcun artista, forse insinuando che qualsiasi cosa si ottenga viene sempre fatta alle nostre spalle, quasi fosse opera di qualcun altro. Lo studio dell'artista è una presenza incessante nell'opera di Nauman, qualcosa che costituisce la fonte di tutta la creatività, la quale a volte sembra essere considerata dall'artista come l'effetto di un gioco linguistico tanto che lo studio stesso diviene un luogo per testare i limiti di qualsiasi definizione dell'arte. Lo studio é anche il luogo in cui l'artista può scegliere se lavorare o meno, lo spazio preferito in cui le sue idee, i suoi progetti e le sue attività si incontrano, si sviluppano si sbrogliano, in un disfarsi estrinsecato e reso letterale dai movimenti dei due danzatori in *Untitled* del 1970/2009 (tav. 24).

Nella produzione artistica di Nauman qualsiasi indagine sulle caratteristiche fisiche dello studio sembra coincidere con una mappatura psicologica e letterale del corpo dell'artista. Spesso la mappatura viene realizzata grazie al suono, come in *Sound for Mapping the Studio Model (The Video)*, esempio del ruolo preponderante che il suono acquisisce in questo processo. L'opera consiste in un video a canale unico che dura poco più di un'ora, in cui Nauman ha estratto e montato insieme tutti i frammenti audio selezionati, che includono eventi sonori, tratti dal più lungo *Mapping the Studio I (Fat Chance John Cage)* (2001; fig. 31). Come suggerisce il titolo della versione a canale unico, è il suono, e solamente il suono, che ci permette di comprendere esattamente lo spazio letterale e metaforico dello studio. Il suono perfora i confini fisici di un corpo nello spazio, riconfigurando l'esperienza che il pubblico fa dell'opera e dell'ambiente circostante. Da *Studio Aids II* del 1967–68 (si veda la lista delle opere in mostra n. 21) a *Days* (2009; si veda la sezione dedicata a tale opera all'interno del presente catalogo), il suono rappresenta per Nauman uno strumento privilegiato di ricerca, e un modo per far entrare in cortocircuito i confini tra spazi, corpi e linguaggi espressivi, trasformando queste entità distinte in insiemi topologici.

Se lo studio è vuoto come la testa dell'artista (o ce l'ha l'osservatore vuota?) allora è perché si tratta davvero di una testa o di una gabbia. Installazioni come *Audio Video Piece for London, Ontario* del 1969–70 (tav. 1), e *Double Steel Cage Piece* del 1974 (tav. 3), sono costruite in modo letterale, in modo da intrappolare il visitatore grazie a seducenti contrappunti visivi e risonanze formali distorte. Se la testa è vuota quanto la stanza vuota, allora torcendosi e allungandosi la testa può svilupparsi in una stanza. Le sue pareti si contraggono e si espandono, fino a rigirarsi all'interno: una testa vuota che collassa dentro di sé, finché sputa se stessa fuori, come acqua da una fontana. Se il getto d'acqua è l'interno della testa, è perché lo spazio vuoto è stato tradotto in un linguaggio liquido. Il linguaggio diviene fluido, l'acqua rimane pazientemente dentro di noi per poter essere emessa in forma di significato, illuminandoci. Un linguaggio infinitamente illuminante, esso stesso una verità a spirale che non porta da nessuna parte.

Forse come segno delle molte felici corrispondenze tra le opere di Nauman e specialmente con l'ultima opera di Marcel Duchamp, *Étant donnés: 1° La chute d'eau, 2° Le gaz d'éclairage* del 1946–66, il passaggio "dato" dal neon (che è senza dubbio un "gas di illuminazione") alle fontane (o cascate), o viceversa, è sempre mediato dal linguaggio. Tale transizione è in primo luogo e principalmente esemplificata dal passaggio da un neon giovanile, *The True Artist Helps the World by Revealing Mystic Truths (Window or Wall Sign)* del 1967 (tav. 22) a *Untitled (The True Artist is an Amazing Luminous Fountain)* del 1968 (tav. 26), le cui lettere ritagliate sono poste lungo il perimetro di un preesistente dettaglio architettonico: una soglia, una finestra o una porta. Una precedente fotografia, incredibilmente evocativa, *Self-Portrait as a Fountain* del 1966–67 (fig. 29), conferma retroattivamente questo passaggio. Ció che è in gioco nel passaggio tra un'opera e l'atra é la vera definizione dell'arte, che viene inizialmente interrogata attraverso un'analisi del ruolo dell'artista, letteralmente incarnato da Nauman, ma anche insistentemente proposta al pubblico. Il bagliore fluttuante e disorientante di *Pink and Yellow Light Corridor (Variable Lights)* del 1972 (tav. 17), ad esempio, distorce la percezione del visitatore inquanto manifestazione letterale, sia affermativa che ironica, dei presunti poteri dell'arte. La definizione dell'arte diviene parte dell'esperienza del visitatore, secondo una logica topologica che si dipana costantemente. Insieme al suono, da cui non si può dissociare, il linguaggio viene usato e abusato da Nauman per creare flussi continui fluttuanti dalle diverse caratteristiche di mezzi espressivi, tecniche, corpi e spazi.

Infine, é la tensione tra gli spazi pubblici e privati di Venezia a costituire una quarta sequenza. Come città che permette la sistematica confusione tra esterno e interno, intesa tra la sua struttura urbana e il modo soggettivo in cui viene esperita, Venezia è ideale per prestarsi al dialogo e all'interazione con l'opera di Nauman. Gli spazi tra le tre sedi espositive, come già gli spazi vuoti di *Fingers and Holes*, non dovrebbero essere considerati dei vuoti, ma parti integranti della struttura della mostra. E' in tali passaggi inesplorati tra opere d'arte e edifici, che l'immaginazione permette al visitatore di connettere le proprie esperienze, reinventando mentalmente l'opera mentre attraversa la città. Non c'è un ordine gerarchico tra i siti i quali, come nel caso delle monadi di Leibnitz, si possono visitare indipendentemente l'uno dall'altro, o in qualsiasi sequenza, escludendo così il bisogno di un ordine obbligato o preferenziale nel muoversi dall'uno all'altro. Lo spazio tra le sedi, come anche il processo individualizzato attraverso il quale ciascun visitatore ne va alla ricerca, ha la stessa importanza: le tre sedi sono come le dita nei buchi della città, ed entrambi sono parte dell'esperienza.

Si dovrebbe notare che le opere incluse in ciascuna delle tre sedi non spiegano la singola composizione di una sequenza tematica. Ciascun sito, al contrario, ospita una combinazione di sequenze, in cui nessuna prevale sulle altre. Le sedi sono organizzate per esporre opere che entrano in risonanza reciproca, per cui gli elementi formali e concettuali che determinano la transizione da un'opera all'altra diventano evidenti al visitatore, ma dipende sempre da lui, condizione essenziale nel caso dell'opera di Nauman, dal fatto, cioé, che presti o meno attenzione. In questo modo, anche solo visitare una delle tre sedi permette al pubblico di esperire la logica che sottende l'intera mostra.

Dato che la mostra vuole suggerire che le relazioni tra materiali e tecniche che costituiscono l'opera di Nauman sono anche di natura topologica, ciascun sito offre la varietà più ampia possibile di soluzioni formali e concettuali ai problemi posti dalle diverse sequenze, e comprende nel modo più esteso possibile opere che coprono l'arco di tempo corrispondente alla carriera dell'artista. Scrivendo a proposito di *Etant Donnés* ... di Marcel Duchamp, Anne d'Harnoncourt e Walter Hopps sostengono che "il numero limitato di opere prodotte da Duchamp costituisce un'*oeuvre* talmente densa e concentrata che si può leggere non solo procedendo in avanti nel tempo, secondo la progressione cronologica della sua carriera, ma anche all'indietro e persino obliquamente." La stessa cosa si può dire di Nauman, e tale criterio mette in evidenza il principio guida della selezione e presentazione delle opere incluse nel progetto. In un certo senso, scegliendo di non esporre le opere di Nauman in ordine cronologico, la mostra condanna se stessa, e l'opera, ad una logica circolare; in altre parole, la mostra condanna il visitatore, come qualsiasi visitatore a Venezia, a iniziare *in media res*, a trovarsi sempre, inevitabilmente, nel mezzo di tutto.

5. Sogni di caffeina (Epilogo)

Nel pieno dell'estate i Giardini si appesantiscono di decadenti alberi di magnolia, pieni di api e di profumo. I fiori dei gelsomini nani sono pronti da cogliere; i delicati vialetti ombrosi di lavanda sono costellati da fitti ciuffi di erba verdissima. L'erba viene tagliata solo durante il periodo della Biennale, per cui il resto del tempo cresce incontrollata, coprendo quanto più terreno il tempo permette, e il risultato è incantevole. Eppure, poche persone vengono a visitarli quando non ci sono mostre in atto. Ci vengono le sporadiche coppiette, le troupe cinematografiche, gli inevitabili turisti smarriti che fuggono la folla estiva sfinita, o gruppi di bambini che si proteggono dalla luce accecante riflessa dalle acque poco profonde della laguna. Pochi passeggiano nei giardini, e ancor meno si avvicinano ai silenziosi edifici dei padiglioni nazionali, una volta giunti alle cancellate in ferro il cui uso si limita a impedire ai visitatori privi di biglietto di accedere agli spazi della Biennale. La maggior parte di loro sembra soddisfatta di sbirciare semplicemente le erbacce che crescono esuberanti e le sagome snelle degli alberi lontani. Senza nulla da mostrare, i giardini perdono poco a poco la ragione per restare esposti. Discretamente, si ripiegano su di loro, perdendo la pelle, affondando, riflettendo, avvolgendosi fino a sparire, restituendo il proprio sè segreto ad una città per la quale non hanno mai avuto una funzione vera e propria. I visitatori casuali sembrano capirlo inconsciamente, e intenti a ritornare sui propri passi verso la città, esitano e iniziano a camminare verso il Canal Grande, lasciandosi alle spalle la cancellata di ferro, finché si fermano. Per un breve momento, si voltano indietro a guardare i giardini, come se guardassero il proprio riflesso più autentico in uno specchio lontano, impossibile. Poi vanno via.

Fonti

Auping, Michael, "Metacommunicator", in *Bruce Nauman, Raw Materials*, catalogo della mostra, Tate, London 2004.

Cassini, Giocondo, *Piante e Vedute Prospettiche di Venezia: 1479–1855*, La Stamperia di Venezia Editrice, Venezia 1982.

Dammicco, Mariagrazia, e Marianne Majerus, *Jardins secrets de Venise*, Flammarion, Paris 2006.

de Bruyn, Eric, "Topological Pathways of Post-Minimalism", *Grey Room* 25 (autunno 2006).

De Sabbata, Massimo, *Tra diplomazia e arte: le Biennali di Antonio Maraini (1928–1942)*, Forum, Udine 2006.

d'Harnoncourt, Anne, e Walter Hopps, "Etant Donnés: 1° la chute d'eau 2° le gaz d'éclairage: Reflections on a New Work by Marcel Duchamp", *Philadelphia Museum of Art Bulletin* 64, n. 299 e 300 (1969).

Gough-Cooper, Jennifer, e Jacques Caumont, "Effemerides on and about Marcel Duchamp and Rrose Sélavy, 1887–1968", in *Marcel Duchamp*, catalogo della mostra, Palazzo Grassi, Bompiani, Milano 1993.

Goy, Richard, *Venice: The City and Its Architecture*, Phaidon, London 1997.

Howard, Deborah, *The Architectural History of Venice*, edizione rivesionata e ampliata, Yale University Press, New Haven 2002.

Martini, Maria Vittoria, "A Brief History of I Giardini", in *Muntadas On Translation: I Giardini, Spanish Pavilion, 51 Venice Biennale*, ed. Bartomeu Marí e Marc Augé, Actar, Barcelona 2005.

Nauman, Bruce, *Please Pay Attention Please: Bruce Nauman's Words: Writings and Interviews*, a cura di Janet Kraynak, MIT Press, Cambridge, Mass. 2002.

Rylands, Philip, e Enzo di Martino, *Flying the Flag for Art: The United States and the Venice Biennale 1895–1991*, Wyldbore and Wolferstand Ltd, Richmond, Va. 1993.

Schulz, Jürgen, *Saggi e memorie di storia dell'arte n.7: The Printed Plans and Panoramic Views of Venice (1486–1797)*, Casa Editrice Leo S. Olschki, Firenze 1972.

Simon, Joan, in *Bruce Nauman: Fingers and Holes*, catalogo della mostra, Gemini G.E.L., Los Angeles 1994.

Simon, Joan, e altri, *Bruce Nauman: Exhibition Catalogue and Catalogue Raisonné*, Walker Art Center, Minneapolis 1994.

Bruce Nauman: mappare lo studio, cambiare il campo visivo

Michael R. Taylor

Nell'estate del 2000 Bruce Nauman ha trascorso sette settimane filmando spezzoni di un'ora nello studio dove lavora sin dal 1989, in un ranch nel deserto del New Mexico. Ha girato in sette zone diverse dello studio per sette notti ciascuna, lasciando che l'attrezzatura registrasse le visioni notturne e i suoni ambientali dello studio, per poi montare la trascrizione in tempo reale degli eventi in un film, *Mapping the Studio I (Fat Chance John Cage)* (2001; fig. 31), della durata di cinque ore e quarantacinque minuti. Il film viene proiettato per la prima volta al Dia Center for the Arts di New York nel 2002, utilizzando sette proiettori con tracce audio multiple disposti in un'installazione che rispecchia le dimensioni della stanza. Il riferimento del titolo al compositore americano John Cage, noto per aver utilizzato combinazioni casuali per determinare la tipologia della sua musica, sottolinea l'aspetto aleatorio dell'opera, in cui le telecamere e i microfoni registrano ciò che accade all'interno e all'esterno dello studio senza alcun intervento o visione da parte dell'artista, ad eccezione del montaggio, in cui Nauman più che aggiungere, condensa le immagini di color grigio tendente al verde dello studio di notte.

Nauman crea anche una colonna sonora che ricorda lo stile di Cage, che accompagna il film con ronzii di mosche, ululati di coyote, latrati di cani, nitriti di cavalli e fischi di treni in lontananza. Lo spettatore sconcertato presume che gli strani rumori provengano dall'esterno dello studio, che sembra una baracca fatiscente, mentre all'interno la calma dello spazio vuoto è periodicamente interrotta dai topi che corrono precipitosamente, dalle falene che svolazzano e da un gatto nero senza coda, con gli occhi incandescenti, che si muove furtivamente tra cavi elettrici, attrezzi e detriti di studio. Il suono e la presenza di queste creature notturne anima ciò che altrimenti sarebbe la banale registrazione di uno studio vuoto, simile ai film *non-action* di Andy Warhol, che ebbero un'enorme influenza sulle prime opere video di Nauman. La vuota fissità del film di Warhol del 1964, *Empire*, ad esempio, qui è sostituita dalla variabilità delle tecniche di sorveglianza, che osservano e registrano ogni movimento dei topi che entrano furtivamente nel campo di ripresa o del gatto nero in cerca di preda, approfondendo l'interesse di Nauman per il comportamento animale già riscontrato nel 1988, ad esempio, nell'opera *Learned Helplessness in Rats (Rock and Roll Drummer)*. Anche se ogni tanto appare sullo schermo una rapida immagine dell'artista intento ad accendere le attrezzature per poi uscire dalla stanza, in generale, però, egli non compare, lasciando così che lo studio stesso sia il soggetto del lavoro.

Secondo Nauman, l'idea di *Mapping the Studio I (Fat Chance John Cage*) è scaturita proprio dai roditori:

> Quell'estate ci fu un grande afflusso di topi di campagna, sia in casa che in studio. Erano così numerosi che anche il gatto si era stancato di loro. Me ne stavo nello studio, frustrato perché non mi veniva nessuna idea nuova, e allora decisi che bisogna lavorare con quello che si ha. E quello che avevo erano il gatto e i topi e una videocamera a raggi infrarossi che per caso si trovava in studio. Perciò la posizionai, e una notte la accesi mentre non c'ero, tanto per vedere che cosa avrei ottenuto.[1]

L'enfasi posta sullo studio come luogo primario di creatività, luogo in cui le idee nascono semplicemente lavorando con "quello che si ha", è uno dei temi dominanti del lavoro di Nauman sin dalla metà degli anni sessanta. Nell'immensa ed eterogenea quantità di opere realizzate nei decenni seguenti, lo studio funge via via da teatro, da prigione e da laboratorio di ripetuti esperimenti volti alla realizzazione di un compito specifico, messi in scena con cura, ma assolutamente irrilevanti. Durante la fase creativa, lo studio di Nauman diventa muto testimone di controlli, interrogatori e persino torture, mentre l'artista convoglia la propria frustrazione e la rabbia per la condizione umana in straordinarie opere d'arte di grande originalità e di forte impatto emotivo.

Nel corso della lunga carriera di Nauman, lo studio appare nelle circostanze più diverse, e spesso sembra assumere un significato ambiguo e polivalente per l'artista stesso, a seconda dell'opera e del contesto specifico. Ad esempio, nell'installazione sonora del 1968 *Get Out of My Mind, Get Out of This Room* (si veda la lista delle opere in mostra n. 20), la frase che compone il titolo, pronunciata ripetutamente dall'artista in una gamma di intonazioni che provengono dagli amplificatori incassati nelle pareti di uno spazio vuoto, proietta sul visitatore la solitudine e l'alienazione dello studio dove l'opera è stata creata. L'opera sembra suggerire che la solitudine della vocazione dell'artista, che richiede di trascorrere innumerevoli ore da soli nello studio, può indurre delusioni paranoiche che trasformano il luogo di lavoro rendendolo minaccioso e inquieto, come anche rappresentare una metafora della mente tormentata dell'artista.

Nell'opera di Nauman lo studio può essere interpretato come luogo piacevole di intimità e riflessione, una via di fuga dalla quotidianità, ma più spesso è visto come un luogo opprimente, come nel caso degli stretti corridoi claustrofobici inizialmente creati a supporto del video *Walk with Contrapposto* (fig. 32). In questo video, girato nello studio nel 1968, Nauman cammina nel corridoio stretto e lungo ancheggiando in maniera esagerata, imitando le pose stilizzate della scultura classica. Nel maggio 1969 questo stesso corridoio, formato da due lunghi muri paralleli distanti cinquanta centimetri l'uno dall'altro, viene ripresentato al Whitney Museum of American Art di New York, in occasione della mostra *Anti-Illusion: Procedures/Materials,* con il titolo *Performance Corridor* (fig. 49). Dal momento che lo spazio espositivo a disposizione dell'opera é limitato, il corridoio diventa, in questo caso, più lungo e molto più stretto, rendono impossibile il passaggio per tutti tranne i più magri dei visitatori.

Tali opere architettoniche, le cui successive variazioni avrebbero incluso luci fluorescenti, specchi, telecamere e monitor per videocassette, segnano l'inizio del duraturo interesse dell'artista per la destabilizzazione della percezione che lo spettatore ha dello spazio e del corpo, attraverso la creazione di opere che sfidano la mente e assalgono i sensi. I corridoi e gli altri ambienti grandi quanto una stanza si possono leggere come surrogati del corpo dell'artista; si può pensare che Nauman sviluppi all'estremo la logica dell'implicito narcisismo del contemporaneo corridoio a specchi di Lucas Samaras (fig. 33), disegnato nel 1966 ma costruito solo nel 1970, quando utilizza le misure e le proporzioni del proprio corpo per definire la forma alta e stretta di questi corridoi compressi, che, dunque, corrispondono al fisico sottile e dinoccolato dell'artista, ampi appena quanto basta per accogliere una persona della sua corporatura.[2]

L'opera di Nauman, quindi, pone in discussione e allo stesso tempo rafforza il concetto dello studio d'artista come luogo privato, quasi sacro, dove l'atto creativo avviene in un'atmosfera di solitudine e riflessione. Fino alla fine del diciannovesimo secolo, lo studio d'artista è spesso considerato un luogo pubblico, sede di incontri tra il pittore o lo scultore e i suoi collezionisti, critici, amici, e modelle, come si può vedere nell'autoritratto allegorico di Gustave Coubert, *The Artist's Studio: A Real Allegory Summing up Seven Years of My Artistic and Moral Life* (fig. 34) del 1854–55. In questo dipinto il corpulento artista tiene in mano pennelli, taglierino e tavolozza: egli è il fulcro dell'atelier cavernoso e scarsamente arredato. Courbet è ben consapevole di essere costantemente in mostra in questo interno sovrappopolato, che egli ha raffigurato come crocevia della società francese contemporanea, in cui intere fasce di questa società sono accolte in studio, per poi essere separate dalla fondamentale figura dell'artista. Mai prima di allora era stata attribuita tanta importanza all'atelier.[3]

La situazione cambia all'inizio del ventesimo secolo, quando il passaggio all'astrattismo porta molti artisti moderni (specialmente individui introspettivi, quasi mistici come Vasily Kandinsky e Piet Mondrian, che equiparano l'opera artistica alla trascendenza spirituale) ad apprezzare la propria riservatezza e a proteggerla da interferenze esterne. Lo studio viene rapidamente trasformato in laboratorio sperimentale, con tanto di antisettici muri bianchi, il cui ingresso è permesso solo a pochi privilegiati, ma è anche un luogo di contemplazione estetica, in cui l'austerità formale delle creazioni dell'artista si ritrova negli ambienti incontaminati e spesso spartani. Viene alla mente la pacata semplicità dell'appartamento di Mondrian a Parigi, al numero 26 in rue du Départ, immortalata nel 1926 dalla straordinaria fotografia di André Kertész (fig. 35), dove anche le foglie e petali del tulipano rosso che l'artista tiene in un vaso vicino all'entrata dello studio sono dipinte di bianco, per timore che il fiore, appassendo, rovini l'immacolata perfezione dello spazio.[4]

Fino ai i primi anni sessanta, quando Nauman studia arte all'University of California, a Davis, prima come pittore e poi come artista concettuale e scultore processuale, utilizzando tecniche e materiali di vario tipo, lo studio dell'artista moderno è stato talmente idealizzato dalla sua rappresentazione fotografica che la presenza dell'artista nello spazio non è più necessaria ad indicare la presenza del genio artistico. Al contrario, l'atmosfera dello studio, inteso come luogo di creatività e illuminazione, dove le cose vengono create e rivelate, è incredibilmente intensificata dall'assenza dell'artista, e dove gli strumenti appena usati e le opere in via di esecuzione caricano lo spazio di energia creativa, talmente potente da oltrepassare quella del singolo scultore o pittore.[5]

Sin dalla Seconda Guerra Mondiale, la mistica dell'atelier d'artista si diffonde ampiamente negli Stati Uniti grazie alla pubblicazione delle immagini di case e studi di famosi artisti moderni come Pablo Picasso, Henri Matisse, Pierre Bonnard e Alberto Giacometti su riviste come *Life*, *Vogue* e *Harper's Bazaar*. Le immagini, scattate da una vasta schiera di fotografi, in particolare Brassaï, Alexander Liberman e Ugo Mulas, utilizzano il linguaggio visivo del documentario fotografico per creare, attraverso le loro attuali abitazioni e atelier, un resoconto fortemente idealizzato dei componenti dell'avanguardia parigina pre-bellica. L'operazione raggiunge l'apogeo nel 1960, con la pubblicazione di *The Artist in His Studio* di Lieberman, libro fotografico di "culto" che presto si diffonde nelle biblioteche scolastiche di arte e nelle abitazioni di aspiranti artisti.[6] Liberman, che aveva lavorato per anni come fotografo e direttore artistico della rivista *Vogue* (e più tardi come direttore editoriale di tutte le riviste *Condé Nast*), dedica quasi venti anni a questo libro, il cui assunto logico consiste nel "mostrare il processo creativo in sé, e in tal modo collegare pittura e scultura con la tradizione della ricerca della verità da parte dell'uomo. Pittori e scultori, come poeti e scienziati, sono cercatori di verità".[7]

Il libro di Liberman affianca le fotografie di artisti moderni come Picasso, Matisse, Giacometti (fig. 36), Georges Braque e Marcel Duchamp in pose ben studiate, al lavoro o al riposo nel loro studio, a immagini sensazionali degli studi stessi. Le fotografie sono accompagnate da brevi note bibliografiche basate su interviste e racconti di aneddoti, dalle quali risulta un ritratto collettivo dell'Avanguardia parigina, inclusi i racconti di imprese personali eroiche e spesso improbabili, che il libro presenta, senza esitazione, come autentiche. Aspetto ancora più importante in questa analisi sono le immagini, come in precedenza quelle di Brassaï, che diffondono l'idea dello studio d'artista come luogo di incanto, creatività ed espressione del prorpio io, rifugio privato, ricco di qualità quasi magiche, tutte espressioni che Liberman cerca di catturare, come un fulmine nella bottiglia, attraverso la tecnica fotografica. Il lettore, incoraggiato dalla prosa entusiasta dei testi, avverte il privilegio di entrare nel luogo più sacro dello studio degli artisti grazie a fotografie che cercano di trasportarci nell'intimità del loro mondo privato, il mondo che secondo Picasso era il punto focale dell'intero universo artistico.[8]

Il fatto che Nauman non era immune né tanto meno ignorasse il costrutto culturale negli anni sessanta che considerava lo studio come misterioso e isolato reame personale in cui l'artista gode di autorità suprema e quasi divina, è evidente in una delle prime opere in cui utilizza il neon. Nell'inverno 1966-67 Nauman crea un'insegna al neon a forma di spirale dal titolo *The True Artist Helps the World by Revealing Mystic Truths* (tav. 22), che installa nella vetrina dello studio in cui si è appena stabilito, una drogheria dismessa di San Francisco. Il messaggio, chiaramente romantico, creato con lettere al neon rosa e blu, rimanda alla dimensione mistica dell'astrazione degli inizi del ventesimo secolo, ma allo stesso tempo contesta la veridicità dell'affermazione in un'epoca di consumismo di massa, guerra del Vietnam e lotta per i diritti civili, un'epoca in cui la presa di posizione parodistica dell'arte Pop e Concettuale scardina i concetti di purezza estetica e il valore compensatorio dell'arte. Più tardi Nauman parla del desiderio di testare la veridicità di questa affermazione, che é

> da un lato un'idea totalmente sciocca e tuttavia, d'altro canto, un'idea in cui credevo. E' vera e non é vera allo stesso tempo. Dipende da come la si interpreta e quanto ci si prende seriamente. Per me é tuttora un concetto molto forte.[9]

La collocazione di questo credo luminoso nella vetrina del negozio senza dubbio confonde e sconcerta i passanti che cercano di capire quale prodotto venga pubblicizzato da quella coloratissima insegna luminosa al neon. In questo modo, il messaggio ambiguo serve a definire lo studio di Nauman, come in precedenza lo studio di Mondrian, come luogo di radicale sperimentazione creativa e, possibilmente, di trascendenza spirituale, luogo in cui l'artista-profeta o veggente predice rivelazioni mistiche.

Nauman si trasferisce a San Francisco nel 1966, poco dopo aver conseguito il diploma di master presso la University of California, a Davis, dove aveva studiato tra gli altri con i docenti William T. Wiley e Robert Arneson, artisti anticonformisti, poi protagonisti del nascente movimento *Funk* della Bay Area, che avevano inculcato nei giovani *protégé* l'idea che un'autentica dedizione alla propria opera e, in particolare, il tempo trascorso nello studio fossero importanti quanto gli oggetti creati. Sviluppando quest'idea, nel 1966 Nauman decide che:

> Ero un artista e mi trovavo nello studio, allora qualunque cosa stessi facendo nello studio doveva per forza essere arte. E ciò che facevo in realtà era bere caffè e camminare avanti e indietro. Allora (si poneva) la questione di come strutturare queste attività in modo da farle divenire arte, o una specie di unità coesa che potesse essere messa a disposizione della gente. A quel punto l'arte divenne più un'attività che un prodotto .[10]

Nauman inizia a creare opere che nascono dalle attività quotidiane di routine nello studio, oltre che da compiti specifici, spesso infruttuosi, che egli stesso stabilisce in modo da tenersi occupato e ammazzare il tempo, che tuttavia esegue e documenta con il distacco clinico e la precisione di uno scienziato che compie esperimenti in laboratorio. Questi compiti ripetitivi includono nel 1967 la creazione di una scultura sempre diversa, giorno dopo giorno e per più di un mese, creata modificando una pila di farina sul pavimento dello studio (*Flour Arrangements*; fig. 47); nel 1967–68, l'esecuzione intensa e fin troppo elaborata di *Dance or Exercise on the Perimeter of a Square (Square Dance)* (fig. 63); nel 1968, il percorrere a grandi passi lo studio o camminare pesantemente, in modo forzato ed esagerato (*Slow Angle Walk [Beckett Walk]* (fig. 50) e *Stamping in the Studio*). Le ultime due opere vengono filmate in uno studio di Southampton, a Long Island, di proprietà di Roy Lichtenstein e Paul Waldman, usando l'attrezzatura video fornita dal gallerista di Nauman a New York, Leo Castelli, che riprende l'artista mentre esegue, senza interruzione per un'ora intera, le azioni ripetitive citate nei titoli.[11] Interrogato qualche anno dopo a proposito di questi esercizi metodici, Nauman ricorda come fosse "un processo noioso e complicato percorrere anche solo un metro",[12] commento che potrebbe facilmente essere applicato al suo sforzo quotidiano nella creazione artistica durante gli anni sessanta, quanto a quello di spostarsi nello studio entro i limiti volontariamente assunti. Solo con la sua telecamera, in uno studio quasi completamente privo di arredi e ancor più di oggetti artistici, Nauman utilizza il corpo, la cosa a lui più accessibile, come materiale di base sia per sculture che per film senza inizio né fine, dato che nelle sue intenzioni devono essere proiettati a ciclo continuo, così da enfatizzare la natura assurdamente banale dei compiti ripetitivi eseguiti di fronte alla telecamera.

L'interesse nel corpo umano come veicolo di idee appare ancora una volta nella straordinaria scultura del 1967, *From Hand to Mouth* (tav. 11), calco in cera del corpo della prima moglie di Nauman. Come suggerisce il titolo, l'impronta inizia dalle dita della mano destra di Judy Nauman, continua con il braccio, e termina con il mento e la bocca. Interpretata come la realizzazione tridimensionale di un'espressione colloquiale, *From Hand to Mouth* è stata spesso paragonata all'opera di Duchamp *With My Tongue in My Cheek* (fig. 37) del 1959,[13] il cui titolo manifesta l'approccio irriverente e scherzoso (*tongue-in-cheek* in inglese, ndt.) dell'anziano artista nei confronti della creazione artistica "seria". L'opera venne paragonata anche all'uso di frammenti corporei colorati nel dipinto di Jasper Johns del 1955, *Target with Plaster Casts* (fig. 38), nella quale è presente una fila di scatole in legno riempite di calchi di labbra, nasi, orecchie, dita e genitali maschili.

Nauman si interessa particolarmente al modo in cui Johns usa parti del corpo e frammenti anatomici in calchi di cera e gesso o impronte fisiche, ad esempio nei disegni impressi a pelle dei primi anni sessanta, che recano le tracce del volto e delle mani dell'artista. Nauman, come Johns, si accosta al corpo in modo spersonalizzato, assegnandogli la funzione di unità di misura, strumento o modello, oppure di oggetto che può essere usato e manipolato a piacimento. La passione per i calchi anatomici aiuta a comprendere l'interesse di Nauman per l'impronta della mano, del braccio, e della mascella inferiore di Judy Nauman, ma il titolo fa riferimento alla tipologia di vita che la coppia condivide, appena sopra la soglia della povertà, ed è affine ai titoli letterali, ma basati su giochi di parole, di Duchamp e Man Ray.

L'influenza di Duchamp nelle prime opere di Nauman è innegabile, nonostante la reticenza dell'artista ad ammetterla, anche se le idee iconoclastiche dell'artista più anziano sono spesso mediate dalle opere di artisti contemporanei come Johns, Samaras, Joseph Kosuth, e Robert Morris. Il rifiuto di Duchamp della pittura "retinica", assieme alla concezione di non finito della sua opera, l'inclusione delle contraddizioni, l'uso di annotazioni e diagrammi e di materiali pungenti e non tradizionali quali il vetro, il filo metallico, il cavo di piombo e la polvere, l'invenzione provocatoria del ready-made, sono elementi che mettono profondamente in discussione le definizioni esistenti di opera d'arte e hanno importanti conseguenze nell'opera di Nauman, nonostante più tardi egli affermi che tali idee erano semplicemente nell'aria a quell'epoca in California. Nauman è tra i pochi artisti della sua generazione ad ascoltare l'appello di Duchamp affinché gli artisti "entrino in clandestinità",[14] esortazione che trova forte rispondenza nell'isolamento che Nauman si autoimpone fin dall'inizio, nei vari studi a San Francisco, Mill Valley, Pasadena, California e, più tardi, in due città in New Mexico, dove continua a professare il "ritiro come forma d'arte".[15]

Sotto molti aspetti, l'approccio di Nauman a Duchamp ricorda l'artista americana Hannah Wilke che, come è noto, dichiara che "onorare Duchamp significa contrastarlo".[16] Nella scultura in piombo del 1966, *A Rose Has No Teeth* (fig. 39), le parole del titolo sono incise a bassorilievo sul lato convesso di una placca di piombo, curvata in modo da poter essere appesa ad un tronco d'albero. Come tutte le sue opere migliori, questo intenso lavoro si può leggere in molti modi, rendendo insufficiente ogni singola interpretazione. Si può dire, tuttavia, che quest'opera sia stata probabilmente creata come arguta risposta alla scultura in piombo di Morris del 1963, *Litanies*, che si riferiva apertamente alle annotazioni ermetiche di Duchamp per l'opera *Large Glass* (1915–23), attraverso l'incisione, su una serie di ventisette chiavi, delle parole della sezione "litanie del carro" dell'ultima opera *Green Box* (1923). Questo rispettoso omaggio è, invece, contestato nell'opera di Nauman, il cui titolo cita un brano delle *Ricerche Filosofiche* di Ludwig Wittgenstein.[17] A mio parere questa strana frase non viene scelta a caso, dato che forma un gioco di parole con il nome del salace alter ego femminile di Duchamp, Rrose Sélavy, e con un'altra opera duchampiana del 1919, *Tzanck Check*, un ingrandimento eseguito a mano dell'assegno di 115 dollari prelevato dalla fittizia "Teeth's Loan & Trust Company" che Duchamp diede al suo dentista, Daniel Tzanck, come pagamento per i trattamenti odontoiatrici.

L'opera *A Rose Has No Teeth* osa suggerire che le espressioni dadaiste di Duchamp hanno perso mordente, forse per l'uso eccessivo che se ne è fatto. Senza dubbio Nauman è infastidito dagli onnipresenti riferimenti alle idee ermetiche dell'artista di origine francese nelle opere di orientamento concettuale degli artisti della West Coast, a seguito dell'epocale retrospettiva su Duchamp tenutasi nel 1963 al Pasadena Art Museum, che Nauman non ebbe l'opportunità di vedere di persona.[18] Questa percezione di sovraesposizione potrebbe spiegare la ragione per cui Nauman aggiunge al disegno del 1967 *Untitled (Study After "Wax Impressions of the Right Knees of Five Famous Artists")* (fig. 40) la frase di coda "Non usate Marchel Duchamp", proponendo, invece, le ginocchia di suoi amici e coetanei Samaras, William T. Wiley, Larry Bell e Leland Bell. Nello stesso anno in cui crea *A Rose Has No Teeth*, Nauman visita una grande mostra su Man Ray al Los Angeles County Museum of Art rimanendo profondamente colpito dall'eclettica serie di opere dell'artista americano e dal suo approccio giocoso al linguaggio e alla produzione artistica:

> C'era una grande mostra su Man Ray a Los Angeles, e andai a vederla. Ricordo che pensai che c'erano cose che anch'io volevo fare e non sapevo se farle e come.

Se avessi dovuto fare performance, dipinti o qualcos'altro. Visitare la mostra di Man Ray mi fece sentire sollevato al riguardo, perché egli sembrava essere a proprio agio sul come lo si fa, sia che fosse una fotografia, un film o un dipinto. Era riuscito in qualche modo a fare tutte queste cose.[19]

La retrospettiva su Man Ray del 1966 è una forza legittimante per il giovane Nauman, ancora intento a forgiare la propria identità artistica dopo la recente laurea alla University of California, a Davis. La mostra, inaugurata il 26 ottobre 1966, esercita su Nauman la stessa influenza fondamentale che la retrospettiva su Duchamp ebbe nel 1963 su artisti della West Coast come John Baldessari, Chris Burden, Richard Pettibone e Ed Ruscha: l'esempio ispiratore di Man Ray lo aiuta a superare l'ansia e il dubbio di come creare opere d'arte a partire dalla gente e dagli oggetti a lui vicini, incluse le attività svolte nello studio che egli registra in performance e film. Man Ray, fonte in precedenza sottovalutata e troppo spesso misconosciuta delle opere e delle idee di Nauman,[20] è la perfetta incarnazione dell'artista che lavora nello studio. L'uso pratico che egli fa dei materiali quotidiani trovati nello studio o nella vicina ferramenta, per costruire opere d'arte sature di significato personale, esercita un impatto decisivo sul giovane artista e lo incoraggia a lavorare con qualunque materiale disponibile, anche se poco ortodosso o improbabile, senza la preoccupazione di sviluppare un preciso stile personale.

L'effetto liberatorio prodotto su Nauman dalla mostra del 1966 proviene in parte dal rifiuto dadaista di Man Ray degli atteggiamenti gerarchici verso i materiali, un rifiuto che gli permette di esprimere le proprie idee con molteplicità di mezzi. Temendo che il pubblico californiano, che vive all'ombra dell'industria cinematografica hollywoodiana, avrebbe associato la sua arte alla fotografia commerciale piuttosto che alla sperimentazione radicale del Dadaismo e del Surrealismo, Man Ray aveva insistito affinché il curatore della mostra, il critico d'arte Jules Langsner, includesse i dipinti ad olio, le aerografie, le sculture, gli oggetti costruiti con vari materiali, le scacchiere con i pezzi degli scacchi, i collage, i disegni, gli acquerelli e i libri, ma non le fotografie, ad eccezione di due serie di "Rayografie".[21] Ignorando le fotografie di moda, il lavoro pubblicitario e i ritratti del bel mondo parigino tra le due guerre, immagini famose per la loro incantevole bellezza e perfezione tecnica, la mostra caleidoscopica di Los Angeles, che presenta trecento opere d'arte, mette in scena, quindi, un altro Man Ray, artista multimediale interessato al linguaggio, in particolare ai giochi di parole e ai giochi linguistici. E' in questo modo che la mostra di Man Ray entra in risonanza con le problematiche indagate da giovani artisti come Nauman, che subito sente una profonda affinità con la libertà e l'eterogeneità dell'opera e delle idee dell'artista americano.

La mostra presenta una grande quantità degli eccentrici oggetti e assemblaggi di Man Ray: i loro titoli, nati da giochi di parole, e la parsimonia dei mezzi utilizzati hanno un profondo impatto sulla successiva produzione artistica di Nauman. Nelle intenzioni di Man Ray questi oggetti spiritosi e sorprendenti (per la maggior parte copie successive di originali persi o distrutti al momento della retrospettiva) devono "divertire, sconcertare, irritare o indurre a riflettere".[22] La mostra include esempi classici come *It's Springtime*, del 1961, allegro assemblaggio di due molle attorcigliate che l'artista ha rimosso dal divano e unito a formare un'incantevole opera di arte cinetica. In un'altra opera, ideata nel 1958, Man Ray ricopre una lunga *baguette* di colore blu cobalto e, formandone due pezzi posizionati uno sopra l'altro, la mette in equilibrio su una bilancia per creare *Pain Peint* (fig. 41), il cui titolo descrittivo gioca sull'omofonia delle parole francesi *pain* (pane) e *peint* (dipinto). L'artista vuole anche evidenziare che il ritornello ripetuto di "*pain*" e "*peint*" produce una fedele rappresentazione onomatopeica dei suoni strombettanti dei clacson dei carri dei pompieri, aggiungendo così un altro livello di significato all'opera.[23]

I giochi di parole verbali e visivi di Man Ray, che evitano l'elegante sofisticazione dei numerosi *jeux de mots* bilingui di Duchamp, hanno una spontaneità immediata, pari a quella degli oggetti e degli assemblaggi caratterizzati da una coraggiosa assertività e da una totale mancanza di pretese. Questi giochi di parole tridimensionali ingannevolmente semplici (Man Ray preferiva chiamarli "giochi di parole plastici"), che spesso venivano considerati solo arguzie irriverenti, erano il più delle volte frutto di un lungo periodo di gestazione, durante il quale l'artista rifletteva a fondo sui significati complessi e sulle associazioni tra titoli e singole componenti.[24] Per Nauman, l'umorismo impassibile di questi oggetti e i loro schietti titoli descrittivi rappresentano la quintessenza dell'americanità, e sono molto più vicini alla sua sensibilità rispetto alle sottili acrobazie linguistiche di Duchamp. "Preferisco Man Ray" ricorda Nauman, "nelle sue opere c'è meno 'elaborazione', più irragionevolezza".[25]

L'influsso di Man Ray si percepisce in un gran numero di opere successive di Nauman, inclusa *From Hand to Mouth* (tav. 11), un'opera che si ispira all'interpretazione letterale, ai giochi di parole e altri giochi linguistici dell'artista americano per rivelare, grazie all'espressione idiomatica del titolo, l'indigenza in cui vive l'artista contemporaneo che cerca di affermarsi. L'artista e critico d'arte Coosje van Bruggen sostiene, inoltre, l'esistenza di una relazione formale tra le serie di sculture, disegni e fotografie di Nauman, intitolate *Henry Moore Bound to Fail* del 1967–70, che mostrano l'artista di spalle, in camicia, con le braccia legate con una corda, e l'assemblaggio di Man Ray del 1920, ora perduto, *The Enigma of Isidore Ducasse*, riprodotto nel catalogo della mostra di Los Angeles in una fotografia in bianco e nero.[26] Man Ray, difatti, aveva utilizzato della stoffa per coprire una forma legata con la corda, omaggio a Ducasse, il precoce poeta francese, nato in Uruguay, che pubblicava sotto lo pseudonimo di "Comte de Lautréamont". L'opera di Man Ray consisteva in un oggetto misterioso, che si presume fosse una macchina da cucire, in onore della famosa frase di Ducasse "bello ... come il casuale accostamento di una macchina da cucire e di un ombrello sul tavolo di una sala di dissezione", avvolta in una coperta militare e fissata con delle corde.[27]

Anche *Light Trap for Henry Moore, No. 1* e *No. 2* (fig. 45), una coppia di fotografie in bianco e nero del 1967, nelle quali Nauman crea delle linee a zig zag facendo oscillare una torcia elettrica nello studio oscurato, richiamano alla mente alcune Rayografie di Man Ray, cinquantaquattro delle quali erano esposte alla mostra di Los Angeles. Le avvolgenti spirali di luce di Nauman, imitando lo stile dello scultore inglese nei disegni dai contorni sovrapposti che raffiguravano i rifugiati nella metropolitana di Londra durante il Blitz, si uniscono a creare una forma scultorea che ricorda vagamente una delle figure sedute di Moore, come anche metà dell'opera in gesso composta di due parti di Nauman, *Mold for a Modernized Slant Step* del 1966. Viste insieme a *Henry Moore Bound to Fail*, queste fotografie sembrano indicare che Nauman percepisca un'affinità tra Man Ray e Henry Moore, due anziani protagonisti dell'arte moderna la cui reputazioni erano allora in declino, ma il cui contributo sarebbe stato apprezzato da future generazioni di artisti e critici di più ampie vedute.[28]

Anche *My Last Name Exaggerated Fourteen Times Vertically* (fig. 55), che Nauman crea nel 1967 con neon di color viola pallido, e un'altra opera al neon creata nell'anno seguente, *My Name As Though It Were Written on the Surface of the Moon* (tav. 15), potrebbero riferirsi a un'opera esposta nella retrospettiva di Man Ray. Nelle opere di Nauman, le lettere manoscritte del nome e del cognome sono completamente sproporzionate, assurdamente allungate nella prima opera e stirate orizzontalmente nella seconda, al punto che la firma risulta di fatto indecifrabile. La visualizzazione distorta del nome dell'artista era stata anticipata dall'opera di Man Ray, *Man Ray 1914* (fig. 42), un gioco di parole che rinnega l'idea dello stile personale distintivo, riproposto con grande rilievo nel catalogo della mostra di Los Angeles, che, a prima vista, sembra un paesaggio cubista. Un'analisi approfondita rivela che le forme approssimativamente parallele e inclinate della composizione, apparentemente astratta, sono quelle delle lettere maiuscole assottigliate del nome dell'artista e dei distinti numeri che compongono l'anno di esecuzione del dipinto.

Infine, quasi tutte le immagini del portfolio *Eleven Color Photographs*, che Nauman crea assieme al fotografo Jack Fulton nel 1966–67, ma che pubblica solo nel 1970, contengono riferimenti alle rappresentazioni letterali di giochi di parole, vocaboli, lettere e modi di dire creati da Man Ray (fig. 46). (L'eccezione è costituita dall'opera *Self-Portrait as a Fountain* [fig. 29], che fa riferimento al famoso orinatoio in porcellana che nel 1917 Duchamp presceglie come *ready-made* e intitola *Fountain).* Come Duchamp, Man Ray dà maggiore importanza all'invenzione mentale che all'abilità tecnica. I suoi giochi linguistici e di parole senza dubbio hanno risvegliato l'interesse di Nauman per gli esperimenti linguistici, un interesse già stimolato dai giochi linguistici di Wittgenstein, e senza dubbio favoriscono la successiva decisione dell'artista di includere anagrammi, scherzi, palindromi, giochi di parole e rebus all'interno di neon e disegni. Il soggetto viscerale e spesso anche brutale di queste opere è lontano dalla giocosa stravaganza di Man Ray, eppure la loro origine si ritrova nell'esperto uso del linguaggio e nella leggendaria arguzia dell'artista più anziano, spesso misto a ironia e all'occasionale battuta acida.

L'intenso e prolungato impegno di Nauman nello studio emerge in questo saggio come uno dei temi centrali della sua produzione artistica. Scenario delle più profonde esplorazioni del significato artistico, lo studio offre un'utile cornice per la comprensione della produzione multiforme e, in definitiva, inclassificabile di Nauman, poiché gran parte del suo lavoro pioneristico, comprendente installazione artistica, scultura, film, video, neon, fotografia e performance, può essere interpretata come una proiezione personalizzata dello spazio privato dell'artista. Ironicamente, il suo interesse per il significato concettuale e metaforico dello studio coincide con il brutale rifiuto, espresso dall'artista francese Daniel Buren, del modello di spazio lavorativo privato dell'artista come privilegiata torre d'avorio, luogo esclusivo dove l'arte viene ideata e creata.[29] Buren propone, quindi, che l'arte venga creata direttamente in strada, come avviene per le sue opere, in cui dipinge e incolla strisce colorate alternate a strisce bianche nei luoghi pubblici e privati più diversi: edifici commerciali, fiancate dei treni e vele delle imbarcazioni.

Per Buren, lo studio dell'artista contemporaneo è una sorta di deposito in cui l'arte viene creata, immagazzinata e, se tutto procede bene, distribuita. Sin dai tempi di Courbet, sostiene l'artista francese, lo studio è diventato un nodo sociale in cui l'artista interagisce con i mercanti d'arte, i collezionisti, i curatori museali e gli altri arbitri del gusto, l'appoggio dei quali è di cruciale importanza per liberare le opere d'arte dal loro purgatorio, cioè l'ambiente in cui sono state create. Secondo Buren, dunque, l'opera d'arte "è vittima di un mortale paradosso al quale non può sfuggire", poiché le pareti intonse, bianche e ben illuminate dei musei e delle gallerie d'arte, in cui l'opera è esposta, sono esattamente il contrario dello studio dell'artista, in cui generalmente si trova una varietà di opere finite, opere in via di esecuzione e opere abbandonate, assieme a un accumulo di mobili, attrezzi e detriti.[30] L'atmosfera dello studio d'artista, che inizialmente ha favorito la produzione artistica, si perde nel momento in cui un dipinto o una scultura viene posta negli spazi immacolati del museo o della galleria d'arte, che mascherano l'ordinaria e alquanto banale realtà della creazione dell'opera.

Le opere di Nauman, tuttavia, sono sempre sopravvissute allo spostamento dallo studio, l'ambiente di produzione, al museo o alla galleria, quello spostamento che Buren teme comprometta l'integrità e capacità di comunicazione dell'arte. Dopo oltre quaranta anni di intense indagini sulla natura dell'arte in relazione a linguaggio, percezione, fenomenologia, e psicologia, Nauman mantiene con decisione la naturale immediatezza dell'opera così come è stata ideata, proprio per il fatto che utilizza, come soggetto e sostanza di una produzione artistica ininterrottamente creativa, ciò che ha a portata di mano negli angoli e interstizi dello studio, incluso il suo corpo, sempre presente. Anziché trasformare questi materiali in opere d'arte esteticamente belle o moralmente incoraggianti, Nauman preserva la relazione tra l'opera e il suo luogo di produzione, così come l'impronta dei propri processi mentali. Santuario, prigione, gabbia, teatro o laboratorio, lo studio rimane il crogiuolo nel quale viene plasmata la sua provocatoria e aspramente scorticata visione dell'umanità.

1 Bruce Nauman, citato in Michael Auping, *A Thousand Words: Bruce Nauman Talks about Mapping the Studio,* "Artforum", 40, 7 (marzo 2002), p. 121.

2 Nauman potrebbe aver visto un altro *Corridor* di Samaras, un disegno datato 9 dicembre 1966, nella mostra "American Sculpture of the Sixties" inaugurata al Los Angeles County Museum of Art nell'aprile 1967. Il disegno, riprodotto anche in catalogo, mostrava una serie di corridoi collegati, fatti di specchi e sfere di cristallo, lunghi circa due metri e mezzo. Si veda *American Sculpture of the Sixties*, a cura di Maurice Tuchman, catalogo della mostra, Los Angeles County Museum of Art, Los Angeles 1967, p. 184.

3 Si veda Michael Peppiatt e Alice Bellony-Rewald, *Imagination's Chamber: Artists and Their Studios*, Little & Brown, Boston 1982, p. 71.

4 Si veda Martin S. James, *Mondrian and the Dutch Symbolists,* "Art Journal" 23, 2 (inverno 1963–64), p. 110.

5 Si veda Jon Wood, *Close Encounters: The Sculptor's Studio in the Age of the Camera*, catalogo della mostra, Henry Moore Institute, Leeds 2001, p. 13. Constantin Brancusi scattò nel proprio studio in vicolo Ronsin 8, a Parigi, delle fotografie emblematiche del passaggio dal ritratto allo studio stesso, in cui la purezza estetica di ciascuna scultura viene sottolineata dalla sua posizione, circondata com'è da un assortimento disordinato di altre opere, molte incomplete, e di attrezzi, in un ambiente di lavoro che rivela la creatività proteiforme dell'artista.

6 Sull'impatto e l'effetto del libro di Alexander Liberman si veda Mary Bergstein, *The Artist in His Studio: Photography, Art, and the Masculine Mystique*, "Oxford Art Journal" 18, 2 (1995), pp. 45–58.

7 Alexander Liberman, *Introduction*, in Liberman, *The Artist in His Studio*, The Viking Press, New York 1960, n.p.

8 Si veda John Richardson, *Picasso's Ateliers and Other Recent Works*, "The Burlington Magazine", XCIX, 651 (giugno 1957), p. 186. Nauman probabilmente conosceva anche le famose foto di Hans Namuth che ritraggono Jackson Pollock mentre lavora con impeto sciamanico nel proprio studio.

9 Nauman, citato in Brenda Richardson, *Bruce Nauman: Neons*, catalogo della mostra, The Baltimore Museum of Art, Baltimore 1982, p. 20.

10 Nauman, in Ian Wallace e Russell Keziere, *Bruce Nauman Interviewed*, 1978, in *Please Pay Attention Please: Bruce Nauman's Words, Writings and Interviews* a cura di Janet Kraynak, The MIT Press, Cambridge, Mass. 2005, p. 194.

11 Si veda Michele de Angelus, *Interview with Bruce Nauman*, maggio 1980, in *ibid.*, pp. 244–45.

12 Nauman, citato in Jane Livingston, *Bruce Nauman*, in *Bruce Nauman: Work from 1965 to 1972*, a cura di Livingston e Marcia Tucker, catalogo della mostra, Los Angeles County Museum of Art, Los Angeles 1972, p. 26.

13 Si veda ad esempio Robert Pincus-Witten, *Bruce Nauman: Another Kind of Reasoning*, "Artforum" 10, 6 (febbraio 1972), p. 32.

14 Duchamp pronuncia la famosa affermazione "il grande artista di domani entrerà in clandestinità" al Philadelphia Museum College of Art nel 1961, nel corso di una tavola rotonda per artisti, intitolata "Dove stiamo andando?" Duchamp affascina il pubblico con un attacco alla dilagante commercializzazione del mercato dell'arte che, sostiene, ha trasformato l'arte in "una merce, come il sapone o i titoli azionari". Secondo Duchamp, "La speculazione economica porta l'arte ad un enorme indebolimento, al degradare del gusto nella bruma della mediocrità", per cui l'unica speranza resta la "rivoluzione ascetica" (un incantevole gioco di parole tra l'estetica e il ruolo da lui adottato, che altrove chiama "monaco dissoluto", che lavora solo nello studio riducendo al minimo gli obblighi sociali) che permetterebbe all'artista di operare al di fuori del sistema delle gallerie in una specie di isolamento eremitico. Si veda John Canaday, *Whither Art?*, "New York Times", 26 marzo 1961, sezione X, p. 15.

15 Nauman, *Bruce Nauman: Notes and Projects*, in Marcia Tucker, *PheNAUMANology*, "Artforum" 9, 4 (dicembre 1970), p. 44.

16 Hannah Wilke, *I Object: Memoirs of a Sugar Giver*, citata in *Übrigens Sterben Immer die Anderen: Marcel Duchamp und die Avantgarde seit 1950*, a cura di Dieter Daniels, catalogo della mostra, Museum Ludwig, Cologne 1988, p. 269.

17 L. Wittgenstein, Ricerche Filosofiche, tr. it. di R. Piovesan e M. Trinchero, a cura di M. Trinchero, Einaudi, Torino 1983, p. 290. Il testo riporta: "'Un neonato non ha denti'. – 'Un'oca non ha denti'. – 'Una rosa non ha denti'. – L'ultima proposizione – si vorrebbe dire – è certamente vera! Più certa, almeno, di quella che un'oca non ha denti. – E tuttavia non è così chiara. Infatti, dove mai una rosa dovrebbe avere i denti?".

18 A proposito dell'effetto a catena provocato della retrospettiva di Duchamp, tenutasi nel 1963, sull'opera degli artisti della West Coast si veda Robert L. Pincus, "'Quality Material ... ': Duchamp Disseminated in the Sixties and Seventies", in *West Coast Duchamp*, a cura di Bonnie Clearwater, catalogo della mostra, Grassfield Press, Miami Beach, in collaborazione con Shoshana Wayne Gallery, Santa Monica, 1991, pp. 87–101.

19 Nauman in conversazione con Coosje van Bruggen (1985), in *Bruce Nauman: Drawings, 1965–1986*, catalogo della mostra, Kunstmuseum Basel, Basel 1986, p. 35, nota 13.

20 Una rara eccezione è costituita dal magnifico saggio di Constance M. Lewallen sulla produzione giovanile di Nauman, in cui Lewallen collega la "incapacità di perseverare in un solo linguaggio espressivo o un'unica direzione" di Nauman alla produzione proteiforme di Man Ray. Lewallen paragona anche l'approccio tecnicamente competente dell'artista più anziano con "un'etica del lavoro tipicamente americana che [Nauman] assorbì non solo dalla famiglia, ma anche dai professori d'arte alla University of Wisconsin, di simpatie socialiste". Si veda Lewallen, *A Rose Has No Teeth*, in Lewallen, *A Rose Has No Teeth: Bruce Nauman in the 1960s*, catalogo della mostra, University of California Press, Berkeley Art Museum e Pacific Film Archive, Berkeley/Los Angeles 2007, p.63.

21 Si veda Carl I. Belz, *A Man Ray Retrospective in Los Angeles*, "Artforum" 5, 4 (dicembre 1966), pp. 22–23.

22 Man Ray, *Objects of My Affection*, in *Man Ray, Objects of My Affection*, catalogo della mostra, Julien Levy Gallery, New York 1945, s.p.

23 Si veda Arturo Schwarz, *Man Ray: il rigore dell'immaginazione*, Feltrinelli, Milano 1977, p. 42.

24 Si veda Brian O'Doherty, *Light on an Individual: Man Ray*, "New York Times", 5 maggio 1963, sezione X, p. 15.

25 Nauman, citato in Livingston, *Bruce Nauman*, cit., p. 11. In questo caso il commento di Nauman è forse ispirato dalla recensione scritta da Ron Padgett sulla retrospettiva di Man Ray al Los Angeles County Museum of Art, in cui il poeta americano dichiara che "Duchamp, pur con tutta la sua tremenda intelligenza, non ha la giocosa perfidia che rende l'opera di Man Ray la cosa gratuita e imprevedibile che è. Man Ray si sarebbe dannatamente divertito a inventare lo xilofono; gli piace far risuonare la nota dissonante, leggermente grossolana". Padgett, *Artist Accompanies Himself with His Rays*, "Art News", 65, 7 (novembre 1966), p. 80.

26 Coosje van Bruggen, *Bruce Nauman,* Rizzoli, New York 1988, p. 111.

27 Comte de Lautréamont (Isidore Ducasse), *Tutte le poesie. I Canti di Maldoror, Poesie, Lettere,* a cura di Gianni Nicoletti, Newton Compton Editori, Roma 1978, p. 316.

28 La maggior parte dei critici non condivide l'entusiasmo di Nauman per la retrospettiva di Man Ray; all'epoca la mostra viene, al contrario, generalmente considerata un fallimento imbarazzante. A proposito dell'accoglienza negativa, spesso ostile, della mostra, si veda Neil Baldwin, *Man Ray: American Artist*, Clarkson N. Potter, New York 1988, p. 335.

29 Si veda Daniel Buren, *Fonction de l'atelier*, 1971, in *Ecrits*, CAPC–Musée d'art contemporain, Bordeaux 1991, pp. 1-195, 205.

30 Buren, *The Function of the Studio*, trad. Thomas Repensek, "October", 10 (autunno 1979), p. 53.

Spazi

Marco De Michelis

"L'artista è l'origine dell'opera. L'opera è l'origine dell'artista"
Martin Heidegger, L'origine dell'opera d'arte, 1936[1]

"Sono lo spazio in cui sono"
Noël Arnaud, L'Etat d'ébauche, 1950[2]

What art may be

Un aspetto del tutto caratteristico dell'inizio folgorante della carriera artistica di Bruce Nauman è rappresentato dalla sua collocazione davvero anomala nel contesto dell'arte americana alla fine degli anni sessanta: marginale rispetto a New York, centro geografico dell'arte americana, e tuttavia protagonista riconosciuto, anche se mai del tutto assimilato, della scena artistica internazionale degli ultimi anni sessanta. Il destino di artista silenzioso sembra stabilito fin dagli anni della sua formazione, ben prima del definitivo trasferimento negli altipiani solitari del New Mexico. Dopo la prima mostra personale nella Galleria di Nicholas Wilder a Los Angeles nel maggio del 1966, quando ancora era studente della University of California a Davis, Nauman è presente dall'anno successivo in quasi tutte le mostre cruciali che documentano il costituirsi della generazione degli artisti postminimalisti americani e, più in generale, la diffusione internazionale dell'arte concettuale. Sono questi, tra il 1966 e il 1969, anni davvero straordinari per l'arte – e non solo per l'arte: quelli in cui prendono forma i primi colossali *Earthwork*, vengono elaborati le tesi e i manifesti dell'arte concettuale come le 35 "Sentences on Conceptual Art"[3] di Sol LeWitt, proposte formule come "Eccentric Abstraction", "Anti Form", "Process Art", "Body Art", "Arte Povera" per descrivere un coacervo spesso incoerente di lavori "in cui l'idea è essenziale, e la forma materiale secondaria, insignificante, effimera, banale, senza pretese e/o 'smaterializzata'".[4] La comunità artistica raccolta nel Lower East Side newyorkese si interrogava sull'opportunità di abbandonare gli spazi tradizionali delle gallerie d'arte e dei musei e non si sottraeva ai grandi temi della politica, dominata in quegli anni dalla contestazione studentesca e dall'opposizione alla guerra in Vietnam.

Nauman partecipava alle mostre, ma continuava a vivere isolato in California: prima a San Francisco, dopo aver completato gli studi presso l'Universiy of California a Davis nell'estate del 1966; poi nella Mill Valley dove aveva subaffittato la casa di un suo ex insegnante, William Wiley; infine dal 1969 a Pasadena, a nord di Los Angeles, prima di trasferirsi definitivamente nel New Mexico nel 1979.[5] L'artista conosce ormai bene l'ambiente newyorkese, ma condivide la vita di quella peculiare comunità artistica californiana che sembrava disdegnare del tutto successo e mercato, preferendo vivere con gli stipendi delle scuole d'arte o con i proventi di altri mestieri, piuttosto che con le vendite nelle potenti gallerie della costa orientale. Come egli stesso ha ricordato: "Andare a New York era contro le regole".[6]

Sulla parete del suo primo studio di San Francisco, ospitato in un ex negozio di alimentari, Nauman appende, nel 1967, un neon circolare sul quale si può leggere *The True Artist Helps the World by Revealing Mystic Truths* (tav. 22), anticipando quasi letteralmente la prima delle trentacinque frasi di Sol LeWitt scritte quasi tre anni dopo: "Gli artisti concettuali sono mistici piuttosto che razionalisti". L'uso del neon, che rimarrà uno dei "medium" prediletti da Nauman nei decenni successivi, coincideva con le pressoché contemporanee sperimentazioni di altri artisti come Dan Flavin, Jasper Johns, Joseph Kosuth e Martial Raysse.[7] In questa occasione, però, Nauman sembra utilizzare la tecnica popolare del neon pubblicitario, quella di cui rimanevano le tracce a testimonianza dell'originaria destinazione commerciale dello studio, per indirizzare un messaggio relativo al significato stesso e al ruolo dell'opera d'arte.

Una delle tante formulazioni offerte dall'artista per spiegare il senso del suo lavoro nella solitudine silenziosa dello studio verso la metà degli anni sessanta è "la ricerca sulle possibilità di ciò che può essere arte".[8] Nauman esplora davvero "la struttura della disciplina",[9] ne interroga il senso. Già durante la permanenza a University of California a Davis, egli aveva abbandonato il progetto di diventare pittore, disciplina alla quale si era inizialmente dedicato come artista. L'arte che egli interrogava era, invece, un'arte "senza tecnica". Il suo significato iniziava semplicemente dalla presenza dell'artista all'interno dello spazio dello studio.

Le fonti alle quali riferirsi si trovavano tutte, in qualche modo, al di fuori delle pratiche tradizionali delle arti figurative. Nauman era, infatti, un appassionato lettore di testi letterari di avanguardia come Samuel Beckett, Vladimir Nabokov e Alain Robbe-Grillet e di testi come le *Ricerche Filosofiche* di Ludwig Wittgenstein (Nauman stesso ricordava: "Ho sempre letto molto. Leggo dei bei pezzi voracemente, e leggerei qualsiasi cosa").[10] In seguito agli studi musicali giovanili, Nauman si dedicò alla scoperta dei compositori minimalisti americani come Steve Reich, Philip Glass e, soprattutto, La Monte Young; negli stessi anni ci fu l'incontro con i protagonisti della nuova danza americana come Meredith Monk, Yvonne Rainer e il gruppo di coreografi raccoltisi attorno alle sperimentazioni di Anna Halprin e del marito Lawrence, architetto paesaggista, ma non per questo meno coinvolto in una sperimentazione che cambierà il volto della danza americana.

Per Nauman, Marcel Duchamp esisteva in uno sfondo impreciso; Man Ray aveva conquistato una più precisa fisionomia in occasione della visita ad una mostra dei suoi lavori tenutasi a Los Angeles; le uniche informazioni su Joseph Beuys erano quelle fornite dal curatore tedesco Kasper König in visita allo studio. Johns e Willem de Kooning, Dada e Surrealismo rappresentavano riferimenti essenziali, ma lontani nello spazio e nel tempo. Certo, le informazioni non mancavano, né sull'arte contemporanea internazionale né, tanto meno, su quanto accadeva sulla costa orientale americana. Tali informazioni venivano, però, filtrate da interrogativi intimamente personali, ancor privi di una risposta, o, potremmo dire, privi di una "teoria".

La Terapia della Gestalt

Jean-Christophe Ammann ha sottolineato, ormai più di vent'anni fa, la "dimensione esistenziale" del lavoro di Nauman, individuata nella capacità dell'artsita di investigare una relazione essenziale tra soggetto e ambiente, come se l'opera stessa risultasse come l'esito di una "indagine".[11] Per Joan Simon, allo stesso tempo, la ricerca di Nauman rivela un carattere davvero "sperimentale", come di un processo che si pone l'interrogativo sul "Dove iniziare e come continuare".[12] Lo "sfondo" di questa attività era lo spazio dello studio, sgombro da materiali superflui per la scarsezza di mezzi finanziari, e a quel tempo il luogo in cui l'artista trascorreva la maggior parte del suo tempo per mancanza di impegni particolari. Come Nauman stesso amava ricordare: "Fui costretto a esaminare-analizzare me stesso e quel che stavo facendo lì dentro".[13]

Nel 1966 lo studio di San Francisco era vuoto, ma era destinato a riempirsi ben presto di una mole impressionante di lavori diversi: sculture in fibra di vetro e altri materiali, perfomance filmate, fotografie, opere al neon, disegni e installazioni. L'unica presenza permanente era quella del giovane artista, convinto che "Se mi trovavo nello studio, qualsiasi cosa facevo era arte".[14] Nell'atto di stabilire un rapporto tra lo spazio dello studio e l'artista alla ricerca di una risposta sul che cosa potesse significare fare arte, Nauman esprimeva un bisogno di riunificazione, un desiderio di riconquistare l'integrità del proprio esistere nello spazio.

Si tratta, è ben chiaro, di un approccio essenzialmente fenomenologico, benché Nauman abbia sempre escluso, per esempio, Maurice Merleau-Ponty dal novero numeroso degli autori conosciuti in quegli anni. Nauman, però, ricorda anche di aver letto un libro destinato ad esercitare una profonda influenza sul suo lavoro: *Gestalt Therapy*, pubblicato nel 1951 da Frederick Perls, Ralph F. Hefferline e Paul Goodman.[15] In questo libro, Perls e i suoi collaboratori riproponevano le teorie ormai classiche della psicologia della Gestalt come strumento terapeutico in grado di ricomporre quella condizione di frammentazione dell'individuo, di "dualismo della sua personalità, del suo pensiero, e del suo linguaggio",[16] la polarizzazione tra anima e corpo, tra cultura e civilizzazione, tra lavoro intellettuale e lavoro manuale, tra individuo e società, così peculiarmente caratteristiche dell'idea stessa di modernità.

Per il terapista della Gestalt, la capacità di "costruire figure" (la cosidetta "*Gestalt Formation")* è determinata dalla parallela capacità di stabilire relazioni significative tra elementi isolati: per dirla con Perls, "da essi facciamo un triangolo";[17] in altre parole, ricomporre l'interazione in cui la "figura" si staglia sullo "sfondo". Perls scrive: "In uno stato di benessere psico-fisico, il rapporto tra figura e sfondo è un processo permanente, ma significativo di emersione e ritirata. L'interazione di figura e sfondo diventa, così, il centro della teoria presentata in questo libro: attenzione, concentrazione, interesse, relazione, eccitazione e grazia sono tutti rappresentativi di una sana formazione di figura/sfondo; mentre confusione, noia, comportamenti coatti, fissazioni, ansia, amnesie, stasi e l'auto coscenza sono indicativi di una formazione figura/sfondo disturbata.[18] Potremmo definire questa condizione disturbata come quella di un individuo che si percepisce come esterno a se stesso, diviso dalla sua stessa esperienza del mondo, che egli considera allo stesso modo di un osservatore estraneo. Come rimedio, *Gestalt Therapy* proponeva una serie di esercizi, di sperimentazioni, destinati a "estendere, o meglio, ad accrescere in voi la consapevolezza di ciò che fate e di come lo fate",[19] ma basandosi sulla premessa che l'individuo e il suo ambiente "non sono due entità indipendenti, bensì *insieme* .... costituiscono un sistema funzionante, di influenza reciproca, totale".[20]

Alcuni di questi esercizi prevedevano la minuziosa descrizione del contesto nel quale il soggetto si trovava, per una precisa presa di coscienza del proprio essere in un luogo (Perls riporta le esclamazioni entusiaste di un paziente: "Mi sento così strano. Il mondo è lì, *realmente è lì!* E io possiedo occhi, *occhi reali*!").[21] Altri esercizi riguardavano l'equilibrio o l'idea di "opposizione" e richiedevano al paziente di immaginare gli eventi accaduti "come in un film proiettato all'indietro" o con "l'immagine capovolta".[22] Un insieme cruciale di esercizi era l'elaborazione di una "tecnica della consapevolezza": "Ora sono consapevole di essere sdraiato su un divano ... Ora sono consapevole di esitare, del fatto che mi sto chiedendo da che parte cominciare ... ora mi sento di nuovo sperduto. Mi torna in mente la raccomandazione di mantenermi nell'ambito delle cose in superficie. Ora sono consapevole di stare seduto con le gambe accavallate ... Concentratevi sulle vostre sensazioni 'corporee' nella loro totalità. Soffermate lentamente la vostra attenzione su ogni parte della vostra persona ...".[23]

Nauman sembra aver perfettamente compreso il significato e la struttura delle pratiche suggerite dalla terapia della Gestalt. In alcuni casi, gli esercizi performativi, ma anche le sperimentazioni sculturali, sembrano ripetere letteralmente le istruzioni di Perls. Al tempo stesso, però, esercizi e sperimentazioni ribaltano profondamente l'intento terapeutico, esaltandone, invece, l'aspetto esperienziale, di conoscenza diretta, di presa di possesso della condizione di frammentazione e di dualità. Gli esperimenti di Nauman non producono risposte, né suggeriscono soluzioni. Non contribuiscono a ricomporre l'armonia dell'interezza, ma hanno come protagonista una irresolubile condizione di disagio e di tensione.

Quando, nelle sculture e nei disegni, Nauman ripetutamente mette a fuoco il problema del rapporto irrisolto tra interno ed esterno, il suo obiettivo non è quello di fare finalmente chiarezza, quanto, piuttosto, "di creare una certa confusione tra la parte interna e quella esterna di un'opera".[24] La sua lista di "cose che puoi fare ad una sbarra diritta: curvarla, piegarla a metà, torcerla"[25] costituisce un'ordinata sequenza di "esercizi" destinati a produrre condizioni di fragile equilibrio, come quello delle sculture realizzate con materiali (gomma, tessuto) che non sono in condizione di mantenere la configurazione voluta, a meno che non siano sospesi, appesi alle pareti dello studio, o semplicemente appoggiati sulla superficie piana del pavimento. Le rozze strutture in vetroresina sono un altro esempio, similarmente e precariamente appoggiate alle pareti dello studio. Se la scultura moderna dei primi decenni del ventesimo secolo aveva perso il piedistallo stabile che la separava da terra, qui sembrava ormai (ma anche nei lavori contemporanei di Richard Serra o Robert Morris, di Eva Hesse o Joel Shapiro) privata perfino della permanenza della sua forma e della sua autonoma presenza nello spazio.

In altri casi esse si propongono come appendici del corpo umano, ma per costringerlo all'esperienza di un instabile equilibrio, piuttosto che per incrementarne la funzionalità nello spazio.

Si pensi a *Slant Step*, lo strano oggetto dal fascino imperscrutabile, simile a uno sgabello o a un gradino, che Nauman aveva casualmente recuperato nel 1965 insieme a Bill Wiley in un magazzino di Mill Valley e poi utilizzato l'anno successivo in occasione di una mostra collettiva che aveva visto coinvolti artisti e poeti della Bay Area. Come lo stesso titolo suggerisce, si tratta di uno scalino obliquo, inutilizzabile appunto per la configurazione inclinata del suo piano d'appoggio, un tema sul quale Nauman ritorna con l'opera *Device to Stand In* (1966; fig. 43), sul quale il corpo umano era destinato ad assumere una posizione faticosamente e innaturalmente instabile. Esempi di questo genere sono innumerevoli: il corpo stesso dell'artista diventa l'occasione per manipolazioni e metamorfosi che ne alterano la fisionomia fino a renderla irriconoscibile, talvolta in deformazioni mostruose, dilatazioni esagerate nello spazio che alterano irreparabilmente le proporzioni originarie del corpo (*Six Inches of My Knee Extended to Six Feet,* 1967 (fig. 44); *Storage Capsule for the Right Rear Quarter of My Body*, 1966). Altre volte fantastiche metamorfosi fanno del corpo stesso dell'artista il soggetto tradizionale della scultura pubblica, come nel caso degli autoritratti (si veda figs. 29 e 53) che trasformano Nauman se stesso in una fontana zampillante, quasi a illustrare un'altra opera testuale che decorava come un'insegna pubblicitaria la vetrina del suo studio-negozio di San Francisco, l'annuncio che *The True Artist Is an Amazing Luminous Fountain* (tav. 26).

In *From Hand to Mouth* (1967; tav. 11), il corpo, ridotto a un troncone mutilato che, dalla bocca, si estende lungo il braccio fino alla mano, raggiunge una condizione di così indefinibile identità da aver alimentato a lungo l'incertezza dell'attribuzione del calco in cera all'artista stesso, piuttosto che, come finalmente è risultato, a quello femminile della moglie Judy. Ancor più estremo sembra essere l'esito a cui Nauman perviene con due fotografie dello stesso anno nelle quali il corpo dell'artista letteralmente si dissolve in una traccia luminosa immateriale che ne avvolge e cancella la figura (*Light Trap for Henry Moore No. 1* e *No. 2*; fig. 45). Se l'obiettivo della terapia gestaltica era quello della ricomposizione di una relazione ordinata tra il sé e l'ambiente che lo circonda, Nauman, invece, sperimenta i limiti estremi della cancellazione dell'identità personale, dilatando fino all'illeggibilità le lettere che compongono il suo nome (*My Last Name Exaggerated Fourteen Times Vertically*, 1967; fig. 55; *My Name as Though It Were Written on the Surface of the Moon,* 1968; tav. 15) o documentando in una fotografia la loro bizzarra trasformazione in cibo e l'atto di essere mangiate da parte del soggetto stesso (*Eating My Words*, 1966–67/1970; fig. 46).

Lo spazio in cui vive e lavora Nauman non è mai destinato ad assumere le sembianze domestiche della casa: di esso non si può dire quello che Gaston Bachelard ha scritto riguardo la casa, e cioè che essa "fornisce un riparo alla *rêverie*, protegge il sognatore, ci consente di sognare in pace".[26] Non è il nido, né il rifugio accogliente, dove trovare protezione rispetto al mondo esterno, piuttosto è il laboratorio enigmatico dove trasformare l'esperienza segreta dell'angoscia, "l'essere frustrato e arrabbiato",[27] in una consapevole "azione investigativa"[28] della propria condizione di artista.

Sculture viventi

Nel 1965, all'University of California a Davis, Nauman aveva proposto una performance (poi ripetuta e riprodotta nel video del 1969, *Wall-Floor Positions*) nella quale l'artista assumeva una dopo l'altra una serie di posizioni diverse, descritte con parole immediatamente associabili a quelle utilizzate dall'artista per descrivere le sue manipolazioni scultoree. Il "Curvare, piegare a metà, torcere" in questo caso veniva trasformato in "Inizia in piedi con le spalle alla parete, poi allontanati dalla parete, poi inchinati, e poi puoi piegarti fino a toccare il pavimento, e poi distenditi, rigirati e alzati in piedi".[29] Nell'arco di un'ora, ventotto posizioni diverse del corpo rispetto alla parete e al pavimento della stanza venivano assunte dall'artista secondo regole arbitrarie, diligentemente rispettate, e conservate per circa un minuto. Il corpo di Nauman si trasformava, in questo modo, in una scultura vivente, usato e manipolato "come un pezzo di materiale",[30] rivelando per la prima volta quell'indifferenza rispetto ai soliti media espressivi che rimarrà una caratteristica peculiare dell'opera di Nauman negli anni successivi.

I numerosi film in sedici millimetri girati nello studio, che hanno come protagonista l'artista stesso, documentano, si potrebbe dire, questo sforzo doloroso e vano di stabilire un'unità armoniosa tra la figura e lo sfondo. Gli esercizi a cui Nauman si sottopone sembrano proporre un'interpretazione disillusa delle pratiche suggerite dagli psicologi gestaltisti. L'artista vi è ritratto, ad esempio, mentre fa rimbalzare alternativamente due palle tra soffitto e pavimento; nell'atto di percorre senza sosta il perimetro quadrato della stanza con movimenti scanditi da un metronomo; o suonando sul violino la stessa nota, ininterrottamente, camminando nello studio, entrando e uscendo dall'inquadratura di ripresa, e, in questo modo, affidando al permanere insistente del suono la testimonianza del procedere dell'azione. Si tratta di azioni ripetute senza una vera progressione, prive di qualsiasi struttura narrativa, scandite soltanto dal tentativo di conservare un ritmo costante dei gesti e dei movimenti, fino al momento in cui, casualmente, questa continuità viene interrotta dall'errore o dalla decisione, altrettanto arbitraria, dell'artista. L'esperimento, dunque, seppur apparentemente destinato a favorire la "presa di possesso" dello spazio da parte dell'individuo, attraverso una vera e propria mappatura dei suoi confini, risultava, comunque, paradossalmente vanificato proprio dalla sua infinita estensione temporale, ulteriormente prolungata quando, nel 1969, Nauman ottenne dal gallerista Leo Castelli la possibilità di utilizzare una videocamera per registrare continuativamente l'azione fino a sessanta minuti. Le affinità con le parallele sperimentazioni di danzatori come Merce Cunningham o Meredith Monk (che Nauman aveva incontrato a San Francisco, e con i quali collaborò nel 1969 ad una performance al Whitney Museum of American Art di New York), sono ben riconoscibili nel tentativo condiviso di trasformare i più semplici movimenti in danza.

Spazi

Nauman aveva già affrontato il problema dello spazio proprio all'interno del suo studio, nel 1966 in occasione della realizzazione dell'opera *Flour Arrangements* (fig. 47): sgomberato da ogni oggetto preesistente, lo aveva utilizzato per realizzarvi una serie di configurazioni temporanee che Benjamin H. D. Buchloh ha descritto come le prime vere "sculture processuali".[31] Per la durata di un mese, Nauman aveva modellato, a intermittenza e in forme diverse, un grande mucchio di farina. Da dall'altro canto, la precarietà delle sculture in vetroresina e in altri materiali veniva così condotta ai suoi esiti estremi da una programmatica rinuncia a costruire degli oggetti statici, sostituita dalla più astratta -e residuale- possibilità di documentare le diverse fasi del lavoro in fotografie in bianco e nero. Il vero soggetto dell'opera è, in questo caso, non tanto la molteplicità delle forme realizzate, quanto, piuttosto, la programmatica processualità dell'azione messa in atto: la trasformazione dello spazio vuoto dello studio nello sfondo di un'azione quotidianamente ripetuta dall'artista, certificata, in qualche modo, soltanto dalla documentazione fotografica di quanto, di giorno in giorno, era accaduto.

Vi è un aspetto cruciale in questi brevi film giovanili e nei contemporanei lavori fotografici di Nauman un aspetto che definirei "dionisiaco", se ripensiamo alla descrizione dello spazio che Friedrich Nietzsche aveva introdotto nella sua opera *La Nascita della Tragedia*, presentandolo come un campo di forza "generato dal dinamismo del moto corporeo".[32] Secondo Nietzsche, l'eccesso di energia, "il traboccare di primigenia gioia", spinge l'artista a divenire, attraverso il suo corpo nello spazio, egli stesso un'opera d'arte. La stretta coincidenza tra il filosofo tedesco e il giovane artista americano non inganni. L'intenzione non è quella di stabilire una diretta dipendenza da uno o dall'altro, del resto mai documentata, quanto, piuttosto, di riconoscere la centralità peculiare e decisiva della nozione di "spazio" nell'opera di Bruce Nauman.

"Spazio" è una parola tutt'altro che neutrale. Essa porta con sé significati complessi e fortemente radicati nella nozione stessa di modernità.[33] L'idea che lo spazio vuoto all'interno di un edificio o quello attorno al volume modellato di una statua costituiscano un problema non era mai stato formulata come tale fino all'inizio dell'età moderna; tale considerazione inizia ad occupare una posizione centrale nella storia e nella filosofia delle arti solo sul finire del diciannovesimo secolo. Bisognerà attendere Constantin Brancusi e la disposizione in qualche modo "architettonica" delle sue sculture all'interno dell'atelier parigino per comprendere che non era più il "pieno" della modellazione plastica, ma lo spazio al suo intorno ad occupare il centro dell'attenzione di artisti come Naum Gabo, Alexander Calder e, finalmente, Lázló Moholy-Nagy.

Lo spazio di Nauman continua ancora oggi a fornire risposte significative ad interrogativi inizialmente proposti sul finire dell'Ottocento, quando storici dell'arte come i tedeschi August Schmarsow ed Heinrich Wölfflin, proponevano, a partire dalle teorie dell'empatia elaborate da Robert Vischer e Wilhelm Worringer, un'idea dello spazio come emanazione della presenza del corpo, come una "struttura" che prende forma attraverso il movimento del corpo, o, ancor più, attraverso lo sguardo fisso dell'uomo che vi assegna un senso e lo interpreta come una proiezione tridimensionale "introflessa" del corpo osservante.[34] E' qui che trova il suo inizio e il suo fondamento teorico la concezione moderna dello spazio come una "proprietà della mente, parte dell'apparato attraverso cui percepiamo il mondo".[35]

Durante un'intervista con Joan Simon del 1987, Nauman spiegò uno dei suoi lavori più importanti e più enigmatici, *A Cast of the Space under My Chair* (1965-68; fig. 48), citando una frase di de Kooning: "Quando dipingi una sedia, dovresti dipingere lo spazio tra i pioli, non solo la sedia".[36] Spostare l'attenzione dal volume "positivo" dell'oggetto, scultoreo o meno, a quello "negativo", cioè al volume immateriale che lo circonda e che lo definisce, costituisce, in realtà, un mutamento di prospettiva di fondamentale importanza. Lo spostamento, tipicamente "gestaltico", dell'attenzione dalla figura all'ambiente è perfino più facilmente riconoscibile in un altro lavoro di Nauman del 1966, intitolato *Shelf Sinking into the Wall*, nel quale lo spazio sottostante lo scaffale, riprodotto in un calco, si materializza fino a staccarsi dalla sua matrice per finire, trascinato dalla forza di gravità, scompostamente ammassato in modo indecente sul pavimento. A ben vedere, il volume sotto la sedia, reso, appunto, misteriosamente solido attraverso la tecnica del calco, persino arcaico nella sua immobile materialità, sembra riconoscibile solamente a prezzo di uno sforzo interpretativo malgrado il suo assoluto realismo.

Ad un'attenta analisi, *A Cast of the Space under My Chair*, rievoca un problema fondamentale della scultura moderna, già formulato nel lontano 1893 dallo scultore tedesco Adolf Hildebrand. Hildebrand aveva cercato di trasferire la nuova problematica dello spazio, in origine essenzialmente architettonica, nei territori delle arti visive e, in particolare, della scultura. Per lo scultore tedesco, che ben conosceva le ricerche di Wölfflin, di Schmarsow, di Vischer e le riflessioni su empatia e visione di Worringer e di Konrad Fiedler, lo spazio costituiva il soggetto principale dell'opera d'arte e la premessa per la sua esperienza da parte dell'osservatore. In una prospettiva le cui radici risalivano a Immanuel Kant e alla sua *Critica della ragione pura,* dove egli aveva affermato il carattere mentale dello spazio, Hildebrand riconosceva il luogo nel quale le arti visive potevano liberarsi finalmente dal giogo antico dell'imitazione della natura, della mimesi. Lo spazio non rappresentava la realtà esterna, le sue caratteristiche e le sue proprietà fisiche, ma un'autonoma costruzione della mente, la proiezione dell'esperienza fisica, totalmente soggettiva, della visione. Per Hildebrand, dunque, la forma artistica poteva esistere solo nel momento in cui questa veniva percepita in uno spazio che rifletteva "l'attività cinetica della nostra immaginazione. Dobbiamo, poi, innanzitutto immaginarlo tridimensionalmente, come spazio vuoto, riempito in parte dai volumi singoli delle cose e in parte dall'aria atmosferica. ... Se i contorni o la forma di un oggetto ne indicano il volume, è possibile anche comporre gli oggetti in modo tale da evocare l'idea di un volume atmosferico da essi delimitato. Il limite di un oggetto è, strettamente parlando, anche il limite della massa d'aria che lo circonda da ogni parte".[37]

Spazi percorribili

All'inizio degli anni settanta Marcia Tucker, in due saggi formidabili che sono tra i più tempestivi contributi critici sull'opera di Nauman, propone un'interpretazione fenomenologica dell'opera dell'artista americano. Tucker osserva che Nauman "non rappresenta o interpreta fenomeni come suono, luce, movimento o temperatura, ma li usa come ... materia prima".[38] In questo modo, l'esperienza reale, fisica e corporea dell'opera, viene collocata al centro dell'interesse di Nauman. Se questo risultava, in qualche modo, già chiaro nei lavori dei quali l'artista stesso era il protagonista, ancor più cruciale risulterà nelle installazioni che, a partire dal 1969, coinvolgono direttamente l'esperienza fisica dello spettatore.

L'anno precedente, Nauman aveva realizzato nel suo studio un angusto corridoio, non più largo di cinquanta centimetri. Nel video *Walk with Contrapposto* (1968, fig. 32) l'artista si addentrava nello spazio di questo corridoio, appena sufficiente per contenerlo, esagerando il movimento oscillante delle anche ad ogni passo. Lo stesso corridoio venne riproposto nel 1969 nella mostra *Anti-Illusion: Procedures/Materials,* presso il Whitney Museum, ma, questa volta, come oggetto scultoreo che i visitatori potevano penetrare, ripetendo, in qualche modo, l'esperienza precedente dell'artista (fig. 49). E' stato lo stesso Nauman a sottolineare il carattere onirico di tale opera ("Si trattava di trovarsi in un lungo corridoio con una stanza alla fine del corridoio ... Era un sogno ricorrente, e ne ho dedotto che doveva essere una parte di me che non avevo identificato.

Mi sembrava importante estrinsecare me stesso")[39] e la claustrofobia determinata dall'estrema ristrettezza dello spazio. In questo modo, l'esperienza dell'artista veniva trasferita a una pluralità di potenziali soggetti, sia pure in modo implicito, dal momento che Nauman evitava di fornire qualsiasi istruzione o spiegazione al visitatore che, a sua volta, assumeva il ruolo del "performer" e vedeva coincidere la propria esperienza percettiva con l'opera d'arte stessa.

Allo stesso tempo, il margine di libertà consentito allo visitatore veniva, però, limitato dalle caratteristiche fortemente "specifiche" del corridoio. Nauman non era interessato a riproporre allo spettatore lo stessa libertà che lo aveva portato all'invenzione dell'opera; egli era interessato, di per sé, a non stimolare una generica esperienza percettiva, ma a riprodurre la stessa peculiare condizione che egli aveva voluto personalmente sperimentare. "Non mi interessava e non volevo presentare situazioni in cui le persone avessero troppa libertà di inventare quel che pensavano stesse accadendo", afferma Nauman, "Volevo fosse una mia idea, e non volevo che fosse la gente a inventare l'arte. Il corridoio era sufficientemente definito. I vari modi di fruirne erano così limitati che la gente era costretta ad avere più o meno le stesse esperienze che avevo avuto io".[40] In risposta al sospetto di una certa perversità intrinseca a queste installazioni, Nauman aveva replicato, in modo perentorio, sostenendo che il visitatore: "Può fare solo quel che io voglio che faccia. Diffido della partecipazione del pubblico".[41] Il carattere sperimentale dell'opera veniva, dunque, ribadito in un modo che non consentiva equivoci, fino al punto da supporre la possibilità di ripeterne gli effetti con altri soggetti, di confermarne i risultati proprio come viene postulato nelle pratiche scientifiche moderne.

Al centro dell'interesse di Nauman non c'era - e non c'è - l'evento esperienziale, quanto piuttosto l'esperienza del disagio, la messa in discussione dell'identità dell'individuo, dei confini tra interno ed esterno, tra pubblico e privato, il dilemma o l'interrogativo che potrebbe produrre una condizione di tensione e richiedere non solo consapevolezza, ma perfino un certo grado di coinvolgimento fisico. Tutte le sue installazioni architettoniche propongono questa condizione. I corridoi, che Nauman ha ripetuto in variazioni numerose nel corso degli anni, sono come trappole in cui il visitatore si infila, senza sospettarne le conseguenze, per trovarsi poi immerso in situazioni che sfuggono a univoche interpretazioni. Suoni improvvisi che pulsano sull'apparato auditivo; pareti che si restringono fin quasi ad immobilizzare il corpo al loro interno; specchi collocati sullo sfondo, in cui il corpo si riflette troncato della testa; monitor televisivi nei quali il visitatore si riconosce ripreso di spalle, nell'atto di avanzare verso il fondo del corridoio e contemporaneamente mentre si allontana dall'immagine proiettata; monitor che mostrano lo spazio del corridoio vuoto nello stesso momento in cui esso è letteralmente ingombro del corpo che vi è penetrato. Il moltiplicarsi e il sovrapporsi di informazioni contrastanti costituiscono due degli aspetti centrali di questi lavori e la causa di una "tensione derivante dal non essere in grado di farle coincidere".[42]

Architetture Mentali

Negli anni settanta, Nauman espose un grande numero di "modelli" di vastissime costruzioni, per lo più grandi tunnel circolari, labirintici ambienti sotterranei o profonde depressioni scavate nel terreno come piramidi rovesciate, ridotti fino a quaranta volte rispetto alle dimensioni reali progettate.[43] Nauman stesso considerava questi progetti come "estensioni delle varie installazioni di corridoi",[44] destinati a riprodurre in scala monumentale, nel caso dei modelli in modo più astratto e concettuale (dato che il visitatore non poteva entrare fisicamente nello spazio, ma doveva immaginare cosa avrebbe significato farlo), quella condizione di tensione tra esterno e interno, tra spazio chiuso e spazio aperto, tra inizio e fine, che l'artista aveva ricercato fin dalle sue prime realizzazioni di ambienti architettonici in scala naturale e, dunque, fisicamente esperibili dall'individuo che le avrebbe "abitate".

In un certo senso, anche la funzione dei disegni appare concettualmente non diversa da quella dei modelli. I disegni di Nauman non sono mai semplicemente "progetti", interpretazioni bidimensionali di un'intenzione progettuale, destinati ad essere usati da altri per realizzare materialmente quanto l'artista ha immaginato. Questo è il destino dei disegni architettonici. Nauman, invece, cerca di prefigurare e di descrivere l'effetto che l'idea realizzata potrà determinare. Michael Auping, citando Douglas Huebler, ha descritti i suoi disegni come "sculture mentali".[45] In alcuni casi sembrano diagrammi, nei quali la funzione dinamica del tempo si sovrappone all'organizzazione spaziale, come, ad esempio, negli studi per il video *Slow Angle Walk (Beckett Walk)* del 1968 (fig. 50), che delineano minuziosamente, come in una notazione coreografica, la sequenza complessa di movimenti che l'artista avrebbe ripetuto davanti alla cinepresa. In altri casi, alla disposizione spaziale degli elementi si sovrappone lo studio degli effetti invasivi dei neon colorati, o i percorsi intricati di immagini che rimbalzano da uno specchio all'altro o da un monitor televisivo all'atro, le dislocazioni e gli spostamenti possibili dell'osservatore, la pianificazione accurata dei diversi punti di vista e dei loro effetti. Alla base di tutto ciò sembrano presiedere più le pratiche della danza e del teatro che quelle dell'architettura.

La complessità concettuale di tutte queste opere risiede nell'intenzione di sovrapporre informazioni contrastanti che ne moltiplichino i significati e ne impediscano una percezione -emozionale, psicologica e fisiologica- unitaria. I modelli di tunnel sotterranei possono essere interpretati come un presagio del "dramma murato" che Bachelard aveva riconosciuto negli spazi oscuri e segreti delle cantine, "muri che hanno tutta la terra dietro",[46] ma sono anche semplicemente grandi sculture nello spazio ortogonale della galleria o del museo. L'osservatore non può sottrarsi a un pensiero che oscilla tra l'immaginazione di quello che davvero accadrebbe se fosse possibile penetrane le viscere opache e isolate dal mondo, se i modelli fossero costruiti in scala naturale, e la percezione dell'impatto reale dei volumi scultурali nello spazio espositivo.

Il desiderio di "creare spazi e forme inquietanti"[47] è una costante esplicita nell'opera di Nauman, lo strumento per innescare un'esperienza cognitiva a partire da una condizione di disagio, un richiamo improvviso al fatto che l'arte solo marginalmente si occupa di "fornire o creare cose belle"[48] quanto, piuttosto, come Wittgenstein gli aveva genialmente insegnato, di "procedere pensando alle cose".[49] Gli spazi triangolari ("Considero i triangoli una tipologia di spazio davvero inquietante, sconcertante"),[50] i tunnel sotterranei, i corridoi tanto stretti da diventare quasi impercorribili, le luci colorate senza ombre che talvolta ne riempiono gli interni, hanno questa funzione: di risvegliare l'attenzione o la consapevolezza e di cercare una risposta alle sensazioni suscitate.

Opere fondamentali come *Double Steel Cage Piece* (1974; tav. 3), una gabbia di maglia metallica percorribile dal visitatore, il cui tema è l'ambiguità di una condizione spaziale che è al tempo stesso racchiusa e trasparente, sembrano sollevare questioni che riguardano non solo il singolo individuo, ma anche una condizione generale dell'esistenza umana. Quanto appena affermato è riscontrabile anche nell'opera *South American Triangle* (1981; tav. 51) che rimane una delle poche creazioni di Nauman in cui viene svelata una relazione diretta con drammatici avvenimenti storici, in questo caso tortura e violenza nel continente latinoamericano. In entrambi i casi, Nauman parla di un personale coinvolgimento così profondo da mettere in dubbio la possibilità stessa di proseguire il percorso intrapreso: "Per molto tempo non ho più fatto nulla in questa direzione perché mi spaventava concentrarmi su temi così gravosi".[51] E ancora: "Ho smesso di lavorare per molto tempo perché l'immagine era veramente forte e molto lontana dalle opere precedenti".[52]

Fin dalle prime opere giovanili, questo tipo di disagio appare un aspetto decisivo dell'opera di Nauman; in esse l'artista metteva alla prova il proprio stesso corpo con azioni che implicavano un'estrema attenzione mentale e sollecitazioni fisiche faticose e coinvolgenti. L'angoscia di cui non cessa di parlare con la sua arte è sempre la sua stessa angoscia. La rabbia e lo smarrimento sulla condizione umana provengono dagli strati profondi dell'anima dell'artista: solo per questo risulta alla fine legittima la pretesa di chiedere agli altri, al pubblico, di condividerne l'esperienza e di percorrere il medesimo cammino alla ricerca di una risposta. La risposta all'invito non sarà sempre positiva. Come Nauman stesso ha riconosciuto, in alcuni casi le situazioni da lui create appaiono intollerabili, tali da portare l'interprete autorevole e osservatore acuto, Arthur Danto, a sottrarsi dall'imperativo di "fare ciò che vedi" che valutava allo stesso tempo proposto e imposto dalla mostra retrospettiva itinerante di Nauman, presentata al Museum of Modern Art di New York nel 1995. Nelle installazioni più drammatiche, Danto individuó l'astuta manipolazione dei sentimenti tipica degli artisti barocchi, con risultati "perentori, invadenti, aggressivi", persino repellenti, piuttosto che una riflessione, sia pur angosciosa, sulla condizione umana.[53]

Marcia Tucker ha recentemente e giustamente osservato che la coincidenza del ruolo dell'osservatore con quello del perfomer, l'ambivalenza tra il "senziente e il percepito",[54] richiama uno dei motivi fondamentali della fenomenologia di Merleau-Ponty:

l'interscambio dialettico tra l'individuo e il mondo che questi occupa, l'ambiguità tra il suo "essere allo stesso tempo vissuto dall'interno e osservato dall'esterno". Quello che Nauman fa con le sue opere è cercare di indurre un'alterazione ai modi in cui l'individuo percepisce il mondo nel quale vive. Come osserva Tucker, però, se "quel che conosciamo del mondo è la somma delle nostre percezioni e delle nostre reazioni fisiche, emotive e intellettive all'ambiente circostante, allora, manipolare efficacemente questi fattori equivale a effettuare un cambiamento virtuale in quel mondo".[55]

Spazi Sonori

Days e *Giorni*, il lavoro più recente di Bruce Nauman, presentato in anteprima in occasione della 53. Esposizione Internazionale d'Arte – La Biennale di Venezia (pp. 145–73), ha le sue origini nei primissimi inizi della carriera artistica dell'artista americano, rivelando una profonda continuità della sua ricerca. Dobbiamo, infatti, risalire fino ai primi anni sessanta, alle esercitazioni giovanili con il pianoforte, la chitarra e il basso, quando Nauman si considerava ancora un possibile musicista; allo studio della dissoluzione delle strutture classiche della musica nell'opera tarda di Beethoven e nella successiva "invenzione" del sistema dodecafonico da parte di Schönberg; all'incontro, avvenuto poco dopo, con la musica di John Cage e con i protagonisti del minimalismo musicale come Reich, Glass e Young. Quello che Nauman vi scopriva era la dissoluzione del tempo e della struttura, sostituiti da un fluire continuo, sottilmente variabile e vibrante, privo di inizio e di fine. Proprio come i movimenti della danza, ordinari e quotidiani, ma enormemente precisi, di Cunnigham e Monk, le costruzioni drammaturgiche di Beckett, e le strutture letterarie che Robbe-Grillet descriveva: "Invece di aver a che fare con una serie di scene collegate da nessi causali, si ha l'impressione che la stessa scena si ripeta costantemente, ma con alcune variazioni".[56]

Nel 1968 Nauman aveva prodotto un'installazione che consisteva semplicemente di una stanza vuota, all'interno della quale una voce registrata borbottava senza interruzione l'invito perentorio: "Esci dalla mia mente, esci da questa stanza" (si veda la lista delle opere in mostra n. 20). L'esperienza visiva veniva sostituita da una sonora che comportava al tempo stesso la collocazione del corpo nello spazio, ossia l'esperienza del visitatore-ascoltatore all'interno di una stanza dalla quale era invitato ad uscire, ma anche una più generale e angosciosa e frantumata condizione di esistere nel mondo, di separazione della figura/mente dallo spazio/sfondo abitato dal corpo. Uscire dalla stanza, per ottemperare all'ordine ricevuto, poteva apparire una soluzione facilmente attuabile; molto meno lo era quella di separarsi da una realtà cosi immateriale come quella della mente. Era proprio questa dualità difficilmente ricomponibile tra spazio e pensiero ad attribuire a quest'opera il carattere di una "scultura esperienziale".[57]

In *Sound Breaking Wall* (fig. 52), un'installazione presentata nella galleria parigina di Ileana Sonnabend nel 1969, una serie di piccoli altoparlanti nascosti nella parete alternavano la registrazione di sussurrii e sospiri quasi impercettibili a quella di risate e tonfi rumorosi. La difficoltà di individuare le fonti sonore e di prevedere lo sviluppo temporale dell'azione sonora produceva la condizione di "minacciosa" incertezza così frequente nella produzione di Nauman. L'anno successivo, nel 1970, presso la galleria torinese di Gian Enzo Sperone, viene presenta un'opera ancor più inquietante: in questo caso, il visitatore, toccando una parete, produceva un suono, ma dislocato su una parete diversa.

Quarant'anni dopo, a Venezia, Nauman realizza una doppia installazione, separata dalle due diverse lingue utilizzate, l'italiano e l'inglese, ma anche dalla loro collocazione in due edifici situati in differenti parti della città. All'interno di ciascuna sede, quattordici altoparlanti ripetono, in sequenze diverse, i nomi dei sette giorni della settimana. Lo scorrere regolare del tempo è alterato dal modificarsi della sequenza dei giorni ed anche, contemporaneamente, dal ritmo, solo approssimativamente uguale, delle diverse voci recitanti. Il visitatore alterna, senza soluzione di continuità, l'ascolto delle singole voci, quando la sua posizione è in prossimità di un singolo altoparlante, con quello della "sinfonia" delle voci sovrapposte, ma non perfettamente sincronizzate, quando si allontana verso il centro della sala. La regolarità delle singole letture, la regolarità del tempo che trascorre, del ciclo settimanale che si ripete senza sosta, viene alterata dalla collocazione del corpo nello spazio, trasformandosi in un brusio difficilmente intellegibile, in un tempo privato della sua trasparente linearità. Le parti e l'insieme ancora una volta si confondono e solo la consapevolezza della posizione della figura individuale nel contesto del mondo indica il percorso di un ordine possibile e, pur tuttavia, inesorabilmente precario. L'angoscia di Nauman, con il passare degli anni, sembra aver placato la violenza e le frustrazioni originarie; non annuncia più l'altalenante convivere del bene e del male, della vita e della morte, dei vizi e delle virtù. Eppure ne rimane una traccia sottile, che scava ancora negli abissi dell'inquietudine. Il tempo si è fermato? Lo sentiamo appena.

1 Martin Heidegger, *L'origine dell'opera d'arte*, 1936, trad. I. De Gennaro e G. Zaccaria Christian Marinotti Edizioni, Milano 2000, p. 3.

2 Noël Arnaud, citato in Gaston Bachelard, *The Poetics of Space*, 1958, trad. Inglese, Beacon Press, Boston, 1969, p.137.

3 Sol Lewitt, *Sentences on Conceptual Art*, "0-9", 5 (gennaio 1969).

4 Lucy R. Lippard, *Six Years: The Dematerialization of the Art Object from 1966 to 1972*, University of California Press, Berkeley 1973, p. vii.

5 Per una cronologia della vita di Nauman negli anni 1964-69 si veda Elizabeth Allison Ferrel, *Chronology*, in *A Rose Has no Teeth: Bruce Nauman in the 1960s*, a cura di Constance M. Lewallen, catalogo della mostra, University of California Press, Berkeley Art Museum e Pacific Film Archive, Berkeley/Los Angeles 2007, pp. 193-213.

6 Nauman, in Michele de Angelus, *Interview with Bruce Nauman*, 1980, in Nauman, *Please pay attention please: Bruce Nauman's Words: Writing and Interviews*, a cura di Janet Kraynak, The MIT Press, Cambridge Mass. 2002, p. 238. Si tratta della più lunga e articolata intervista concessa da Nauman, all'interno del contesto del California Oral History Project della Smithsonian Institution, Archives of American Art, Washington D.C. 1980. Nauman è stato e rimane un artista poco loquace e, a differenza di altri suoi contemporanei, poco propenso alle elaborazioni teoriche. Sono le interviste rilasciate nel corso dei decenni a costituire uno strumento essenziale per interpretare le sue idee e le sue intenzioni.

7 Si veda Coosje van Bruggen, *Bruce Nauman*, Rizzoli, New York 1988, p. 15.

8 Nauman, citato in *ibid.*, p. 7.

9 Nauman, in de Angelus, *Interview with Bruce Nauman,* cit., p. 285.

10 Nauman, in Christopher Cordes, *Talking with Bruce Nauman: an Interview*, 1989, in Nauman, *Please Pay Attention Please*, cit., p. 362.

11 Jean-Christophe Ammann, *Wittgenstein and Nauman*, in *Bruce Nauman*, catalogo della mostra, Whitechapel Art Gallery, London 1986, pp. 21–29.

12 Joan Simon, *Nauman Variations*, in Nauman, *Please Pay Attention Please*, p. 11.

13 Nauman, in Willoughby Sharp, *Two Interviews*, 1970, in *Bruce Nauman*, a cura di Robert C. Morgan, The John Hopkins University Press, Baltimore/London 2002, p. 237.

14 Nauman, in Joan Simon, *Breaking the Silence: an Interview with Bruce Nauman*, 1987, in Nauman, *Please Pay Attention Please*, cit., pp. 322-323.

15 Si veda Lorraine Sciarra, *Bruce Nauman*, 1972, in Nauman, *Please Pay Attention Please*, cit., p. 166. Il libro è a cura di Frederick S. Perls, Ralph F. Hefferline, Paul Goodman,*La Terapia della Gestalt. Vitalità e accrescimento nella personalità umana*, (New York, 1951), trad. I. J. Sanders e F. Liuzzi, Astrolabio, Roma 1997.

16 Perls, Hefferline e Goodman, *Gestalt Therapy*, cit., p. 28.

17 *Ibid.*, p. 29.

18 *Ibid.*, p. 30.

19 *Ibid.*, p. 311.

20 *Ibid.*, p. 345.

21 *Ibid.*, p. 313.

22 *Ibid.*, p. 319.

23 *Ibid.*, pp. 357-8.

24 Nauman in Sharp, *Two Interviews*, cit., p. 237.

25 *Ibid.*, p. 242.

26 Gaston Bachelard, *La poetica dello Spazio*, (Paris 1958), trad. E. Catalano, Edizioni Dedalo, Bari 1975, p. 34.

27 Nauman, in de Angelus, *Interview with Bruce Nauman*, cit., p. 239.

28 Nauman, in Ian Wallace e Russel Keziere, *Bruce Nauman Interviewed*, 1978, in Nauman, *Please Pay Attention Please*, cit., p. 188.

29 Nauman, in Sciarra, *Bruce Nauman*, cit., p.161.

30 Nauman, in Sharp, *Two Interviews*, cit., p. 242.

31 Benjamin H. D. Buchloh, *Process Sculpture and Film in Richard Serra's Work* in Buchloh, *Neo-Avantgarde and Culture Industry: Essays on European and American Art from 1958-1975*, The MIT Press, Cambridge Mass 2000, p. 414.

32 Friedrich Nietzsche, *La Nascita della Tragedia*, (1872), Adelphi Edizioni, Milano 1984, p. 144.

33 Si veda a questo proposito Adrian Forty, ad vocem *Spazio*, in Forty, *Parole e edifici: un vocabolario per l'architettura moderna*, Pendragon, Bologna 2004, pp. 267-291.

34 Su August Schmarsow, Robert Vischer e Wilhelm Worringer si veda *Empathy, Form and Space*, a cura di Maligrave e Ikonomou, The Getty Center, Santa Monica CA 1994.

35 Forty, *Spazio*, cit., p. 267.

36 Simon, *Breaking the Silence*, cit., p. 324.

37 Adolf Hildebrand, *The Problem of Form in the Fine Arts*, in *Empathy, Form and Space*, a cura di Maligrave e Ikonomou, cit., p. 239.

38 Marcia Tucker, *PheNAUMANology* in "Artforum" 9, 4 (dicembre 1970), pp. 38-44; ripubblicato in *Bruce Nauman*, a cura di Morgan, cit., pp. 21-27. Il secondo saggio è Tucker, *Bruce Nauman*, in Jane Livingston e Marcia Tucker, *Bruce Nauman: Work from 1965 to 1972*, catalogo della mostra, Los Angeles County Museum, Los Angeles,1973, pp. 31-48.

39 Nauman, citato in Amei Wallach, "Artist of the Showdown", in *Bruce Nauman*, a cura di Morgan cit., pp. 36-42. Pubblicato originariamente in *Newsday*, 8 gennaio 1989.

40 Nauman, citato in van Bruggen, *Bruce Nauman*, cit., p. 18.

41 Nauman, in Sharp, *Two Interviews*, cit., p. 235.

42 Nauman, in de Angelus, *Interview with Bruce Nauman*, cit., p. 265.

43 Il valore 1:40 è riportato in Wallace e Keziere, *Bruce Nauman Interviewed*, p. 186. In De Angelus, *Interview with Bruce Nauman*, cit., p. 276, Nauman parla di una scala 1:12 per i modelli di tunnel.

44 Nauman, in de Angelus, *Interview with Bruce Nauman*, cit., p. 278.

45 Michael Auping, *Projection and Displacement*, in *Bruce Nauman: Drawings for Installations*, catalogo della mostra, Sperone Westwater, New York 2008, pp. 7-12. Si veda anche *Bruce Nauman. Drawings. Zeichnungen 1965-1986*, catalogo della mostra, Museum für Gegenwartskunst, Basel 1986.

46 Bachelard, *La poetica dello Spazio*, cit., p. 48.

47 Nauman, in Bob Smith, *Bruce Nauman Interview*, 1982, in Nauman, *Please Pay Attention Please*, cit., p. 298.

48 Nauman, in Simon, *Breaking the Silence*, cit., p. 332.

49 Nauman, in Sharp, *Two Interviews*, cit., p. 245. E' noto l'interesse di Nauman per Wittgenstein e la sua conoscenza delle *Ricerche Filosofiche* del filosofo austriaco. Si vedano ad esempio Ammann, *Wittgenstein and Nauman*, e Robert Storr, *Beyond Words*, in Kathy Halbreich e Neil Benezra, *Bruce Nauman*, Walker Art Center, Minneapolis 1994, pp. 47-66.

50 Nauman, in Simon, *Breaking the Silence*, cit., p. 332.

51 Nauman, in Smith, *Bruce Nauman Interview*, cit., p. 299.

52 *Ibid.*, p. 300.

53 Arthur C. Danto, *Bruce Nauman*, in *Bruce Nauman*, a cura di Morgan cit., p. 150. L'articolo era stato originariamente pubblicato in "The Nation", 8 maggio 1995.

54 Tucker, *PheNAUMANology*, cit., p. 23.

55 *Ibid.*, p. 27.

56 Alain Robbe-Grillet, citato in Ingrid Schaffner, *Bruce Nauman through Samuel Beckett*, in *ibid.*, p. 168.

57 Kraynak, *Bruce Nauman's Words*, in Nauman, *Please Pay Attention Please*, cit., p. 1.

L'analogia diventa arte: le infinite traiettorie della ricerca di Bruce Nauman

Erica F. Battle

Uno dei miei metodi di lavoro utilizza la tensione tra due tipi di informazioni che non collimano – non è solo l'oggetto che si sperimenta e contempla; è l'oggetto in relazione ad altri brani di informazione con i quali si ha a che fare.

Bruce Nauman[1]

Analogia : Topologia

In *Bruce Nauman: Topological Gardens*, le analogie abbondano. Quando si tenta di rapportarsi con approccio curatoriale alla quarantennale carriera di Nauman, qualsiasi aspirazione a identificare un'unica linea di continuità presto lascia spazio, fortunatamente, alla realizzazione che la sua produzione artistica è un universo di cui non si riesce a tracciare la mappa. La prassi artistica di Nauman rende impossibile la specificità, tipicamente modernista, del mezzo espressivo e nega l'importanza tradizionalmente attribuita ad una cronologia precisa. La caratteristica comune dei testi critici su Nauman, pubblicati nel corso dei decenni, è, infatti, una premessa simile alla seguente: la sua è una carriera basata su deviazioni di rotta, aberrazioni e disparità.[2]

La risposta più semplice a questa difficile situazione consiste nell'affermare che Nauman continua a porre domande diverse sul mondo e sul proprio ruolo d'artista, grazie ad approcci altrettanto diversi, utilizzando un'economia di mezzi espressivi che si rivela allo stesso tempo di ampio respiro materiale e di grande densità concettuale. L'arte di Nauman ci ha insegnato ad evitare il percorso lineare a favore di cerchi, di labirinti diagrammatici e, in termini topologici, della mappatura di una rete di punti fissi nell'andamento oscillante di una prassi artistica in evoluzione. Per la sua stessa natura, *Topological Gardens* afferma che la possibilità di esplorare l'arte di Nauman, dal punto di vista della cronologia e del variare delle forme, dipende dall'identificazione di *topoi* che facciano da guida in entrambi i casi.

Eppure, anche l'idea di definire un singolo *topos* che rappresenti Nauman è problematica: l'attaccamento a una tematica ben definita può essere utile fino a un certo punto. Ciò che serve, invece, è un paradigma che offra allo stesso tempo continuità ed elasticità, proprio come i tre temi selezionati per questa mostra. Tali "sequenze", come le ha definite Carlos Basualdo nel suo saggio contenuto nel presente catalogo, si intrecciano dentro e fuori, sopra e sotto, negli spazi pieni e vuoti dell'opera di Nauman e attraverso la quarta presenza della mostra: la topografia di Venezia. Sono temi che si definiscono a coppie – Fontane e Neon; Teste e Mani; Suono e Spazio – e sono anch'essi definiti per analogia.

Il pensiero analogico, che alcuni ritengono stia alla base del ragionamento cognitivo,[3] offre un metodo affascinante per esaminare l'arte di Nauman, che spesso nasce dalla tensione tra significati pragmatici e possibilità semantiche, sia che l'opera abbia a che fare specificamente col linguaggio o confonda le aspettative dell'osservatore attraverso la sua realtà fisica. Nel libro su Nauman, pubblicato nel 1988, Coosje van Bruggen definisce molte sculture giovanili dell'artista, tra le quali *From Hand to Mouth* (1967, tav. 11), come delle "analogie formali".[4] Allo stesso modo, anche le prime opere testuali di Nauman mostrano una propensione per il linguaggio analogico che, come sottolinea Michael Auping, è il "tipo di messaggio in cui Nauman si concentra alla fine degli anni sessanta; affrontando direttamente o indirettamente i soggetti/analogie espressi in *Codification*, a volte forgia, ma, più spesso, mette alla prova la relazione tra le parole, le forme e il loro significato".[5] In *Codification*, opera di testo del 1966, Nauman scrive, inoltre, la frase "Analogic and digital codification", confondendo, nel gioco di parole, "analogia" e "analogico".[6]

La ben nota storia del raggiungimento della maturità dell'artista, che descrive il momento decisivo durante il terzo anno di studi alla University of Wisconsin a Madison, quando Nauman abbandona gli studi di matematica strutturale per proseguire gli studi nell'ambito dell'arte, mette ancor più in evidenza la capacità dell'artista di pensare per analogie. Nauman conserva un certo interesse per la matematica, anche dopo aver compiuto il passaggio accademico, tanto da affermare, in un'occasione, di aver subito un'influenza duratura da un professore di matematica specializzato in topologia algebrica.[7] Sia i concetti matematici espliciti (come dimostrazioni, variazioni e linee sghembe) che le loro applicazioni metaforiche appaiono continuamente nel processo artistico di Nauman.[8] L'artista porta con sé e, quindi nella sua opera, un'innegabile soddisfazione nel risolvere i problemi che perdura dai primi esperimenti con film e video, e nei successivi quarant'anni di attività.

Le relazioni analogiche che si possono identificare nel corso del tempo in molteplici linee parallele nella produzione scultorea, nelle installazioni, nelle performance, nelle opere al neon e sonore di Nauman, sono il fulcro e il tessuto connettivo di Topological Gardens. In tale mostra, localizziamo la nostra versione della logica di Nauman, e cioè che la tensione che guida la sua opera non deriva da un oggetto o un'esperienza isolata, ma dall'"oggetto in relazione ad altri brani di informazione con i quali si ha a che fare.[9] Gli "altri brani di informazione" che proponiamo sono le tre sequenze che collegano tematicamente le opere esposte, ma anche i contorni geografici e sociali di Venezia. Comprendendo tre sedi sparse nelle isole che s'interconnettono a comporre la città (il Padiglione degli Stati Uniti, al centro dei Giardini, a sud-est; l'Università Iuav di Venezia, sede dei Tolentini, nelle vicinanze di Piazzale Roma, a nord-ovest; gli spazi di Ca' Foscari Esposizioni dell'Università Ca' Foscari, situati tra le due sedi sopra elencate, nei pressi di una cruciale curva del Canal Grande), la mostra propone percorsi concreti che abbracciano la città come uno spazio olistico. I possibili accostamenti tra le singole opere presenti nelle stesse sedi e le connessioni più ampie che attraversano la geografia della mostra permettono un'interpretazione, un'esperienza e una percezione dell'arte di Nauman che s'intrecciano strettamente all'esperienza di Venezia. Le fontane e i neon delle opere di Nauman, ad esempio, entrano in relazione analogica con le fontane e le insegne dei negozi negli spazi pubblici cittadini.

Un'analogia elementare inizia da un presupposto (la fonte) che viene seguito da un'altra serie di informazioni (l'obiettivo). Anche basandosi su un modello comparativo necessariamente dualistico, le analogie non implicano un pensiero puramente antitetico, ma rappresentano *linee* continue di pensiero che vanno da ciò che è ovvio e già stabilito fino a ciò che è ambiguo e indefinito. La struttura della mostra nelle tre sedi è altrettanto libera da costrizioni; le sequenze concettuali che si dipanano nelle opere di Nauman non sono presentate come corollari contenuti in esclusiva in ciascuna sede. Come un diagramma di Venn, formato da tre cerchi semitrasparenti in cui la possibilità di isolare un singolo tema è definita da varie combinazioni dei punti di intersezione, la mostra opera nelle zone d'ombra in cui l'arte di Nauman prospera, e che i visitatori sono lasciati non a chiarire, ma ad approcciare e navigare per conto proprio.

Ripetizione, trasformazione, rielaborazione, revisione, sono parole chiave per la prassi artistica di Nauman. Per questa ragione, consideriamo *Topological Gardens* solo una delle commutazioni di un universo che resta aperto alla possibilità di letture assiomatiche alternative. Così postuliamo che, nonostante le opere selezionate si estendano necessariamente al di là di se stesse, fungendo, come tutte le opere di Nauman, da significatori di interi percorsi e possibili tangenti nell'interpretazione della sua prassi artistica, qualcosa di particolarmente illuminante nel modello topologico dello spazio e nel metodo analogico di comprensione ci salva dal tentativo paradossale di chiudere il circuito. Fontane e Neon; Teste e Mani; Suono e Spazio, non sono quindi situazioni chiuse, ma categorie aperte. Sono i punti fissi da cui possiamo partire, ma le traiettorie sono infinite.

Fontane : Neon

Un momento esemplare dell'incontro tra il primo modernismo e la sua controparte contemporanea è l'apparizione di Nauman trasformato in fontana nella fotografia *Self-Portrait as a Fountain*

(1966-67/1970, fig. 29). Come afferma Michael Taylor nel suo saggio contenuto nel presente catalogo, Nauman crea l'immagine (e probabilmente la serie di opere successive a quest'opera che sviluppano il tema della fontana) facendo inevitabilmente riferimento all'orinatoio iconico di Marcel Duchamp del 1917. Eppure, la metafora che mette in relazione la fontana con l'artista/creatore ha una storia più lunga, che va dagli artisti più accademici ai più innovatori, da Ingres a Pablo Picasso. La persistenza di questa immagine retorica è in parte dovuta all'aspettativa che l'artista possieda la capacità divina di creare, all'infinito. La consapevolezza dell'artista di essere, allo stesso tempo, capace e responsabile della rigenerazione dell'ispirazione è stata ripetutamente espressa in forma di acqua, che può fluire da una brocca, da una fontana o da un ruscello. Ci si aspettava che alcune di queste rappresentazioni raggiungessero il livello di purezza incontaminata e di perfezione accademica che si riscontra nell'opera *La Source* di Ingres (1856; Musée d'Orsay, Parigi).

In *Self-Portrait as a Fountain*, e nella fotografia in bianco e nero immediatamente successiva, *The Artist as a Fountain* (1966–76, fig. 53), Nauman svela, tuttavia, che la metafora acquatica è un'aspettativa insidiosa, qui impersonata irriverentemente dall'artista stesso che posa come "fonte". Spruzzando acqua dalle labbra increspate e mostrando il torso nudo, o mettendosi in posa come una fontana nel giardino, Nauman si presenta come l'artista al massimo dell'ambizione e dell'atteggiamento sacrilego. Usando il proprio corpo come fontana, Nauman elimina la distanza posta dai suoi predecessori tra se stessi e le loro floride metafore (o gli sgradevoli orinatoi); il suo corpo interpreta la sua relazione ambivalente verso le aspettative della società, di storici dell'arte e non solo. Forse questa è la ragione per cui nel 1968 l'opera *Self-Portrait as a Fountain* è stata scelta per enucleare l'annuncio di Nauman al mondo dell'arte newyorkese, venendo riprodotta nella cartolina inviata dalla Leo Castelli Gallery in occasione della prima personale dell'artista a New York. Sul retro si legge un invito altrettanto chiaro, scritto a mano: "Per favore, sabato 27 gennaio, venite all'inaugurazione della mostra di Bruce Nauman".[10]

Il *topos* della fontana appare saltuariamente nella produzione artistica di Nauman per i primi tre anni, dal 1966 al 1968, anche se si può dire che gli interrogativi sul ruolo dell'artista contenuti nelle opere legate al tema della fontana si può dire che siano alla base della maggior parte della sua "produzione" successiva. (L'artista riprende il tema in questione in modo esplicito, creando fontane scultoree funzionanti, realizzate in altre forme, anche negli anni novanta e verso la metà del primo decennio del nuovo secolo). Soffermandoci sulle opere esposte alla mostra inaugurale del 1968 da Castelli, notiamo che su una delle pareti, insieme alle opere legate al tema della fontana, appaiono opere eseguite in una incredibile varietà di linguaggi espressivi (fig. 54). In *Neon Templates of the Left Half of My Body Taken at Ten-Inch Intervals* (1966; fig. 13), in *The True Artist is an Amazing Luminous Fountain (Window or Wall Shade)* (1966) e in *Self-Portrait as a Fountain* (fig. 29), Nauman ribadisce le indagini analogiche sul proprio io. Creata dopo *Self-Portrait as a Fountain*, l'insegna semitrasparente in Mylar, in tonalità rosa, che costituisce *The True Artist is an Amazing Luminous Fountain (Window or Wall Shade)*, trasferisce il tema della fontana nell'ambito del metodo della produzione di insegne. Il disegno preparatorio del 1966 per quest'opera, *The True Artist is an Amazing Luminous Fountain (Design for Around the Edge of a Window or Wall of These Proportions)*, segna il primo momento in cui Nauman mette per iscritto la sua ambiziosa e ambivalente dichiarazione d'artista, citando il tema della fontana insieme alle parole "luminoso" e "vero artista".

Premettendo che questi termini hanno a che fare sia con un interesse che con una critica del ruolo intellettuale di Nauman in quanto artista, molte delle prime opere al neon rivelano tracce di altri aspetti della sua identità, sia fisica, come in *Neon Templates*, o nominale, come in *My Last Name Exaggerated Fourteen Times Vertically* (1967, fig. 55). Entrambe le opere sono state incluse nella mostra di Castelli, come anche il fotomontaggio *My Name As Though It Were Written on the Surface of the Moon: Bbbbbbbbbbrrrrrrrrruuuuuuuuuucccccccccceeeeeeeeee* (1967, fig. 56) che successivamente avrebbe ispirato la realizzazione di un'altra insegna al neon, sempre basata sul nome. A proposito di queste prime manifestazioni del legame tra identità e creazione oggettiva, Marcia Tucker scrive nel 1970 che "L'interesse per l'aspetto fisico del proprio io non è semplice egocentrismo artistico, ma uso del corpo per trasformare l'intima soggettività in dimostrazione oggettiva".[11] Seguendo la nostra logica analogica, la "dimostrazione oggettiva" porterebbe a connettere le fontane, animate fisicamente o meno, direttamente con i neon che citano il nome dell'artista; entrambi i gesti cancellano il divario tra l'identità dell'artista e i suoi oggetti. Anche se i neon che riportano il nome di Nauman sembrano impugnare la problematica autoriale, ogni sospetto di serietà viene rapidamente dissipato dal senso dell'umorismo che sottende la facezia sul giovane artista che cerca di "farsi un nome". Forse, in reazione all'aspettativa di creare uno stile personale identificabile, Nauman attenua l'impatto del proprio nome nei neon, sia allungando le linee che costituiscono visivamente il cognome in parabole di un freddo viola pallido in *My Last Name Exaggerated Fourteen Times Vertically,* sia ripetendo le lettere del suo nome per creare la prospettiva inclinata del neon caldo blu-bianco di *My Name As Though It Were Written on the Surface of the Moon* (1968, tav. 15).

La maggior parte della produzione giovanile al neon di Nauman è strettamente legata alla costruzione di insegne, come evidenzia *The True Artist is an Amazing Luminous Fountain (Window or Wall Shade)*, che anticipa l'insegna iconica al neon creata l'anno successivo per la facciata del suo studio di San Francisco, un ex negozio: l'opera a spirale *The True Artist Helps the World by Revealing Mystic Truths (Window or Wall Sign)* del 1967 (tav. 22). Qui, tuttavia, Nauman elimina simpaticamente la frase "è un'incredibile fontana luminosa" dalla dichiarazione, affidandosi, invece, alla risplendente insegna al neon per rapportare le precedenti incarnazioni della frase e inserendovi al suo posto frasi aggiuntive altrettanto intimidenti: "aiuta il mondo" e "verità mistiche". Nauman espone *The True Artist Helps the World by Revealing Mystic Truths (Window or Wall Sign)* nella vetrina dello studio, un'ex drogheria affacciata sulla strada, offrendo ai passanti più attenti, l'opportunità di distinguere la sua dichiarazione d'artista tra altri neon che popolano il paesaggio urbano. In *Topological Gardens*, l'insegna ronzante è appesa a rovescio rispetto al visitatore che entra nel Padiglione degli Stati Uniti, proprio per ripropone l'installazione nella posizione originale: un'insegna rivolta verso la strada, che veniva vista a rovescio da chi entrava nello studio dell'artista.

L'ingresso del Padiglione degli Stati Uniti è contrassegnato anche da un secondo elemento che connette fontane e neon. *Untitled (The True Artist Is an Amazing Luminous Fountain)* (tav. 26) si curva sopra la porta d'entrata ed occupa lo spazio nell'intercapedine della soglia tra l'esterno e l'interno dell'edificio. L'opera consiste in un'altra insegna, originariamente eseguita nel 1968 utilizzando una specifica tipologia di lettere realizzate con un materiale allora disponibile in commercio, il cartongesso *Upson*, e realizzata per Venezia in lettere in alluminio stampato, prodotte industrialmente, scelte da Nauman per questo contesto specifico. Queste opere, come anche la versione a tenda di *The True Artist Is an Amazing Luminous Fountain* che le precede, rivelano l'interesse iniziale di Nauman per la creazione di opere d'arte che rispondano direttamente ai suggerimenti architettonici di uno specifico luogo.

Le insegne al neon, ideali per attirare l'attenzione su un messaggio per poi sovvertirlo, si dimostrano punto di partenza perfetto per le ricerche formali, linguistiche, umoristiche e provocatorie di Nauman. La possibilità di commercializzare idee invece che prodotti - o idee come prodotto dell'artista - è un concetto che interessa Nauman, sebbene qualsiasi collegamento tra il suo modo di utilizzare il neon e la padronanza del linguaggio commerciale della Pop art è negato dal contenuto sovvertito e sovversivo delle sue opere. Giocando con il linguaggio dell'anagramma, l'opera *None Sing Neon Sign* del 1970 (tav. 16) riflette sulla propria manifestazione come oggetto d'arte. Altri neon testuali, come *Raw War*, opera eseguita lo stesso anno (fig. 57), utilizzano i palindromi per cercare di ottenere un linguaggio politico nel momento in cui le lettere lampeggiano per rivelare la connessione tra le due parole. I neon testuali di Nauman, essendo esercizi di ragionamento analogico, richiedono che sia l'osservatore a creare il collegamento persistente, a volte pungente. Nel 1982, al Baltimore Museum of Art, la curatrice Brenda Richardson organizza una mostra incentrata solamente sui neon, per la quale Nauman crea l'installazione permanente di grandi dimensioni *Violins Violence Silence*, come anche una versione più piccola per interni (fig. 58).[12] In entrambe le opere, le versioni in neon delle parole del titolo, scritte sia regolarmente che all'indietro, sono sovrapposte e sottoposte a sequenze lampeggianti che complicano il significato implicito nella frase assonante, le cui interpretazioni possono spaziare dalla filastrocca per bambini a un'allusione al mito di Nerone che suona la lira mentre la città di Roma brucia.

Violins Violence Silence apre la strada alla realizzazione di installazioni pubbliche di neon di grandi dimensioni, come *Vices and Virtues* (tav. 27), le cui date di esecuzione, 1983–88, riflettono l'iter dell'opera, dalla proposta, al rifiuto iniziale, alla realizzazione finale per la Stuart Collection presso l'University of California a San Diego. Composta essenzialmente da una lista dei proverbiali sette vizi e sette virtù, l'opera difficilmente potrebbe essere più laconica; eppure il progetto una volta proposto incontra resistenze, a causa dell'interpretazione polemica delle parole da parte dello staff del teatro, dei funzionari locali e dei giornalisti.[13] L'opera *Vices and Virtues*, le cui lettere si allungano fino a due metri e dieci, viene, infine, installata sul Charles Lee Powell Laboratory dell'università.

Vices and Virtues è stata ricreata per *Topological Gardens*, adattata nelle dimensioni per essere montata sopra il fregio esterno dell'edificio neoclassico sede del Padiglione degli Stati Uniti. I vizi e le virtù, nozioni facenti parte della conoscenza culturale comune, sono accoppiati e sovrapposti; "Anger" (ira), ad esempio, si fonde con "Fortitude" (fortezza), dando all'opera una propria articolazione interpretativa. Una sequenza lampeggiante a intervalli prefissati accende le virtù in senso orario e i vizi in senso antiorario, producendo un numero apparentemente infinito di cambiamenti di significato. Ogni tanto, tutte le parole si illuminano e si affermano in pochi lampi spettacolari. E' in quel momento che Nauman sembra valutare la condizione umana, concludendo che l'uomo è in grado non solo di praticare individualmente alcuni vizi e virtù, ma anche di incarnare, attuare e ispirare simultaneamente queste quattordici caratteristiche.

Teste : Mani

Il passaggio alla successiva traiettoria tematica di *Topological Gardens* evidenzia l'impossibilità di isolare una sequenza dalle altre: la sezione dedicate a Teste e Mani inizia con dei neon e si conclude con delle fontane. Negli anni ottanta, quando la produzione di neon raggiunge l'apice, Nauman realizza insegne al neon che presentano corpi elettrificati o parti che li compongono: teste, mani, genitali maschili e figure sottili, a volte impegnate in atti violenti e/o sessuali. Teste contorte e torturate, illuminate a colori vivaci, ficcano le dita l'una nell'occhio dell'altra, come nel caso di *Double Poke in the Eye II* (1985; tav. 4), o divorano l'una il naso dell'altra, come in *Eating Buggers (Version II)* (1985; tav. 5). Nauman spesso traccia i contorni dei corpi in neon a partire dalla propria ombra, il che spiega i tratti spaventosamente gonfiati e simili a quello dei fumetti che, privati di qualsiasi specificità creano l'interscambio tra comico e grottesco. Come se fossero neon cinetici, *Double Poke in the Eye II* e *Eating Buggers (Version II)* lampeggiano per rappresentare il ripetersi delle azioni del mangiare o colpire, in un flusso inquietante di fermo immagine. Un comportamento tanto indecoroso viene paradossalmente contraddetto dalle linee pure e dalle superfici sterili delle scatole di alluminio che nascondono la maggior parte dell'apparato elettrico dell'opera. (Molte delle opere di testo al neon di Nauman, invece, lasciano appesi o lasciano spuntare cavi e trasformatori in modo disordinato).

Alla richiesta di spiegare la ragione del passaggio dal pensiero matematico alla creazione di oggetti, Nauman replica: "L'arte mi ha permesso di lavorare sia con la mente che con le mani".[14] Molte opere di Nauman presentano una relazione analogica in cui teste, mani o entrambe fungono da significanti rispettivamente del pensare e del fare, per cui l'atto mentale e quello fisico della creazione sono continui come le superfici topologiche del corpo. Teste e mani sono presenti sia come soggetto dell'opera che come significanti di questo concetto per tutta la carriera di Nauman, e sono presenti nella mostra in molte versioni e in vari materiali. Separate o insieme, fungono da avvincenti distillati dell'atto di produrre arte e delle complessità di pensiero e comunicazione.

In *Human Sexual Experience* (1985; tav. 14), le luci intermittenti al neon rendono esplicito lo scopo per cui l'indice di una mano si inserisce nel cerchio formato dall'altra. Tale movimento provocatorio si può associare direttamente alla scultura *Untitled (Hand Circle)* del 1996 (tav. 25), nella quale mani in bronzo, saldate, riproducono lo stesso gesto, ma facendo anche un arguto riferimento alle teste, quelle del pubblico: la scultura è appesa all'altezza dello sguardo, come se minacciasse di ficcare un dito nell'occhio dello spettatore. A tali opere, esposte negli spazi di Ca' Foscari Esposizioni dell'Università Ca' Foscari, si unisce *Untitled (#358)* del 1986 (tav. 23), una costruzione sospesa di schiuma poliuretanica e cartone composta dalla sagoma della testa di Nauman e dai vari arti curiosamente attaccati con pezzi di legno e *double clip*. *Untitled (#358)* rispecchia ulteriormente l'uso giocoso che l'artista fa della propria ombra, qui materializzata in una sagoma in schiuma poliuretanica originariamente tracciata per creare alcuni neon figurativi dello stesso periodo. Posizionandola sospesa come

Untitled (Hand Circle), le articolazioni e le membra dell'opera *Untitled (#358)* sono confuse dalla dissezione e ricomposizione della forma originale; tale posizione anticipa i successivi caroselli sospesi di Nauman, nei quali si vedranno animali dagli arti riarrangiati, teste che pendono dal fil di ferro e dondolanti teste-fontane in resina.

Nauman progetta molte delle sue opere scultoree in modo che siano visibili ad altezza dello sguardo, attivando, così, una specie di rapporto esperienziale uno a uno, che non fa altro che aumentare l'aspetto provocatorio dell'opera. In questo modo l'artista controlla l'interazione tra il corpo del visitatore e le sue sculture, come accade per le varie versioni di teste che pendono dal soffitto appese ai cavi. In *Four Pairs of Heads (Wax)* del 1991 (tav. 10), le coppie di teste, troncate all'altezza del collo, sono appese a una distanza sufficiente da permettere al visitatore di girarci attorno, mentre due di esse sono attaccate a una barra d'acciaio orizzontale facendo pensare al teatro dei burattini. A differenza di opere strettamente connesse a quest'ultima, come *Ten Heads Circle/Up and Down* e *Ten Heads Circle/In and Out* (fig. 59), entrambe del 1990, in cui le teste sono realizzate in colori che ricordano quelli delle caramelle, *Four Pairs of Heads (Wax)* fa penzolare teste per lo più color pelle, con pezzi di cera color rosso sangue attaccati ai crani vuoti dalle cavità cerebrali spaventosamente visibili. Ogni coppia di teste è legata assieme dal cavo metallico che sfrega e incide la cera, evocando una brutalità che aiuta a realizzare che queste non sono solo teste che pendono, ma sono anche trofei (*hanging heads* in inglese, letteralmente teste appese, ndt.). Forse questo spiega perché, quando una serie di teste di Nauman venne esposta alla galleria Castelli nel 1990, un critico soprannominò l'artista "Maestro del Frammento Morboso".[15] In *Hanging Head for Leo* (1990; tav. 13) la testa si materializza in bronzo, come un pendolo incombente.

Nauman lascia che le tracce del processo di fusione con cui realizza le teste di cera rimangano perfettamente visibili come nel caso delle fusioni prodotte a metà degli anni sessanta mentre studiava per il master in arte. Una cucitura visibile unisce il viso e il retro di ciascuna testa; a volte, il tubicino per la respirazione rimane nella bocca, evocando la difficoltà fisica sopportata dal modello. In alcune teste dalle bocche spalancate Nauman inserisce una fusione della propria lingua.[16] Come in una maschera mortuaria, gli occhi sono sempre chiusi. Quando le teste non sono appese, esse subiscono scocciature come quelle subite dalle opere al neon come *Double Poke in the Eye II* e *Eating Buggers (Version II)*: lingue ficcate negli occhi, lingue che leccano teste, nasi rovesciati che si incastrano, teste fuse assieme. In *Five Pink Heads in the Corner* del 1992 (tav. 8), Nauman accatasta cinque teste posizionandole con la faccia al muro, impedendo al visitatore di percepire il consueto fulcro dell'informazione visiva, il volto. Proprio perché relegate significativamente nell'angolo, esse esprimono la vergogna; nel Padiglione, la loro ignominia è connessa per analogia alle teste che dondolano dai cavi, come in "*hanging your head*" (espressione fraseologica equivalente allo "stare a capo chino dalla vergogna", ndt.).

Alla fine degli anni ottanta e all'inizio degli anni novanta, il tema delle teste accatastate continua ad essere presente in altre sculture in cera e viene anche trasferito su video. *Perfect Balance (Pink Andrew with Plug Hanging with TV)* del 1989 (fig. 60) è un'opera composta da una testa di cera appoggiata su un monitor appeso, che mostra l'immagine di una mano col dito medio alzato. In opere come *Andrew Head/Andrew Head Stacked* del 1990 (fig. 61) le teste di cera, impilate come fossero la base minacciosa di un palo totemico, iniziano a trovare corollari in opere video della metà degli anni novanta come *Think*, *Work* (fig. 62), e *Jump*, in cui la testa di Nauman appare in coppie di monitor sovrapposti. In *Think* del 1993 (tav. 20), Nauman si filma mentre salta su e giù, e la sua testa compare e scompare dall'inquadratura fissa della cinepresa mentre l'artista urla il monosillabo che dà il titolo all'opera. Un monitor mostra il suo moto cinetico nella direzione giusta, mentre un altro lo trasmette capovolto; gli ordini aggressivi, insistenti, e senza fiato ("Pensa! Pensa! Pensa!"), non essendo sincronizzati, creano una cacofonia per cui l'ordine pragmatico di Nauman è immediatamente ostacolato dall'impossibilità di trovare un momento per pensare entro il raggio di ascolto di questo monologo interrotto. *Think* e altri video della serie "Raw Materials" ricordano i precendenti film nei quali Nauman riprende se stesso nello studio mentre compie azioni ingannevolmente semplici. Forse, nel caso di video come *Think*, Nauman si stava ponendo la stessa domanda fondamentale su cui aveva già meditato nel 1967 mentre sedeva nel suo studio: come inventare arte.

Mentre *Think* accoglie i visitatori e gli studenti al loro ingresso nella sede Iuav dei Tolentini, al Padiglione degli Stati Uniti sono esposte due opere dello stesso periodo formate da due coppie di monitor sovrapposti.[17] Sul canale video inferiore di *Coffee Spilled and Balloon Dog* del 1993 (tav. 2), un prestigiatore si serve dell'abilità manuale tipica del mestiere per creare un cane a partire da un palloncino trasparente. Vestito di nero, ad esclusione delle mani e del volto, e posizionato in piedi su uno sfondo nero, la maggior parte del suo corpo scompare, mentre la testa sembra disincarnata come quelle appese nella stanza accanto. Le mani, inquadrate solo fino ai polsi, ricordano i gesti topologici di opere presenti nel Padiglione, come *Fifteen Pairs of Hands* del 1996 (tav. 7), in cui fusioni in bronzo smerigliato delle mani di Nauman compiono variazioni di gesti interpretabili all'infinito. Sullo schermo superiore, una tazza di caffè cade ripetutamente al rallentatore e si schianta sulla superficie immacolata di una tovaglia bianca. In questo caso, mentre il confronto tra il rovesciare il caffè e il dare la forma di un cane al palloncino è un'analogia facilmente identificabile nei concetti di distruggere e il creare con le proprie mani, sia la tazza di caffè che il palloncino sono, invece, figure topologiche. Così come una tazza di caffè è omeomorfa della ciambella (come sottolinea Basualdo nel saggio presente in questo catalogo, ricordando le sculture giovanili di Nauman che riproducono una tazzina da caffè e relativo piattino), anche il palloncino è un paradigma topologico: può cambiare forma senza accumulare materia o perdere la sua essenza.

In *Washing Hands Normal* (1996; tav. 28) Nauman si riprende mentre si lava le mani con un'energia che supera quella necessaria a ottenere la pulizia. Esprimendo i movimenti delle superfici topologiche viste in *Fifteen Pairs of Hands, Washing Hands Normal* paragona, inoltre, il suono del flusso costante dell'acqua che scorre nel lavandino a una fontana. Nell'ala opposta del Padiglione degli Stati Uniti la sorgente è realizzata in due fontane funzionanti, *Three Heads Fountain (Three Andrews)* (fig. 26) e *Three Heads Fountain (Juliet, Andrew, Rinde)*, entrambe del 2005 (tav. 21). Le teste in resina, appese in gruppi di tre, sono bucate in vari punti per spruzzare acqua dagli occhi e dalle orecchie, oltre che dalla bocca. L'acqua, sputata, spruzzata e lasciata sgocciolare, cade in una vasca fatta del materiale più grezzo e sbrigativo: una cornice di legno e del rivestimento per stagni. Qui Nauman abbandona qualsiasi nozione classica o metaforica della fonte, e la sostituisce con un gioco di parole: si tratta letteralmente di sorgenti (*fountainheads* in inglese, ndt.). Come tali, chiudono il cerchio, riportandoci all'inizio.

Suono : Spazio

Le sculture sospese di Nauman richiamano le sovrapposizioni tra le categorie proposte per la mostra. In *Hanging Carousel (George Skins a Fox)* del 1988 (tav. 12), ad esempio, il tema visivo delle mani ci riporta alla categoria delle Teste e Mani, mentre il congegno del carosello rotante ci spinge avanti, verso Suono e Spazio. Questo terzo passaggio analogico di "Topological Gardens" costituisce un'accoppiata apparentemente smaterializzata, più concentrata sulla modalità che sul soggetto dell'arte. Eppure suono e spazio fanno parte integrante degli interessi formali di Nauman, imbrigliati dall'artista come oggetti dalla forza attutita. In un brano spesso citato, egli paragona l'effetto che desidera ottenere con le sue opere all'"essere colpito in faccia con una mazza da baseball. O meglio, essere colpito alla nuca. Non vedi mai arrivare il colpo che ti tramortisce".[18] Questo momento drammatico si realizza generalmente nelle opere che manipolano suono e spazio come strumenti di un'esperienza da cui non si può prescindere.

Hanging Carousel (George Skins a Fox) manifesta un impulso provocatorio simile a quello delle teste appese. Qui, le forme animali in poliuretano, adoperate in tassidermia, sono legate, grazie ai cavi avvolti attorno ai colli inanimati, alle estremità di fulcri d'acciaio che si estendono in quattro direzioni. Il carosello, che ruota sia in senso orario che antiorario grazie ad un motorino dotato di timer, con il suo malinconico agitarsi distrugge qualsiasi attinenza con una giostra. Al centro, un monitor sospeso trasmette uno spezzone di un filmato in cui viene mostrato l'ex vicino di casa di Nauman, George Stumpff, mentre scuoia una volpe. L'incredibile abilità di Stumpff riporta al tema delle mani; scuoiare una volpe è un atto manuale di distruzione (uccisione, scuoiamento), ma anche di creazione (creare qualcosa di nuovo, come suggeriscono le forme tassidermiche). Le forme di poliuretano, che Nauman inizia a usare negli anni ottanta in collage, caroselli e sculture, senza la finitura di pelle sono figure stranamente rudimentali. Nel complesso, la scultura sembra suggerire la possibilità di interazione, ma le sue braccia, come un mulino a vento in azione, sono troppo minacciose per avvicinarsi troppo.

Lo scuoiamento è citato anche nell'installazione *Flayed Earth Flayed Self (Skin Sink)* del 1973 (tav. 9), nella quale Nauman utilizza del nastro adesivo per dividere pavimento e pareti in sei sezioni, secondo uno schema a girandola. Il testo che accompagna l'opera, pubblicato inizialmente come libretto per la Nicholas Wilder Gallery di Los Angeles, fa riferimento alla sbucciatura e scoprimento della terra e del sé nel tentativo di divenire privo di limiti a dispetto del contenimento. Numerose pagine bianche precedono e seguono il testo nel libretto, come se Nauman volesse far pensare alla propensione che lo spazio negativo ha di caricarsi positivamente nell'universo infinito.[19] L'uso che Nauman fa del nastro adesivo per mappare, contenere, e implodere lo spazio del pavimento è intrinsecamente legato alle precedenti mappature dello studio, come in *Dance or Exercise on the Perimeter of a Square (Square Dance)* del 1967–68, in cui l'artista permette alla struttura di un quadrato di nastro adesivo, mappato sul pavimento dello studio di Wiley, di guidare, limitare e dirigere i suoi movimenti scanditi da un metronomo (fig. 63). Dopo aver prodotto *Flayed Earth Flayed Self (Skin Sink),* Nauman costruisce i cerchi concentrici di *Cones Cojones* (1973–75, fig. 64), che, secondo un collage di testi accompagnatori, evocano sezioni coniche, inserite una nell'altra, che dal centro della terra si proiettano verso l'esterno. In entrambe le opere, il visitatore deve trovarsi al centro per percepire, attraverso la cinestesia suggerita dai testi, le forze naturali che spingono lo spazio a sottostare ai moti topologici di espansione e contrazione. Il testo per *Flayed Earth* include giochi di parole che sembrano anticipare un'altra dimensione spaziale dell'opera di Nauman, che ci riporta al discorso sugli oggetti appesi: "Sospensione della fede, sospensione di un oggetto/oggetto di sospensione —appendere".[20] La sospensione stranamente rafforza le teste appese, i monitor, le sculture, i caroselli di Nauman; essa inizia a manifestarsi per la prima volta in una serie giovanile di modelli di tunnel, passaggi e trincee, costruiti principalmente in gesso. In *Model for Trench and Four Buried Passages* del 1977 (fig. 65), ad esempio, anelli concentrici in gesso e fibra di vetro intrappolano il pavimento e sono appesi al soffitto all'altezza dello sguardo, impedendo di vedere completamente la scultura. Nauman afferma in un'occasione che i modelli dovevano essere esperiti con la consapevolezza che sarebbero potuti essere costruiti in scala naturale: nel guardarli "avresti avuto un'altra informazione e cioè che se fossero stati costruiti sarebbero stati alti tre metri e saresti potuto entrare".[21] *Smoke Rings (Models for Underground Tunnels)* del 1979–80 (tav. 18), presente in *Topological Gardens*, è un'opera formata da due modelli in gesso poggiati sul pavimento, i cui tunnel impossibili hanno un difetto cruciale: non hanno entrata né uscita.

I giochi di permesso e divieto di accesso sono temi esperienziali presenti in molte opere di Nauman, nelle quali lo spazio è declinato in corridoi, stanze sigillate, capsule, stanze d'isolamento, il cui interno spesso è ripreso da telecamere di sorveglianza. Nauman ha sottolineato che i modelli per tunnel sotterranei e le opere che allo stesso modo complicano le normali relazioni spaziali hanno a che fare con la dimensione sociale dello spazio:

> Immagino che una delle parti più importanti di gran parte di molti lavori riguardi la differenza tra spazio privato e spazio pubblico e il modo in cui è psicologicamente diverso stare in una stanza con un gruppo di persone, oppure da soli .... Ad esempio, se ti trovi in un posto e poi entra altra gente, allora la tua percezione di quello spazio cambia, oppure il modo in cui agisci nello spazio e come ti collochi nello spazio quando non conosci nessuno . . . Perciò una delle cose principali che ho pensato, rispetto alla ricerca del limite, è come imporre la tensione di quel tipo di trasformazione, tra il tuo spazio e la necessità di condividerlo socialmente.[22]

Nonostante il loro conferito interesse per la socializzazione, le opere corridoio di Nauman e gli ambienti scultorei come *Double Steel Cage Piece* (1974; tav. 3), sono incredibilmente antisociali: essi sono pensati non per incoraggiare l'interazione, ma per aumentare l'imbarazzo dell'aspettativa altrui, quando l'individuo viene esibito in pubblico. Come Marco De Michelis analizza dettagliatamente nel saggio presente in questo catalogo, esse mettono in atto la classica tecnica di adescamento degli esperimenti psicologici sull'illusione: si entra in uno degli stretti corridoi di Nauman per curiosità e forse sfida, ma una volta al loro interno le possibilità di movimento sono immediatamente limitate. In *Double Steel Cage Piece*, lo spirito audace che entra nella struttura in rete d'acciaio diviene spontaneamente parte dell'oggetto, ed è visibile a chi è presente nella stanza, per cui qualsiasi pretesa di autonomia viene invertita in soggettività imposta.

L'interesse di Nauman nel garantire o negare l'accesso allo spazio è in analogia con la decisione di fornire o ostacolare il passaggio di informazioni. In *Audio Video Piece for London, Ontario* (1969–70; tav. 1), ad esempio, la telecamera di sorveglianza, posta di lato, oscilla in una stanza adiacente, ma sigillata per il visitatore: ciò che appare nel monitor è essenzialmente uno spazio privo di contenuto, il cui significato è galvanizzato dall'isolamento. Nauman, quindi, trasforma uno spazio contenuto e inaccessibile, anche se palesemente vuoto, in un oggetto di desiderio. Qui come in *Double Steel Cage Piece*, che possiede a sua volta una stanza interna sigillata, Nauman eleva lo status del vuoto.

Quando poi Nauman garantisce l'accesso, spesso mette alla prova la resistenza fisica e psicologica dell'ignaro partecipante. Negli anni settanta, operando a partire dall'interesse per la fenomenologia, inizia a progettare esperienze volutamente disagevoli tramite la realizzazione di corridoi e ambienti che presentano luci intense dai colori stridenti come in *Green Light Corridor* del 1970 o *Yellow Room (Triangular)* del 1973 (fig. 65). In *Topological Gardens* questo effetto è esemplificato da *Pink and Yellow Light Corridor (Variable Lights)* del 1972 (tav. 17), con i suoi strati di luci fluorescenti rosa e gialle che si estendolo lungo un portico del chiostro dei Tolentini all'Università Iuav. Le luci sono programmate in modo tale che nello stesso momento in cui le luci rosa fluorescenti oscillino dal 100% al 30% di energia, le gialle passino dal 30% al 100%, e viceversa. La luce vacillante getta un'aura inquietante nell'intera architettura dello spazio.

In opere audio e video apparentemente innocue per i sensi, la durata, la ripetizione senza fine, e il volume stesso del suono di cui Nauman si serve, spesso rendono l'esperienza del vedere o partecipare un atto di resistenza. In *End of the World* (1996; tav. 6), la musica emessa da chitarre *lap steel* e *pedal steel* appare inizialmente gentile, persino nostalgica, evoca una qualche astratta idea atmosfera country del West; con il passare del tempo, però, il sonoro delle tre proiezioni aumenta e satura i sensi. Nauman produce effetti simili, adoperando il suono come corollario dello spazio, in opere che utilizzano sia registrazioni audio che ambientazioni costruite, come *Get Out of My Mind, Get Out of This Room* (1968; si veda la lista delle opere in mostra n. 20), mettendo uno in contrasto con l'altro.

Quest'ultima opera presuppone la costruzione apposita di una stanza stretta, quadrata, con altoparlanti nascosti che proiettano con forza la voce di Nauman, sussurrante e rauca, per formare il comando ripetuto "Esci dalla mia testa, esci da questa stanza" fino a raggiungere una forza minacciosa. Mentre l'architettura permette l'accesso, il sonoro pretende l'espulsione. Molti ambienti, opere sonore e installazioni video di Nauman presentano simili paradossi dell'esperienza, in cui, come ha commentato Janet Kraynak, la partecipazione "emerge come un'idea opprimente che è *a spese* del pubblico".[23] Molte opere in mostra presso l'Università Iuav attingono a questo aspetto della produzione artistica di Nauman, in cui l'informazione data dall'artista e le reazioni sensoriali e psicologiche dello spettatore entrano in conflitto.

Get Out of My Mind, Get Out of This Room è una delle cinque registrazioni audio che Nauman ha raggruppato in una raccolta intitolata *Studio Aids II* (1967–68; si veda la lista delle opere in mostra n. 21). Le altre quattro registrazioni (*Violin Tuned D.E.A.D.*; *Rolling on the Studio Floor*; *Jumping*; *Walking in the Studio*), che alludono in vario modo o ripropongono il suono delle azioni dei film e dei video girati da Nauman nello studio, sono trasmesse una dopo l'altra in un'installazione sonora all'ingresso dell'Università Iuav.[24] L'uso e il riutilizzo da parte di Nauman dei suoni ovattati del rotolare, saltare e camminare ha finalità simili all'uso del disegno; come egli afferma, "Io disegno per elaborare le opere, per capire come procedere. Poi a volte faccio un disegno dopo la realizzazione dell'opera per spiegare a me stesso cosa è davvero stato fatto".[25] Come i disegni sono a volte tracciati, coperti di annotazioni e ridisegnati in seguito alla realizzazione dell'installazione che illustrano, il suono può essere modificato, declinato, riutilizzato e nuovamente registrato.

Nauman ha riproposto la stessa idea in opere recenti, tra cui le numerose versioni di *Mapping the Studio I (Fat Chance John Cage)* del 2001 (fig. 31). Tra tutte le varie realizzazioni della prima proiezione a sette canali, *Sound for Mapping the Studio Model (The Video)* (2001; tav. 19), a canale unico, dimostra, in particolare, la preferenza di Nauman di riprendere un soggetto per portarlo ad un altro livello di manipolazione editoriale. *Sound for Mapping the Studio Model (The Video)* venne creato a partire dallo stessa registrazione girata dalla videocamera di sorveglianza a infrarossi usata per *Mapping the Studio I*, ma i nastri sono stati rimontati per collegare i momenti di maggior azione nel video e i rumori ambientali distinguibili nelle registrazioni audio, i quali, tuttavia, non sono sincronizzati. La non corrispondenza tra le informazioni visive e quelle uditive mette in evidenza quanto l'una sia dipendente dall'altra; il video sembra un esercizio di dissociazione e sospensione. In questo caso, la tendenza di Nauman a riutilizzare suoni e immagini è inestricabilmente connessa allo spazio dello studio, fonte inesauribile di materia prima per la maggior parte della sua produzione artistica. Riferendosi a opere giovanili create nello studio, come *Composite Photo of Two Messes on the Studio Floor* (1967; fig. 67), Coosje van Bruggen scrive nel 1980 che questa ingegnosità "era anche una forma di economia artistica – Nauman non voleva lasciare inutilizzati nessuna idea o materiale".[26] Lo studio, punto di partenza per indagare cosa significhi esattamente fare arte, ha fornito il soggetto, la struttura, lo spazio e i suoni che appaiono ripetutamente nell'opera di Nauman. Noto per essere una persona estremamente schiva, l'artista considera lo studio come uno spazio in cui può scegliere di coincidere con il resto del mondo; anche se si tratta di uno spazio sacrosanto, il suo funzionamento interno viene trasformato nel tessuto della sua arte.

Anche le opere più recenti di Nauman, *Days* e *Giorni* (pp. 145–73), sono il risultato della struttura dello studio e insieme della mutazione dei suoni. Per queste opere Nauman scrive sia in inglese che in italiano, dei copioni che elencano in ordine sparso i giorni della settimana. Tali copioni vengono poi recitati per circa dodici minuti alla volta da lettori appositamente ingaggiati. Nauman ha programmato il sonoro in modo da essere trasmesso da sette paia di altoparlanti direzionali, montati con dei *double clip* a dei cavi d'acciaio, appesi al soffitto e fissati al pavimento. *Days* e *Giorni*, di cui si parla in altre sezioni del presente catalogo, creano una specie di corridoio sonoro in cui le voci acquistano e perdono chiarezza, evanescenti tranne che per la presenza di altoparlanti piatti e quadrati. Come l'opera composta da parole *Vices and Virtues* presentata precedentemente (tav. 27), le nuove installazioni acustiche, seppur costituite dalla serie di informazioni più semplice e culturalmente nota, attraverso la loro sequenza programmatica, orchestrano i giorni della settimana in un concerto di voci ondeggianti, dissolvendo l'interesse dei visitatori per i significati pragmatici. Questi ultimi, invece, devono obbligatoriamente abbandonarsi alla sensualità dello spazio, saturo di suoni.

Nauman : Venezia

In questa descrizione di *Topological Gardens*, il punto d'arrivo coincide con un momento precedente. Proprio mentre l'opera *Giorni* veniva registrata a Venezia come seconda reiterazione di *Days*, collegando la creazione dell'opera alle circostanze della preparazione della mostra, *Untitled* è stato ricreato a febbraio 2009 esattamente nel luogo in cui viene esposto durante la mostra, all'interno, cioè, degli spazi di Ca' Foscari Esposizioni presso l'Università Ca' Foscari (fig. 68). Nauman aveva originariamente scritto le istruzioni per la performance inclusa in *Untitled* come proposta per la Biennale di Tokyo del 1970. Anche se non vi partecipò personalmente, l'artista ricorda la descrizione fatta da Sol LeWitt della performance registrata, così come era stata esposta in Giappone. Tipico esempio della perenne difficile condizione delle performance, la natura effimera di *Untitled*, realizzata finora un'unica volta, ci ha lasciato solo due fonti certe a cui riferirsi: le istruzioni originali scritte da Nauman, e la fotocopia di un disegno. Quest'ultimo riporta tratteggiate le posizioni dei danzatori, i segni sul pavimento fatti col nastro adesivo e il progetto per costruire un'impalcatura da cui riprendere la performance. A noi sono toccate, però, le munizioni migliori: la disponibilità dell'artista a considerare l'idea di rivedere, ricreare, rimettere in scena e rifilmare *Untitled* non solo all'interno della mostra, ma anche all'interno della città dove l'opera è presentata. Così Venezia emerge come la quarta categoria concettuale della mostra, meno come *topos* in sé e più come ambiente motivante; la relazione analogica tra Venezia e Nauman si proietta nelle traiettorie precedenti di Fontane e Neon; Teste e Mani; Suono e Spazio, tessendole insieme grazie allo spazio e all'esperienza che se ne fa.

Per chi ha esaminato attentamente le performance basate sulle istruzioni di Nauman, create tra fine degli anni sessanta e l'inizio degli anni settanta, l'espressione "Ingaggiare un danzatore" è una direttiva dai toni familiari. L'ingaggio di professionisti per registrarne i loro movimenti è un qualcosa che ritorna in tutta la carriera di Nauman, ne sono esempio nella mostra i musicisti di *End of the World* (tav. 6), il prestigiatore di *Coffee Spilled and Balloon Dog* (tav. 2), e George Stumpff in *Hanging Carousel*

(George Skins a Fox) (tav. 12). Seguendo lo spirito di questa divisione del lavoro, abbiamo ingaggiato alcuni studenti dell'Università Iuav perché prendessero parte alla ri-creazione di *Untitled*.

Le istruzioni di Nauman per eseguire la performance sono rigorose e accurate (si veda il testo insieme alla tav. 24): tenendosi per mano, due danzatori distesi a faccia in giù fanno ruotare i corpi lungo una linea retta, rotolando in modo circolare su una superficie definita da un motivo a stella racchiuso nel perimetro di un quadrato (tav. 24). La telecamera, inizialmente immobile mentre i danzatori si muovono, comincia, poi, a girare con loro, creando l'impressione che stiano rotolando sul posto mentre il motivo a stella si muove sotto di loro. Segue una rotazione inversa della telecamera, che nasce da una motivazione pratica: la necessità di srotolare il cavo elettrico. Anche in *Hanging Carousel (George Skins a Fox)* è presente la stessa logica: prima la rotazione in senso orario, poi in senso antiorario per districare i cavi elettrici del monitor. In questo modo i movimenti spaziali di entrambe le opere sono determinati dalla tensione tra l'idea che la guida e la realtà contingente che impone delle restrizioni, proprio come accade per *Double Steel Cage Piece* (tav. 3), un'opera che attrae i partecipanti e allo stesso tempo li soppone a una notevole compressione fisica.

Rotolare sul pavimento e mantenere il proprio corpo in linea con quello di un altro danzatore, il tutto mentre si compie un movimento circolare, è essa stessa un'azione empiricamente difficile, anche quando viene eseguita da danzatori esperti che cercano di compierla con esattezza. Molte performance di Nauman, allo stesso modo, implicano una specie di sopportazione donchisciottesca, sia che richiedano ai danzatori di eseguire compiti superflui da sviluppare per un lungo periodo di tempo sia che richiedano semplicemente il compimento di movimenti ripetitivi fino all'inevitabilmente sfinimento. Nauman spesso prende in considerazione questa possibilità nelle sue istruzioni, presentate, alle volte, più come studi di fattibilità.[27] In un'occasione l'artista ha affermato che nell'allestire le situazioni per performance, film o video, "Ho sempre voluto fare attenzione a che la struttura includesse tensione a sufficienza, sia che venisse da un errore casuale o dalla stanchezza che fa sbagliare ... che ci fosse una qualche struttura programmata nell'evento ... credo che i pezzi ben riusciti lo siano per questo motivo, e quelli che non sono riusciti abbiano fallito perché non c'era sufficiente struttura in loro".[28]

In *Untitled* la tensione strutturale cresce progressivamente. I danzatori iniziano il movimento in senso orario sopra il motivo a stella seguendo fedelmente le istruzioni. Le mani che si toccano al centro sono l'asse che ne guida il movimento, e la loro presa intrecciata ricorda le mani topologiche esposte in un'altra sede della mostra. In un ritmo calcolato, le mani si muovono in cerchio sopra lo schema definito dal nastro adesivo quando, all'improvviso, anche la telecamera sospesa su di loro inizia a girare, seguendo il loro ritmo per creare l'impressione di movimento sotto i loro corpi. Osservando i danzatori muoversi sul tappeto bianchissimo segnato col nastro adesivo, ci rendiamo conto che in pratica stanno esibendosi sopra un disegno. I loro movimenti, e la danza tra loro e la telecamera, sono decisamente in accordo; la tensione che Nauman ha attentamente integrato è presente per ora più nelle nostre menti che nella performance, nel momento in cui ci rendiamo conto della possibilità di fallire e ci chiediamo, a proposito dei danzatori: "Per quanto tempo ancora possono proseguire?". Anche la rotazione intermittente della telecamera mette i loro movimenti in prospettiva: nel mantenere come richiesto una linea retta nello schermo, i danzatori sono continui in alcuni momenti, esitanti in altri. Alla fine, col trascorrere dei trentadue minuti, lo sforzo fisico di mantenere la precisione dei movimenti inizia a portarli allo sfinimento. Le mani dei danzatori si staccano, e la linea creata dai loro corpi si spezza in strane angolazioni. Nella registrazione della performance è evidente che i danzatori condividono lo stesso impegno morale; entrambi continuano l'azione, nessuno dei due vuole cedere per primo (fig. 69 e 70). In questo modo condividono la percezione di Nauman secondo cui la domanda da porre non è mai perché, ma quanto e per quanto tempo.

Per tutto il tempo, il pavimento arancione a terrazzo veneziano e la base in pietra del caminetto antico, elementi preesistenti nella stanza che fa parte degli spazi espositivi di Ca' Foscari Esposizioni, entrano ed escono dall'inquadratura. Filmare *Untitled* nello stesso luogo in cui sarebbe stato esibito al pubblico si è dimostrato importante per Nauman, come lo è stato in altri esempi delle sue istruzioni per performance.[29] Nel desiderio di coerenza spaziale, la distanza tra la performance dal vivo e la sua controparte filmata viene meno, quasi per non privilegiare una a scapito dell'altra.

In quanto fusione degli anni settanta e del primo decennio del ventunesimo secolo, *Untitled* degli anni 1970/2009 è un esempio caratteristico della sincronicità che guida *Topological Gardens*, che trova nelle opere di Nauman create nel corso di quattro decenni, al posto della cronologia, uno "stile di conoscenza"[30] che collega analogicamente i *topoi* della sua attività artistica. La mappatura analogica di Fontane e Neon; Teste e Mani; Suono e Spazio dà forma alla mostra e guida questa particolare lettura dell'opera di Nauman. I punti d'accesso, definiti in parte dall'ondeggiante categoria di Venezia, non intendono definire un percorso o definire una reazione, quanto aprire l'arte di Nauman al campo dell'esperienza. La nostra interpretazione è inevitabilmente soggetta ad ulteriore estrapolazione, da parte del pubblico, del lettore e dell'artista, dal momento che quest'ultimo continua ad operare.

In questo modo la nostra logica analogica spiega le possibilità di sostituzione, confronto, e reinvenzione: una ridefinizione delle premesse di base del percorso verso nuove variazioni. Nauman spinge a questo tipo di pensiero ciclico, la cui conclusione è effimera, rimpiazzata da un nuovo compito a portata di mano, una nuova forma del problema, ma sempre nella reiterazione dei punti essenziali dell'arte: pensare, lavorare, creare. Un brano tratto dal testo scritto da Nauman per *Flayed Earth* (tav. 9) sembra riconoscere la necessità di trovarsi sempre pronti:

HO MANI VELOCI LA MIA MENTE È ALL'ERTA/
STRINGO IL MIO CORPO PRONTO PER L'ISPIRAZIONE/
ANTICIPAZIONE NESSUN SEGNO RESPIRAZIONE/
NESSUN RESPIRO PENSO NE' AVANTI NE' INDIETRO
PRONTO MA SENZA ASPETTARE SENZA/
ESSERE IN GUARDIA SENZA ESSERE PREPARATO.[31]

Per sempre artista/fontana, Nauman si erge perpetuamente sul limite, pronto a procedere verso la prossima incarnazione, seguendo le infinite traiettorie della sua arte.

1 Nauman, citato da Coosje van Bruggen, *Bruce Nauman*, Rizzoli, New York 1988, p.108. In tutto questo capitolo del libro, van Bruggen cita brani delle sue conversazioni con l'artista avvenute nel giugno 1985 e nell'aprile 1986.

2 Si vedano *Bruce Nauman: Work from 1965 to 1972*, a cura di Jane Livingston and Marcia Tucker, catalogo della mostra, Los Angeles County Museum of Art, Los Angeles 1972, p. 10; Neal Benezra, *Surveying Nauman*, in *Bruce Nauman: Exhibition Catalogue and Catalogue Raisonné*, a cura di Neal Benezra e Kathy Halbreich, Walker Art Center, Minneapolis 1994, p. 16; e Christine Hoffman, *Denk Dank (Think-Thank)* in *Bruce Nauman: Theaters of Experience*, a cura di Susan Cross, catalogo della mostra, Guggenheim Museum Publications, New York 2003, p. 54.

3 La ricerca di ragionamenti analogici spiega chiaramente che tale tipo di logica trova applicazione in moltiplici campi di studi inclusi diritto, educazione, scienze politiche, matematica e linguistica. Basandosi sugli esempi, le strategie cognitive come le analogie consentono un modo di pensiero comparativo che può contribuire a costruire principi di insegnamento e più ampi ragionamenti pertinenti ad una miriade di discipline. Per articoli che certificano tale diversità che contiene allo stesso tempo come soggetto appropriate ed accessibili definizioni di ragionamenti analogici si vedano: Emily Sherwin, "A Defense of Analogical Reasoning in Law", *University of Chicago Law Review*, 66, 4 (autunno 1999): 1179-97; Marijke Breuning, "The Role of Analogies and Abstract Reasoning in Decision-Making: Evidence from the Debate over Truman's Proposal for Development Assistence", *International Studies Quarterly*, 47, 2 (giugno 2003): 229-45; Lyn D. English e Patrick V. Sharry, "Analogical Reasoning and the Development of Algebraic Abstraction", *Educational Studies in Mathematics*, 30, 2 (marzo 1996): 135-57.

4 Coosje van Bruggen, *Bruce Nauman*, cit., p. 109.

5 Michael Auping, *Metacommunicator*, in *Raw Materials*, catalogo della mostra, Tate Publishing, London 2004, p. 9.

6 Si veda Nauman, *Please Pay Attention Please: Bruce Nauman's Words. Writings and Interviews*, a cura di Janet Kraynak, The MIT Press, Cambridge, Mass. 2002, p. 49.

7 Si veda Michele de Angelus, *Interview with Bruce Nauman*, 1980, in *Please Pay Attention Please: Bruce Nauman's Words, Writings and Interviews* a cura di Janet Kraynak, The MIT Press, Cambridge, Mass. 2005, p. 213. "Credo di aver imparato un bel po' di matematica, mi piaceva: mi interessava molto non la matematica pratica, ma la comprensione della struttura della matematica, per cui continuai a studiarla. Penso avesse a che fare col modo in cui era insegnata. Per un paio d'anni mi trovai in una classe poco numerosa con un insegnante particolarmente bravo, specializzato in topologia algebrica, che spiegava molto bene".

8 Si veda Nauman, *Notes and Projects*, "Artforum" 9, 4 (dicembre 1970), p. 44. Ripubblicato in *Please Pay Attention Please*, a cura di Kraynak, cit., p. 58.

9 Nauman, citato in Van Bruggen, *Bruce Nauman*, cit., p. 108.

10 Si veda *Bruce Nauman 25 Years Leo Castelli*, a cura di Susan Brundage, Rizzoli New York 1994, n.p.

11 Marcia Tucker, *PheNAUMANology*, "Artforum" 9, 4 (dicembre 1970). Ripubblicato in *Bruce Nauman*, a cura di Robert C. Morgan, The John Hopkins University Press, Baltimore e London 2002, p. 23.

12 Si veda Brenda Richardson, *Bruce Nauman: Neons*, catalogo della mostra, Baltimore Museum of Art, Baltimore 1982, p. 92.

13 Per una illuminante testimonianza diretta del processo durato cinque anni, dalla ideazione alla realizzazione, di *Vices and Virtues*, si veda Mary Livingston Beebe, *Landmarks: Sculpture Commissions for the Stuart Collection at the University of California, San Diego*, Rizzoli, New York 2001, pp. 128-141.

14 Nauman, citato in Van Bruggen, *Bruce Nauman*, cit., p. 7.

15 Adam Gopnik, *Bits and Pieces*, "The New Yorker", 14 maggio 1990.

16 Si veda la scheda n. 397 del *Catalogue raisonné*, che descrive anche il particolare processo di fusione.

17 In *Topological Gardens* i monitor cubici sovrapponibili utilizzati in origine da Nauman per queste opere sono stati sostituiti da schermi piatti montati a parete in serie sovrapposte. La decisione di usare monitor a schermo piatto è stata presa per questo contesto particolare dal gruppo dei curatori in accordo con tutti gli stretti collaboratori di Nauman, e dimostra l'atteggiamento dell'artista verso l'aggiornamento tecnologico come progresso accettabile nella presentazione delle sue opere, in considerazione del veloce cambiamento degli standard tecnologici.

18 Bruce Nauman citato in Ingrid Schaffner, *Circling Oblivion/Bruce Nauman through Samuel Beckett*, in *Bruce Nauman*, a cura di Morgan, cit., p. 163.

19 Si veda Nauman, *Flayed Earth Flayed Self (Skin Sink)*, Wilder Gallery, Los Angeles 1973, n.p.

20 *Ibid.*

21 Nauman, in de Angelus, *Interview with Bruce Nauman*, cit., p. 278.

22 *Ibid.*, p. 278.

23 Janet Kraynak, *Dependent Participation*, in *Grey Room,* 10 (inverno 2003/Mit press 2003) p. 24.

24 Anche se l'opera *Get Out of My Mind, Get Out of This Room* era stata inizialmente inclusa come una delle cinque tracce audio che in origine componevano *Studio Aids II*, l'artista ha deciso, d'accordo con il team curatoriale, di separarli in due esperienze distinte presso la sede Iuav ai Tolentini.

25 Nauman, citato in Auping, "Projection and Displacement", in *Bruce Nauman: Drawings for Installations*, catalogo della mostra, Sperone Westwater, New York 2008, p. 7.

26 Si veda van Bruggen, "Sounddance", 1988, in *Bruce Nauman*, a cura di Morgan, cit., p. 48.

27 In un'opera senza titolo del 1969, Nauman incarica un danzatore di eseguire ogni giorno della mostra per trenta minuti un esercizio, con il seguente avvertimento: "Aggiungo una nota cautelare extra: ho lavorato su questo esercizio ed è difficile. Non fare l'errore di assumere qualcuno che non sia fisicamente o mentalmente in grado di affrontare questo problema". Nauman citato in *Please Pay Attention Please*, a cura di Kraynak, cit., p. 53.

28 Nauman, citato in de Angelus, *Interview with Bruce Nauman*, p. 247–48.

29 Si veda, ad esempio, il testo per un'opera senza titolo del 1969, in *Please Pay Attention Please*, a cura di Kraynak, cit., p. 51. Il libro di Kraynak include anche un certo numero di istruzioni per performance che contengono le parole "ingaggiare un danzatore" o annotazioni a proposito della possibilità di diventare troppo stanco per continuare.

30 de Angelus, *Interview with Bruce Nauman*, p. 268.

31 Nauman, *Flayed Earth, Flayed Self (Skin Sink)*, n.p.

Days/Giorni

Passione, patire

Carlos Basualdo

Fa freddo e la città è piena di pioggia la mattina del 13 giugno 2008, un'altra improbabile giornata estiva a Venezia. E' ancora presto quando, dopo l'inevitabile vagare che è parte ineludibile dell'esperienza veneziana, arriviamo a destinazione allo studio Waterland, nome quanto mai appropriato, nelle vicinanze del Ghetto in Cannaregio, il vasto sestriere nella zona nord-ovest della città. Camminiamo in fretta, schivando i turisti nell'uscire da Lista de Spagna, la trafficata zona pedonale che collega Rialto alla stazione ferroviaria, per addentrarci in un vicolo stretto che termina in un ingresso chiuso da un cancello. Attraversiamo un ponticello di legno, saliamo una rampa di scivolosi scalini di pietra, e suoniamo il campanello. Al di là del portone massiccio ci sorprende la vista di uno splendido giardino arcadico con piscina, irregolare e quasi suburbano per quanto è trascurata la distribuzione del verde. Un curato vialetto lastricato in pietra, furiosamente luccicante per la pioggia e vivacizzato da un gran numero di giochi per bambini, attraversa con discrezione il giardino. Oltrepassiamo un piccolo triciclo arrugginito e un grande pallone di plastica dai colori sbiaditi. Attraversiamo una porta a vetri ed entriamo in casa, dove il proprietario dello studio ci accoglie in un salone il cui pavimento veneziano a riquadri deve gareggiare con i numerosi vestiti appesi, i giocattoli, i passeggini e persino con gli animali imbalsamati per attirare la nostra attenzione. Tutto è umido, leggermente caotico, ma assolutamente allegro. Sulla destra si trova una serie di alte porte di legno; di fronte al giardino una rampa; verso il retro un'altra porta, piuttosto modesta, che si apre su uno studio di registrazione perfettamente attrezzato: la scoperta più insolita, non si può fare a meno di pensare, nel mezzo di un'isola medievale.

Ci troviamo lì per registrare le voci di *Giorni*, versione italiana di *Days*, un'installazione sonora che Bruce Nauman ha appena terminato nello studio in New Mexico. Dalle nove e trenta del mattino fino quasi alle sei di sera arriva una processione apparentemente infinita di persone, tra cui alcuni miei studenti universitari, il preside della Facoltà di Design e Arti dello Iuav, artisti e amici vari. Uno per volta, a turno, entrano nello studio, siedono su una panca e leggono ad alta voce la traduzione in italiano delle due versioni del testo che Nauman ha scritto per l'opera, un elenco modificato dei giorni della settimana. Nauman e il tecnico del suono se ne stanno dietro una parete in vetro insonorizzata e ascoltano tranquilli, fornendo di tanto in tanto indicazioni precise agli interpreti. La lettura di ciascuna versione del testo richiede circa venti minuti, così Nauman trascorre poco più di mezz'ora con ciascuno dei lettori. Conclusa la registrazione, il lettore esce dallo studio e ci raggiunge per un po' di tempo nella stanza esterna, per il pagamento, la firma di moduli, e per sedersi a chiacchierare. A mezzogiorno ci fermiamo per un pranzo abbondante; al termine della giornata, cessata finalmente la pioggia, attraversiamo il Canal Grande per andare a cena a casa di Massimo Magrì, professore di filmografia presso la Facoltà di Design e Arti dell'Università Iuav.

Conosciamo a memoria i giorni della settimana, ne conosciamo intimamente i nomi e l'ordine in cui tracciano senza pretese lo scorrere del tempo, al punto da dimenticare di pensarli come un modo relativamente arbitrario di scandire le nostre esistenze. Essi sono diventati, in un certo senso, un'armatura invisibile alla quale abbiamo demandato la facoltà di decidere chi incontrare e cosa fare, dove andare e quando riposare. Anche se non ce ne rendiamo conto, essi sono, tuttavia, parte di noi finché siamo al mondo, finché l'uso che facciamo del tempo costituisce la sostanza del nostro pensare.

Se martedì rifiutasse di seguire lunedì, se domenica cadesse arbitrariamente nel mezzo della settimana, chi saremmo?

Leggere per la prima volta la lista dei giorni trasformata da Nauman mi fa sentire come se scendessi lungo scale ripide senza l'aiuto del corrimano. Ma questa volta non è il mio corpo a richiedere la sua presenza rendendomi acutamente consapevole di ogni movimento potenzialmente pericoloso, è piuttosto la mia coscienza che, esitante, inizia a diffidare di sé. Sembra che tutti i lettori presenti quel giorno nello studio nelle vicinaze del Ghetto provino lo stesso senso di calmo disorientamento. I lettori si sentono sommersi dalle loro stesse voci, come da un fiume in piena che rompe gli argini. Quando, entrando di tanto in tanto nello studio, li osserviamo in silenzio mentre registrano, ciò che percepiamo e udiamo è la pura sostanza espressiva delle loro voci, temporaneamente libera dai contenimenti imposti dalla coscienza.

Nelle definitive installazioni di *Days* e di *Giorni*, ogni voce viene emessa da due altoparlanti posti uno di fronte all'altro. Sono in tutto sette le coppie di altoparlanti, sistemati in due file parallele, una disposizione che inevitabilmente ricorda un corridoio. Come in *Raw Materials*, installazione sonora di Nauman presentata alla Turbine Hall della Tate Modern di Londra nell'autunno 2004, gli altoparlanti permettono di orientare il suono. La tipologia di altoparlanti utilizzato in *Days* è sottile, quadrato, di colore bianco avorio ed emette suoni in entrambe le direzioni; attaccati con comuni morsetti metallici a due cavi di acciaio tesi tra pavimento e soffitto, sono posti all'altezza dello sguardo, il che li rende simili a degli specchi vuoti, opachi. Quando l'opera è in funzione, si sentono tutte le voci all'unisono, ma poiché gli altoparlanti sono direzionabili, si può ascoltare ciascuna voce isolatamente. In verità le si percepisce non tanto come "voci" quanto come "persone": persone che occupano la stanza, ci spingono da una voce all'altra, ci forzano con gentilezza ad affrontare gli specchi vuoti nei quali si riflette un tempo privo di sequenza o costrizioni. Sembra che ogni voce, libera dal tempo, ci chiami come una sirena accecata.

In *Days*, come in molte altre opere di Nauman, la ripetizione è adoperata per accrescere la natura espressiva del singolo elemento ripetuto; ciò la rende chiaramente diversa dall'uso della ripetizione tipica del Minimalismo, che rende espressivo l'insieme a scapito del singolo elemento. L'opera di Jasper Johns, le bandiere, i bersagli e la maggior parte delle straordinarie serie di numeri iniziate a metà degli anni cinquanta, potrebbe costituire un precedente plausibile. Anche per Johns la ripetizione rende problematico un ordine apparentemente naturale, così che ciascun numero viene finalmente liberato dalla tirannia della serie e può esistere di per sé, permettendo un'esperienza visiva puramente soggettiva. Nei dipinti di Johns, i singoli numeri, diventando nuovamente delle cifre, al di là della logica forzata di un ordine sequenziale, sono soggetti alla pura forza dell'interpretazione. Alle voci che compongono *Days*, libere dalla costrizione del tempo, viene concesso di diventare intimamente personali, al punto che finiamo per vederci riflessi nelle loro sconfinate emozioni.

Nella versione in lingua inglese, *Days*, le voci sono ripetute continuamente, cosicché la sequenza non ha inizio né fine, come in numerose opere precedenti di Nauman. Alla base di *Giorni* sta, invece, una logica diversa: una sola voce apre la sequenza, poi una seconda, alla quale, successivamente, si aggiungono tutte le altre voci che, alla fine, diventano ritornano ad essere due e poi una sola. La durata del risultante ciclo è leggermente più lunga del tempo di lettura che il testo richiede. Le prime voci che si ascoltano sono quelle di due giovani studentesse, l'ultima appartiene all'uomo più anziano del gruppo. La sequenza evoca chiaramente il passare del tempo, che si misura non tanto in giorni quanto in tempo vissuto. Le voci femminili che aprono la sequenza vibrano di aspettative e sensualità; verso la fine, il contrappunto tra due voci maschili esprime uno stato d'animo più cupo. Forse per la prima volta nella lunga carriera di Nauman il fattore determinante nella durata dell'opera sembra essere puramente soggettivo. Non sorprende, quindi, il fatto che questa struttura renda l'opera al tempo stesso più musicale e più emotiva, come se l'intenzionalità dell'artista portasse il contenuto espressivo delle singole voci ancora più lontano.

Mentre *Days* sembra evocare il trascorrere del tempo stesso, il tempo che passa, serpeggiando, dipanandosi dentro e sopra di noi, *Giorni* allude allo scorrere della vita, la nostra vita, che inesorabilmente affonda nel tempo. *Days* potrebbe avere le sue origini nell'esperienza dello studio vuoto dell'artista, dove il tempo non smette mai di scorrere e il suo scorrere assume la forma di un'interrogazione senza fine circa la natura dell'opera e dell'arte. *Giorni*, tuttavia, appartiene all'esperienza della passione e della resistenza. La radice latina della parola "passione" è la stessa del verbo italiano "patire", il cui significato è sopportare, resistere. Sopportare lo scorrere del tempo, resistere a una passione passeggera; vivere e poi scomparire; è passione nel vero senso della parola, sembra dirci quest'opera, quel che si esperisce intensamente nell'eterna sottomissione delle nostre identità proteiformi.

-----Messaggio inoltrato-----
Da: **Susanna Carlisle**
Data: Mercoledì 26 novembre 2008, 18:55
A: Bruce Nauman
Oggetto: Days

Ciao Bruce,

anche se ho visto/ascoltato *Days* alcune settimane fa nel tuo studio, la mia reazione alla tua installazione ha continuato a ritornarmi in mente. Bruce [Hamilton] pensa che ti possa interessare conoscere le mie riflessioni, per cui ecco, questo è quello che mi sta passando per la testa.

Le voci che arrivavano da un unico altoparlante nella tua sala computer creavano un senso di tedio, che mi sembrava essere quello che tu cercavi di ottenere fin dall'inizio, ma quando ho ascoltato le voci provenire da tutte le casse nell'arena spaziale che hai creato, la mia reazione mi ha sorpreso. Ho sorriso perché sentivo che *Days* era finalmente in grado di esalare. Dopo averle sperimentate in forma essenzialmente compressa, ero sbalordita dalle relazioni ampie e complesse che le voci trasmettevano. Non provavo alcun tedio, ma piuttosto un potente impeto di godimento viscerale. Alla fine sono riuscita a sperimentare la straordinaria musicalità insita in ciascuna versione. Per me, la versione italiana e quella inglese sono caratterizzate da ritmi, tessiture e personalità culturali differenti.

Poiché nella versione inglese le voci sono state registrate in luoghi diversi, a livelli diversi, e in momenti diversi, penso che ciascuna voce simbolicamente sottolinei la natura individualista dello spirito americano. È più audace della versione italiana e sembra una stratificazione delle diverse energie che colorano il nostro paese. Musicalmente mi ricorda John Cage, Steve Reich e Cecil Taylor, suoni spesso discordanti, ma con una struttura di base sempre in movimento. Il linguaggio potrebbe avere qualcosa a che vedere con il nervosismo. Lunedì, martedì, ecc. creano un inglese americano lineare, laborioso e audace, ma che manca dell'elasticità, flessibilità e finezza dell'italiano parlato.

Poiché le voci italiane sono state tutte registrate allo stesso tempo e nello stesso luogo, sembra che nel suono ci siano un flusso costante, ripetizione e armonia. Ha più a che fare con una voce corale, quella di un coro di chiesa o un coro lirico. È più raffinata della versione inglese, un po' come lo è la consuetudine italiana di dilungarsi durante i pasti rispetto all'abitudine tipicamente americana di consumare la colazione in piedi, il pranzo al volante e la cena di fronte alla televisione. Non so perché mi colpisca tanto. Penso che la lingua italiana parlata sia più musicale, abbia una maggiore espressione volumetrica che non l'inglese. Forse il fatto di aver registrato le voci insieme nello stesso luogo ha creato una trama più armoniosa in cui ciascuna voce si estende e ritorna indietro allo stesso modo???

Penso che usando un semplice mezzo, voci che pronunciano i giorni della settimana, tu sia riuscito a intessere un arazzo sonoro che riflette la personalità di ciascuna cultura. È anche importante che chiunque entri in *Days* abbia l'alternativa di ascoltare singole voci. Tu ci hai offerto un tale spazio. Tuttavia penso che l'impatto dell'opera derivi dall'integrazione dell'insieme, certamente più intenso della somma delle sue componenti.

Inutile dirlo, *Days* è provocatorio e molto bello! Grazie per avermi dato l'opportunità di vederlo/ascoltarlo in anteprima. So che ci sono altre cose alle quali ho pensato, ma al momento mi sfuggono. Per favore fammi sapere se desideri un maggiore contributo.

Abbi cura di te, Susanna

Bruce Nauman, biografia breve

Bruce Nauman nasce nel 1941 a Fort Wayne, in Indiana. Durante il suo programma undergraduate presso l'Università del Wisconsin a Madison, Nauman studia matematica e fisica prima di cambiare il suo indirizzo in arte sotto l'insegnamento di Italo Scanga e di altri docenti. Nauman consegue il Master in Arte presso l'Università della California a Davis; fanno parte dello staff della facoltà artisti quali William T. Wiley Robert Arneson e Wayne Thiebaud, che supportano il suo crescente desiderio di investigare la produzione artistica al di là dei suoi iniziali dipinti astratti. Presso l'Università della California Nauman sperimenta la fusione di oggetti in fibra di vetro e resina di poliestere, decidendo di lasciarne le superfici grezze per mettere in risalto il processo di fusione. Durante gli anni trascorsi a Davis, Nauman realizza le sue prime due performance, una delle quali prevede l'utilizzo di un tubo fluorescente come estensione del proprio corpo nell'atto di simulare azioni quotidiane; tale performance viene in seguito registrata in video.

Al termine degli studi universitari, Nauman occupa il monolocale di un ex drogeria a San Francisco dove si concentra sull'atto e sul processo del fare arte, fotografando giochi di parole visivi e azioni quotidiane. Una vecchia insegna al neon di una birra presente in questo ex negozio serve da ispirazione per il celebre neon *The True Artist Helps the World by Revealing Mystic Truths (Window or Wall Sign)*. Allo stesso tempo ingenua e sarcastica, questa dichiarazione fu l'inizio di un ironico discorso riguardante il ruolo dell'artista all'interno della società, motivo tuttora presente nell'opera di Nauman. Il Philadelphia Museum of Art ha recentemente acquistato questa significativa opera del 1967 per la sua collezione permanente. Successivamente Nauman si trasferisce nello studio del suo ex docente, Wiley, nella Mill Valley in California, all'interno del quale si dedica alla realizzazione di diversi film che lo ritraggono nell'atto di camminare intorno allo spazio alterando i suoi movimenti corporei. Nauman inizia a raccogliere l'attenzione dei critici nel 1966, dopo la sua prima mostra personale presso la Nicholas Wilder Gallery di Los Angeles, e con l'invito a partecipare alla collettiva di Lucy Lippard intitolata *Eccentric Abstraction* presentata a New York. Nel 1968 si registra il primo debutto di Nauman a New York con una mostra personale presso la Galleria di Leo Castelli; tale mostra venne presto seguita da un'altra mostra presso la Konrad Fischer Galerie a Düsseldorf. Nel 1972–73, il Los Angeles County Museum of Art ed il Whitney Museum of American Art organizzano la prima grande retrospettiva del suo lavoro, *Bruce Nauman: Works from 1965–1972*, una mostra che viaggia in Italia, Svizzera, Germania, Olanda ed altri luoghi negli Stati Uniti.

Influenzato fin dall'inizio dalla filosofia e dalla letteratura - dalle *Investigazioni filosofiche* di Ludwig Wittgenstein e dall'opera *Molloy* di Samuel Beckett - Nauman esamina costantemente il sistema razionale del linguaggio, i confini spaziali e corporali, la durata e la psicologia, attraverso la realizzazione di sculture, video installazioni e la costruzione di ambienti. Alla fine degli anni Sessanta, Nauman si dedica alla produzione di opere al neon come anche alla costruzione di corridoi, filmando, a volte, le sue performance all'interno di questi ultimi. Le grandi ambientazioni costruite all'inizio degli anni Settanta includono spesso camere di video sorveglianza e monitor che dominano dall'alto e registrano gli spettatori al loro interno. Nauman continua a realizzare grandi sculture ed installazioni durante gli anni Settanta e gli inizi degli anni Ottanta, mappando lo spazio con nastro adesivo oppure evocando limitazioni fisiche e psicologiche attraverso la creazione di passaggi e di tunnel. Per un periodo di dieci anni Nauman interrompe il suo lavoro con i video, una forma d'arte che avrebbe ripreso nuovamente verso la metà degli anni Ottanta, per dedicarsi alla realizzazione di numerose installazioni video multi-canale, che esplorano, ancora una volta, il linguaggio e l'uso metaforico di labirinti, come anche la presenza di ratti e clown. All'inizio degli anni Ottanta, Nauman introduce l'iconografia di animali a grandezza naturale fusi nella cera che sospende come delle formazioni a carosello. Gli anni Novanta vedono la produzione di sculture raffiguranti teste e mani umane in cera e bronzo, video installazioni ed un sostenuto lavoro con i neon. All'inizio del XXI secolo, i video, le installazioni sonore e le sculture di Nauman si sviluppano intorno a temi ricorrenti durante tutta la sua produzione artistica a partire dagli anni Sessanta.

Le mostre nei musei hanno continuato a tracciare la pratica di Nauman, così come lo hanno fatto le celebri mostre personali tra le quali ricordiamo: *Bruce Nauman, 1972-1981* tenutasi presso il Rijksmuseum Kröller-Müller, a Otterlo in Olanda e presso la Staatliche Kunsthalle a Baden-Baden nella Germania dell'Est nel 1981; la retrospettiva organizzata dal Walker Art Center a Minneapolis che viaggia tra il 1993 e il 1995 a Madrid, Los Angeles, Washington D.C., e New York. Nel 2006-07 *A Rose Has No Teeth*, una mostra dei suoi primi lavori, viene presentata presso l'Art Museum dell'Università della California a Berkeley, al Castello di Rivoli Museo d'Arte Contemporanea di Torino e presso la Menil Collection a Houston in Texas. Tra le prestigiose collettive che hanno incluso l'opera di Nauman ricordiamo la Biennale di Venezia nel 1978, 1980, 1999 e 2007, così come le diverse edizioni di Documenta nel 1972, 1977, 1982 e 1992. Raccogliendo una molteplicità di premi durante la sua carriera per la sua pratica artistica eccezionalmente vasta e concettualmente provocatoria, Nauman ha ricevuto il Wexner Prize nel 1994, il Leone d'oro insieme a Louise Bourgeois alla 48. Biennale di Venezia nel 1999, ed il Praemium Imperiale per le Arti Visive nel 2004 in Giappone. Il San Francisco Art Institute e il California Institute of the Arts hanno conferito a Nauman un dottorato honoris causa in Arte. Nauman attualmente vive in New Mexico insieme a sua moglie, la pittrice Susan Rothenberg.

Acknowledgments

For those of us who have spent time in Venice for any certain period of time, the trials and tribulations that often accompany an extended interaction with such a fascinating city do not escape the memory. Perhaps this accounts for my initial perplexity when my colleague, Michael R. Taylor, the Muriel and Philip Berman Curator of Modern Art, forwarded the official invitation to propose an exhibition for the U.S. Pavilion in the 2009 edition of the Venice Biennale. Knowing that I have been teaching at the Università Iuav di Venezia since 2004, Michael imagined that his suggestion might spark my enthusiasm. It did, but only after I overcame an initial wave of apprehension. As part of the curatorial team that organized the 2003 edition of the Biennale, I remember the impossible heat of that blazing summer, the simmering crowds, the bewildering installation process, and the endless, sleepless nights of the week before the opening. It was hard for me to imagine going back to Venice to relive these moments while working on a complex, large-scale exhibition.

One could say that the quick answer to all of my hesitations was Bruce Nauman. At that time in the summer of 2007, the Museum embarked on the journey to acquire one of his most iconic works, the 1967 neon sign that carries the mythical inscription: *The True Artist Helps the World by Revealing Mystic Truths (Window or Wall Sign)*. With Nauman very much on our minds, it became clear that Venice was a suitable city for exploring his work—a city full of accidental beauty and inviting complexity, where use determines form, and form determines social interaction in a circular and spiraling logic. Venice is both an overexposed city of tourists and a place full of secrets, where what is hidden is revealed in the same movement as that which is thought to be evident becomes obscured. The context of organizing an exhibition for the U.S. Pavilion proved to be an opportunity to understand Venice while rediscovering Nauman's work—and in doing so, unpacking the very notion of national representation. It was readily evident that there would be no better chance and no context more suitable in which to study Nauman's work.

Anne d'Harnoncourt fully understood all of the possibilities and complexities involved in such an endeavor from our very initial conversations. Twenty-one years ago, the Philadelphia Museum of Art organized an exhibition of the recent work of Jasper Johns at the Pavilion, and the temporal distance from that occasion had not extinguished the delights and sorrows of that project in her mind. She therefore responded to our curiosity with a delighted caution that took very little to become ardent enthusiasm. She supported us, as a director but also as a curator, in a way that was hers and unique, and her constant advice and involvement in the project meant the world to us. In a museum that is proud to be the home of the most comprehensive collection of works by Marcel Duchamp and to offer its audience the possibility of exploring Jasper Johns's work in a room solely devoted to him, the choice to work with Bruce Nauman was self-evident. All three of these artists share a basic philosophical position about the possibilities of art and the role of the artist. Their work is, as Anne would say, "about ideas," and the way in which those ideas are connected to an intuitive yet systematic questioning of the very definition of what art is or could be.

Since we had never met Bruce Nauman, we looked to his long-time dealer, Angela Westwater, to guide us in the delicate task—the first of many—of presenting our initial ideas to Bruce and his studio assistant, Juliet Myers. Working with Angela Westwater has certainly been an extremely rewarding aspect of this project, and her graceful directness has provided sound orientation through the sometimes-labyrinthine preparations for the exhibition. Acting both as a contemporary Virgil and Beatrice, she has firmly and tactfully helped us tour both heaven and hell. The kind collaboration of Angela's gallery staff, especially Michael Short and Jennifer Burbank, should be noted as well.

Encouraged and enthused by the artist's support, we worked round the clock to put forth a proposal to the Bureau of Educational and Cultural Affairs of the U.S. Department of State (ECA). After the selection process, in which the Federal Advisory Committee on International Exhibitions unanimously recommended our project, we were met with the cooperative spirit of Colombia Barrosse, Cultural Programs Division Chief. Working with Colombia and the State Department has truly been both a privilege and pleasure for the Museum.

If Venice is indeed a labyrinth full of unexpected Minotaurs distractedly waiting in the most charming corners, then again guidance is absolutely key, and Marco De Michelis was undoubtedly the thread that led the way. In his former role as Dean of the School of Art and Design at the Università Iuav, he supported this project from its very first stages, understanding it to be a unique opportunity for a collaboration between the U.S. Pavilion and two of the most prestigious educational institutions in Venice—Iuav and Università Ca' Foscari—even though this type of partnership had very few antecedents. His thoughtful contributions both to this catalogue and to my own thoughts on Nauman took place in the form of innumerable conversations on both sides of the Atlantic. Finally, it is Marco's richly textured voice that we hear at the end of the sequence of *Giorni*—Nauman's sound installation that the artist produced working with students in Venice that we are premiering in this exhibition.

Putting together an exhibition that will take place thousands of miles away from its organizing institution is no easy task and required much time and passionate dedication of the Museum staff. After Anne's passing, Gail Harrity, the Museum's Interim Chief Executive Officer, and Alice Beamesderfer, Interim Head of Curatorial Affairs, carried the torch with an unwavering commitment. Without their support at that crucial and extremely critical time, we would not have been able to accomplish our goals. A large team was assembled in Philadelphia to work on the preparations for the show, led by the patient enthusiasm of Erica F. Battle, whose responsibility in the realization of the project is, simply stated, enormous. Systematically tackling the myriad aspects regarding the exhibition and its catalogue, Erica's reassuring presence, and her truly invaluable curatorial input, kept us all, as one may say, on safe ground—no little feat, when talking of Venice. In the Modern and Contemporary Art Department she was first aided by Lauren Bergman, our former Administrative Assistant, who, in the project's early stages, hand-delivered the proposal to the Department of State in Washington, D.C. Roberta Nuzzaci joined the department from Italy as a Curatorial Intern, and became absolutely indispensable for the project, playing the invaluable role of mediating the Museum's many communications with Venice. Jennifer Wilkinson, Research Assistant, greatly helped us by devoting herself to coordinating multiple aspects of the catalogue, from rights and reproductions to editorial matters.

Realizing the many facets of this extremely complex project ultimately involved Museum staff beyond our Modern and Contemporary Department. We found consistent, diligent, and priceless help in the wise advice and passionate persistence of Suzanne F. Wells, Director of Exhibitions Planning, and Zoe Kahr, Assistant Director of Exhibitions Planning; the endless resourcefulness and good will of Jack Schlechter, the Museum's Installations Designer, as well as the meticulousness of Kate Higgins in the project's early stages; the dedication and exactitude of Wynne Kettell, Associate Registrar for Special Exhibitions; and the expert advice and technical assistance of Stephen A. Keever, Manager of Audio-Visual Production. Sherry Babbitt, the William T. Ranney Director of Publishing, guided us through the intricacies of creating this catalogue under the tightest of schedules; David Updike, Editor, and Richard Bonk, Book Production Manager, crucially stepped in to assist the production of the book in its final moments. Ruth Abrahams, Director of Editorial and Graphic Design, aided with the vision and production of the exhibition brochure and additional printed materials. In the Conservation Department, Sally Malenka, Conservator of Decorative Arts and Sculpture, both advised us about the care needed for Nauman's objects and researched components for works that were refabricated for this occasion. Kelly O'Brien, Director of Individual Giving, assisted by Emily Magnuson, Major Gifts Assistant, capably led the undertaking of fundraising for the exhibition. Joseph J. Rishel, the Museum's Gisela and Dennis Alter Senior Curator of European Painting before 1900, also provided us with invaluable guidance, support, and, perhaps most importantly, constant inspiration.

Norman Keyes, Interim Director of Marketing and Public Relations, as well as Elisabeth Flynn, Senior Press Officer, fully dedicated themselves to working with the press in regards to this project. In this arena of media relations, the Museum worked with John Melick, Antoine Vigne, and Kellie Honeycutt of Blue Medium, who provided useful insights into the intricate workings of the Biennale and much organizational efforts for and leading up to the Vernissage.

Without the collaborative spirit of many individuals and institutions in Venice, a show of this kind would be lost in translation. The three institutions that worked with the Museum to host *Topological Gardens* stand out in this regard. At the Peggy Guggenheim Collection, Philip Rylands, Director, and Chiara Barbieri, Manager of Publications and Special Projects, along with many others on staff, welcomed our ideas and helped endlessly to ensure that they came to fruition at the U.S. Pavilion. At the Iuav, we found early and enthusiastic support in Rector Carlo Magnani and former Dean Marco De Michelis, whose steadfast encouragement was upheld by Medardo Chiapponi, Dean, and the technical advice and aid of Ciro Palermo, Ufficio Tecnico—all of whom allowed us to transform their main lecture hall and other student spaces into a site for the exhibition. At Ca' Foscari, Rector Pier Francesco Ghetti and Giuseppe Barbieri, Exhibitions Director and Chair of the History of Art and Conservation Department, generously opened the doors of the newly renovated Exhibition Spaces at Ca' Foscari to host the artist and the Museum. There, Stefania Amerighi, Project Manager, tirelessly worked with our staff on planning for all elements of installation.

In addition, the following individuals aided us immeasurably with on-the-ground coordination that proved essential to the project: Jill Weinrich, On-site Coordinator, helped us in installation; Gilda Zaffagnini of Nexa was responsible for the wonderful events planned in celebration of the artist; and Eleonora Charans, Project Coordinator, assisted with the initial planning for the exhibition, the coordination of trips to Venice with the artist and Museum team, and the production of *Giorni*. We thank Bruce Hamilton, Nauman's technical advisor, for lending us his expertise to install *Giorni* and *Days* in Venice.

We would also like to thank various staff members of the 53rd International Art Exhibition—La Biennale di Venezia, who have bravely galvanized the organization of all seventy-seven pavilions this year: Paolo Baratta, President, and Andrea del Mercato, General Director, of the Fondazione La Biennale di Venezia; Beate Barner, Head of the Press Office for Visual Arts; Roberto Rosolen, National Pavilion Participation Manager; and Manuela Lucà Dazio, Managing Director, Visual Arts and Architecture Department.

We also owe our gratitude to those that contributed to the making of this superb catalogue: Mischa Leiner, assisted by Franck Doussot, at CoDe. New York, provided the creative and careful design; David Frankel meticulously edited the contents, which Elena Cimenti painstakingly translated with alacrity; Marguerite Shore swiftly generated the English translation of Marco De Michelis's essay. Roberta Nuzzaci found another way to help the project by acting as an Italian proofreader. In the Museum's Photography Studio, Graydon Wood, Andrea Nuñez, and especially Jason Wierzbicki provided much help with images. The essays by the catalogue authors who have been mentioned in their additional capacities—Michael R. Taylor, Marco De Michelis, and Erica F. Battle—are also joined by an account by Susanna Carlisle, who wrote to Bruce of her experience hearing his new sound installation. We are thankful to her for agreeing to publish her intimate and lucid text.

The lenders to *Topological Gardens* have shown their incontrovertible appreciation of Bruce Nauman by generously dedicating their works for a six-month loan period to the exhibition—for which our thanks is unending. Though enumerated on the Lenders to the Exhibition page, many individuals in institutions and otherwise are especially thanked: Alfred Pacquement, Director at the National Museum of Modern Art, Centre Georges Pompidou, Paris; Sir Nicholas Serota, Director at the Tate, London; Glenn D. Lowry, Director at the Museum of Modern Art, New York; Madeleine Grynsztejn, Pritzker Director, and Elisabeth Smith, James W. Alsdorf Chief Curator, at the Museum of Contemporary Art, Chicago; Sjarel Ex, Director at the Museum Boijmans Van Beuningen, Rotterdam; Richard Koshalek, Director, and Kerry Brougher, Chief Curator, at the Hirshhorn Museum and Sculpture Garden, Smithsonian Institution, Washington, D.C.; Maxwell Anderson, The Melvin and Bren Simon Director and CEO, and Lisa Freiman, Senior Curator of Contemporary Art, at the Indianapolis Museum of Art; Mary Livingston Beebe, Director of the Stuart Collection at the University of California, San Diego; Udo Kittelmann, Director of the National Gallery, Berlin; and Dr. Eugen Blume, Head of the Hamburger Bahnhof, which oversees the Sammlung Marx.

We are also greatly appreciative of the Emanuel Hoffmann Foundation; the Friedrich Christian Flick Collection; and the François Pinault Foundation. Many individuals also parted with their exquisite examples of Nauman's works, including: Dorothee and Konrad Fischer; Jack and Nell Wendler; Marc and Livia Straus; Donald Young; Isabel and Agustín Coppel; Rachel and Jean-Pierre Lehmann; anonymous private collectors; and the artist. We are also thankful that Joseph D. Ketner, former Chief Curator at the Milwaukee Art Museum, thoughtfully and generously offered us the use of neon exhibition copies from his show *Elusive Signs: Bruce Nauman Works with Light*, and, together with the Stedelijk Museum, Amsterdam, he can be credited for the presence of *My Name As Though It Were Written on the Surface of the Moon* (1968) in the exhibition.

Throughout the two-year journey of planning this exhibition, Juliet Myers has remained a constant fulcrum of enthusiastic and sound advice. As Nauman's studio assistant of twenty-two years, Juliet worked closely with the curatorial team and dedicated a constantly increasing amount of time to this project—for which our gratitude is unending. Juliet not only facilitated the extraordinarily copious details involved in this project but also fostered our efforts to realize an exhibition that would, in all of its aspects, appropriately honor Bruce in Venice.

Absolutely nothing has been more rewarding than working with Bruce Nauman. Only ten days after Anne died unexpectedly on June 1, 2008, Bruce arrived in Venice for a crucial planning trip. Working with him has allowed us to stay as close to Anne as is imaginable. Her deep and sincere admiration for his work corresponded intimately with the close attention that Bruce has given to the project, and with the patience with which he has treated our unending questions. Working for Anne gave us the distinct feeling that we were constantly learning, so that every minute spent with her became precious. The experience of working with Bruce has been exactly like that. We knew from our first conversations how much we would miss our constant interaction with him once the show opened.

Finally, it is very clear for us that we would not have been able to devote ourselves fully to this exhibition without the loving support of our families: Mónica Amor, Lucas and Maya Emilia Basualdo, Sarah Powers and Emma Rose Taylor, and Steven Battle. For those who are here as much as for those who are not, this is our way of honoring you all.

Carlos Basualdo
Keith L. and Katherine Sachs Curator of Contemporary Art

Fabrication and Production Credits

A number of works of art were produced and/or refabricated specifically for *Bruce Nauman: Topological Gardens*. The U.S. Commissioners and the Philadelphia Museum of Art would like to thank the following people, who showed tremendous dedication to the production and fabrication of these works:

***Vices and Virtues*, 1983–88**
Exhibition copy fabricated by Neon Casale, Casale Sul Sile, Treviso, Italy: Franco Gobbo, Owner, Project Manager, and Coordinator; Christian Gobbo, Project Assistant; Raffaele Grigoletto, Project Assistant; Christian Grosso, Project Assistant; Stefania Rosina, Project Assistant; Nico Massarin, Project Assistant; Franca Massarin, Administrative Director; Leda Biasin, Administrative Officer

Support structure fabricated by Extra Pubblicità, S. Biagio di Callalta, Treviso, Italy: Leonardo Leodari, Head Manager; Gianluca Biagini, Project Manager; Marco Bellini, Executive Manager; Massimo Leodari, Technical Officer; Paolo Rizzo, Production Manager; and Davide Mazzariol, Site Manager.

Templates for neon letters and timing device were provided by Jacob Fishman of Lightwriters Neon, Inc., Northbrook, Illinois.

The cooperation and enthusiasm shown by Mary Livingston Beebe, Director, and Matthieu Gregoire of the Stuart Collection at the University of California, San Diego, were fundamental to the remaking of *Vices and Virtues* for the U.S. Pavilion.

***Untitled*, 1970/2009**
Filmed at the Exhibition Spaces at Università Ca' Foscari, February 10, 2009
Director: Massimo Magrì
Assistant to the Director: Federica De Rocco
Production: Alberto Osella & Partners
Technical support: Movie People
Dancers: Carlotta Borasco, Elena Dell'Acqua, Irene Giubilini, and Monica Soccol
Choreographer: Silvia Salvagno

***Giorni*, 2009**
Recorded by Waterland Music Studio, Venice, June 13, 2008
Sound Engineer: Cristiano Verardo
Project Coordinator: Eleonora Charans
Participants in recording: Valentina Barboni, Laura Bruni, Daria Carmi, Marco De Michelis, Claudia Di Lecce, Francesco Perrone, Gianandrea Poletta, Anita Sief, Tommaso Speretta, and Daniele Zoico

The Philadelphia Museum of Art is additionally thankful to Jacob Fishman for creating an exhibition copy of *Human Sexual Experience*, and to Gibbs Connors, Philadelphia, for creating the template for Nauman's sign *Untitled (The True Artist Is an Amazing Luminous Fountain)* for the U.S. Pavilion's main entrance.

These endeavors would not have been possible without the support and close consultation of the artist and Juliet Myers of the Nauman Studio, New Mexico.

Photography Credits

All photographs courtesy the owners/lenders and the following:

Courtesy the artist: repros. pp. 146–47

© 2009 Artists Rights Society (ARS), New York / ADAGP, Paris / Succession Marcel Duchamp; photograph Jacques Faujour, © CNAC/MNAM/ Dist. Réunion des Musées Nationaux / Art Resource, New York: fig. 37

Robin Bernhard: figs. 19, 21

Bildarchiv Preussischer Kulturbesitz / Art Resource, New York: plate 2

© Giorgio Colombo, Milan: fig. 52

Donald Young Gallery, Chicago: fig. 59

Courtesy Donald Young Gallery, Chicago; photograph Tom Van Eynde: plate 21, fig. 28

© Fondazione La Biennale di Venezia – ASAC: figs. 17–18, 22–24

Collection David Geffen, Los Angeles; © Jasper Johns/Licensed by VAGA, New York: fig. 38

The J. Paul Getty Museum, Los Angeles; © Estate of André Kertész: fig. 35

Konrad Fischer Galerie: plates 23, 28

Courtesy Leo Castelli Gallery, New York; © Estate of Rudy Burckhardt / Artists Rights Society (ARS), New York: fig. 54

© 2009 Man Ray Trust / Artists Rights Society (ARS), New York / ADAGP, Paris: figs. 41–42

Museum für Moderne Kunst, Frankfurt; photograph Rudolf Nagel: fig. 60

© The Museum of Modern Art / Licensed by SCALA / Art Resource, New York: plate 20

Courtesy Philadelphia Museum of Art; photograph Pasquale Barisano: plate 24; figs. 68–70

Courtesy Philadelphia Museum of Art, © Michele Lamanna 2008: repros. pp. 158, 172–73

Réunion des Museés Nationaux / Art Resource, New York; photograph Hervé Lewandowski: fig. 34

Réunion des Museés Nationaux / Art Resource, New York; photograph Philippe Migeat: plate 18

© 2008 Philipp Scholz Rittermann: plate 27 (top row, two center images)

Lynn Rosenthal: fig. 20

© Jason Schmidt 2009: repros. pp. 148–49

Uwe H. Seyl, Stuttgart: fig. 62

© The Solomon R. Guggenheim Foundation, New York; photograph David Heald: plate 16

Courtesy Sperone Westwater, New York: plates 3–8, 13–15, 19, 26–27; figs. 4, 13–15, 31–32, 39, 43–51, 53, 55, 57–58, 61, 63, 65–67

Courtesy Sperone Westwater, New York; photograph Tom Powell: plate 10

Courtesy Sperone Westwater, New York; photograph Michael Short: fig. 64

Graydon Wood: plate 22

List of Illustrations of Works by Bruce Nauman

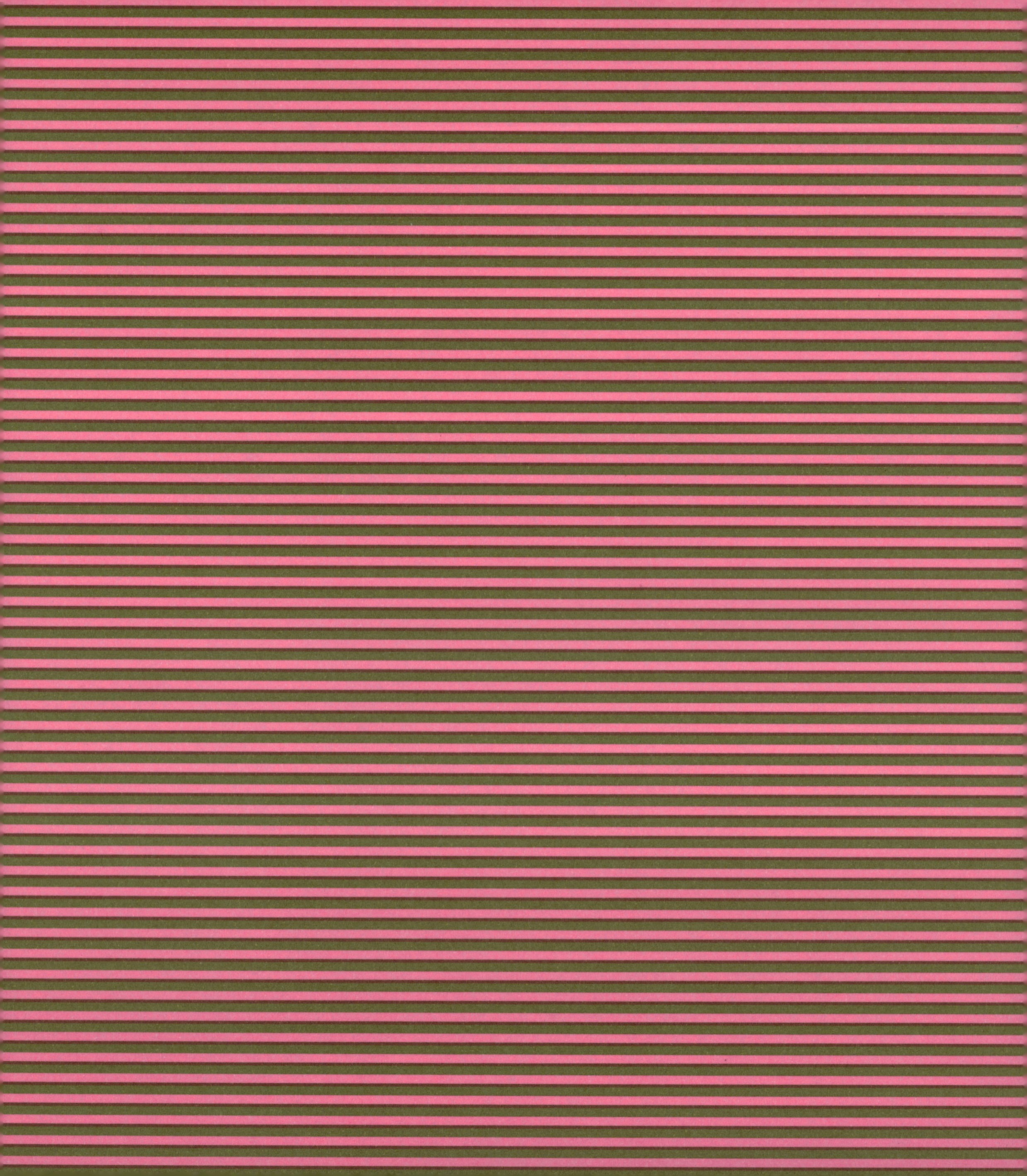